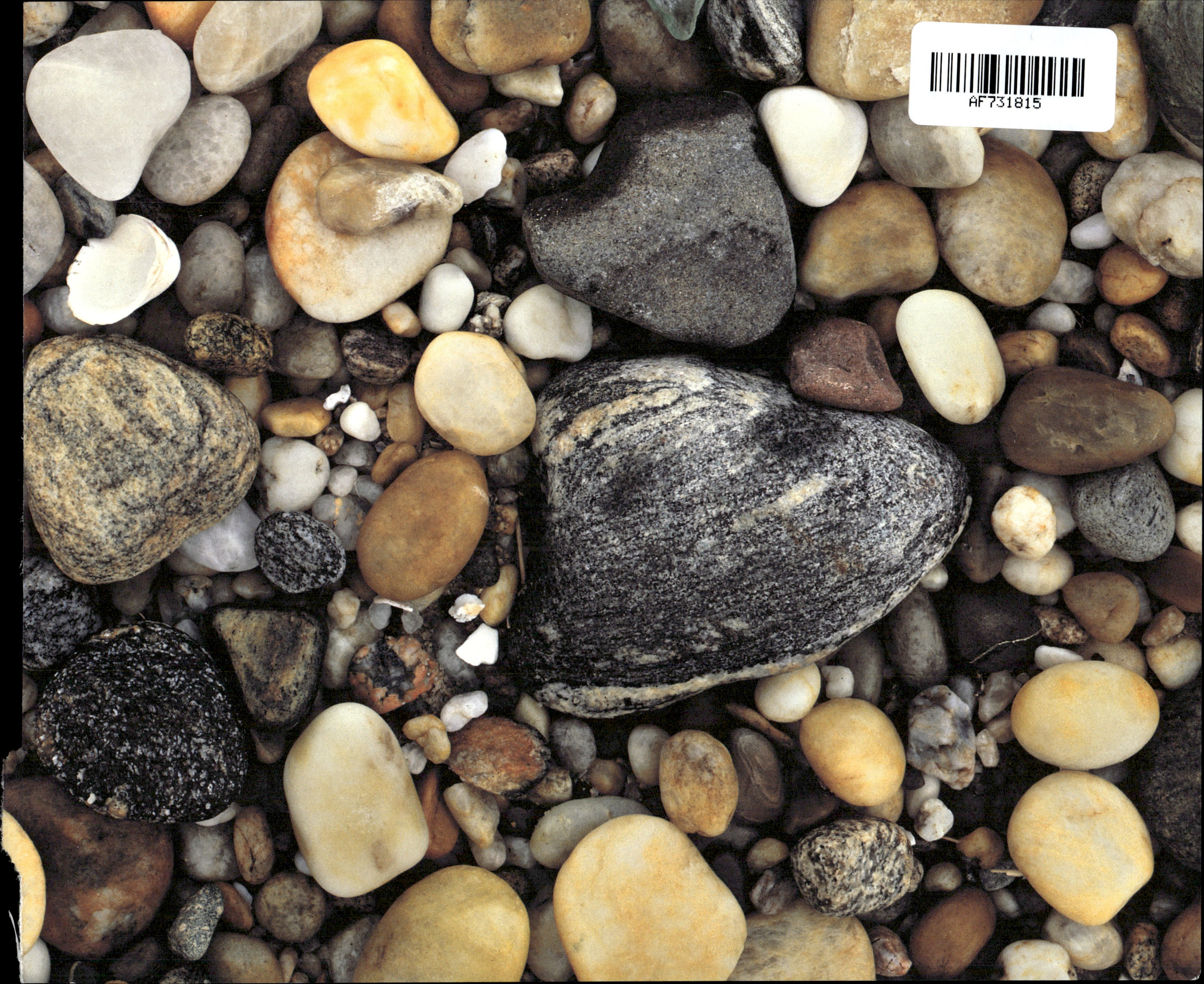

# Between Sea and Sky

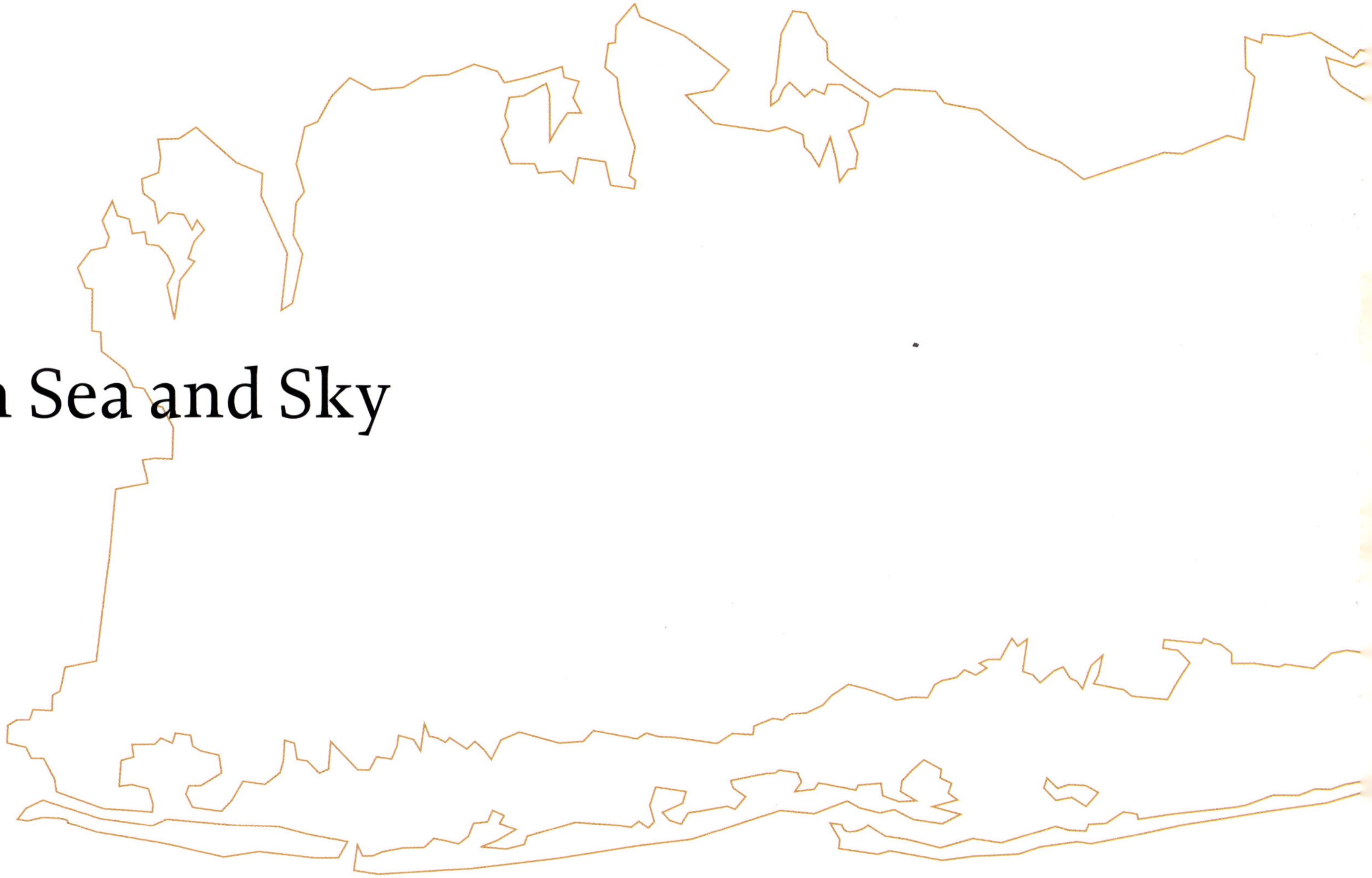

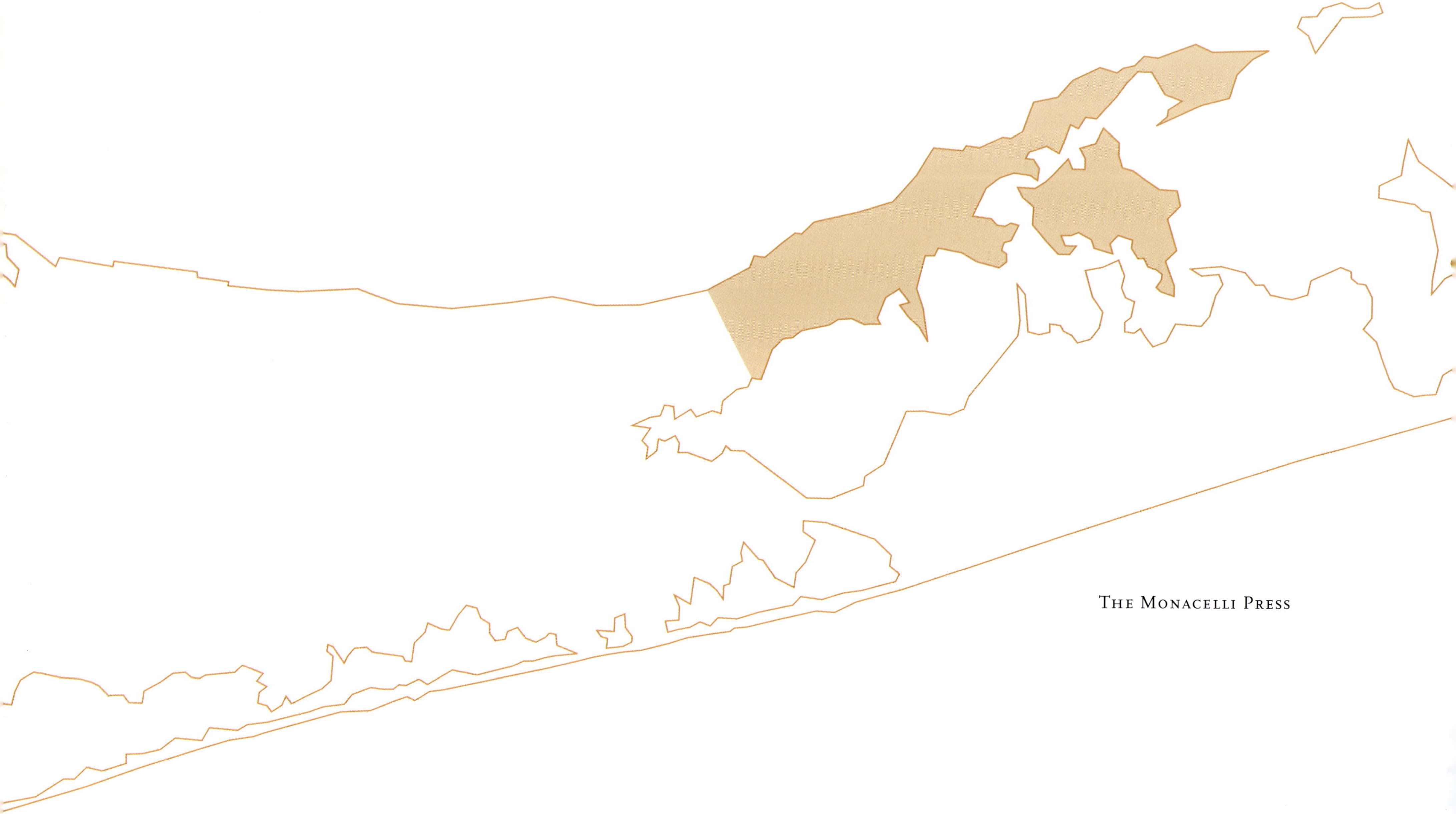

THE MONACELLI PRESS

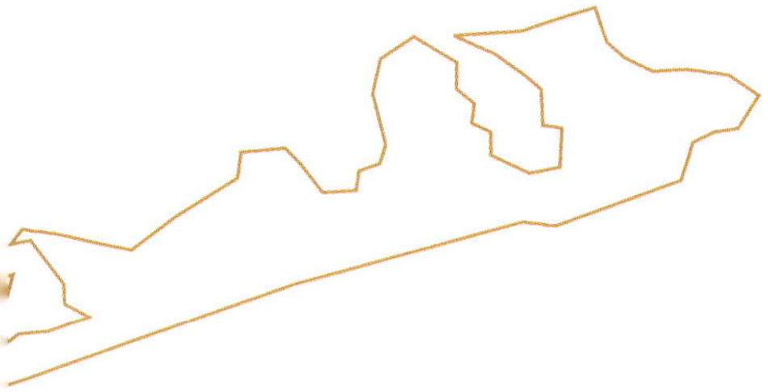

# Landscapes of Long Island's North Fork

Jake Rajs

Essay by Jesse Browner

Afterword by Joshua Y. Horton

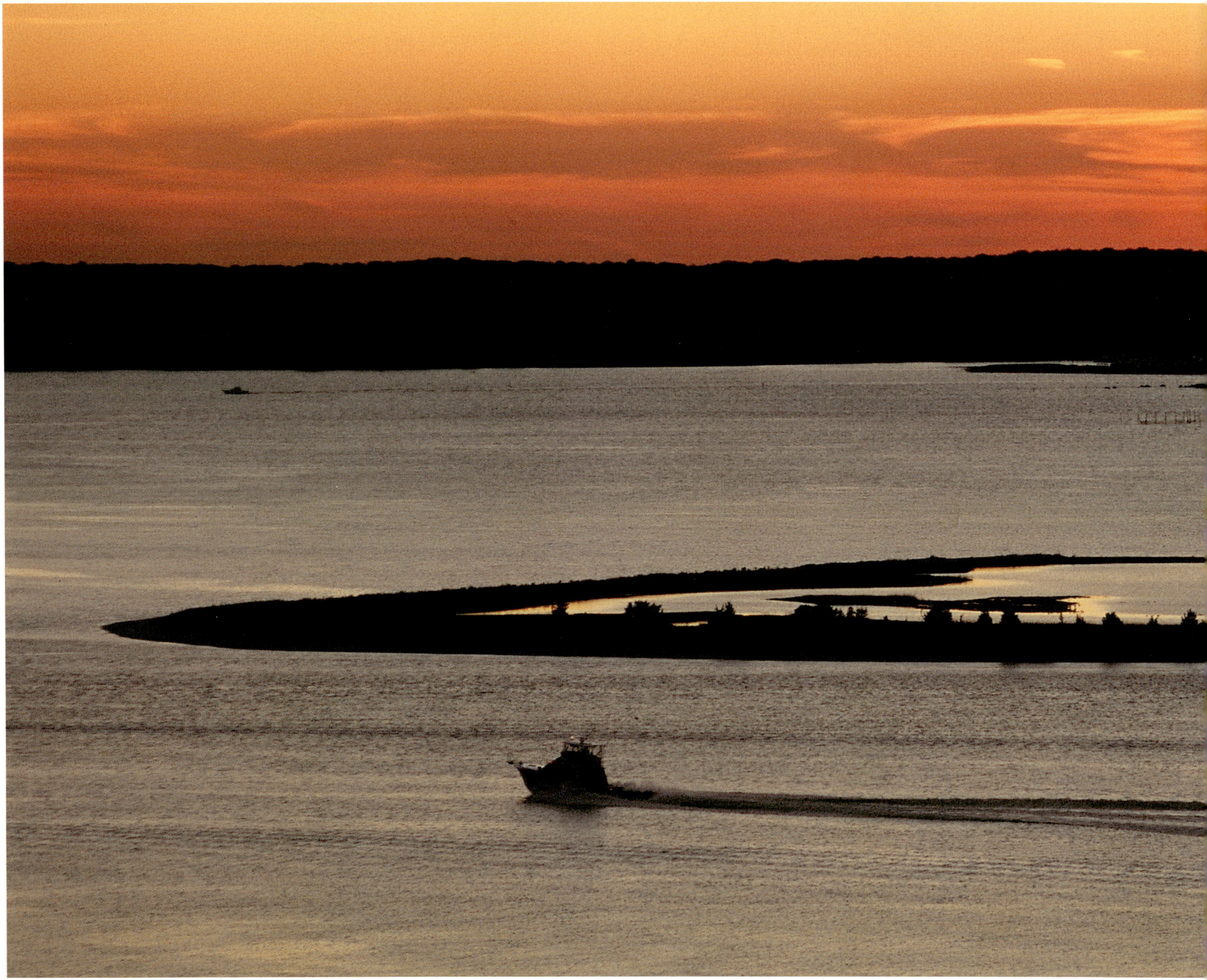

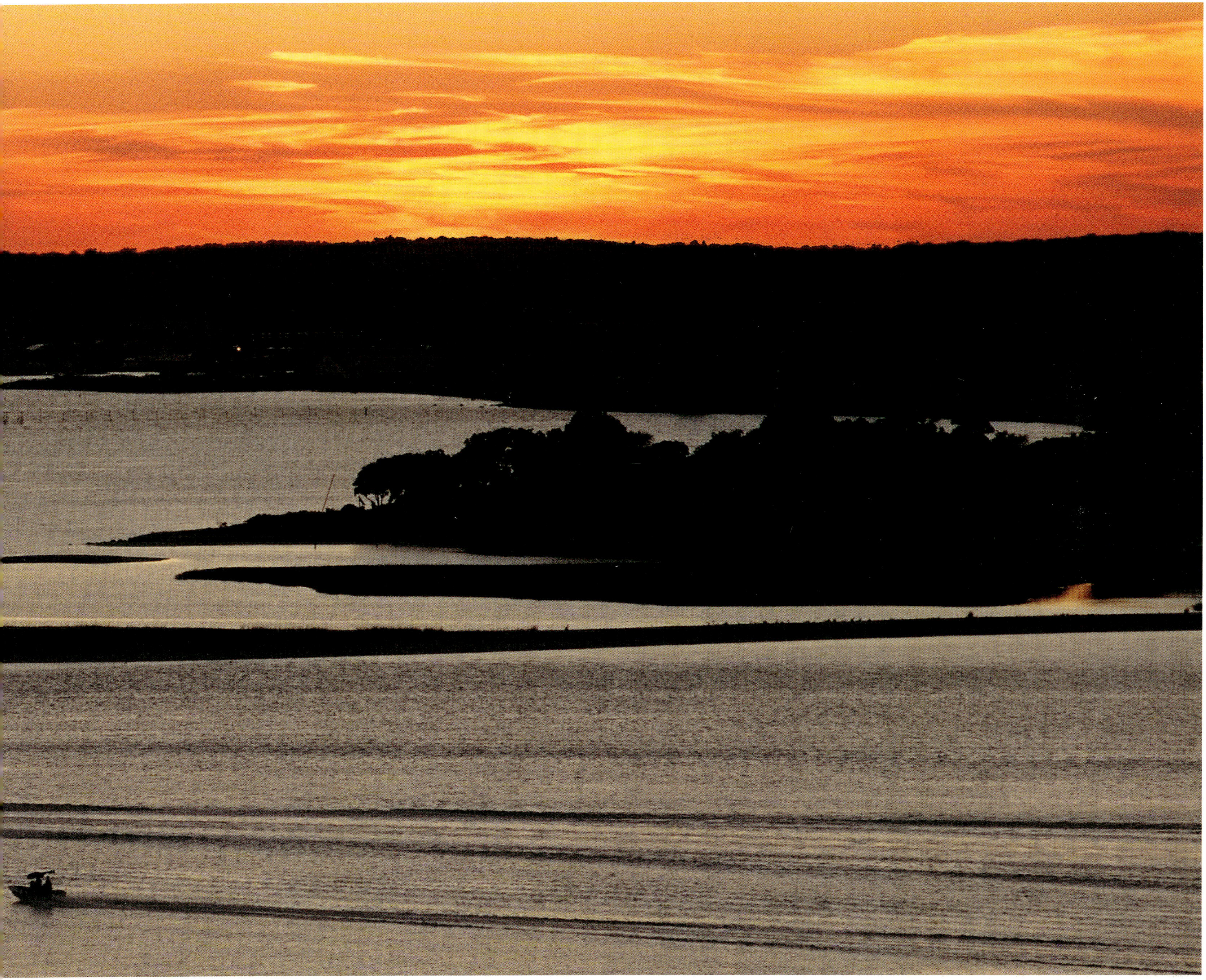

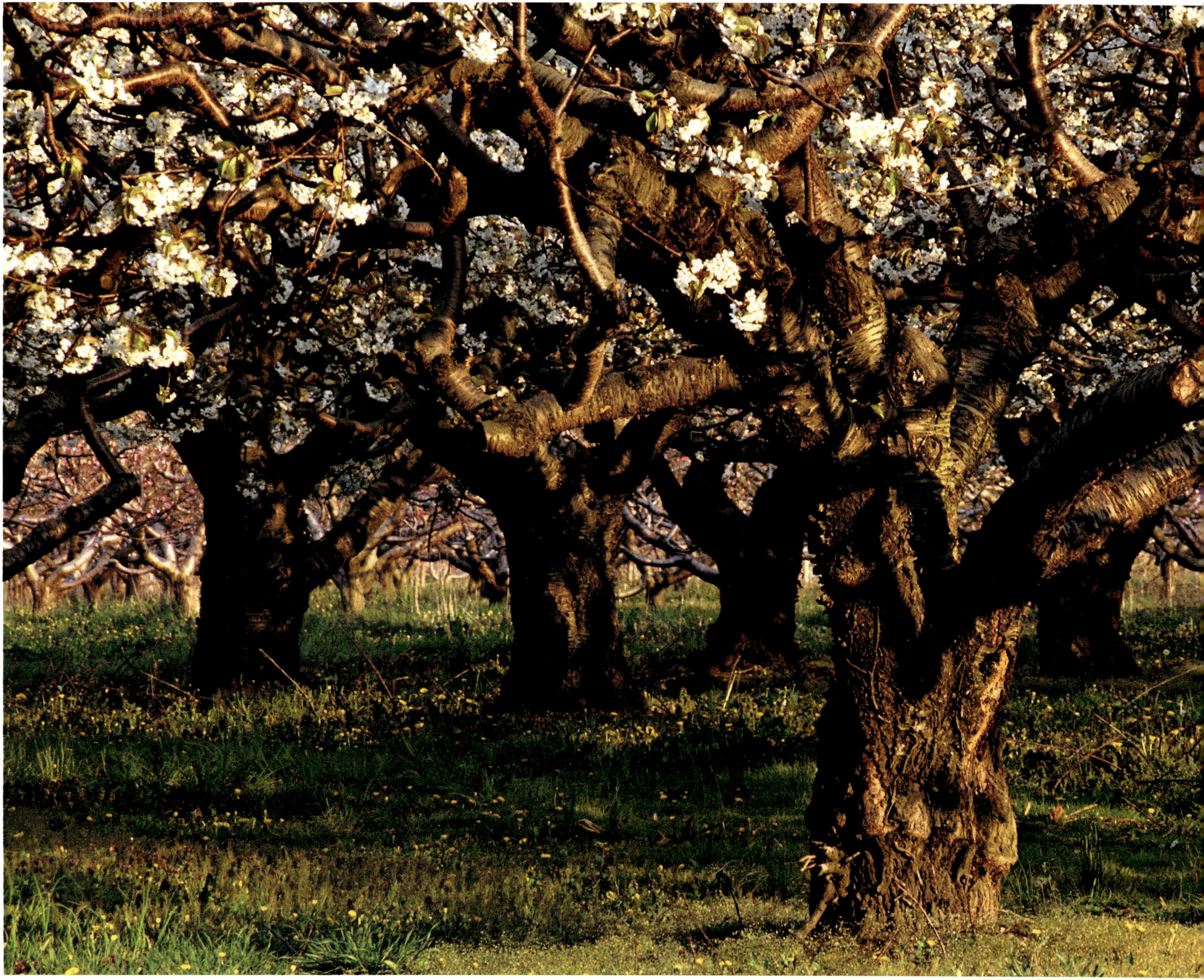

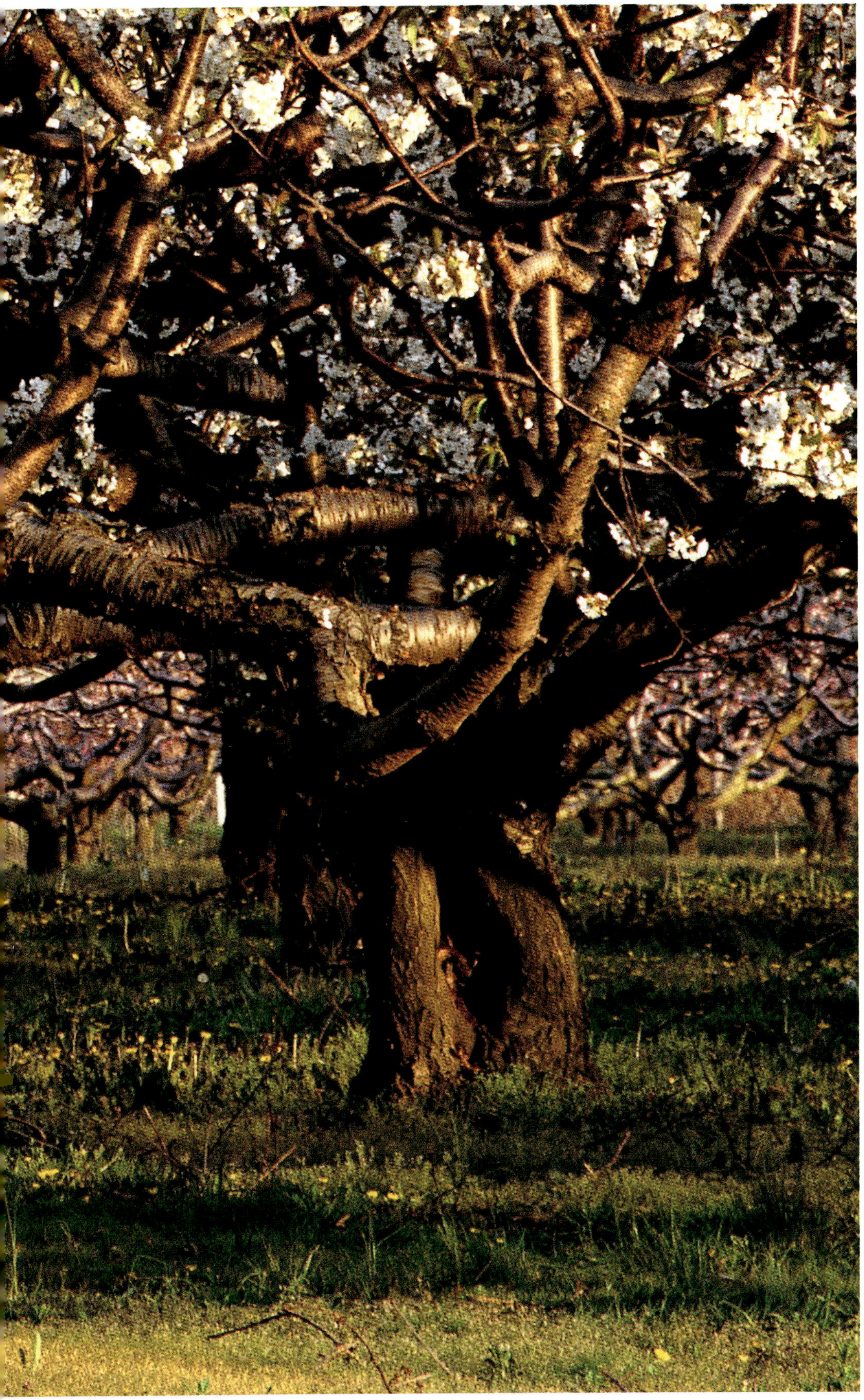

To Amy

We met by the sea.
I appreciate your love, passion, joy, respect, and support.

In memory of Sam

You believed in my art.
We shared friendship and a love of travel.

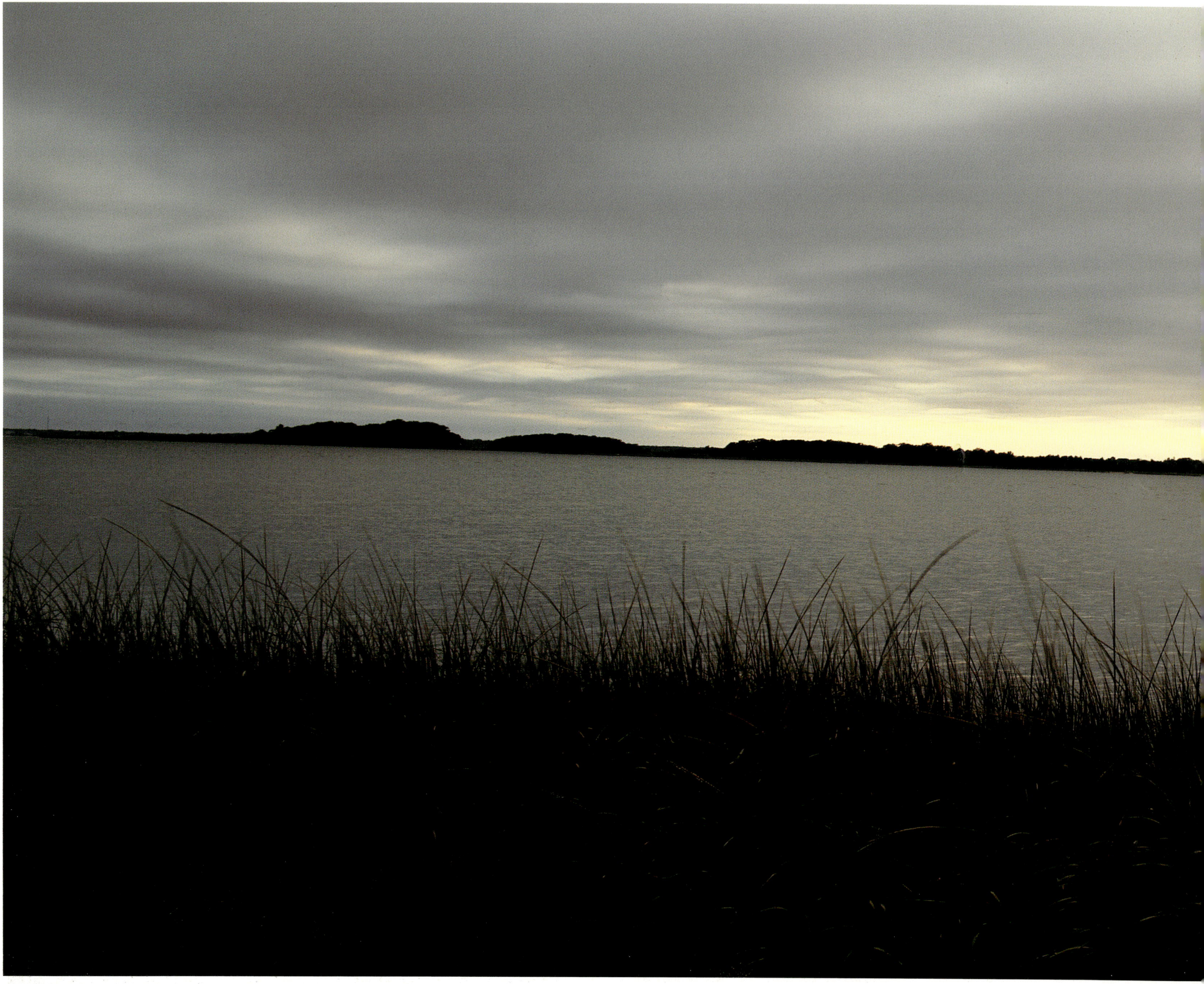

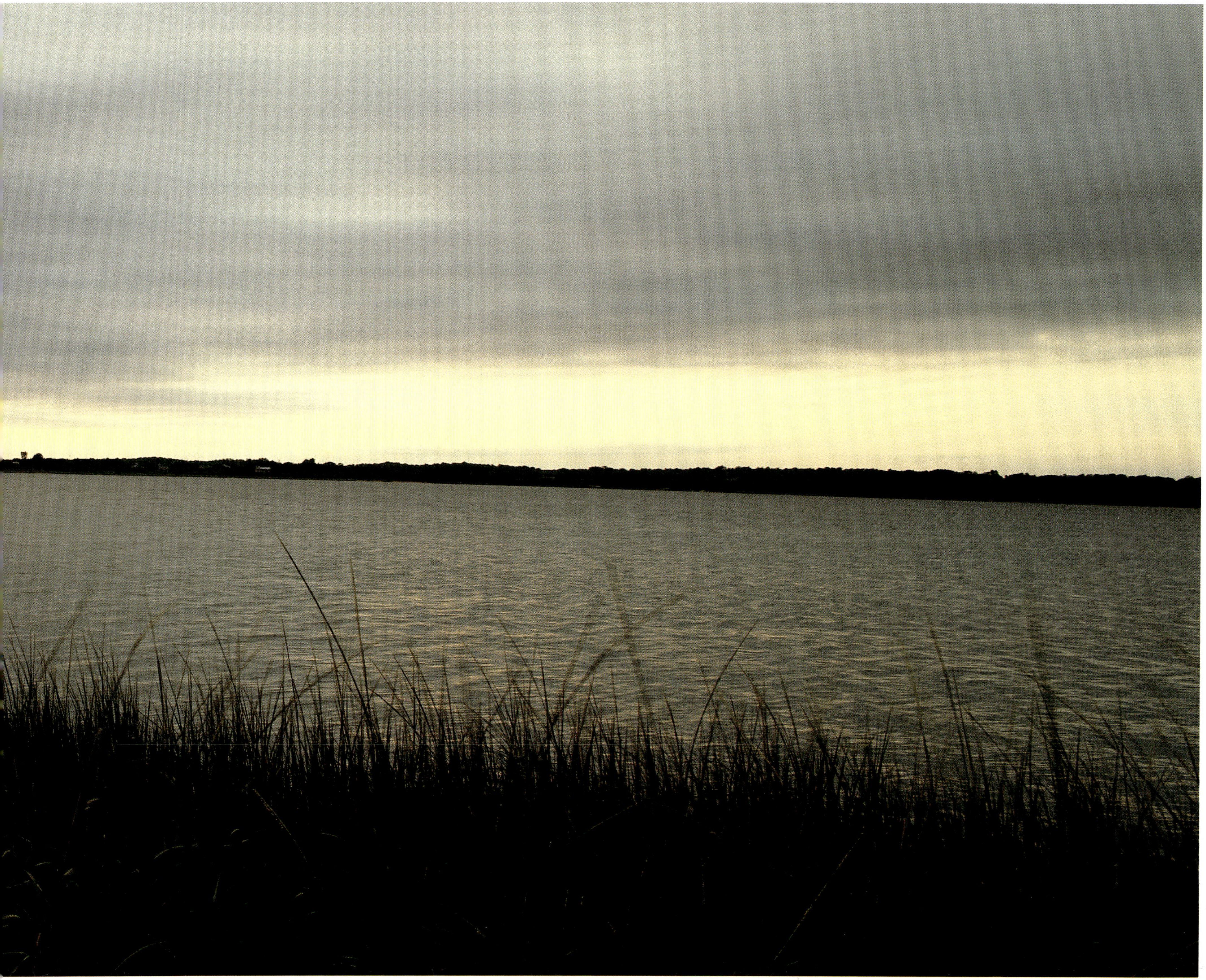

# Sea Change

DAWN, HALLOCK'S BAY. A heavy mist hangs low upon the still water. Although there is not the least breath of wind, the cordgrass whispers in the salt marsh. A great blue heron tiptoes in the shallows, head bowed, lost in thought. A horseshoe crab glides slowly past, through water so crystalline as to be nearly invisible. From its perch atop a twenty-foot pole, an osprey solemnly considers its options, gives its wings an unhurried stretch, and leaps into the incipient sunrise. At the far end of the bay, a lone clammer stalks chest-deep at a stately, measured pace, unconsciously mimicking the heron. The sun emerges from the Atlantic, rises over the low palisade of red cedar and blackjack oak on the barrier beach, and awakens a family of long-tailed ducks, grunting to life in the bulrushes. The mist rises like a curtain on the new day.

Are we at the far end of the world, or at the beginning of time? Although Hallock's is only a hundred miles from Manhattan, a certain disconnect is forgivable. The North Fork of Long Island tends to disorient everyone encountering it for the first time. The initial impulse that comes to anyone asked to describe the North Fork is to define it by what it is not: It is not the Long Island of Brooklyn and Queens, New York City's gritty, multiethnic outer boroughs; nor is it the Long Island of the popular imagination, a daunting sprawl of decultured suburbs and gridlocked freeways. Much less is it the Long Island of its celebrated twin, the South Fork, home of money-saturated Hamptons, polo-playing fundraisers, and media-besotted beautiful people. It is a place quite apart, not two hours from the throbbing metropolis yet apparently suspended in its own bubble of time and space.

Paumanok, one of several Algonquin names for precolonial Long Island, was once believed to refer to the land's vague resemblance to a fish, as Walt Whitman famously pointed out in *Leaves of Grass*. While it is unlikely that the island's thirteen tribes had much interest in what their homeland looked like from outer space, the fact is that it does indeed resemble some sort of marine creature—a pilot whale, perhaps, or a shark—facing west, with Jamaica Bay as its mouth and the North and South Forks as its upper and lower tail fins, suspended between the Long Island Sound and the Atlantic Ocean. The mouth of the Peconic River, where it empties into Flanders Bay at the city of Riverhead, marks the dividing point between the twin forks. Between them lie Peconic Bay and its three islands: Robins, Shelter, and Gardiners. From Riverhead, the North Fork extends like a great spindly finger some forty miles eastward, ending at Plum Gut, a turbulent channel of water between Orient Point and Plum Island. Beyond that are Block Island Sound and the open Atlantic.

By far the most common way of entering the North Fork is to drive the length of the Long Island Expressway to its terminus at Riverhead, and then to take the old colonial road, Route 25, all the way to the point. It is not an auspicious beginning, as the Riverhead segment of Route 25 is lined today by mile after mile of strip malls, factory outlets, big-box stores, and auto dealerships. But then something unexpected, and almost miraculous, happens near the Southold town line. Four lanes narrow to two, the road begins to dip and curve as a country road should, and development gives way to farm stands, church steeples, plowed fields, orchards, vineyards, and quaint—but not too quaint—hamlets and villages. Through Laurel, Mattituck, Cutchogue, Peconic, Southold, Greenport, East Marion, and Orient, the last fifty years or so seem to melt away until, at last—even if this is your very first visit—you begin to understand why childhood memories retain their golden fondness deep into disillusioned adulthood. For this is where it all began. This is how it was, and how it is, and how it may yet survive to be.

It is precisely that quality of the land—simultaneously timeless, in the moment, and embellished by memory—that Jake Rajs captures in his photography. His vision propels us upward to the restless sky, outward to the unfathomable sea, and inward to the slumbering soul.

As you push on eastward, the contours of the land begin to make themselves felt. To the south, deep inlets, lined with salt grass and stands of white oak and swamp maple, push inland from the bay almost to the road. To the north, vast flat, open fields rise gently to the wooded bluffs overlooking the Sound. At Dam Pond, between East Marion and Orient, the wasp-waisted peninsula contracts to the width of the causeway, bringing Connecticut, Shelter Island, and Montauk into stunning, simultaneous view. It then widens out into wooded hills to the north and broad, flat fields to the south, many reclaimed long ago from aboriginal wetlands and none more than a few scant feet above sea level.

Nowhere on the North Fork are you ever more than a mile or two from the water; its presence is the one overwhelming constant of North Fork reality, from the comparative mildness of its winters and the pale translucence of its light to the ubiquity of boatyards, fish markets, and dinghies for sale roadside. Water defines the North Fork the way a mountain is defined by its own slopes, both delimiting it from and connecting it to all that surrounds it. It is not always easy to determine where one begins and the other ends.

---

One thing is certain: water has been the North Fork's defining element since the very beginning. During the last ice age, the Wisconsin Glacier extended from Canada to its terminal position down the central spine of Long Island. Over the millennia, the glacier advanced and retreated, scouring the land and creating outwash plains and recessional moraines, including the one that defines the Sound shore of the North Fork. When the glacier retreated definitively back to Connecticut some twenty thousand years ago, it left behind kettle lakes and some of the richest, deepest stone-free soil on the East Coast. It did not take long for the native peoples of the region, themselves recent arrivals from Asia and the North American west, to discover and exploit the pristine natural bounty of their new, and newly temperate, home. This was the first and last time that the word "discover" could be used in its fullest sense in relation to the migration of nations through North America.

The four Algonquin-speaking tribes of the East End—the Shinnecock and Montauk of the South Fork, the Manhanset of Shelter Island, and the Corchaug of the North Fork—could plausibly have served as the models for the archetypical, or stereotypical, peaceable children of nature painted by early European colonists. On the North Fork especially, they had everything they could possibly desire for a full, healthful, prosperous existence. The bays provided an essentially limitless supply of porgy, weakfish, flounder, fluke, alewives, and turtles; vast underwater beds of eelgrass nurtured scallops, oysters, clams, mussels, and crabs. Corn, fertilized by menhaden seined from the shallows, grew readily and in abundance. Dense forests of oak, maple, and white pine were rich and uncontested foraging and hunting grounds, teeming with white-tailed deer and wild turkey. The related tribes were at peace with one another and held a virtual monopoly on purple and white wampum, cylindrical beads painstakingly manufactured from the shells of quahogs and traded as far west as Ohio. For centuries, the only dark cloud on the Corchaugs' horizon was the recurrent threat of raids by the Pequots, their overlords across the Sound in Connecticut, as commemorated in the real meaning of the name Paumanok—"land of tribute."

By the 1630s, the Dutch in New Amsterdam and the English of the Massachusetts Bay and New Haven colonies had been trading with the East End natives for a decade, but their dreams of establishing permanent colonies there remained stymied by the warlike Pequots. Only when the Pequots were decimated by war in 1637 did it become possible for the Europeans to expand into eastern Long Island. In 1640, the Reverend John Youngs, a native of Southwold, in Suffolk, England, led a small group of nonconformists from New Haven into Peconic Bay and founded Southold, the oldest English town in New York (a claim that remains disputed by Southampton). Although they had a strongly stockaded village—the remains of which can still be seen by Down's Creek on Fort Neck—Corchaug resistance was nonexistent, and the natives were soon confined to a small reserve on Indian Neck. When even that was denied them, they seemed to melt away like spring snow. The last Corchaug, David Hannibal, died in 1936.

What the English found on the North Fork were not the typical hardscrabble challenges encountered by most early colonists. The Corchaugs had cleared hundreds of acres of prime farmland—known locally as the "Broad Fields"—sparing their usurpers the arduous task of hacking farmland out of the primeval forest. The creeks were lined with ample provision of salt hay for the newcomers' plow horses; freshwater springs were abundant; the woods offered fine mature oak for housing and white pine for shipbuilding. With all these riches at their disposal, the New Haven colonists rapidly spread across the peninsula and most readily adapted themselves to the lives of prosperous, settled farmers and landowners, raising wheat, rye, and corn. For the next 250 years, the North Fork essentially slept, the principal thrust of its historical trajectory reflected in the catalog of land transfers among the descendents of the original settlers, whose names—Horton, Wickham, Tuthill, Wells, Latham—dominate local politics, farming, and tombstone inscriptions to this day. In the words of local historian Wayland Jefferson, "There are no epic adventures to be told and no pretense is made that this history recounts events of major importance."

Of course, no history, howsoever supine, is entirely without defining moments, and even that of the North Fork has a few of its own. Let me parse the highlights. In 1664, Southold was compelled—very reluctantly—to sever its ties to Connecticut and become subject to the Duke of York and thus, eventually, a part of New York state. In the 1690s, Captain Kidd plied the waters of the bay, burying his treasure somewhere on or near Gardiners Island. Throughout the Revolutionary War, Southold remained under British occupation; while many of its inhabitants were loyalists, more than half fled to Connecticut. In 1838, the hamlet of Winter Harbor incorporated and changed its name to Greenport, becoming home port to a large whaling fleet that prospered throughout the early and mid-nineteenth century. In 1844, the railroad came to the North Fork, with its terminus at Greenport, opening markets for local produce in New York City and bringing the first tourists. By the late nineteenth century, Orient had become a popular and sophisticated resort, and artists had begun to settle in Peconic, including Edward August Bell and Irving Wiles, founder of the Peconic school. Albert Einstein spent several summers in Cutchogue in the 1930s.

And that's about it. Though not entirely unaffected by world events, the people of the North Fork remained essentially untouched by most of the revolutionary changes that roiled the rest of civilization through those turbulent centuries.

But change slowly began to make itself felt in the modern era. With the waning of the whaling industry, the North Fork economy was primarily agricultural, with potatoes as its mainstay. Irish and Polish farmers moved in for the first time in the early twentieth century, just as competition from newly opened lands in the West inaugurated a steady decline in prices. Cauliflower and asparagus were reliable cash crops for a time, but cheap Californian produce soon made them unprofitable as well. By the 1950s, with land values soaring and potato prices plummeting, the old farming families began converting to fruit and industrial sod, or selling out to developers. The original Wickham farm fell to a golf course. A planned extension of the Long Island Expressway would have plowed a six-lane highway through the heart of the North Fork to a suspension bridge extending from East Marion to Old Saybrook, Connecticut, effectively destroying the region's rural character. Although community opposition and high costs scotched the Atlantic Expressway, development pressures and the ongoing hardships of the farming community seemed destined to extend the suburbanization of central Long Island to its easternmost extremity.

And then, in 1973, John Wickham sold seventeen acres of potato field to Alex and Louisa Hargrave. The Hargraves had something special in mind for their tiny farm—something that represented both the continuity of the land's age-old agricultural traditions and a bold, even reckless innovation. The North Fork, with so little history of its own, suddenly had a unique new future before it.

---

About ten years ago, my wife and I rented an old farmhouse for the summer, way out in the middle of the fields on Cutchogue's Oregon Road. It had few of the luxury amenities that many summer people look for, but we were thrilled with the bucolic location. Behind the house, potato fields stretched all the way to the middle road; before it, wave after wave of yellow corn seemed to roll and crackle as it rose over the summer into a bright green forest, into which our children gleefully disappeared for hours at a time. The occasional tractor was the only traffic we ever saw from our front porch, and half a mile down a dusty farm path lay the bluffs, beaches, and inviting waters of the Sound.

We had a lazy, memorable summer, and decided to rent the same house the following year, but when we returned to Oregon Road, we had to drive its full length three times before we could find it. We were looking for potatoes and corn as our reference point, and the potato and corn fields had vanished. In their place was a vineyard—the same hundreds of acres were now under tidy parallel rows of merlot and chardonnay. It was a change of clothes that the landscape of the North Fork has been trying on with inexorable frequency in recent years.

In 1975, the Hargraves opened their winery, the first on Long Island, with seventeen acres of cabernet sauvignon, pinot noir, and sauvignon blanc. Twenty years later, thirty-five commercial vineyards accounted for 1,800 acres of former potato fields; by 2006, that number had grown to sixty vineyards and 4,000 acres; and it continues to grow with considerable international investment. As Louisa Hargrave has noted, it is a perfectly natural confluence: "Long Island wines are grown in a cool, temperate climate that protects the elements that make aromatic, smooth, highly energized wines with great natural balance."

It could reasonably be argued that the triumph of wine production has been one of the single most pivotal events in the history of the North Fork since the arrival of the railroad, or even of the first English colonists. Many would no doubt take exception to the notion that the arrival of the vineyards saved the North Fork, but there's no denying that, as local journalist Denise Civiletti rightly points out, "Long Island wineries [have become] central players—if not *the* central players—in our evolving North Fork economy."

Before the Hargraves, suffering farmers had few willing takers for their increasingly valuable land other than developers. Today, with conservation easements, land trusts, and tax incentives, vast tracts that might otherwise be lost forever are being preserved for agriculture. The preservation of the land and the growing environmental consciousness of those who control it have led, in turn, to a sudden—some might say fervid—interest in the North Fork among tourists, and especially wealthy weekenders from New York City, who a decade ago might not even have been able to place it on the map. The North Fork had been "discovered"—again. While that, understandably, might not sit well with those who are being priced out of their ancestral homeland, there is no doubt that it has created a viable, self-sustaining, and vibrant economy that will ensure the survival of all that makes the peninsula unique in the first place—its beaches, its wetlands, its villages, and its waters.

It is a sea change that is still in the making, and no one knows where it may all lead. Given the North Fork's vast, largely untapped potential as an idyllic leisure ground so close to the country's greatest city, it may all seem inevitable in retrospect. Those who have been in on its secrets want to preserve their Brigadoon as they always knew it; newcomers stand mouth agape at its splendors and seek to put their own stamp on it. The process seems to have settled into a comfortable compromise on the North Fork. Standing on the corner of Front and Main in Greenport on a summer's afternoon, watching the colorful (and very civic-minded) motorcycle clubs roar through town, it is still hard to grasp that real estate prices have doubled and doubled again in the past ten years.

Outside curiosity about the North Fork is at an all-time high, reflected in a remarkable efflorescence of world-class eating establishments that specialize in local produce; gleaming fleets of pleasure craft and the well-heeled marinas to accommodate them; and a recent moratorium on development as local governments scramble to adjust to the new realities. On the North Fork, old and new seem, for now, to be cohabiting harmoniously and fruitfully—a phenomenon movingly rendered in Jake Rajs's photographs.

There are, as of this writing, no bottlenecks on the LIE off-ramps, byways remain blissfully clear even in the high season, and day-trippers may still find themselves sharing the road with a laconic tractor or two. On any given summer's day, it is still not unusual to find oneself entirely, almost preternaturally, alone on a great stretch of white sandy beach, disturbed only by the urgent passage of Canada geese. The local kids still fish and leap from the public dock at the end of Greenport's Fifth Street, as they have always done. Victorian manors still share the waterfront with unwinterized bungalow colonies that have been there since they were giving it away. The fishing fleet, though reduced, is still an intrinsic part of the local economy, and small boats still pull up behind Alice's Fish Market at dawn each day to unload their catch. It remains very difficult to find a hip nightclub anywhere in the vicinity—let alone a publicist or a paparazzo—and those hoping to do a little celebrity spotting may have to content themselves with one of the reclusive architects and artists who have colonized Orient village. All that may change as the money and the monied continue to pour in, but for the moment, at least, the North Fork remains what it has always been—a sleepy, dappled, and blessed backwater. The North Fork has awakened, it is true, but it is still basking in the golden mist of its ancient slumber, somewhere between a dream and a sunrise.

JESSE BROWNER

# Sound

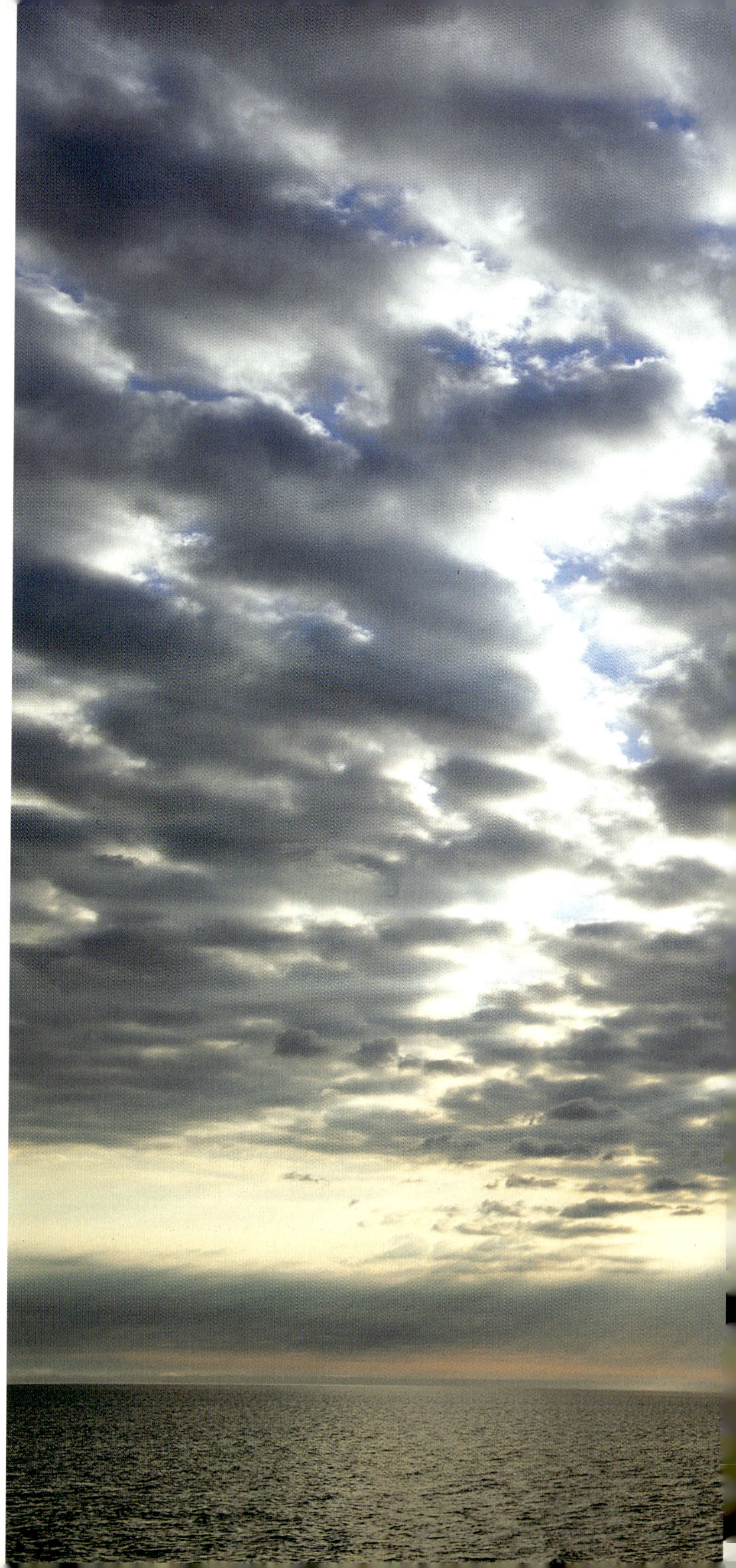

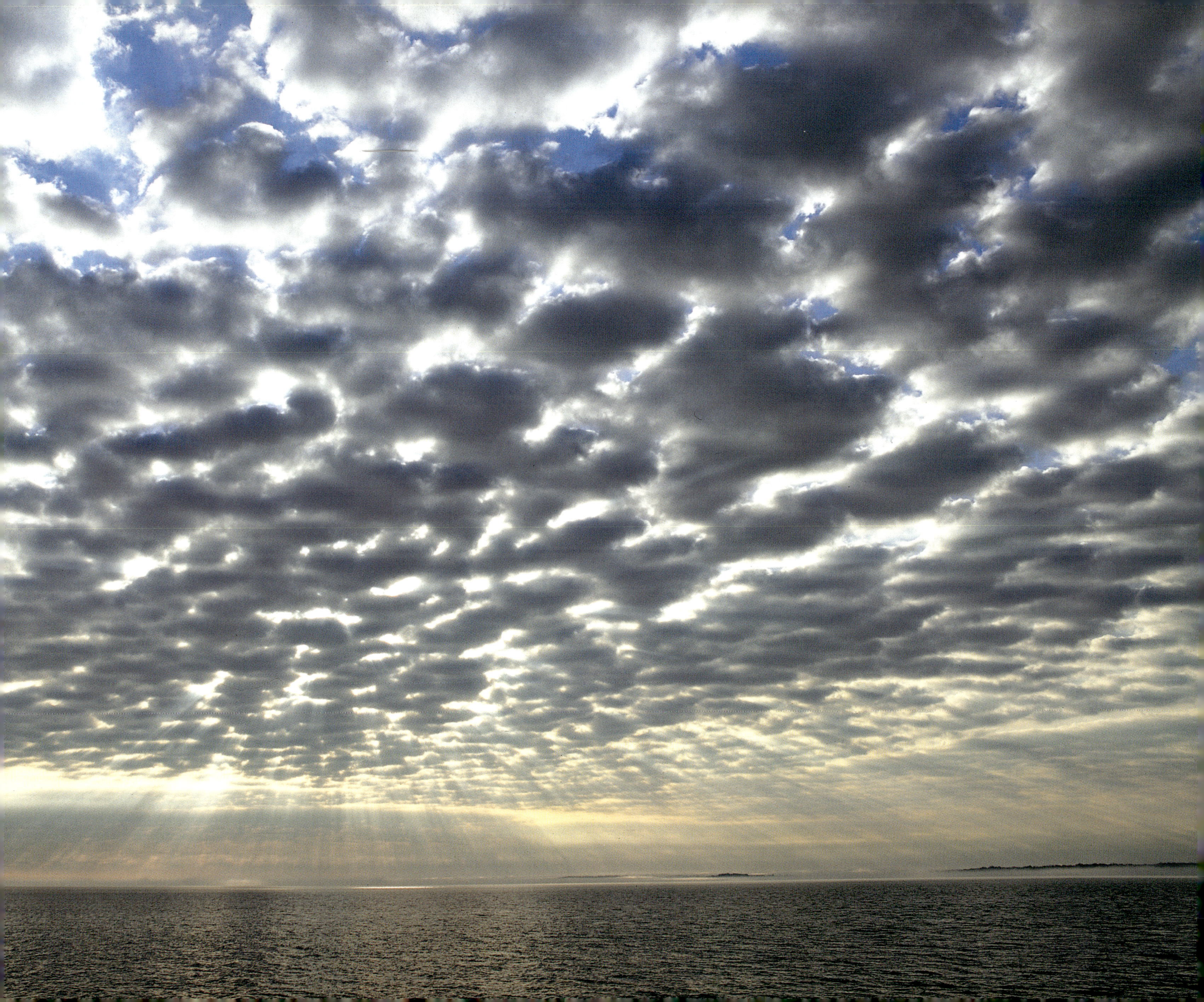

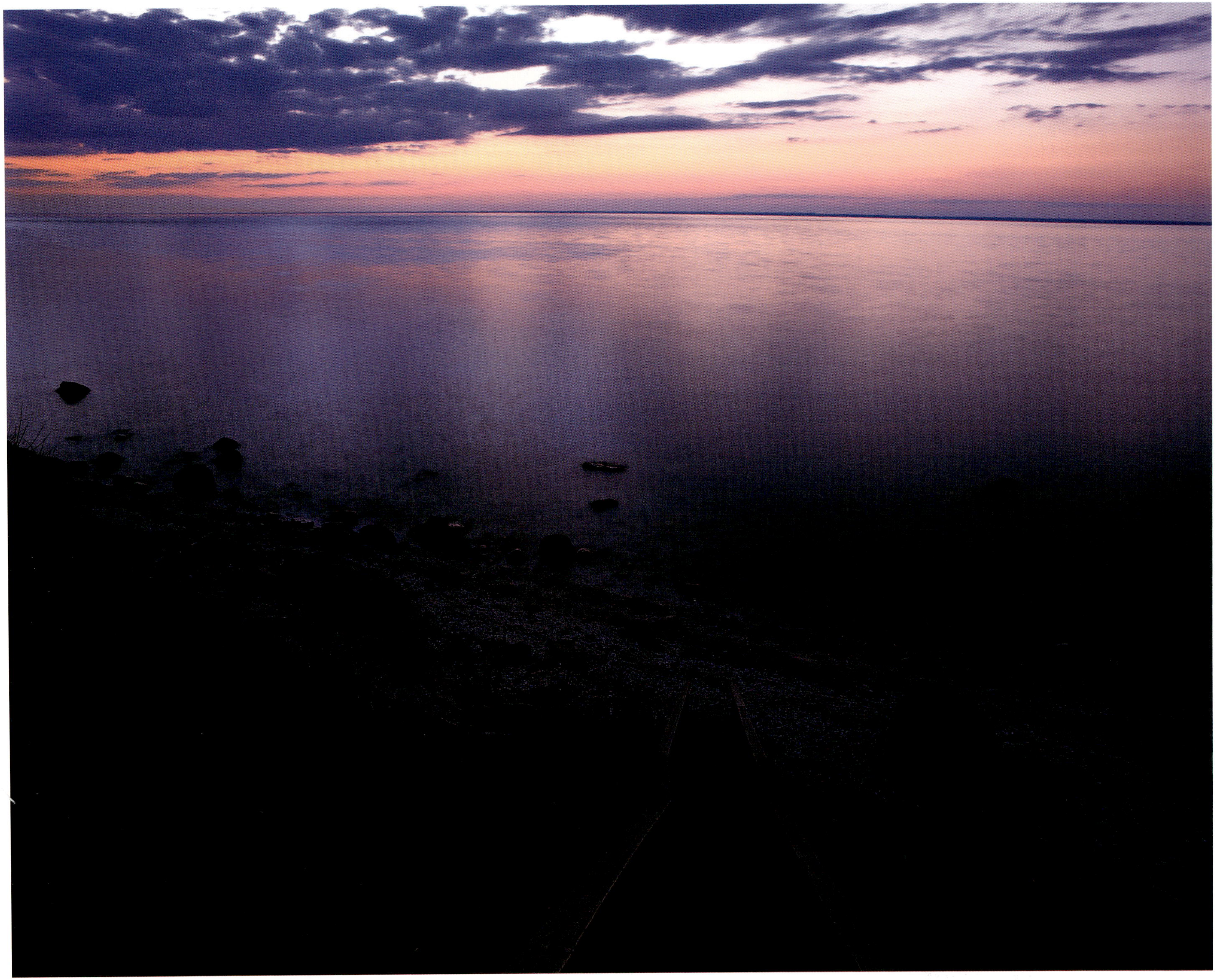

View from Horton's Point Lighthouse Mattituck Inlet, Mattituck → Goldsmith's Inlet, Peconic Park

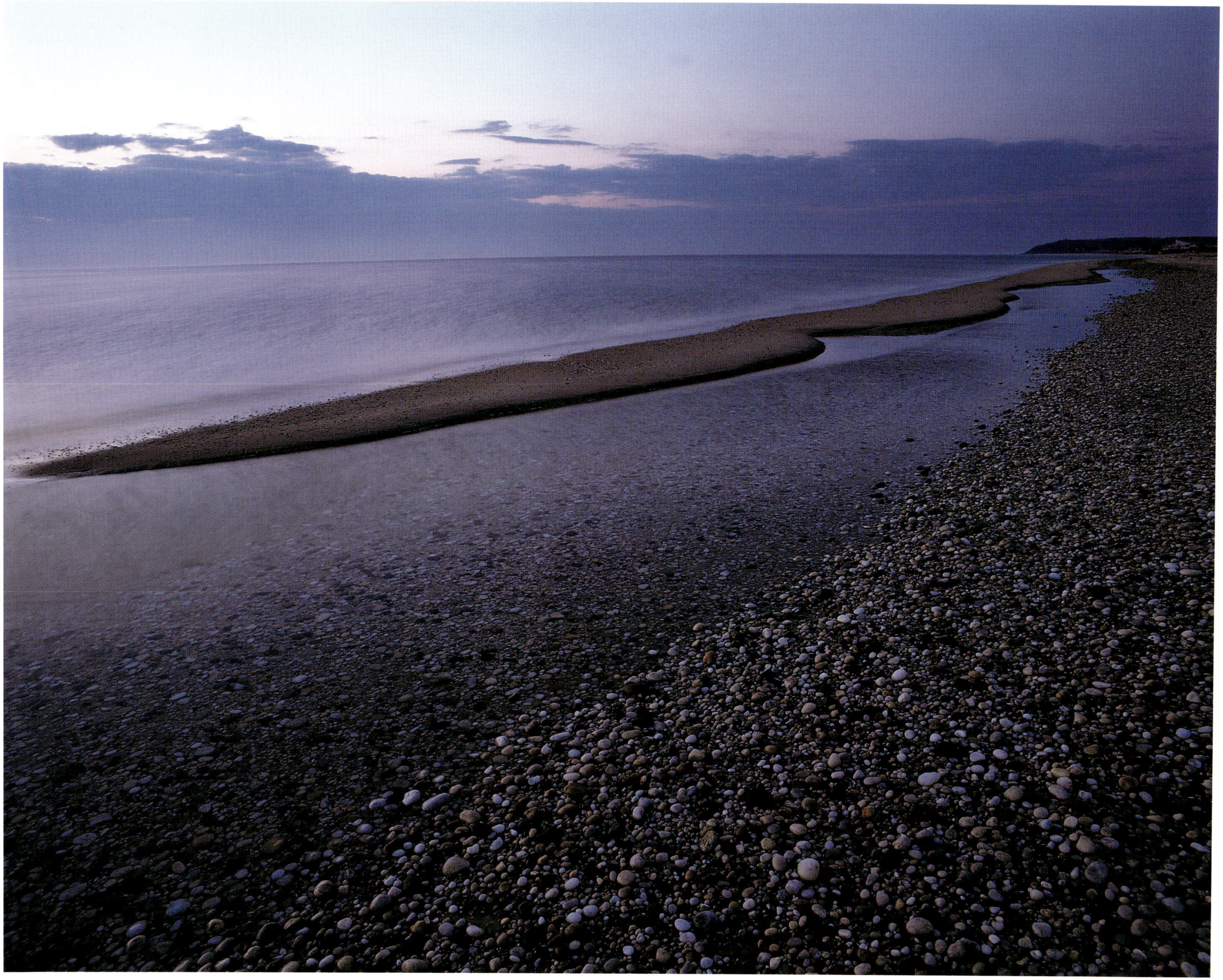

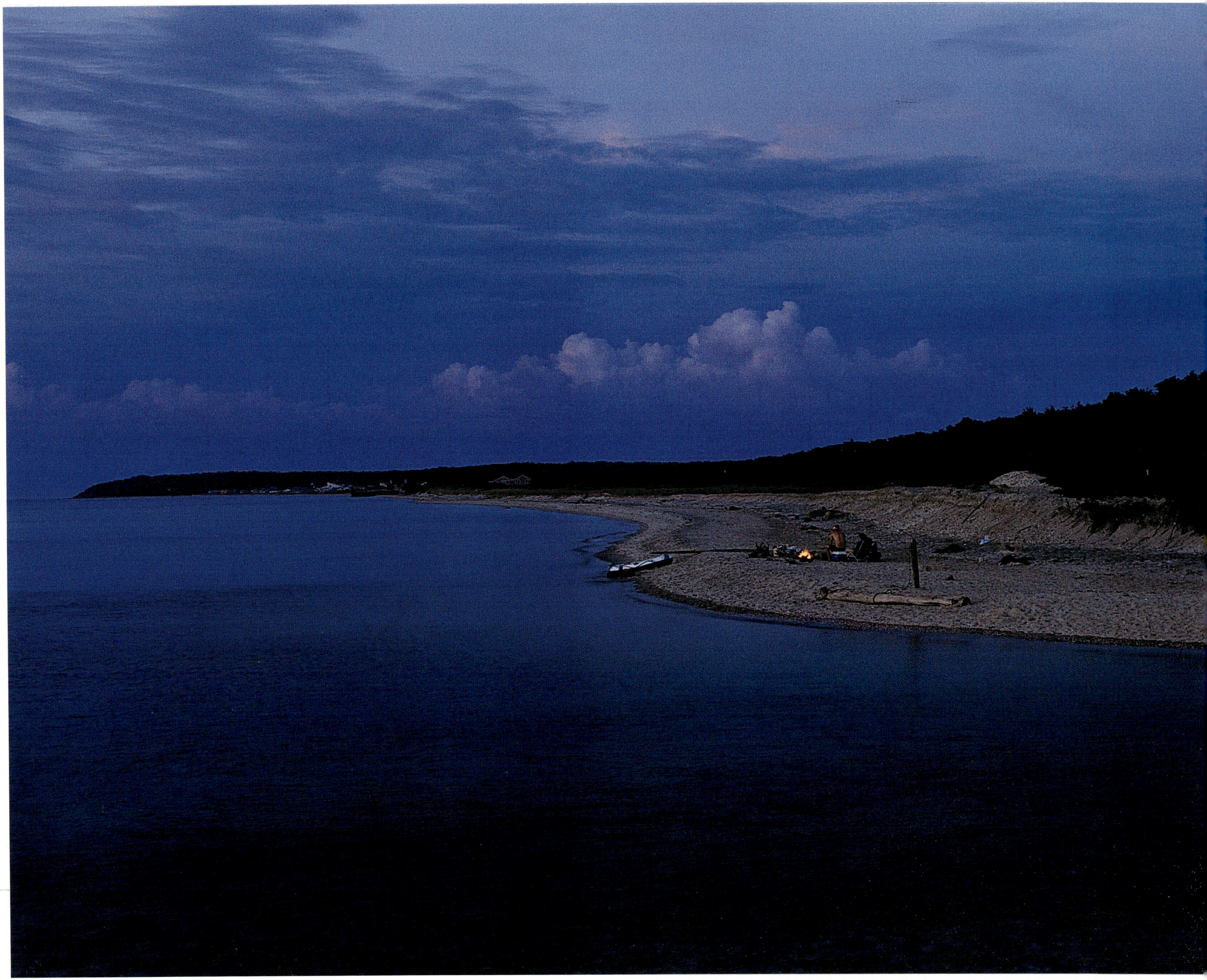

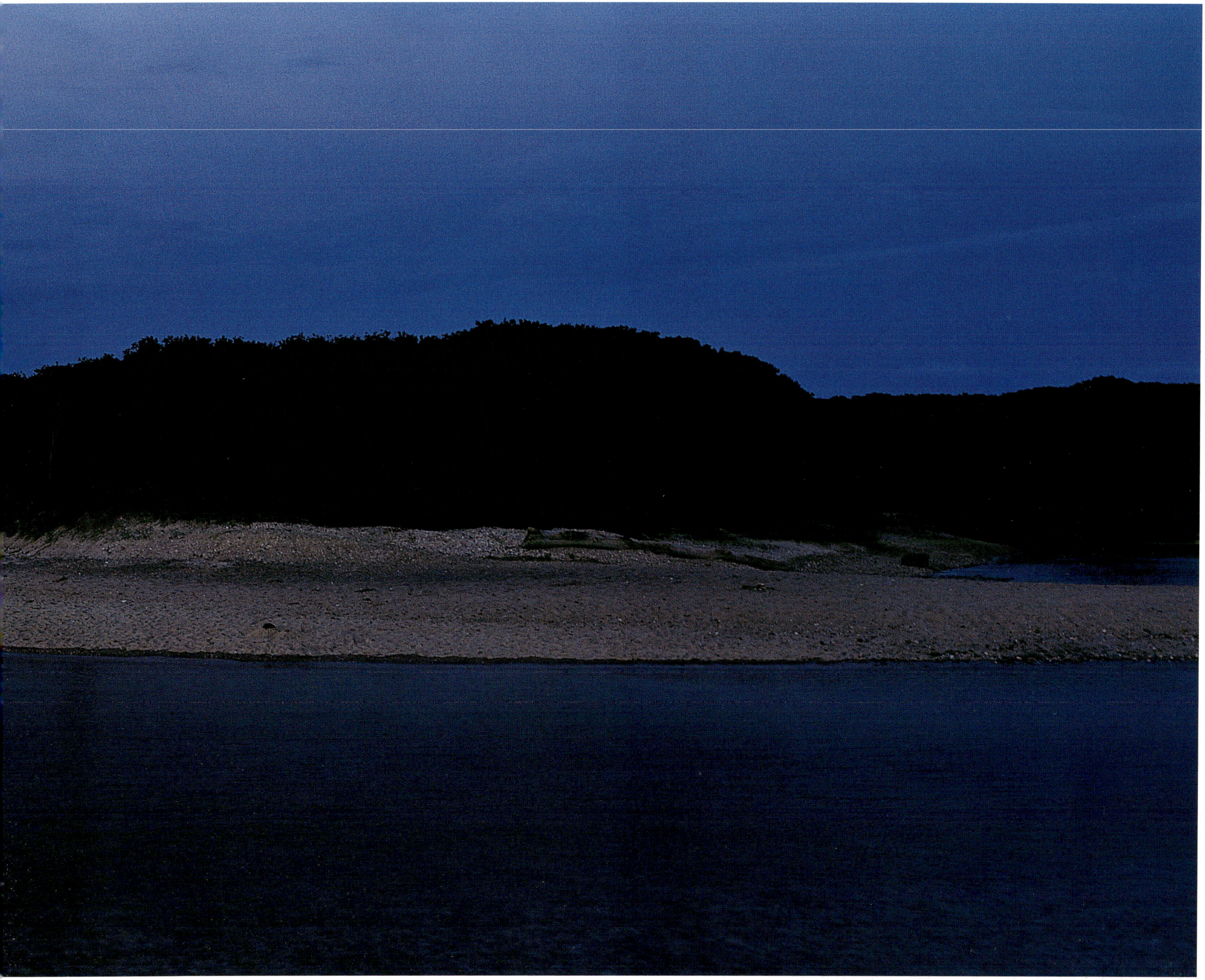

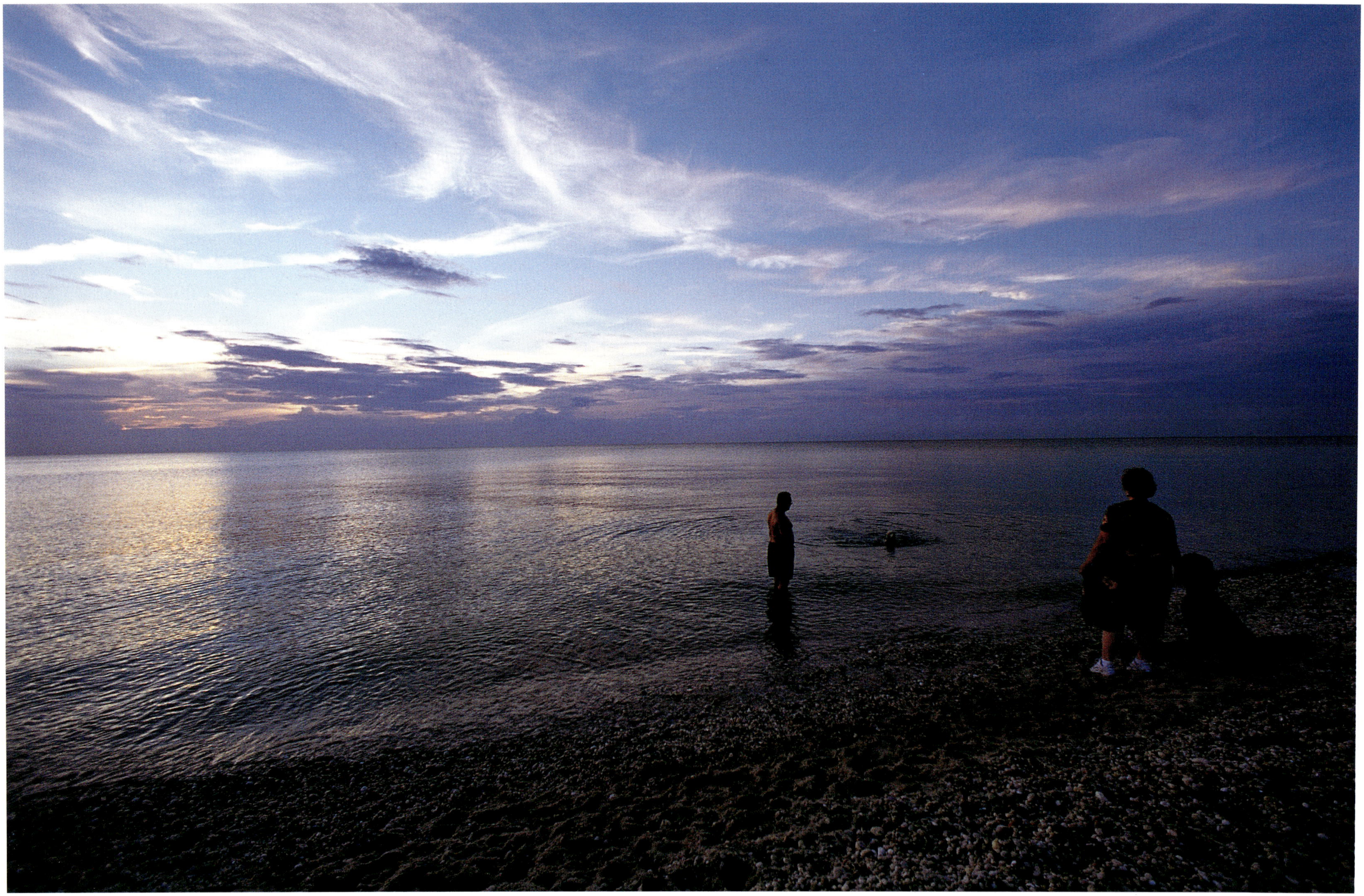

Goldsmith's Inlet, Peconic Park    Town Beach, Southold

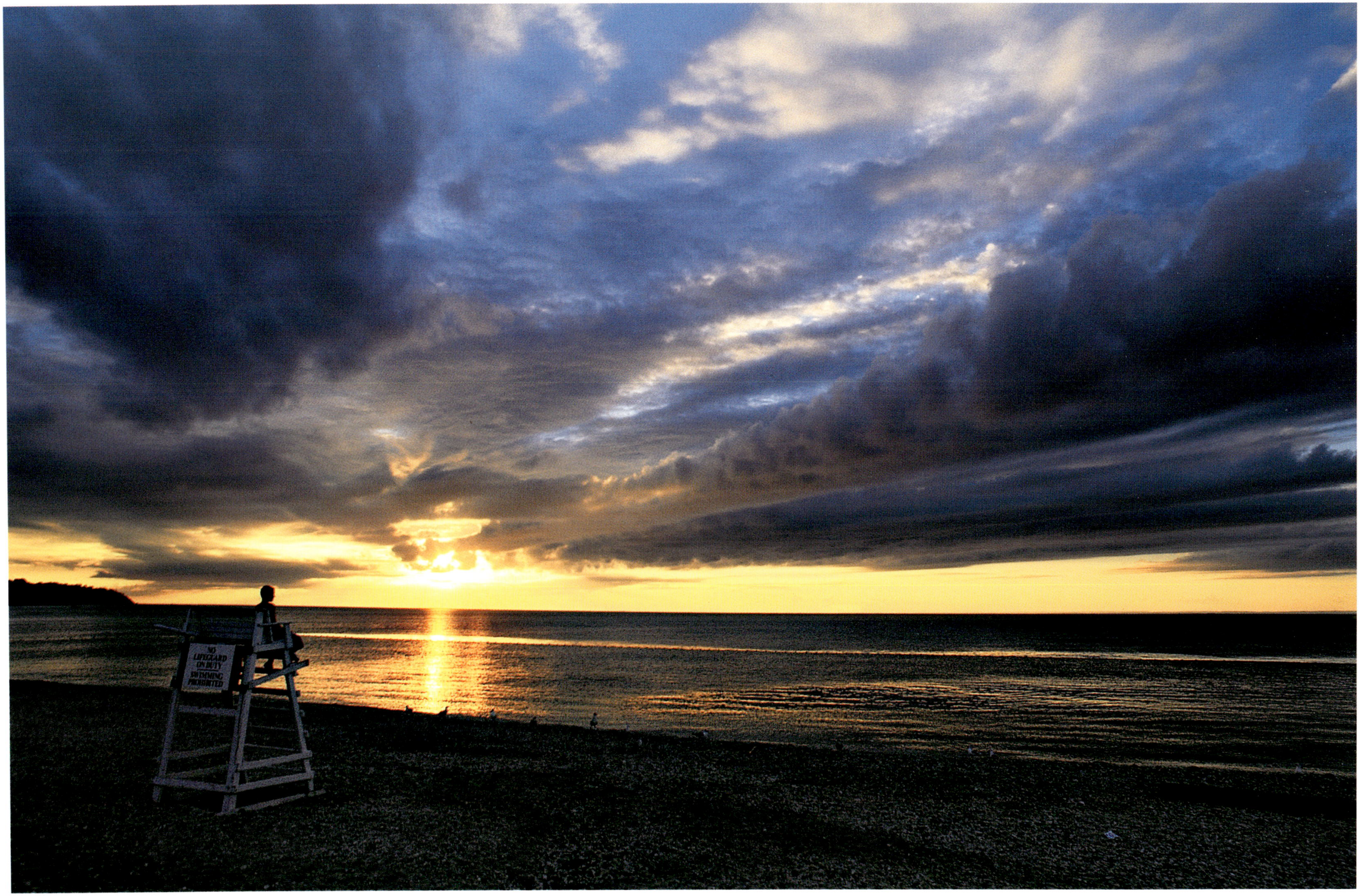
NO
LIFEGUARD
ON DUTY
SWIMMING
PROHIBITED

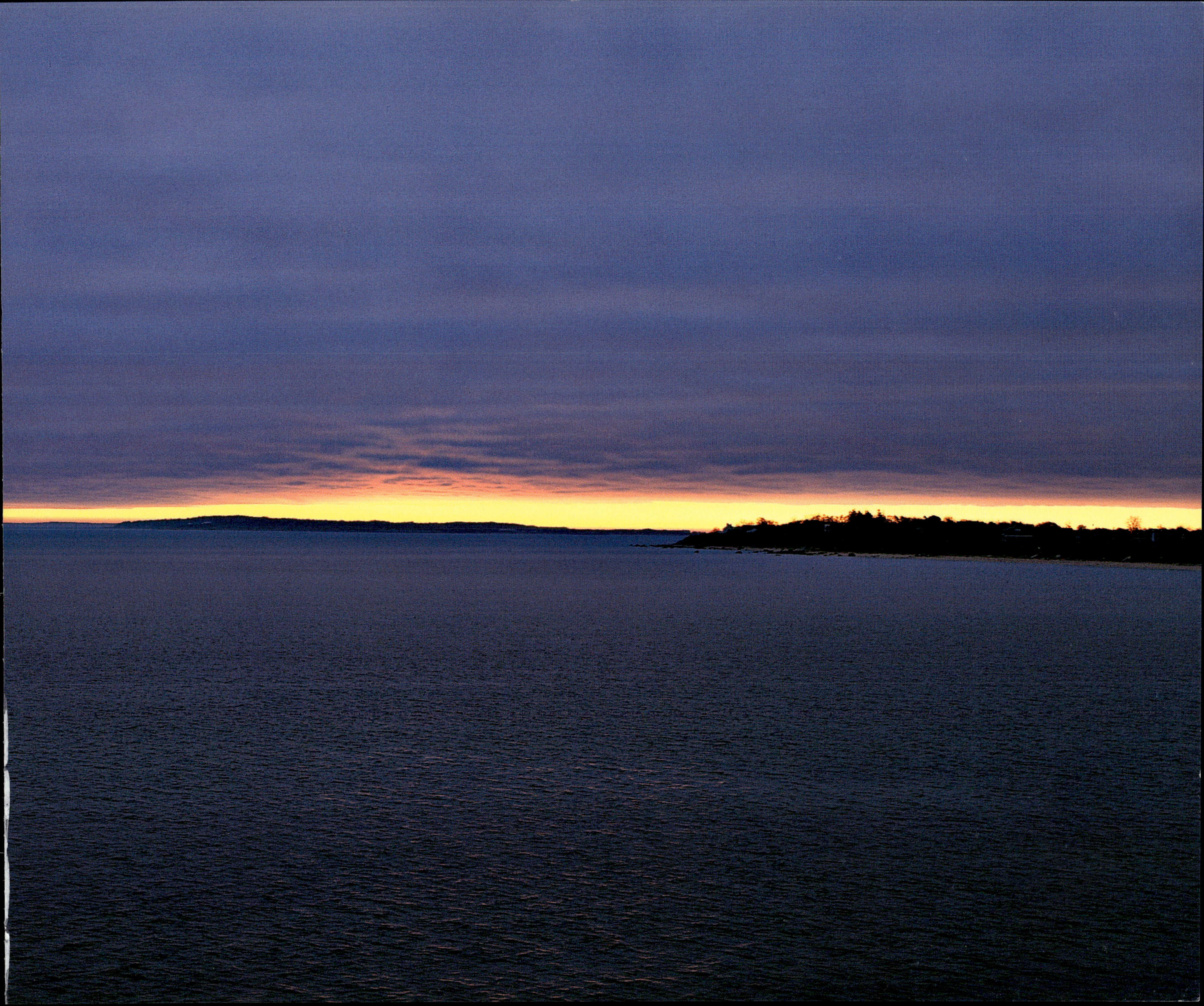

Birch Beach, Cutchogue

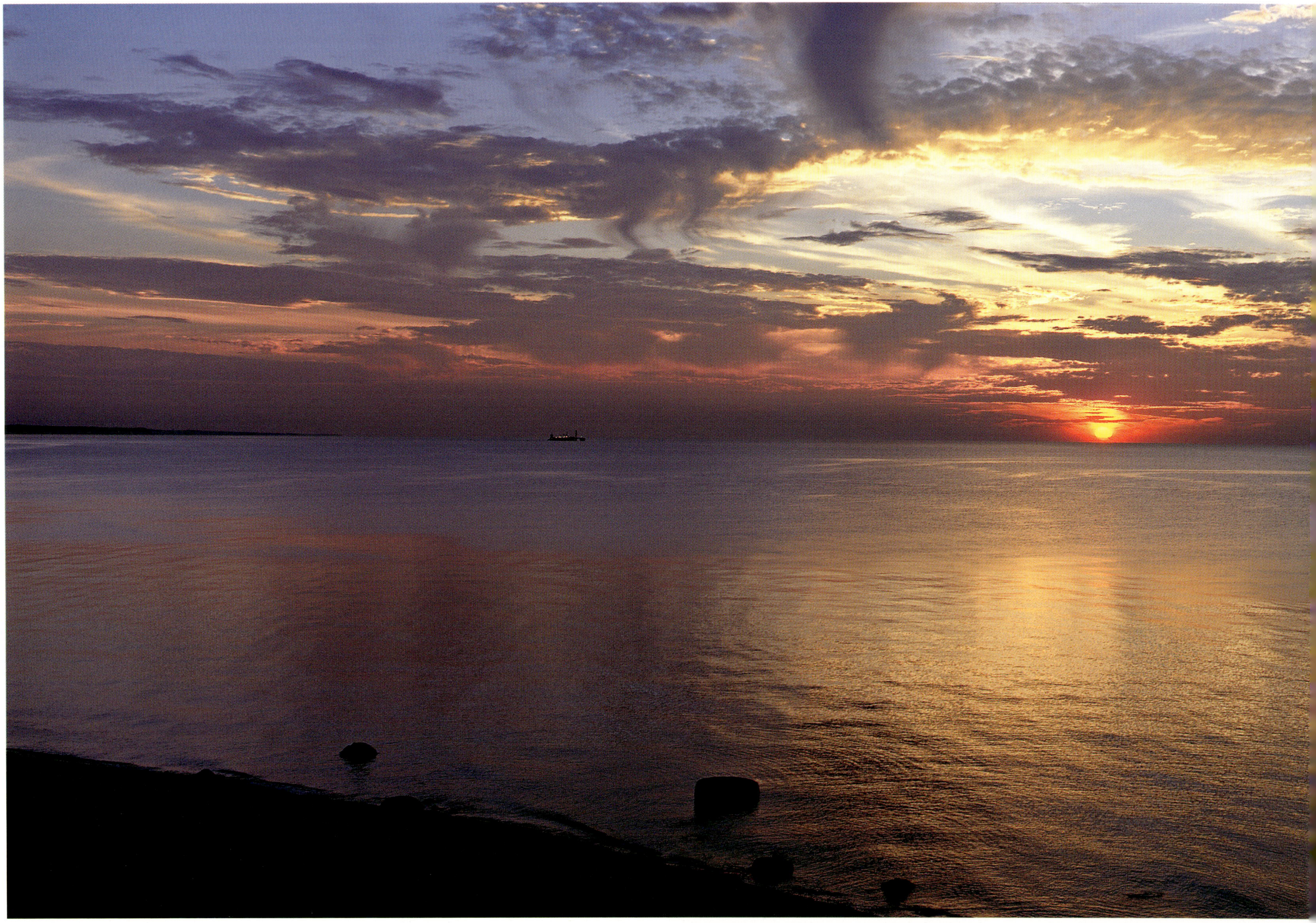

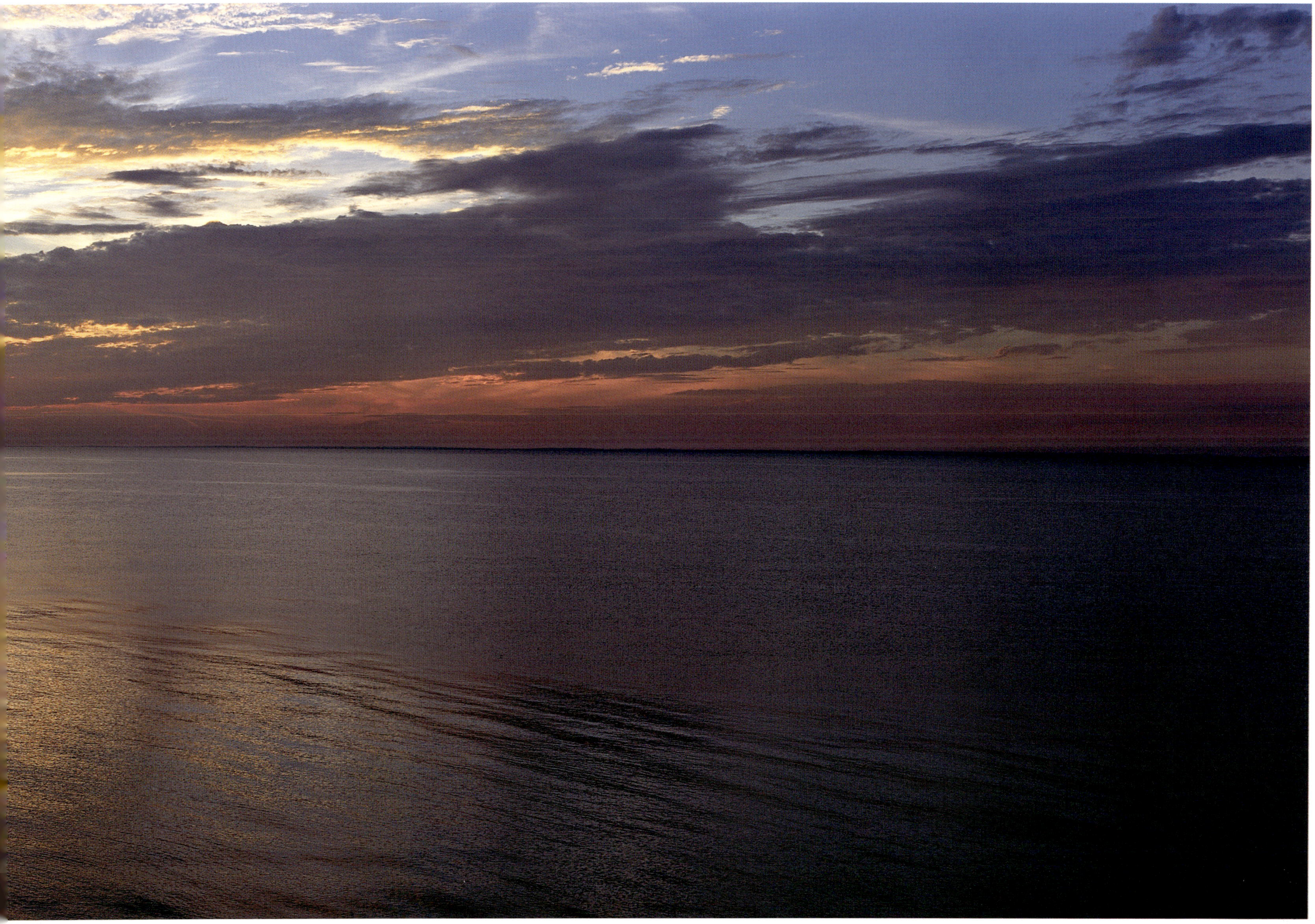

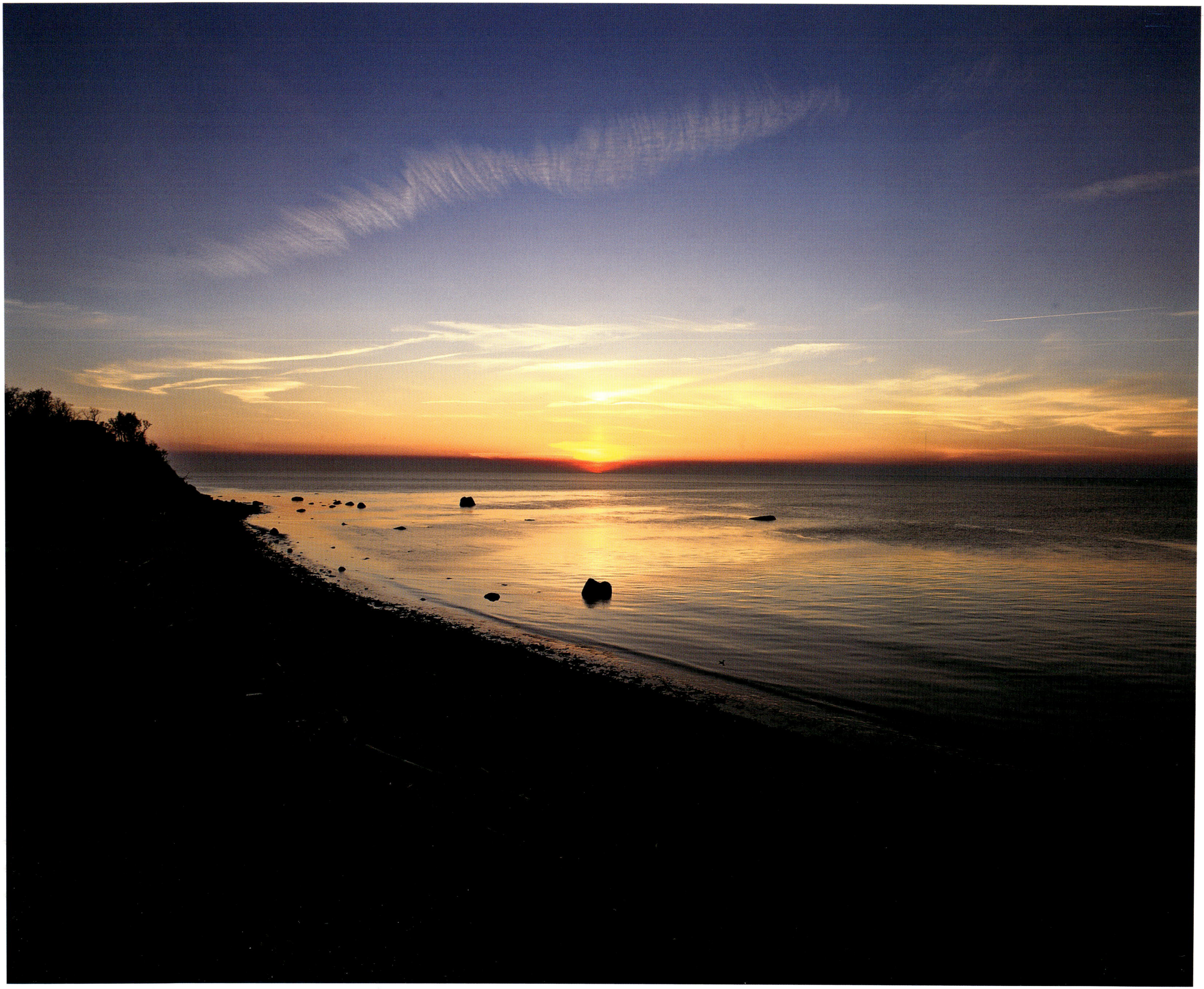

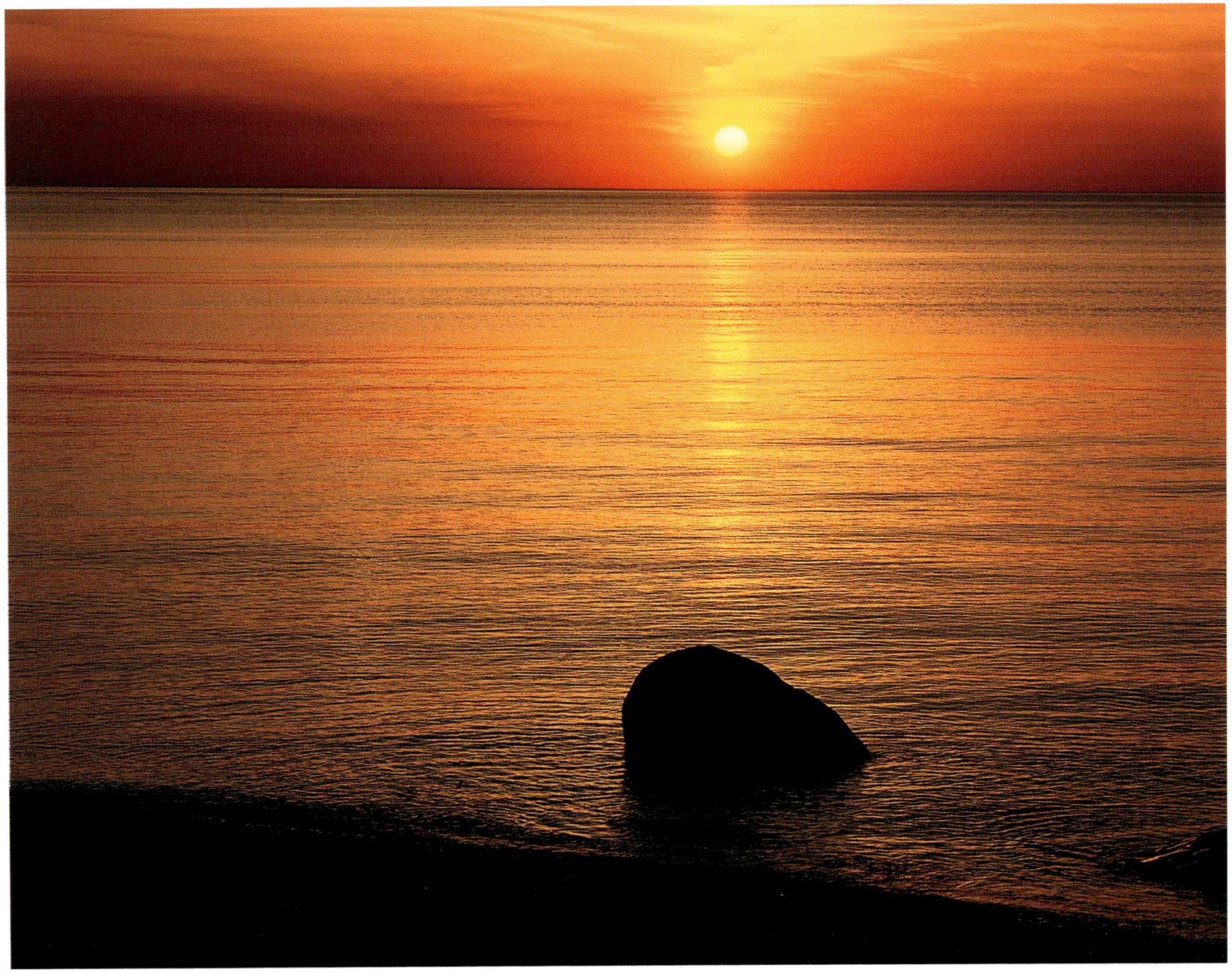

Orient Southold

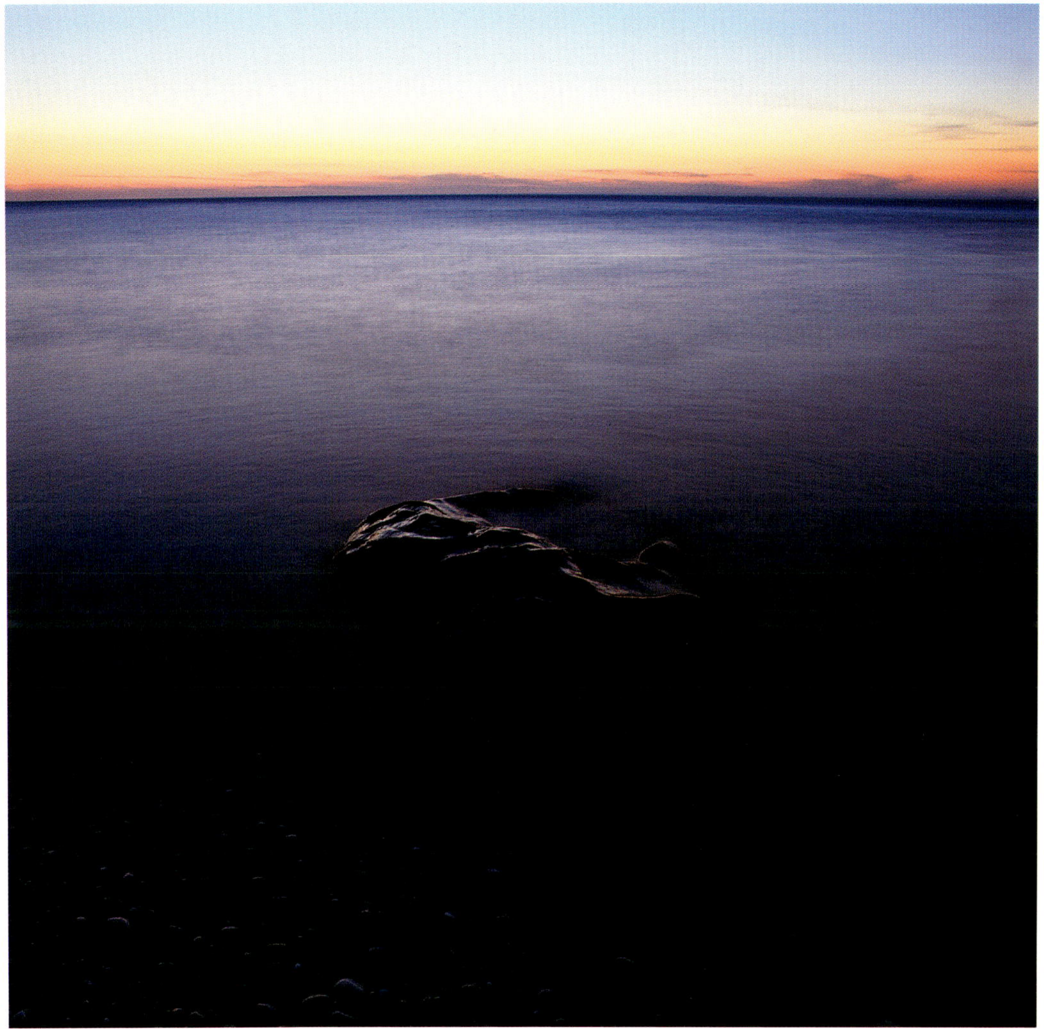

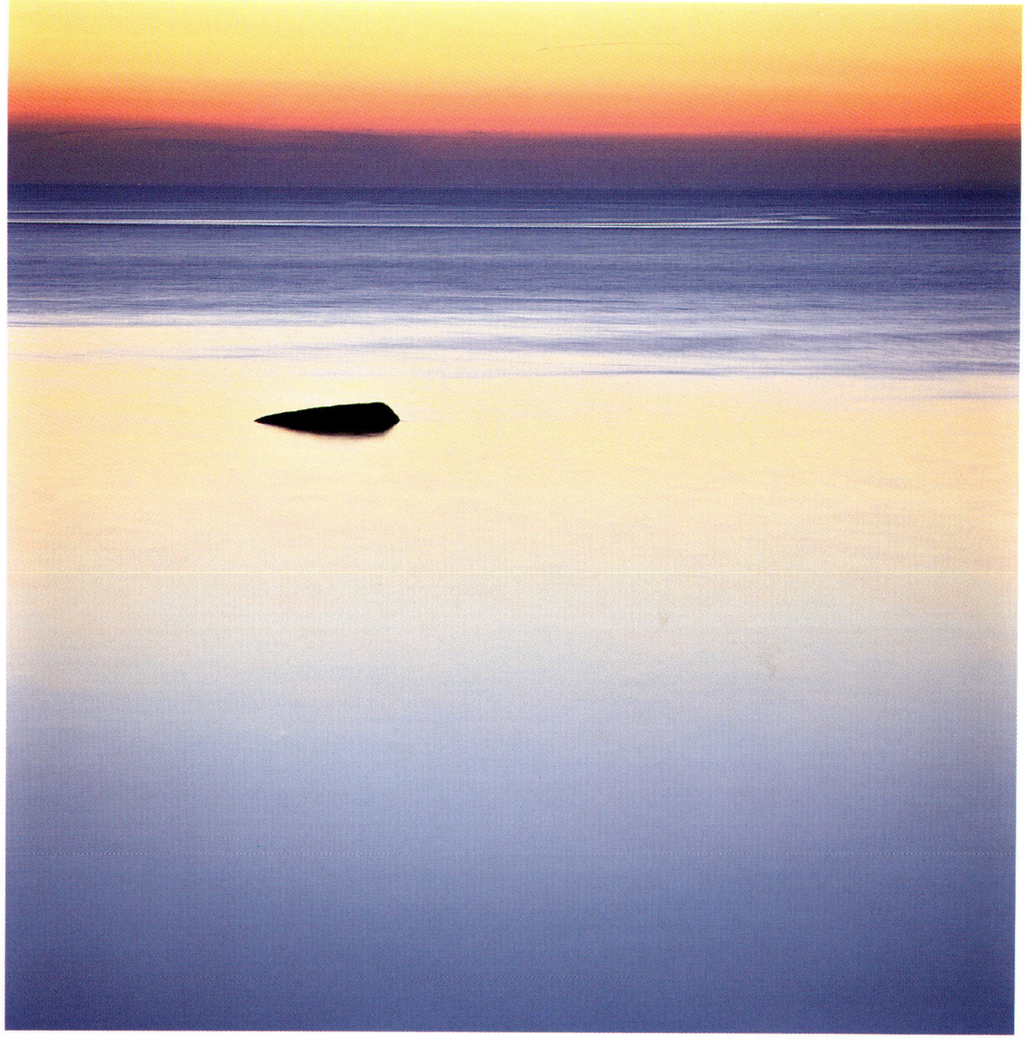

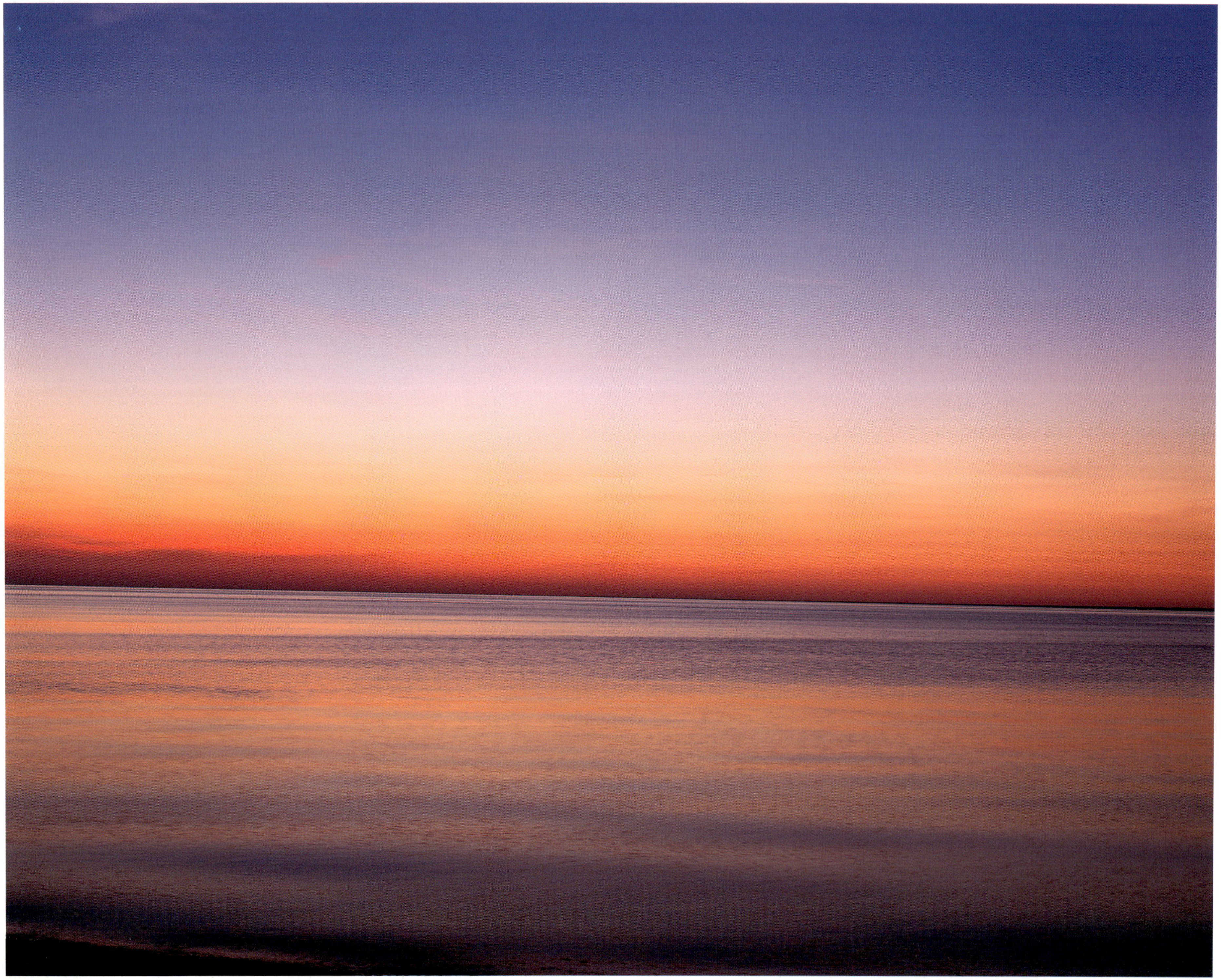

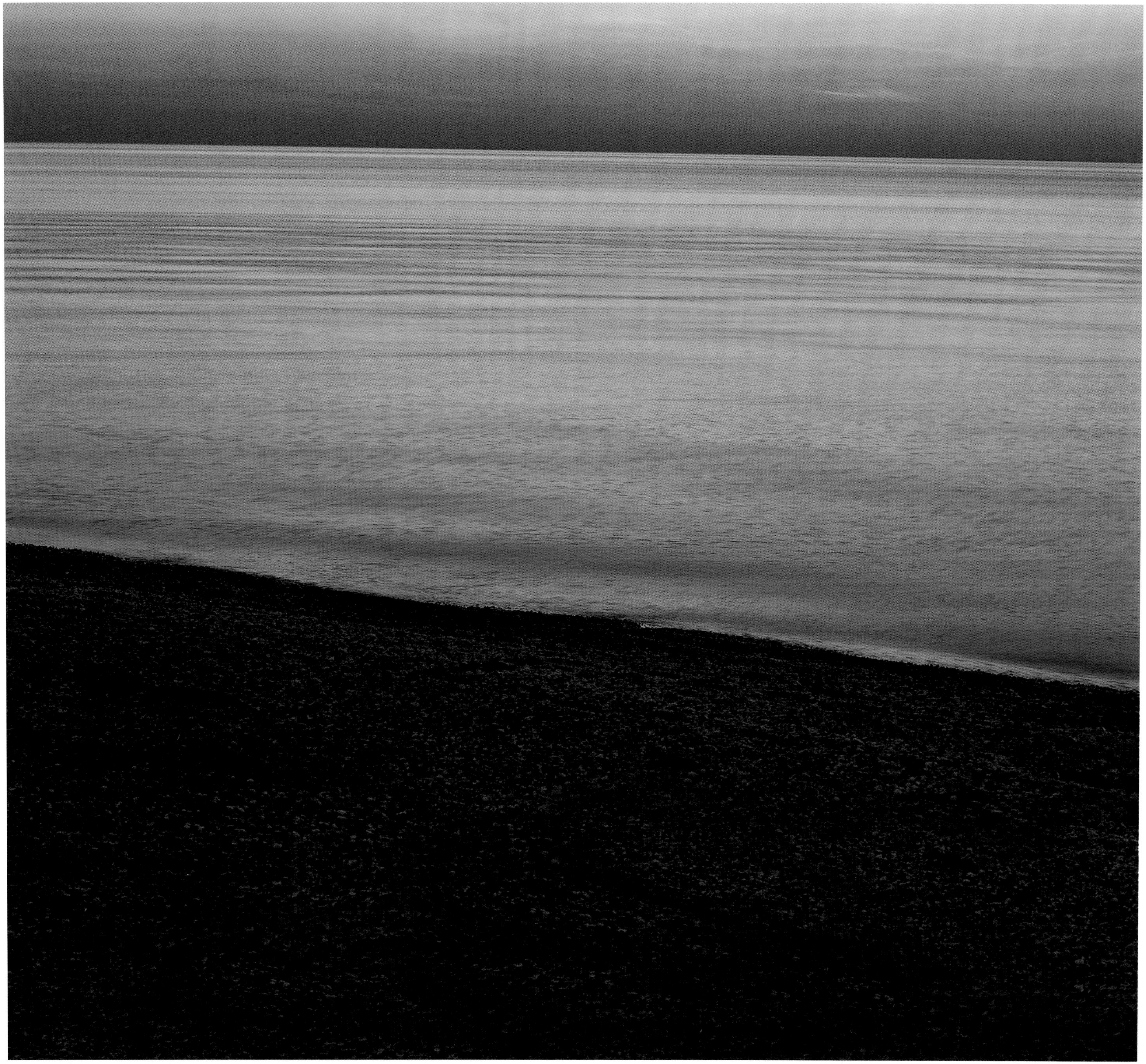

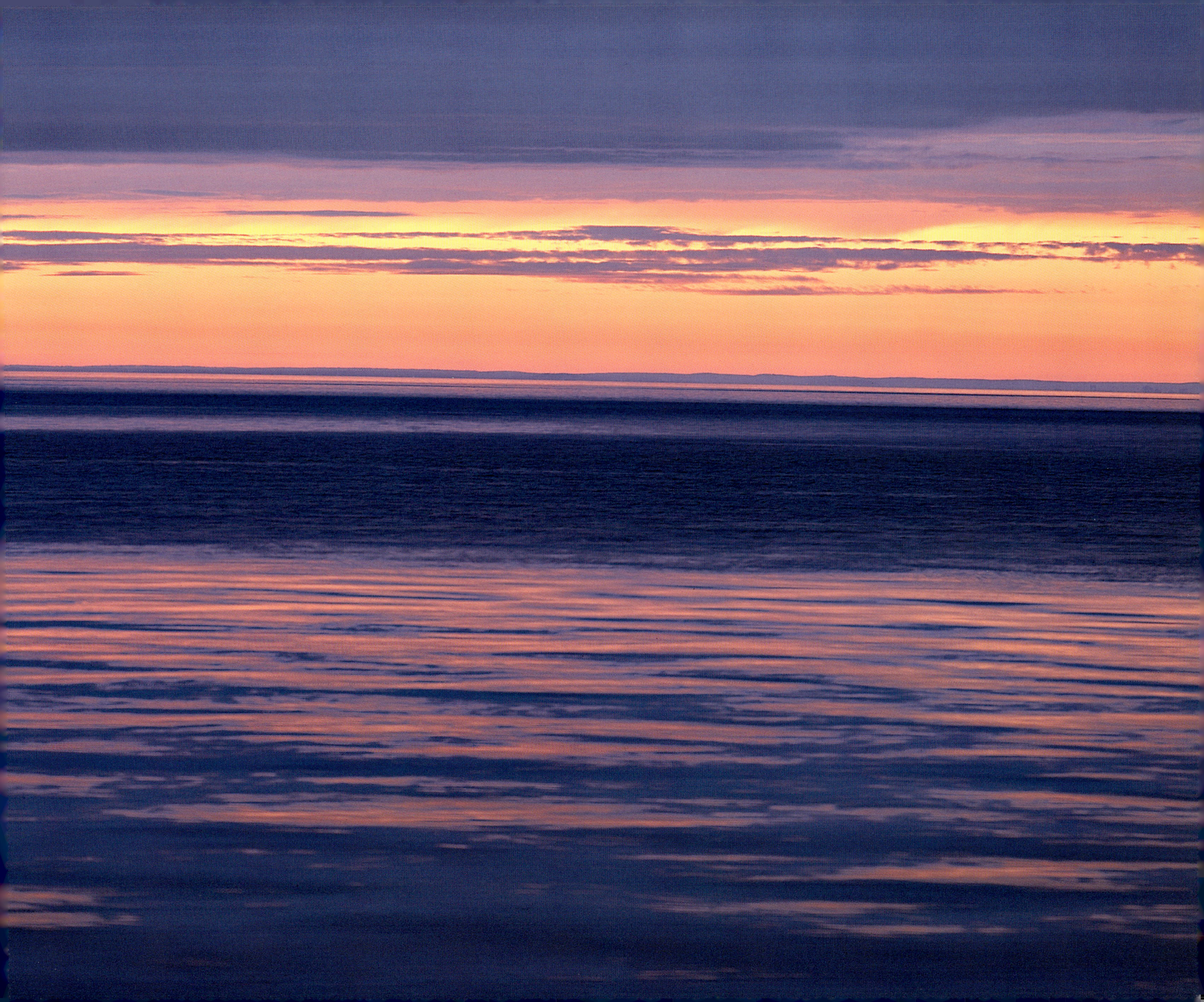

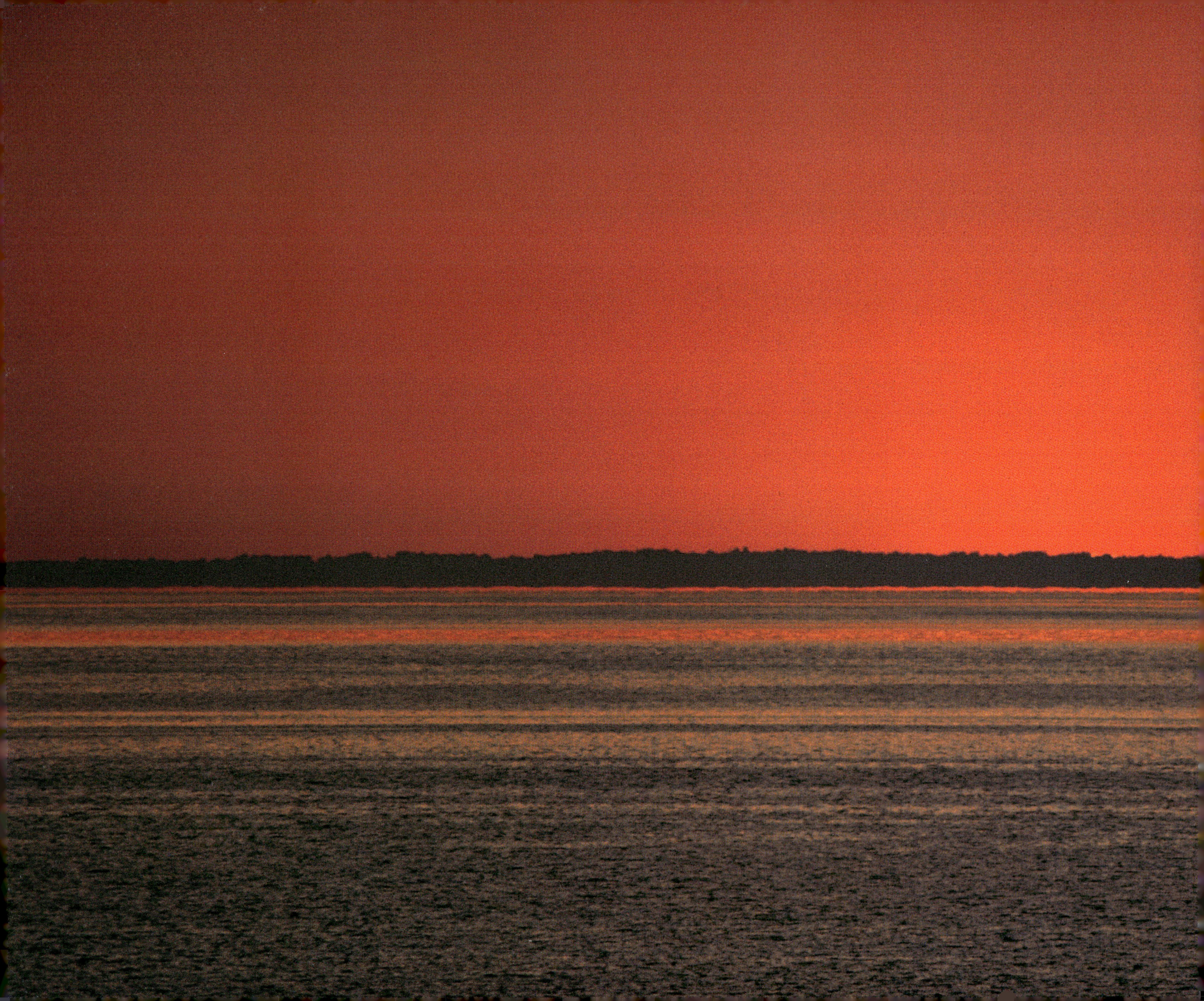

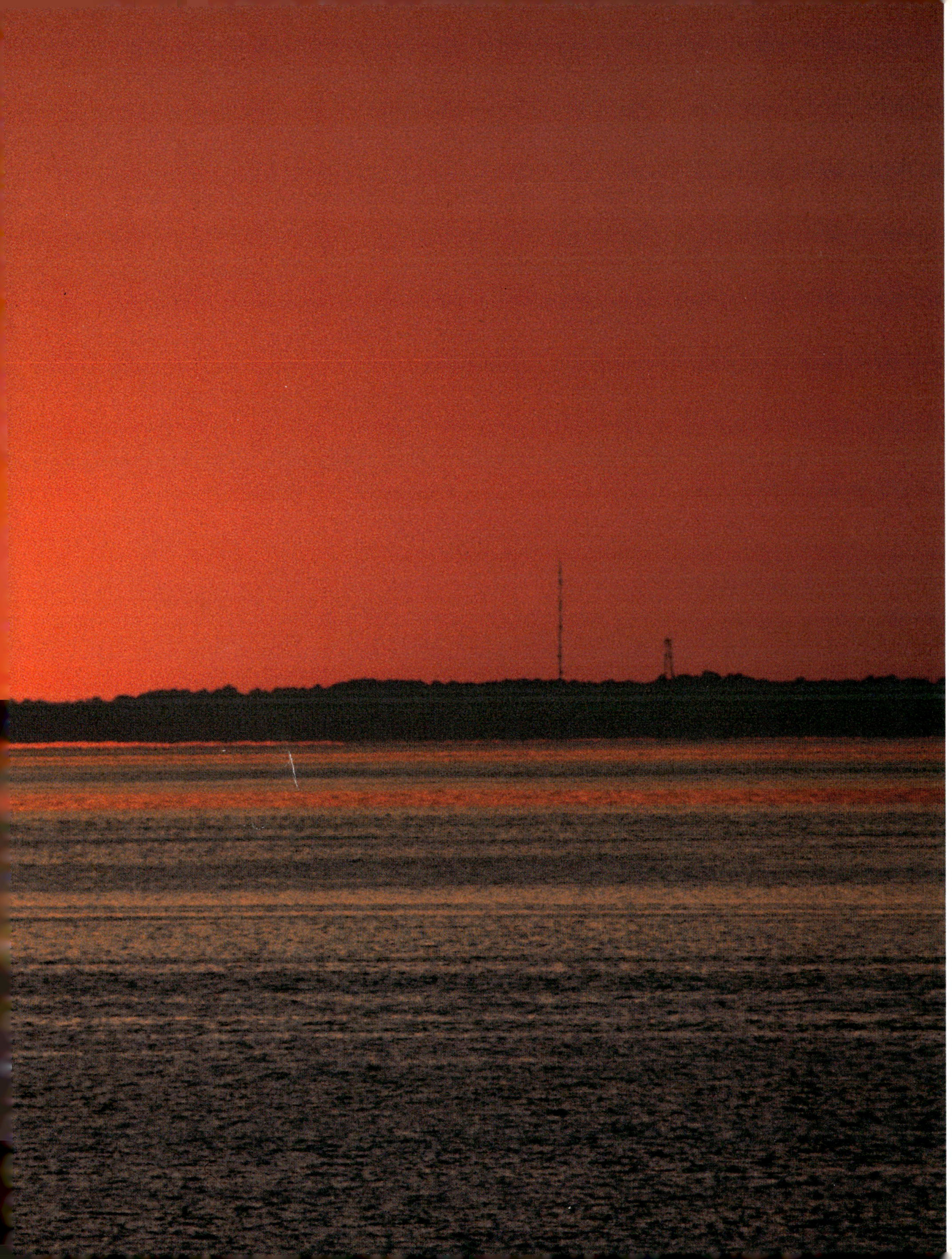

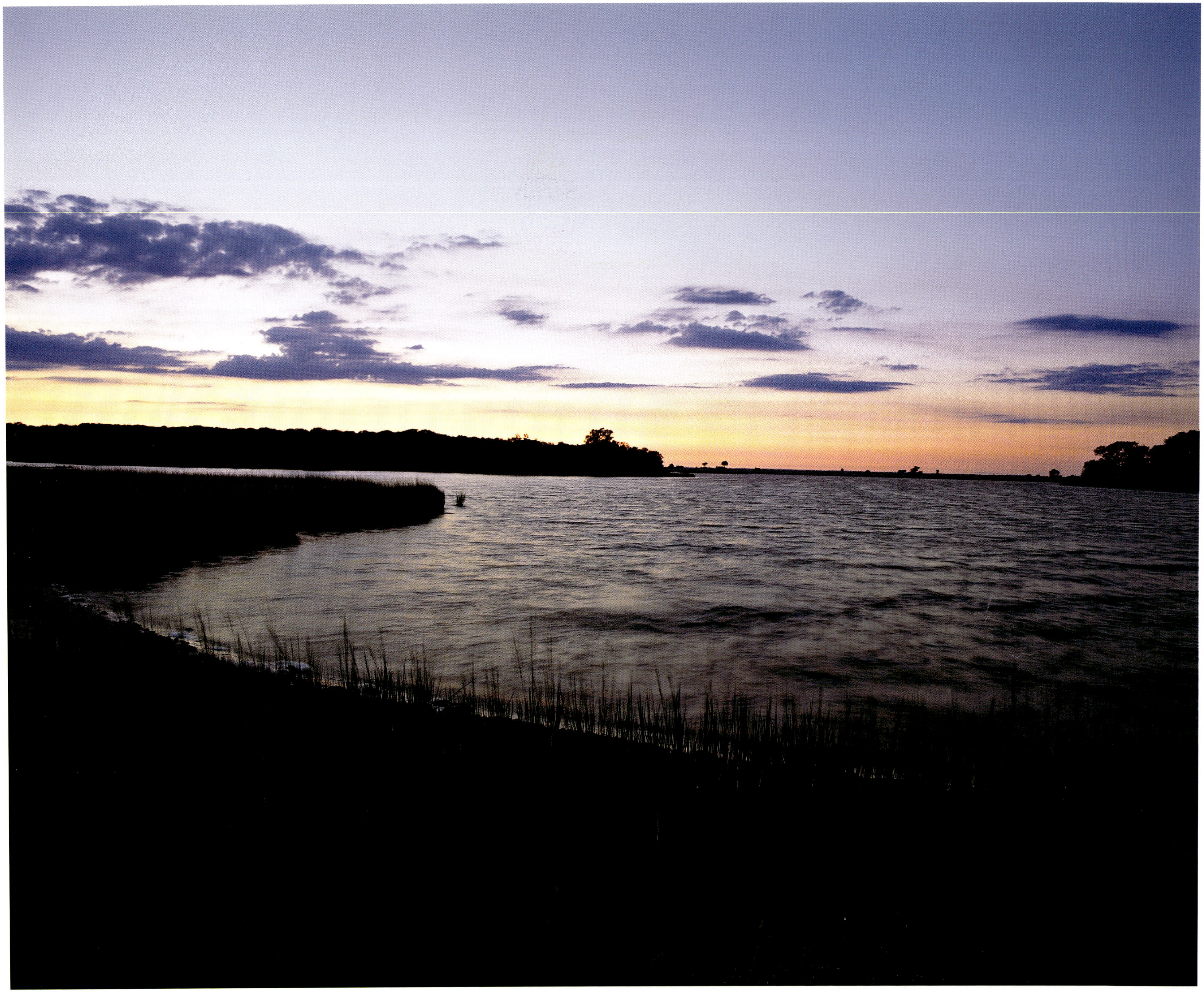

Dam Pond, East Marion Birch Beach, Cutchogue

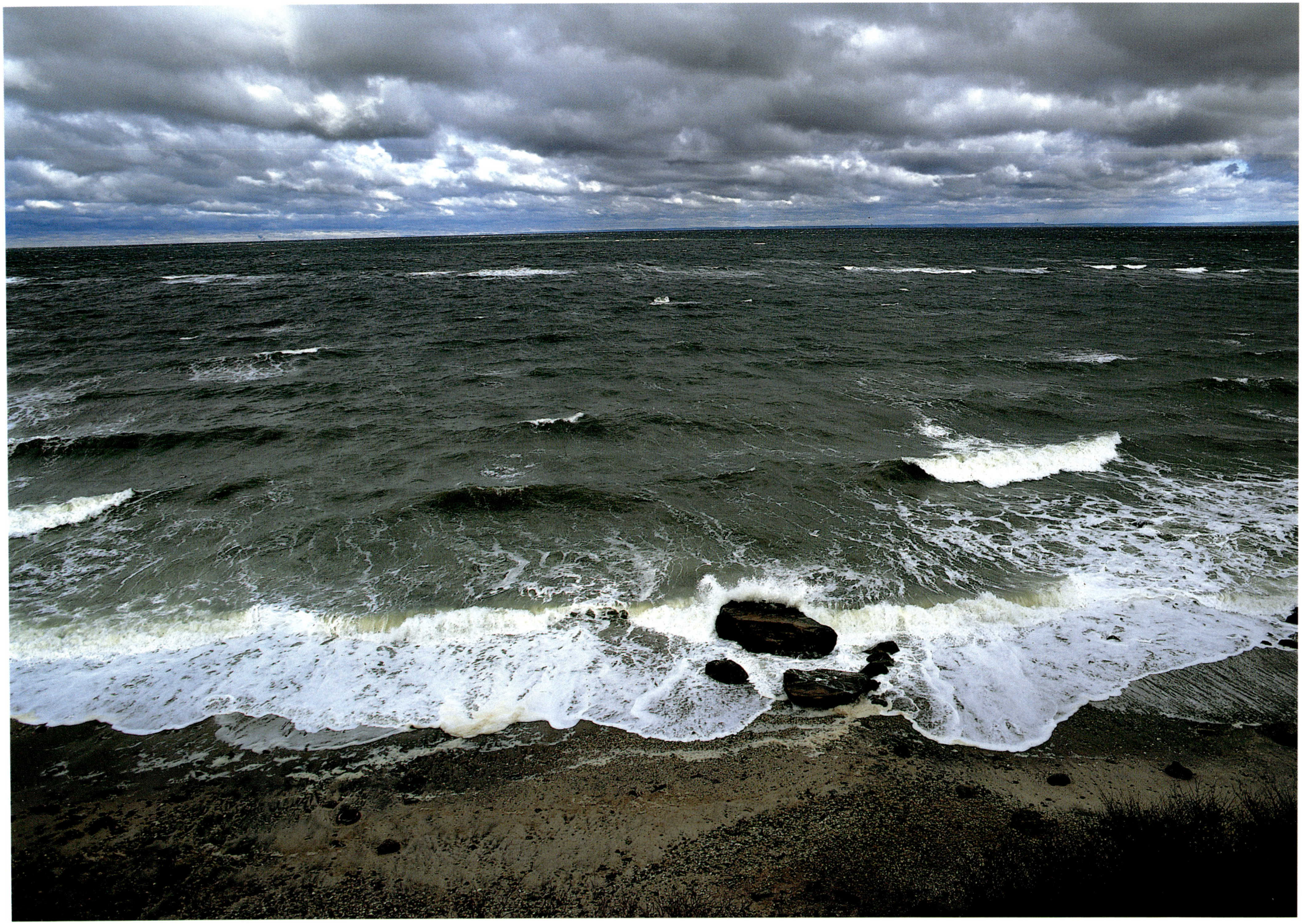

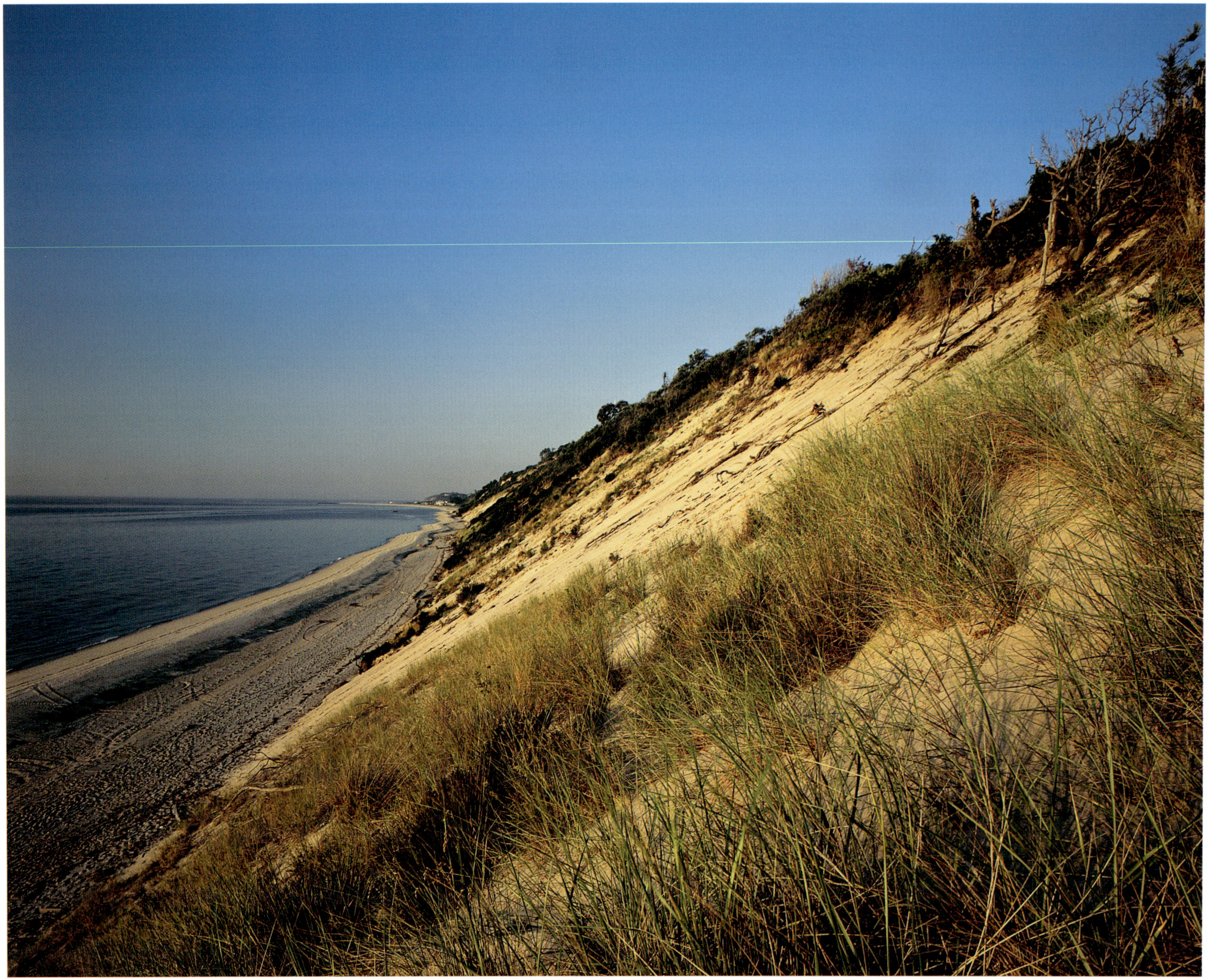

Mattituck

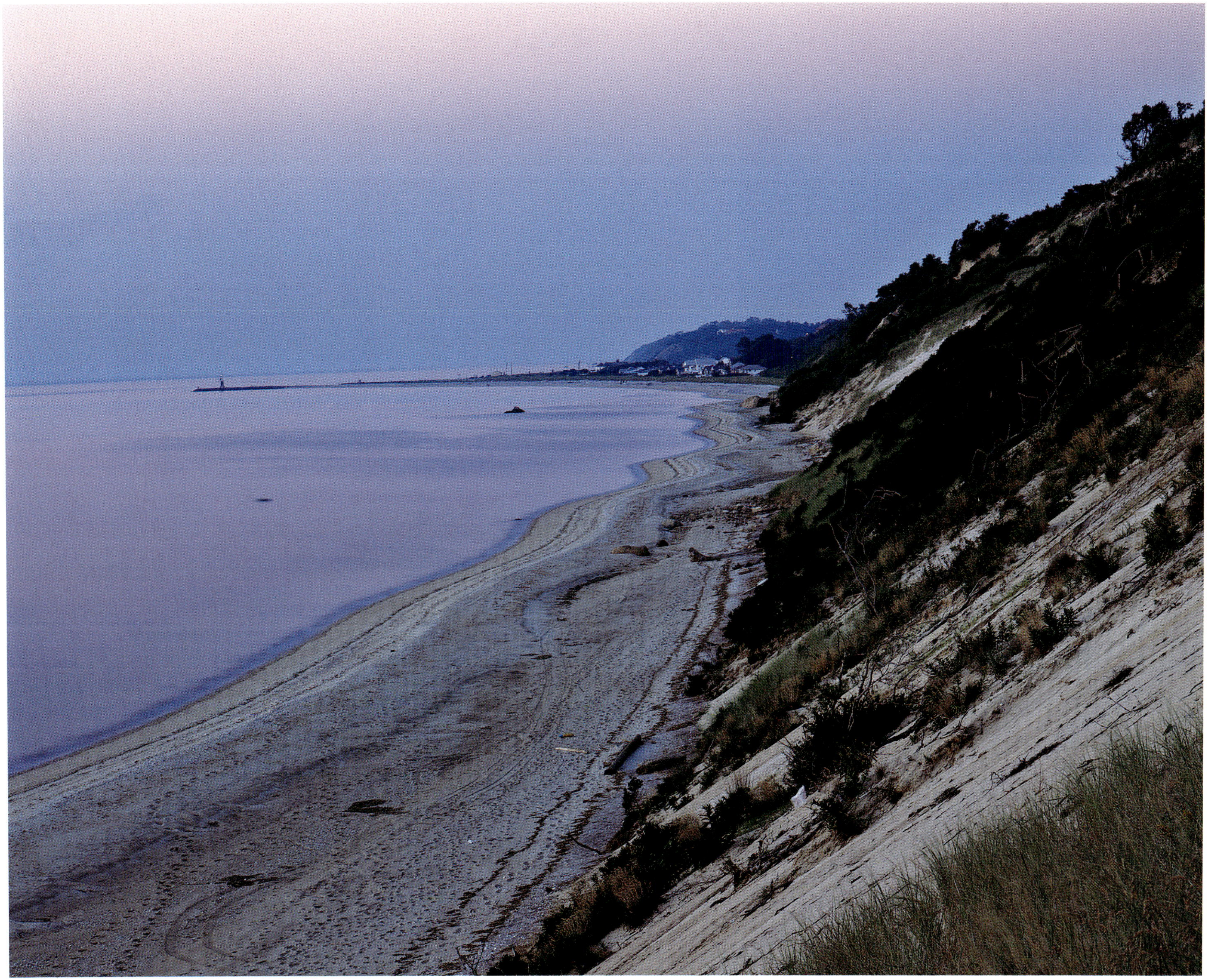

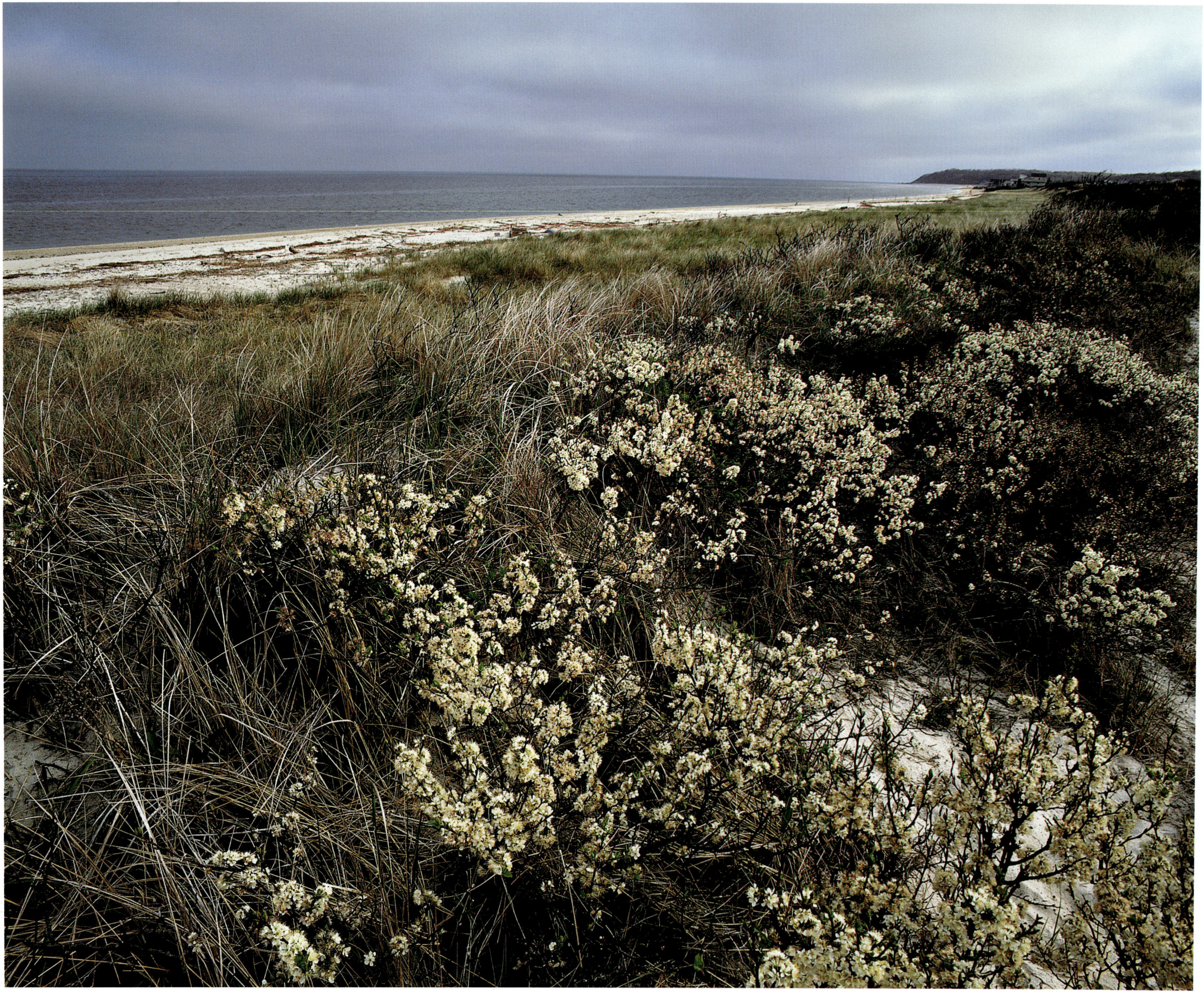

Peconic Dunes, Peconic

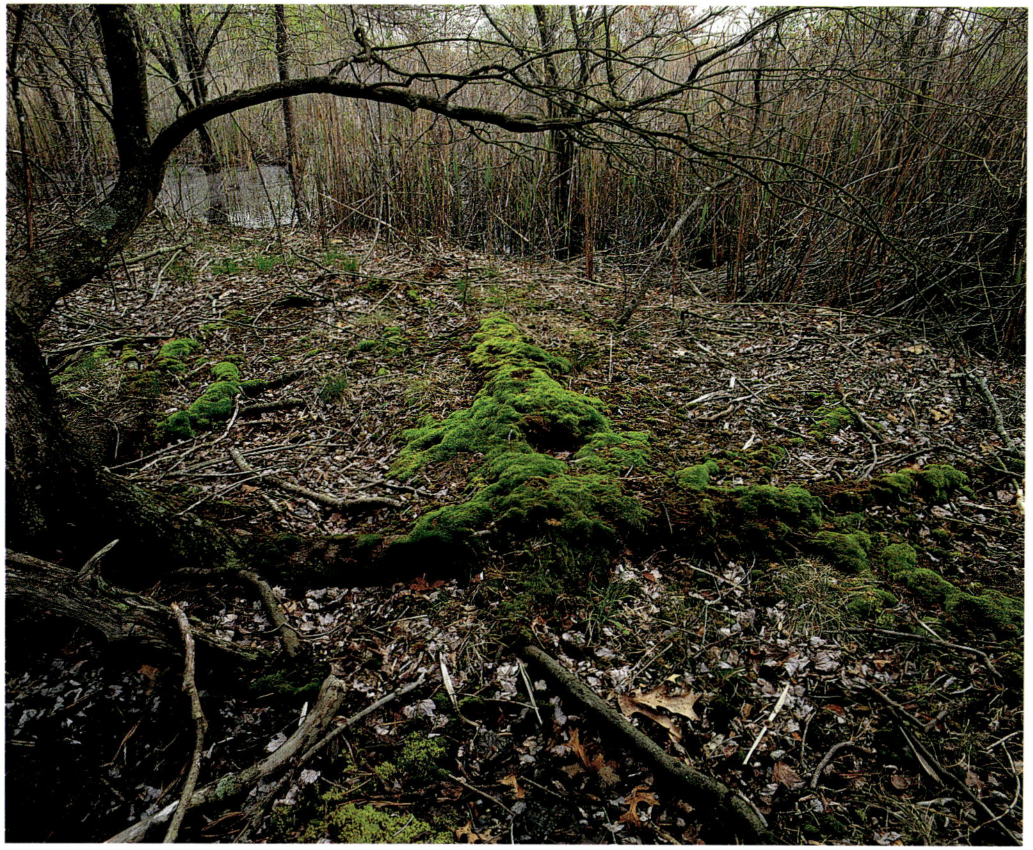

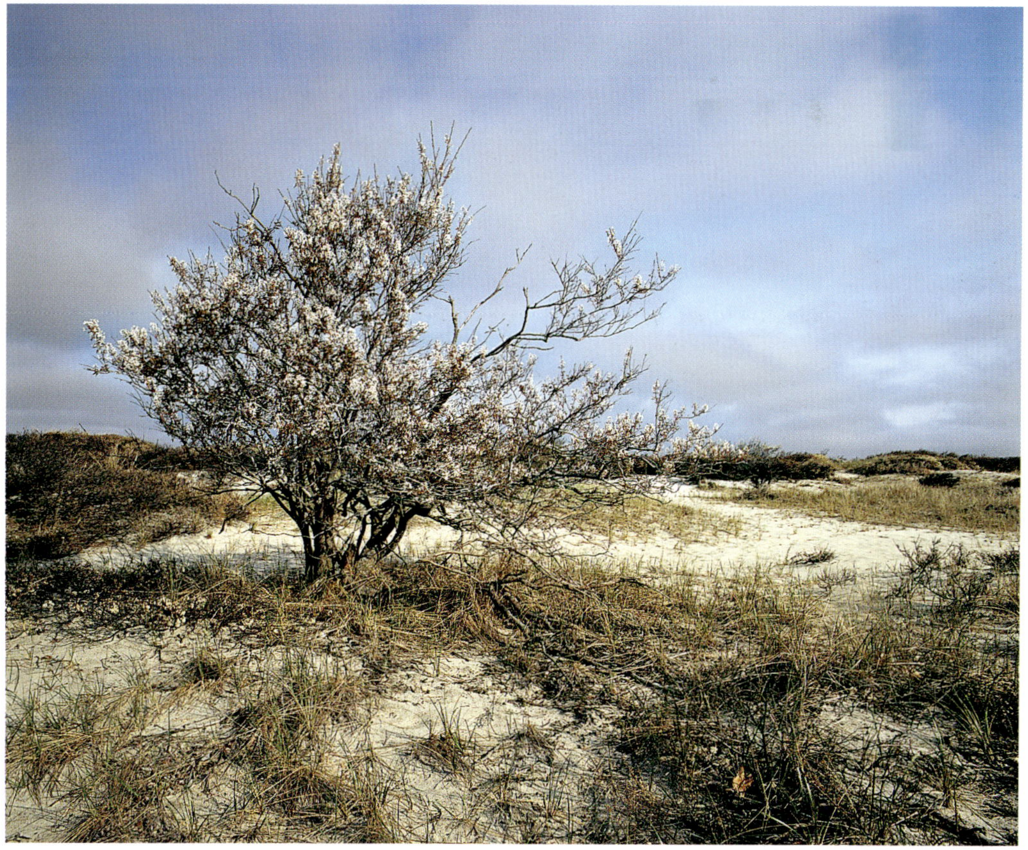

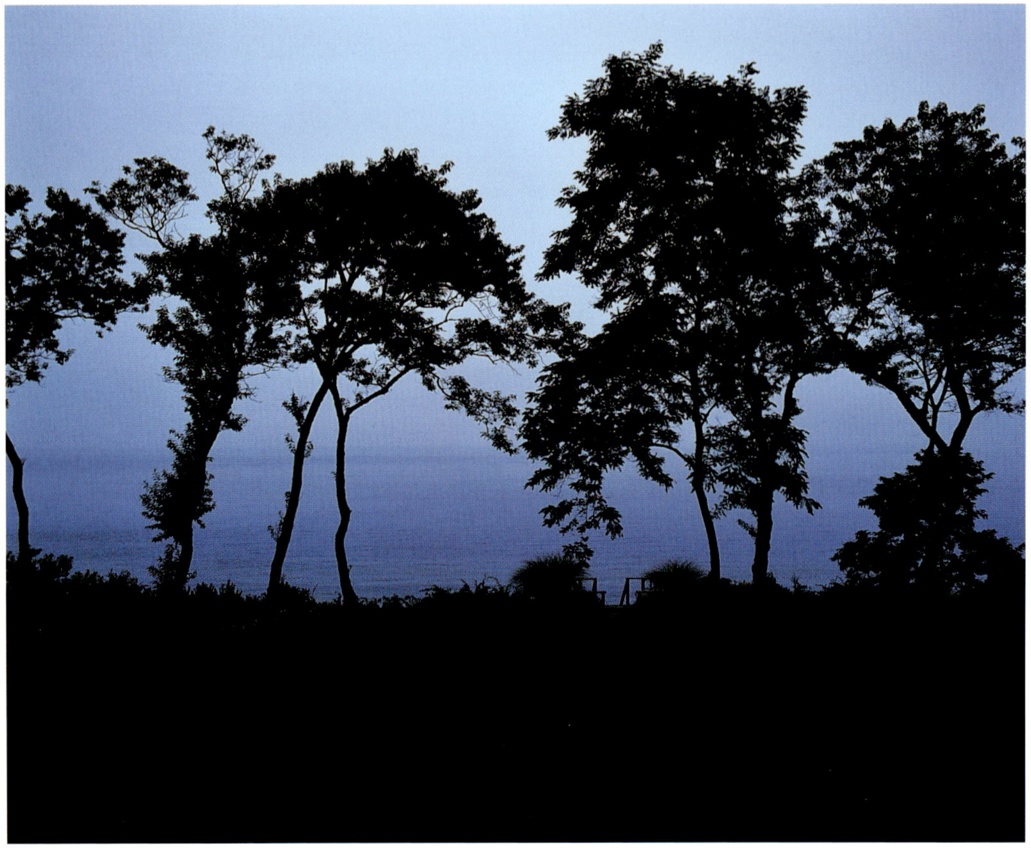

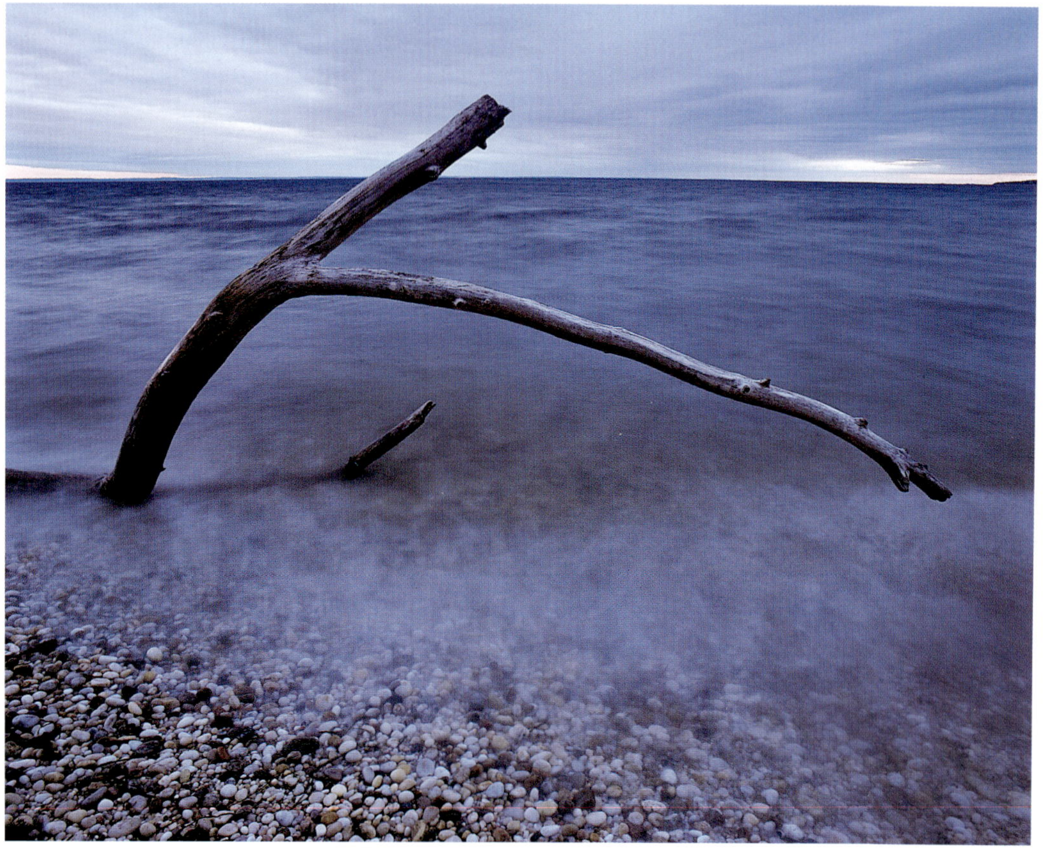

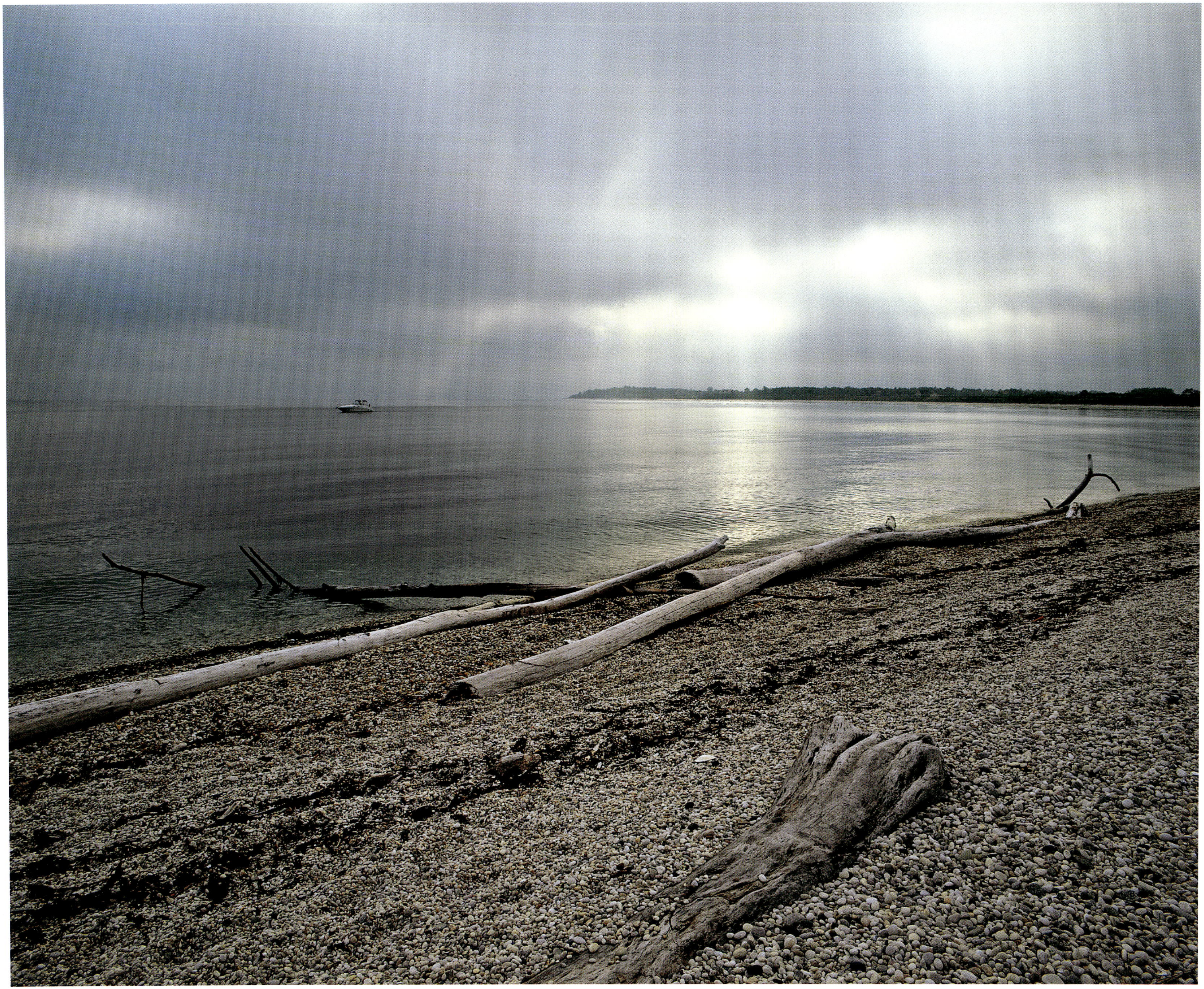

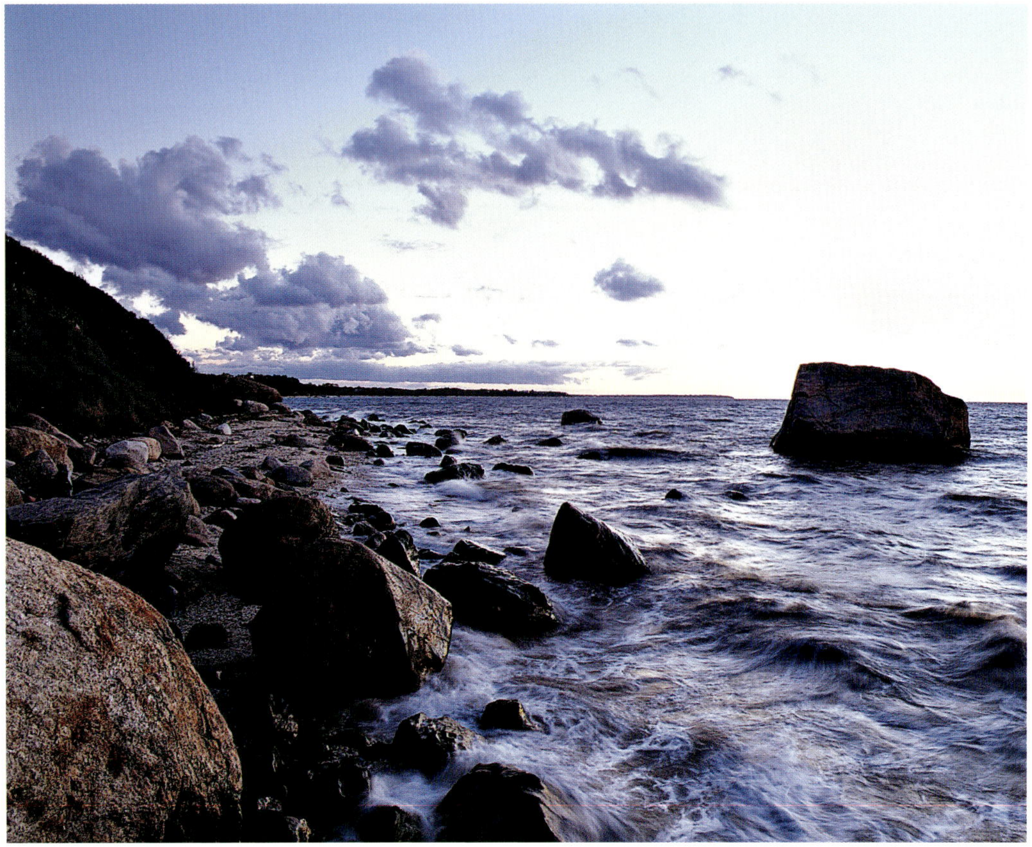

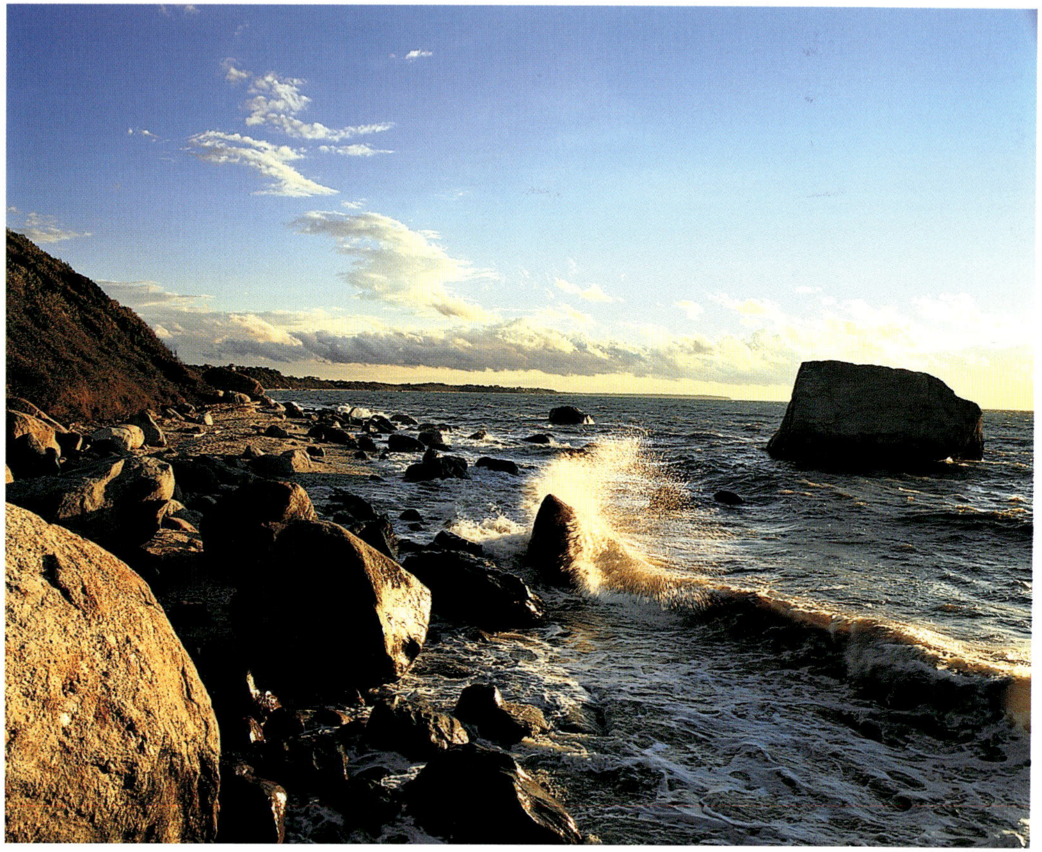

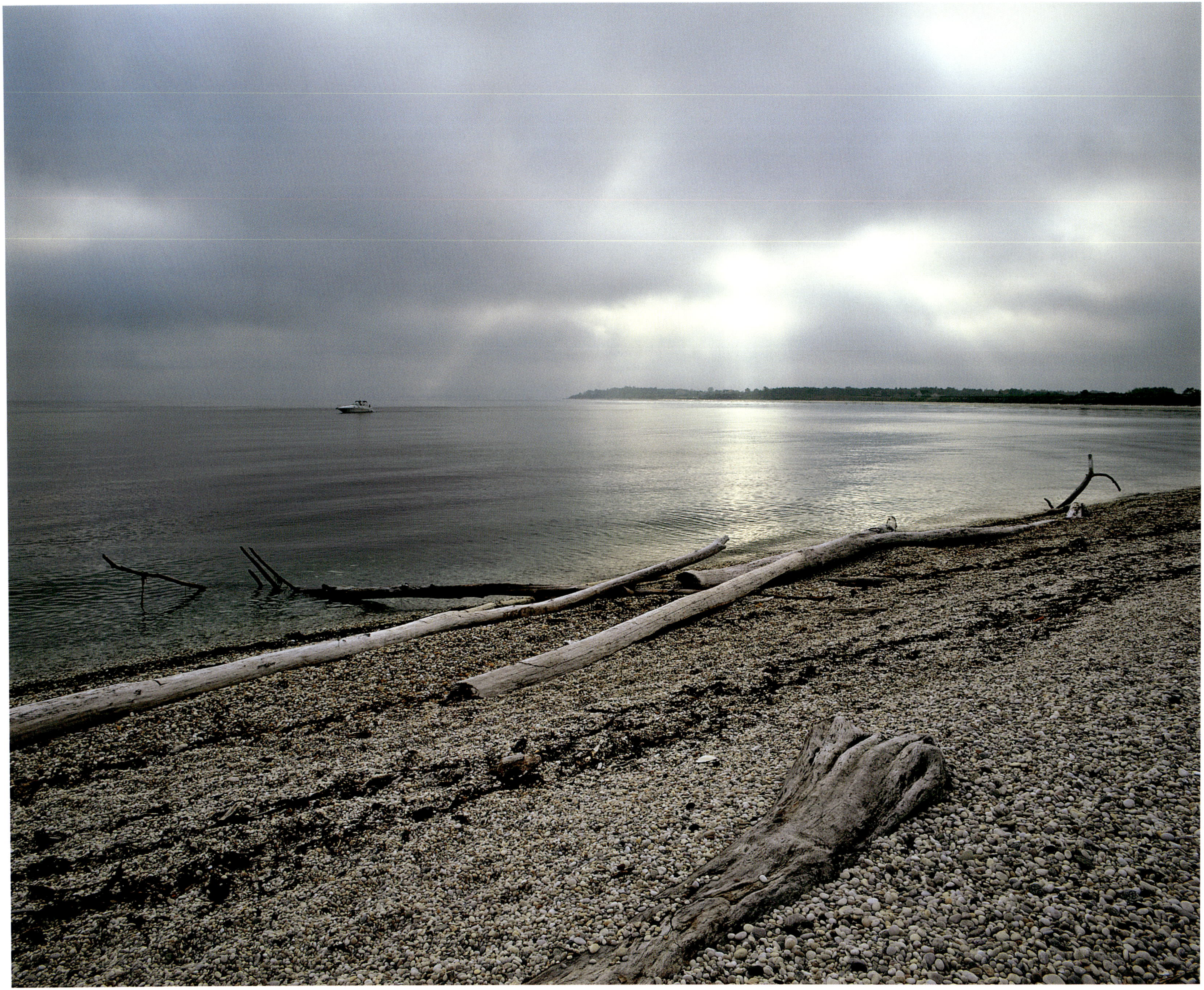

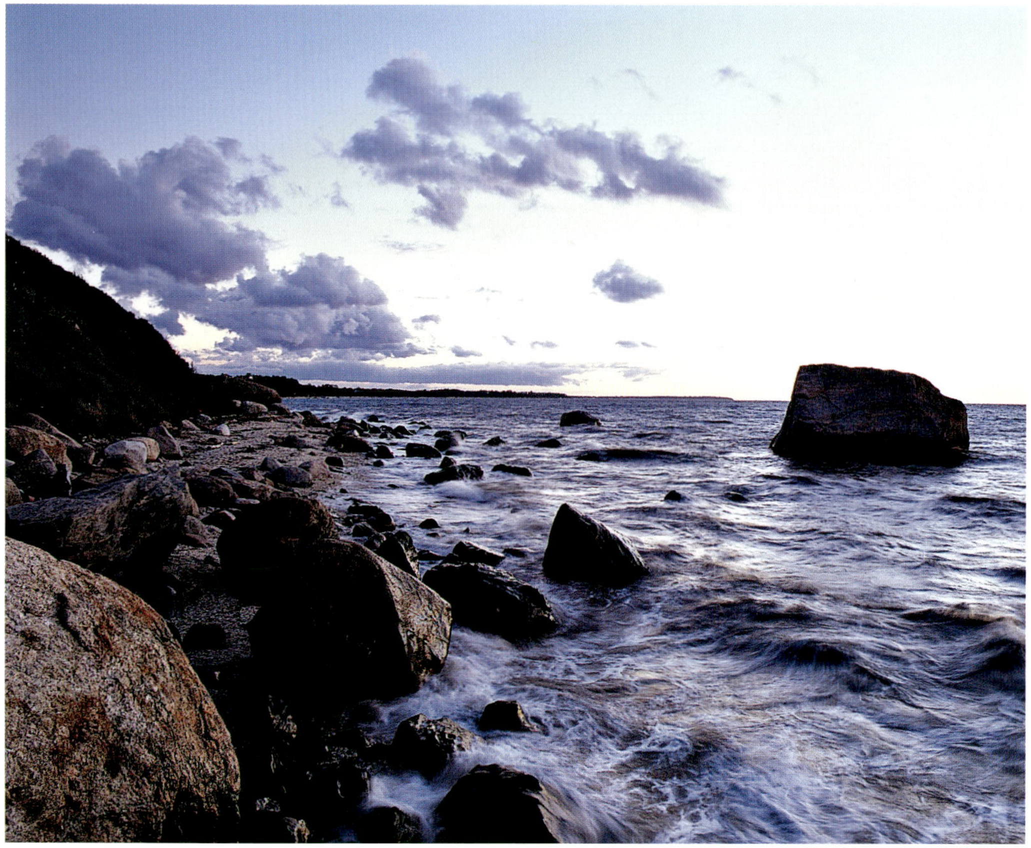

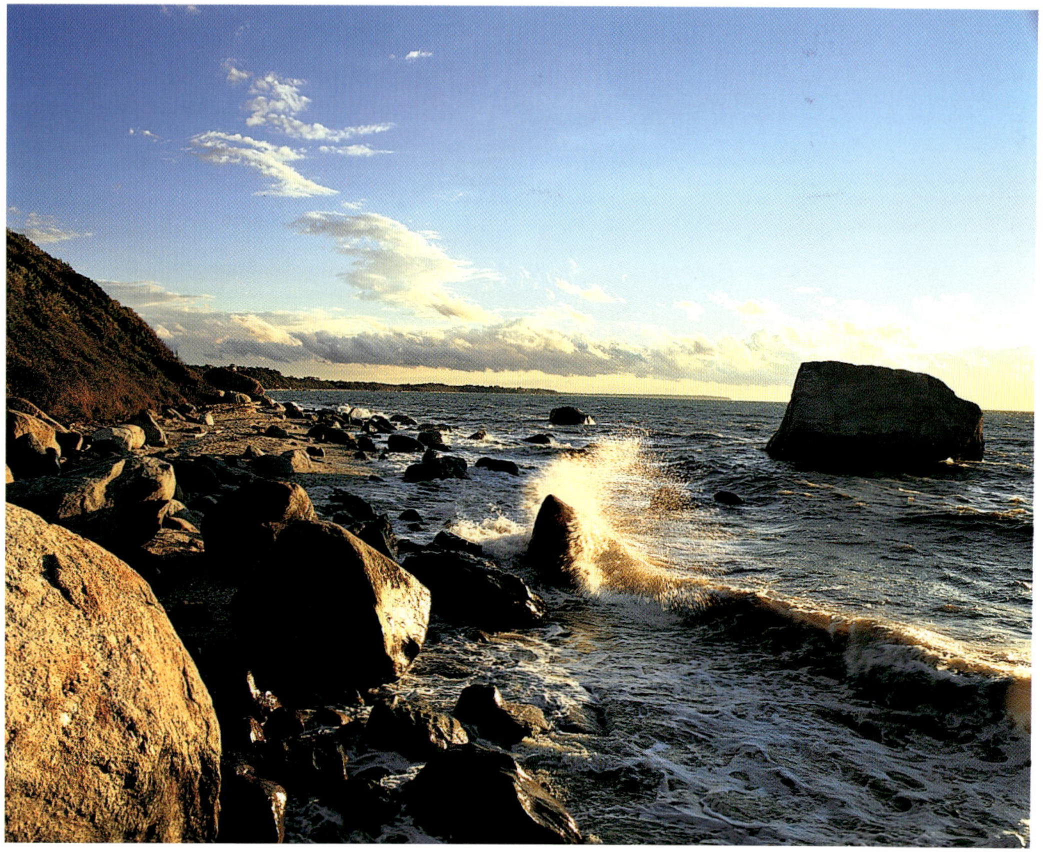

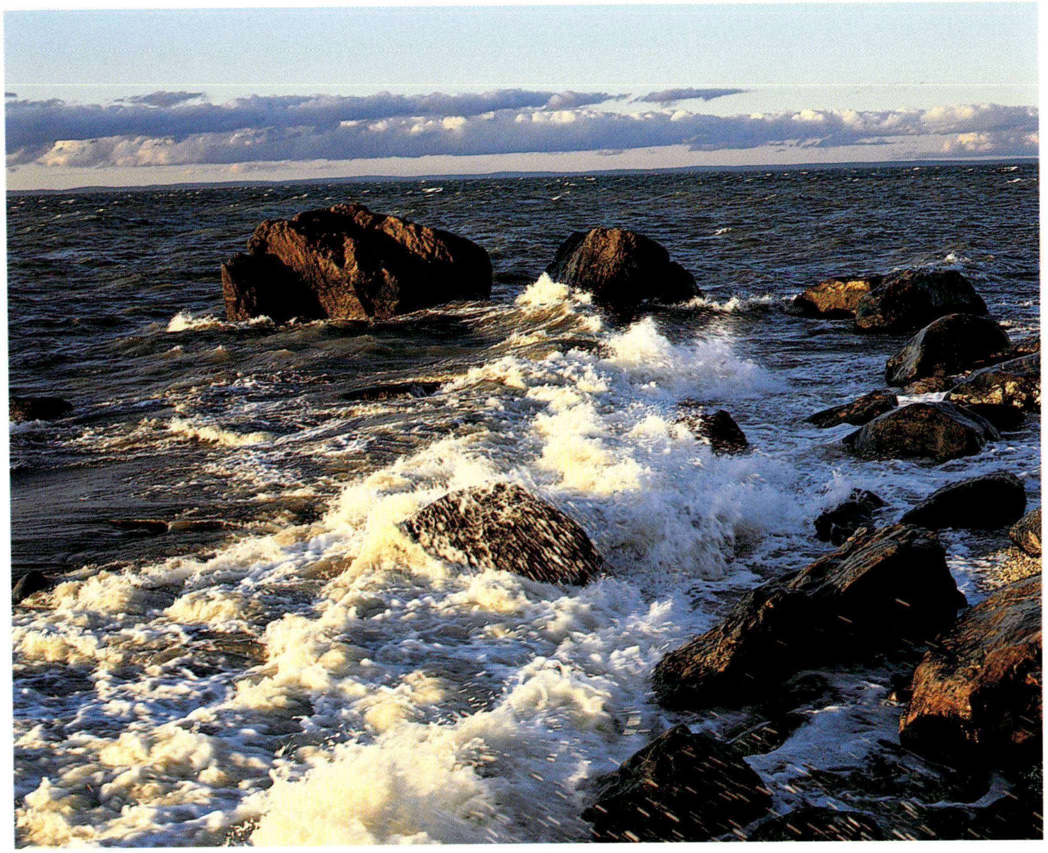

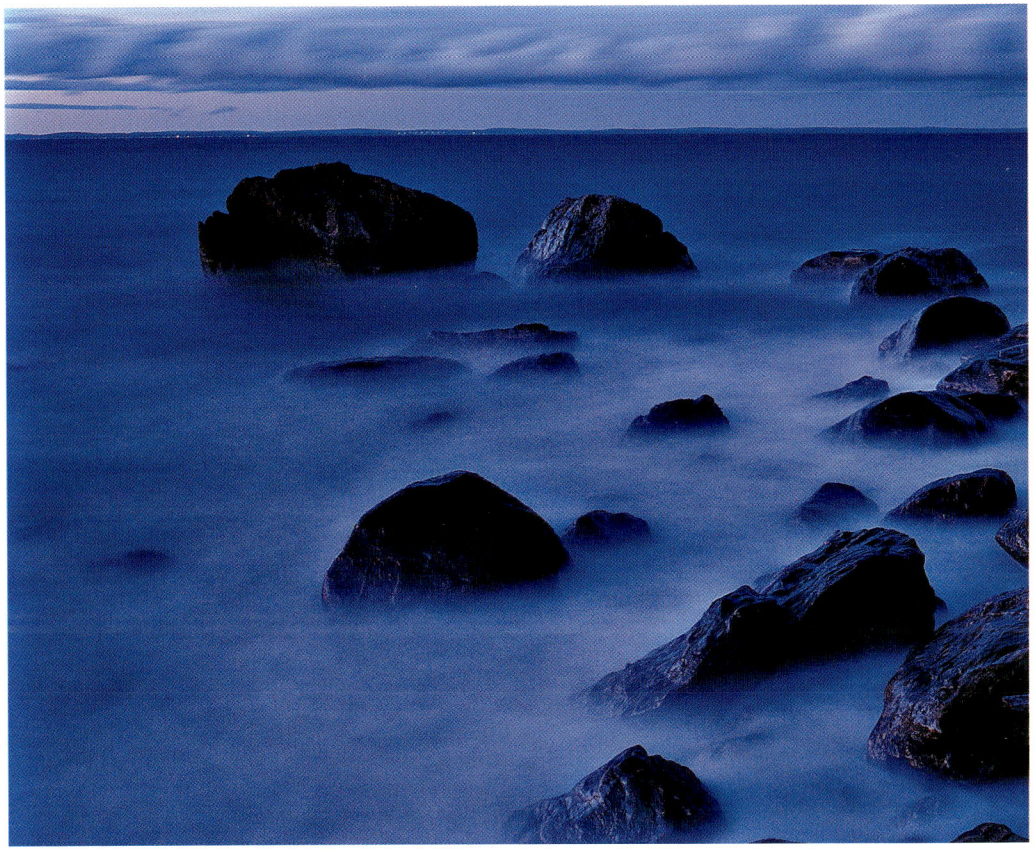

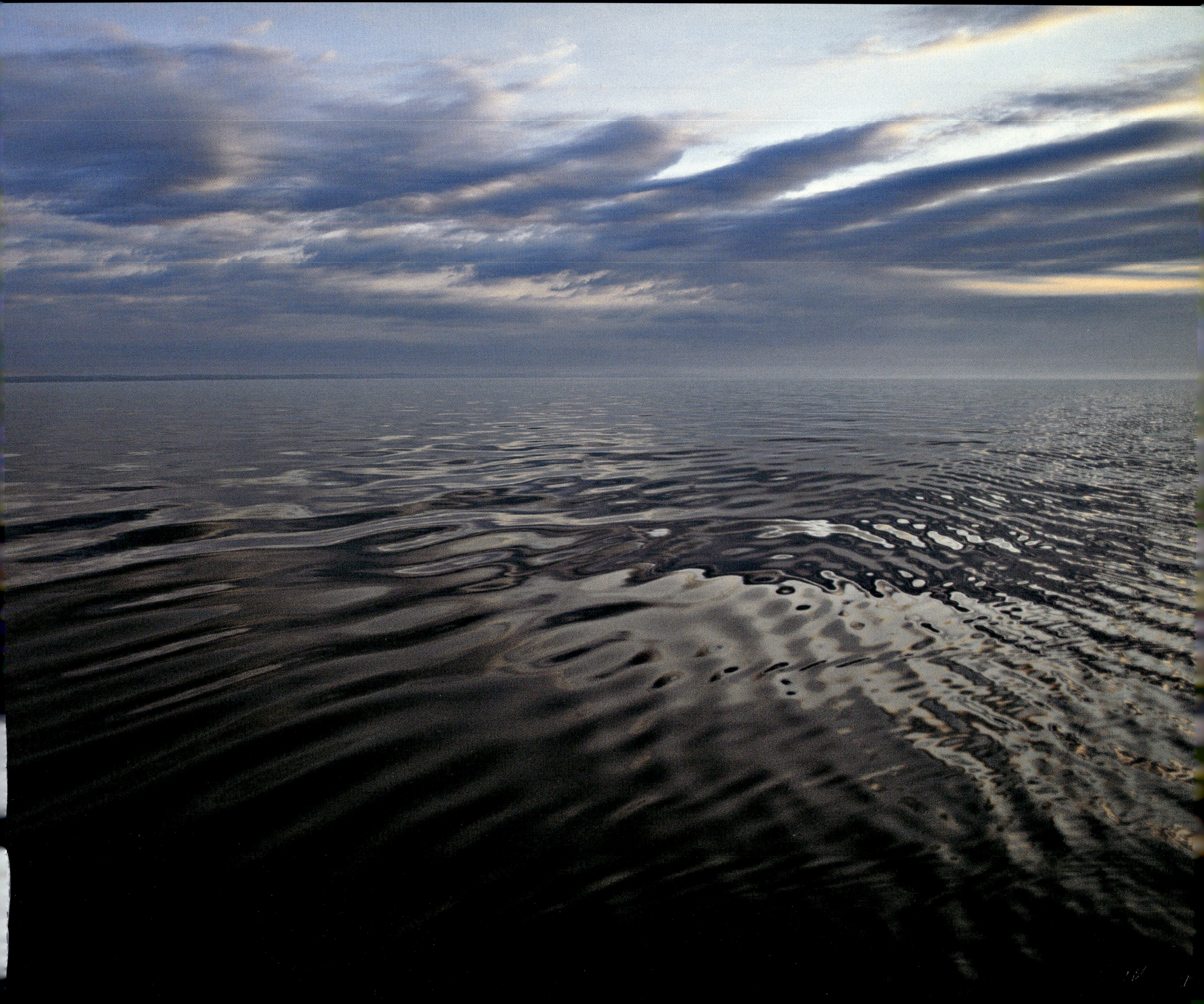

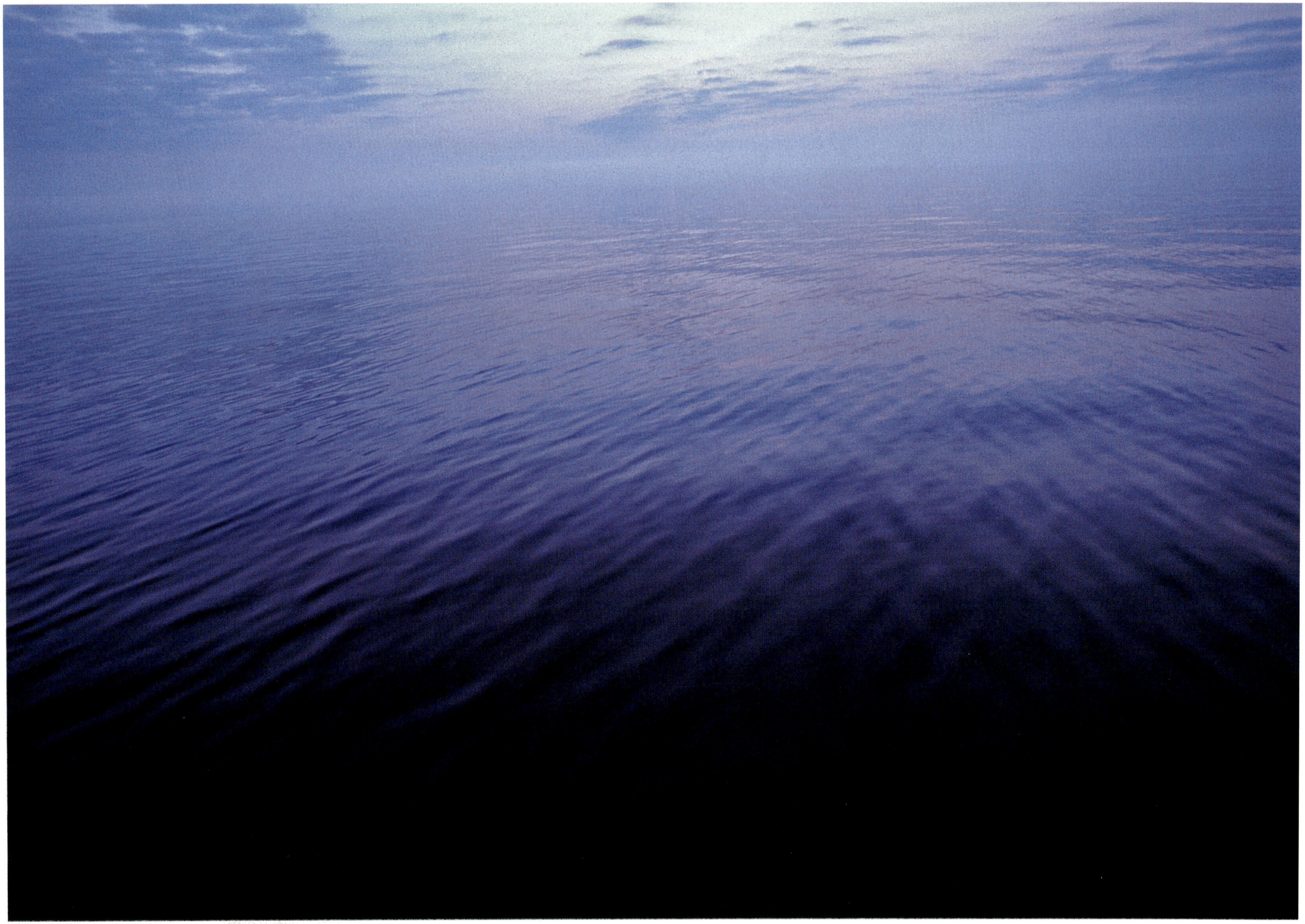

Fishing on the Sound

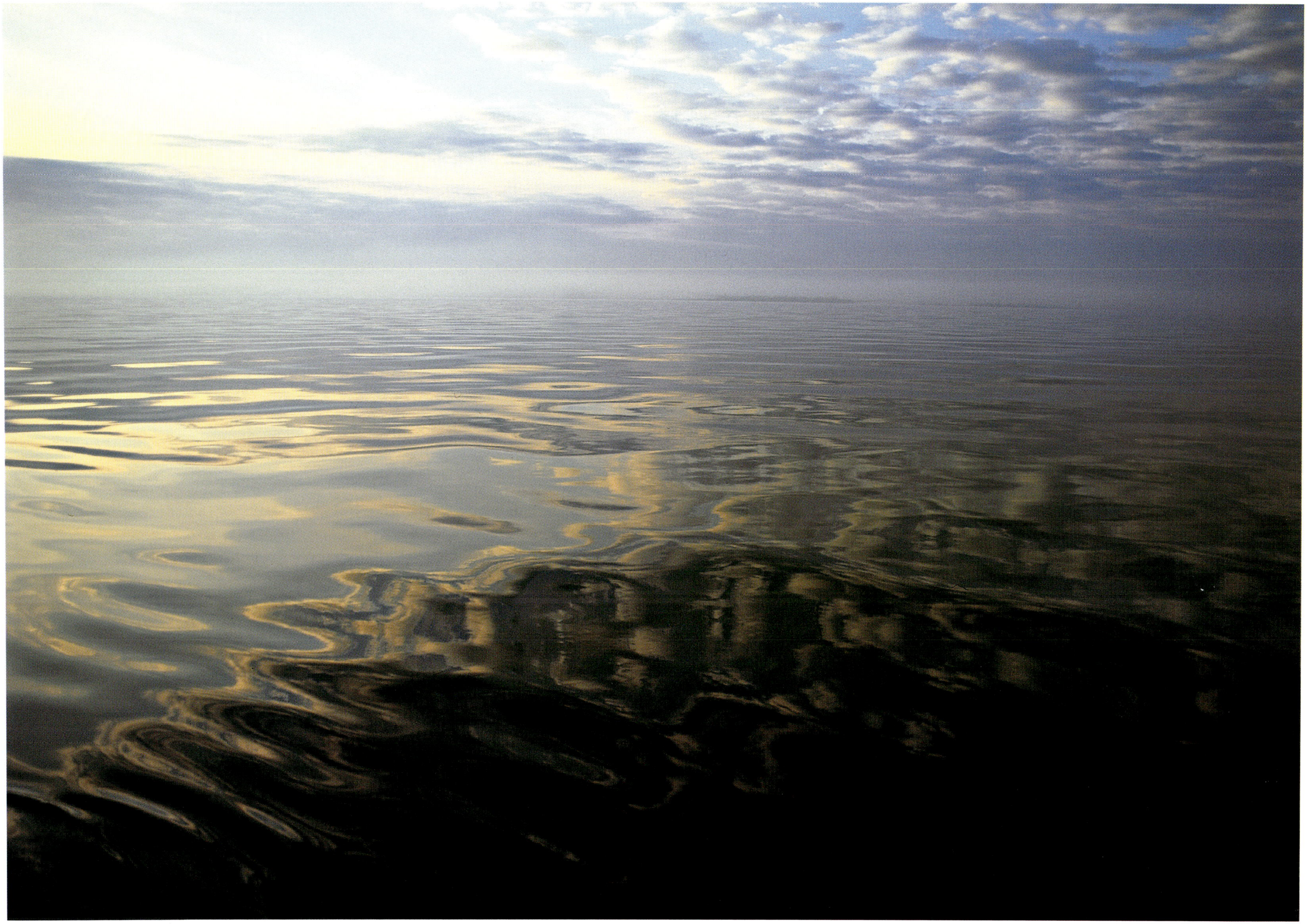

Birch Beach, Cutchogue

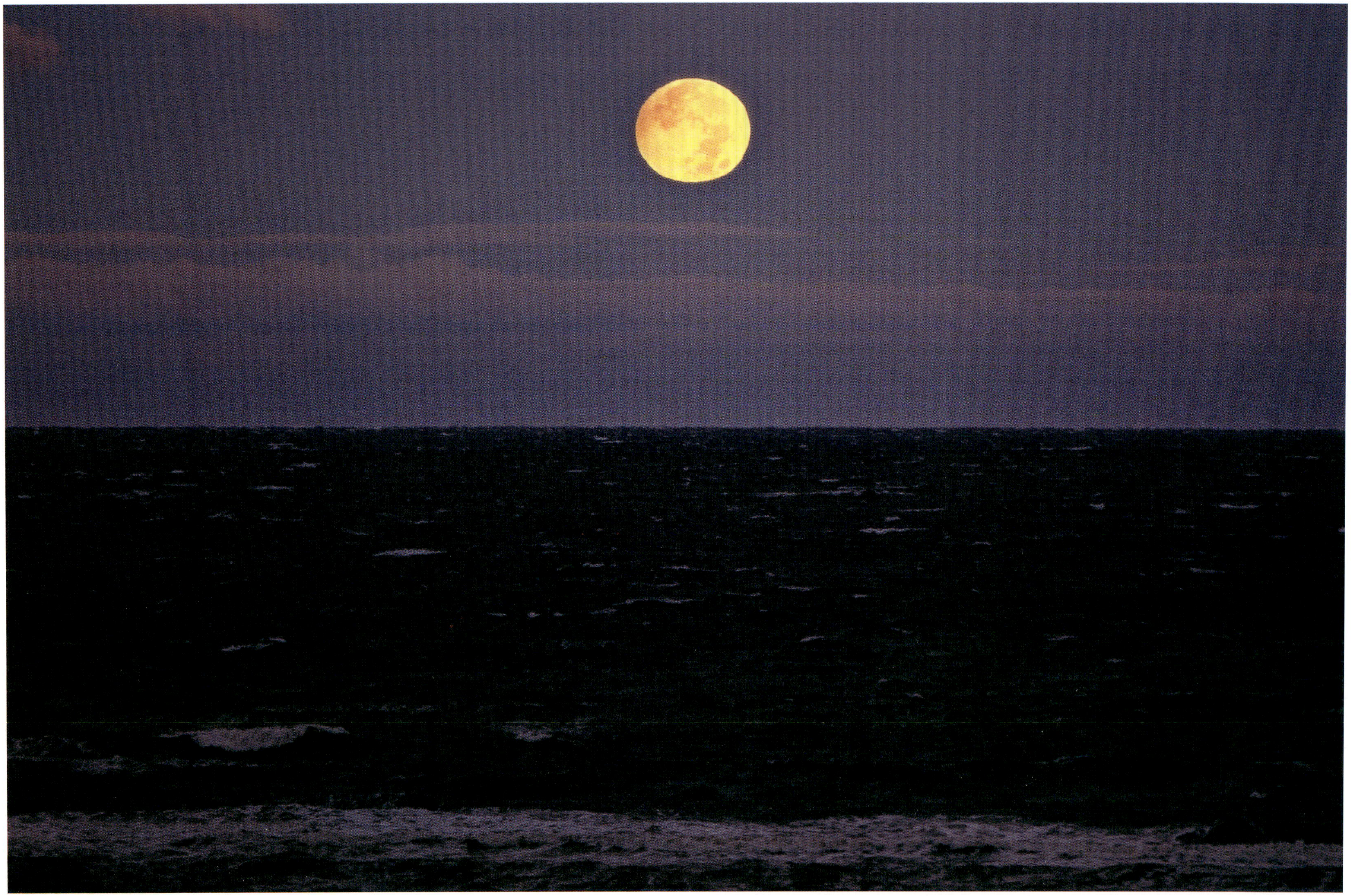

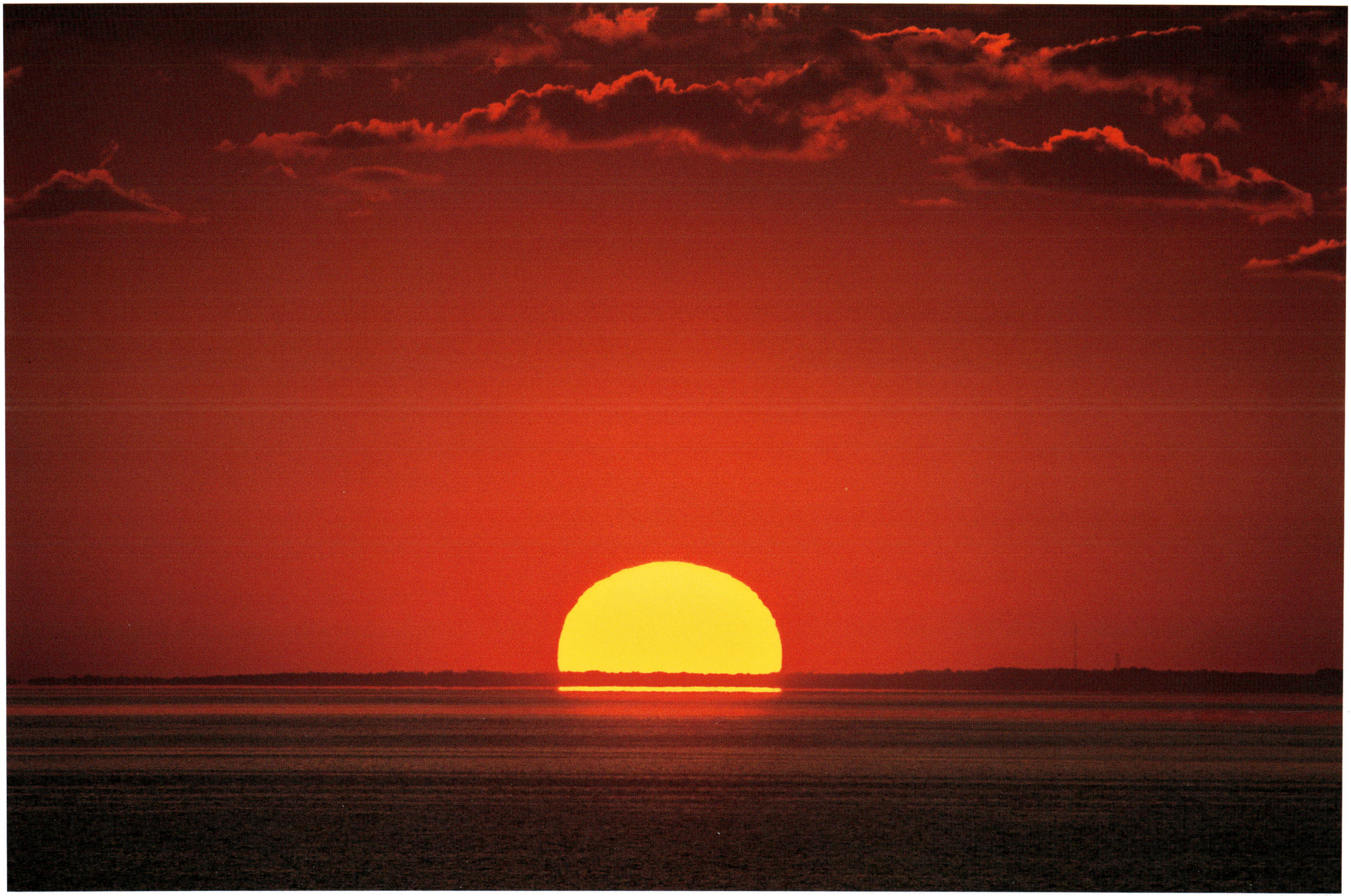

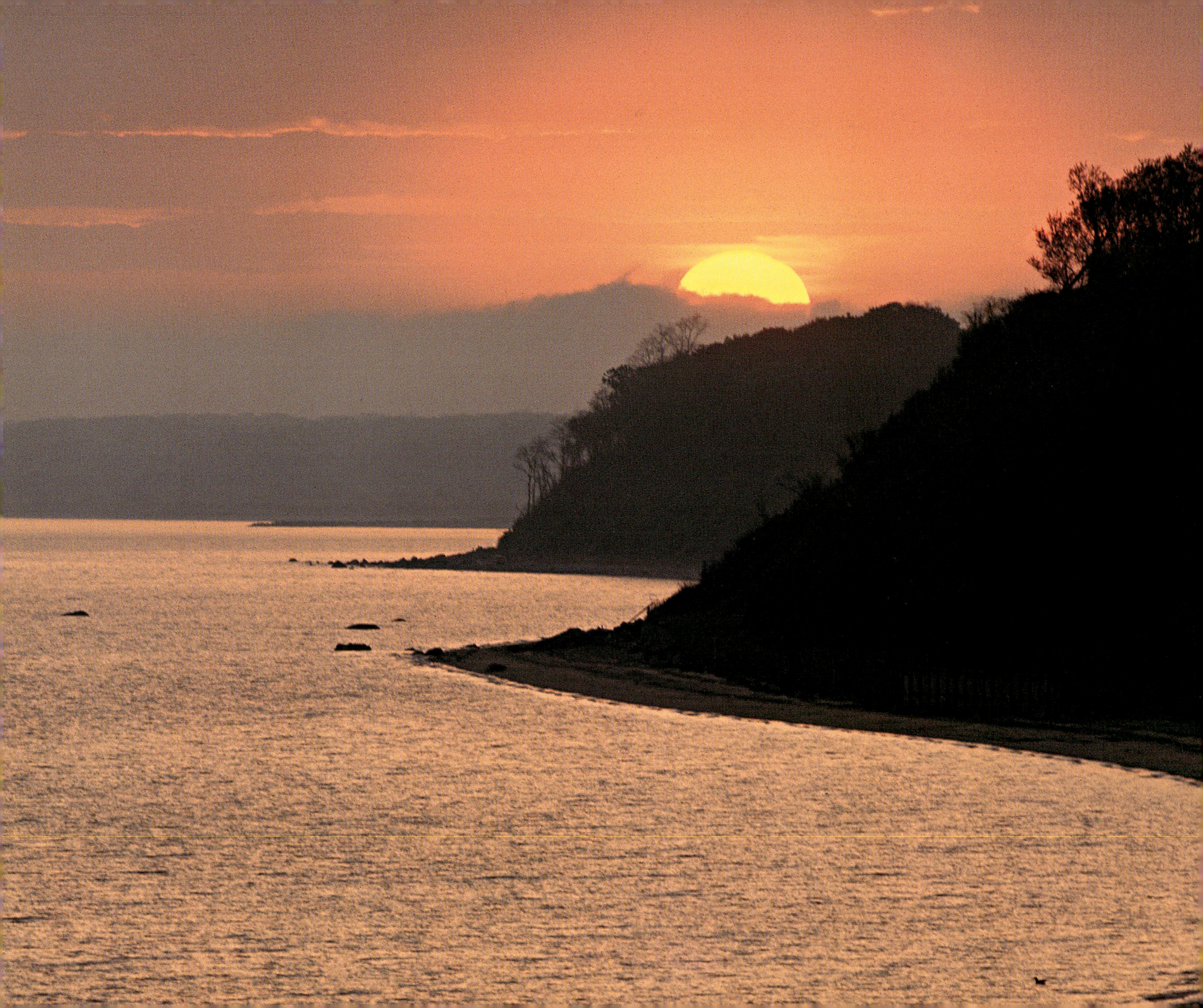

Bluffs, Cutchogue

Bluffs, Cutchogue

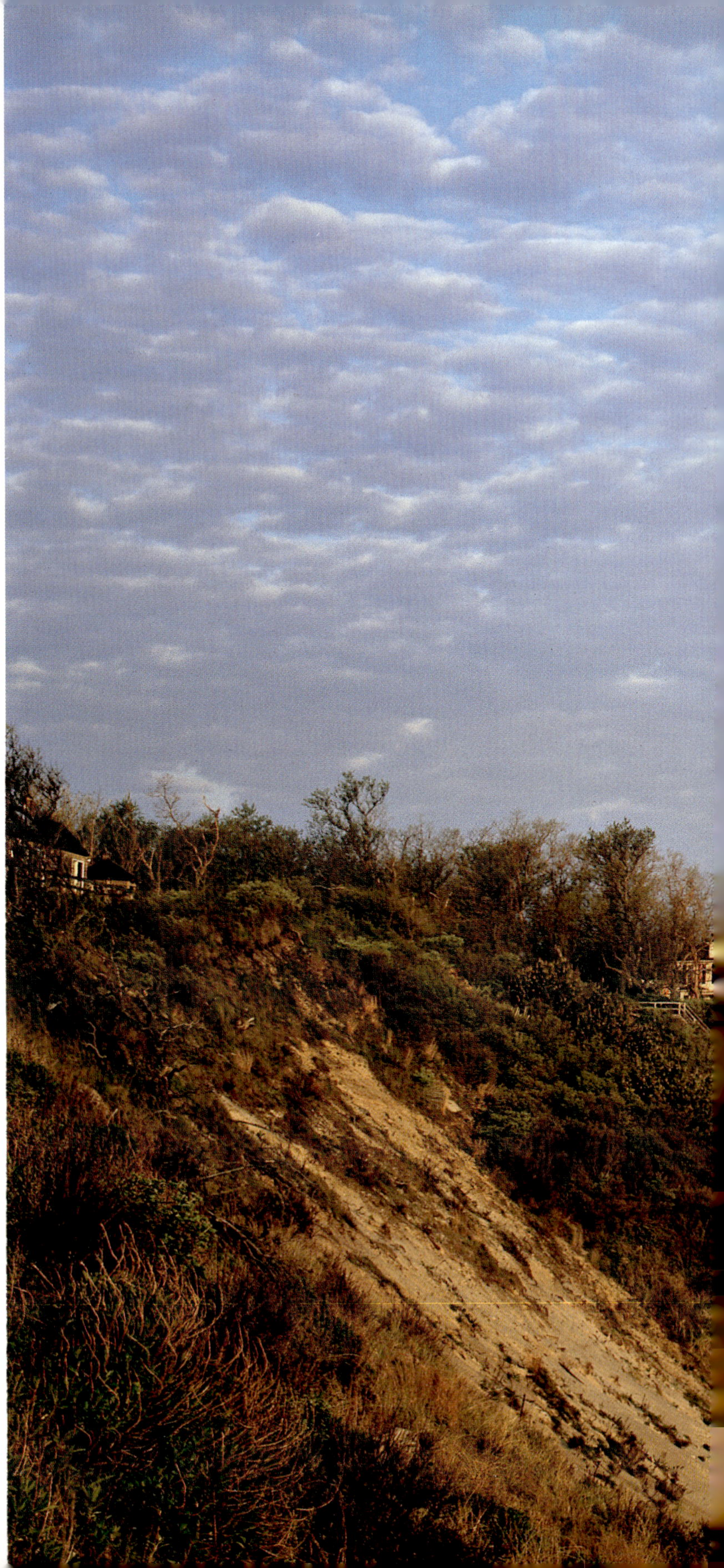

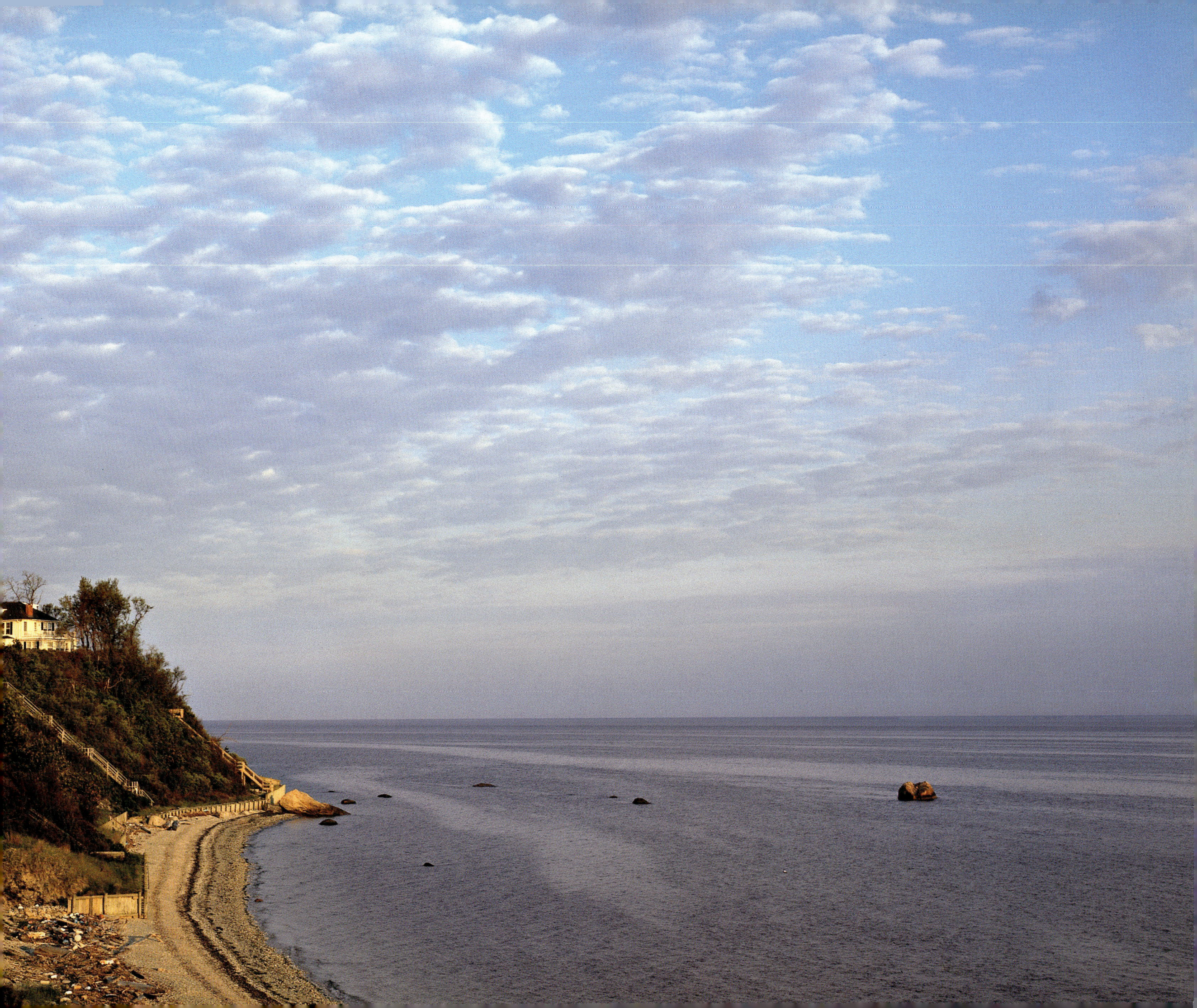

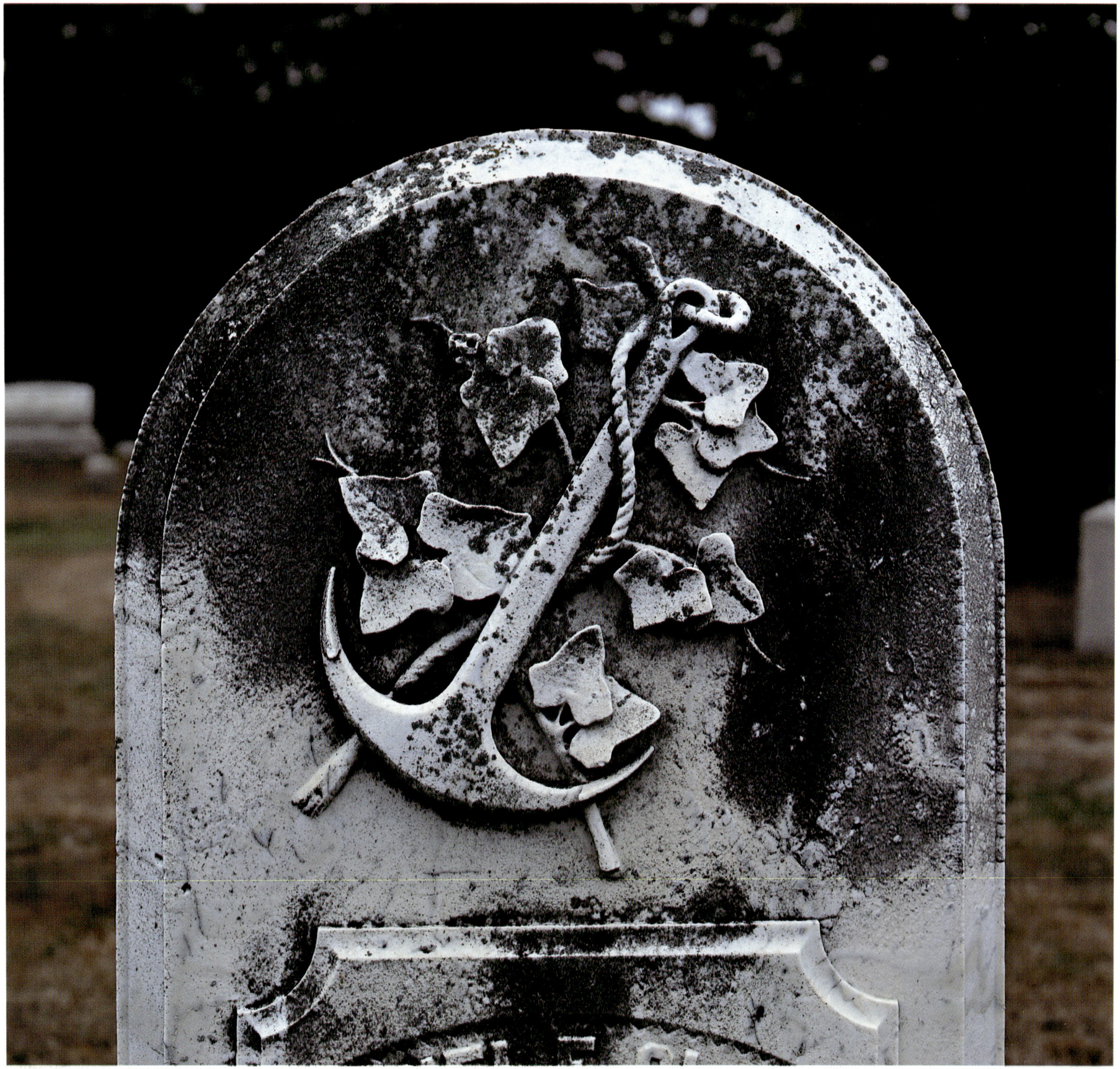

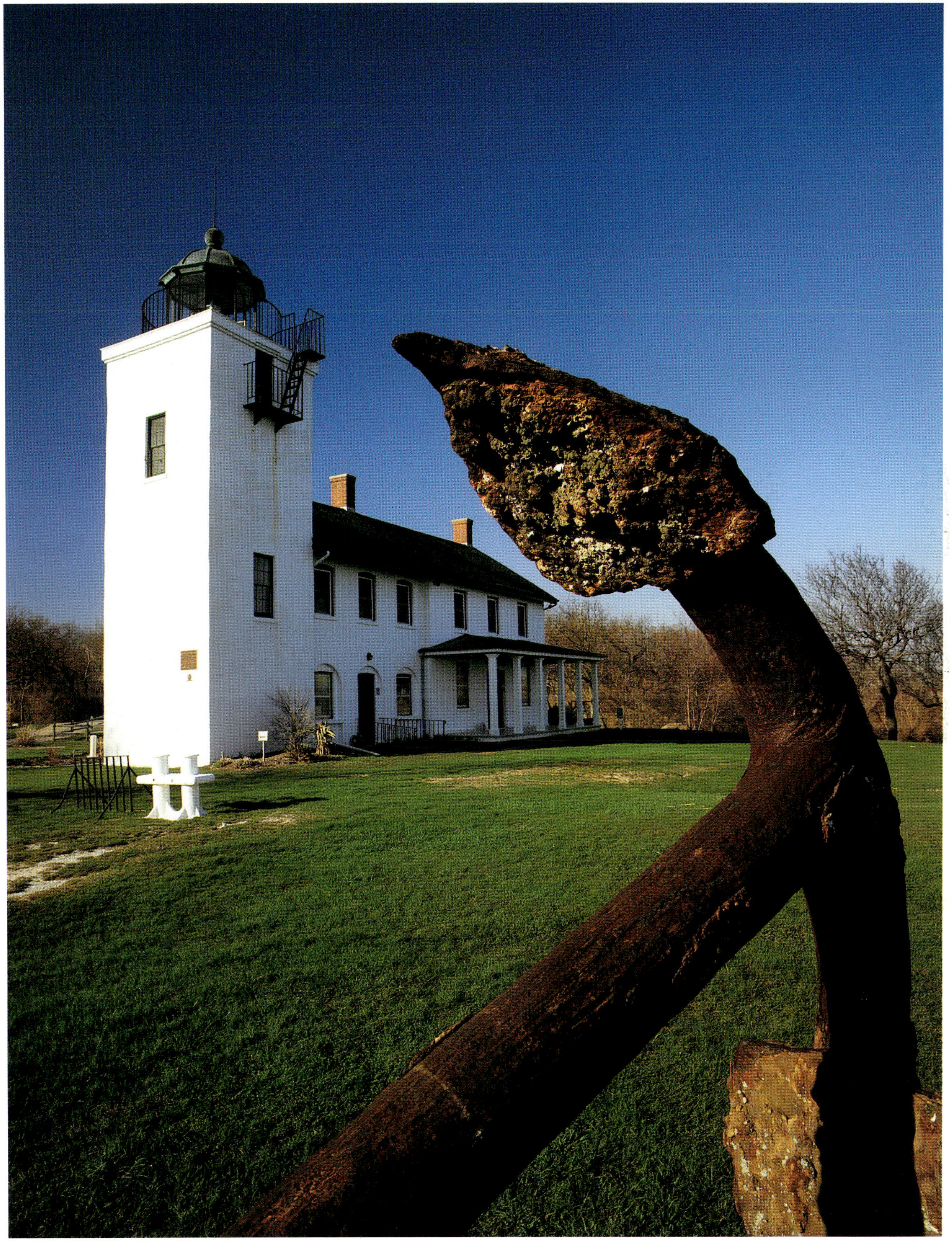

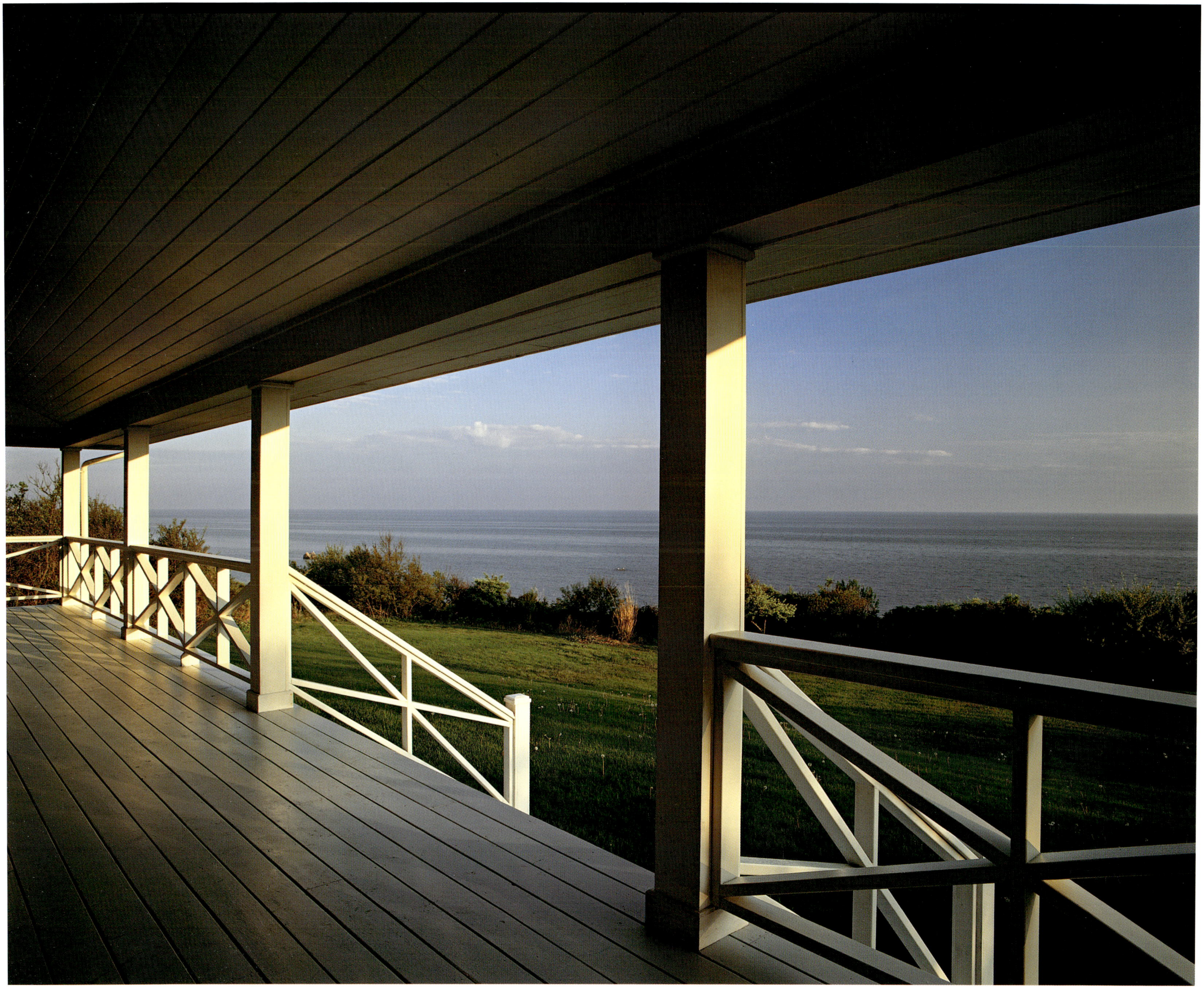

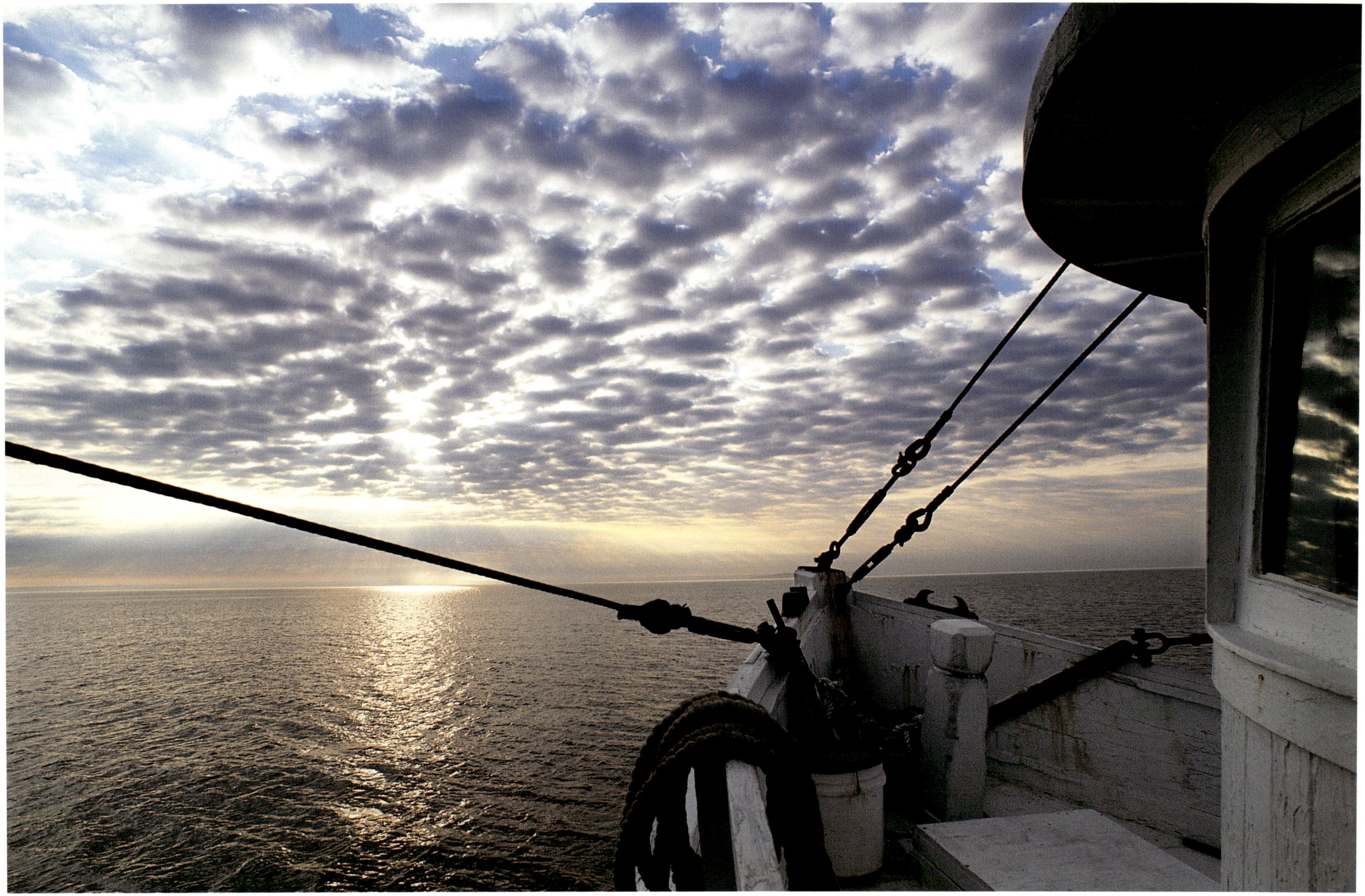

Fishing boat at dawn

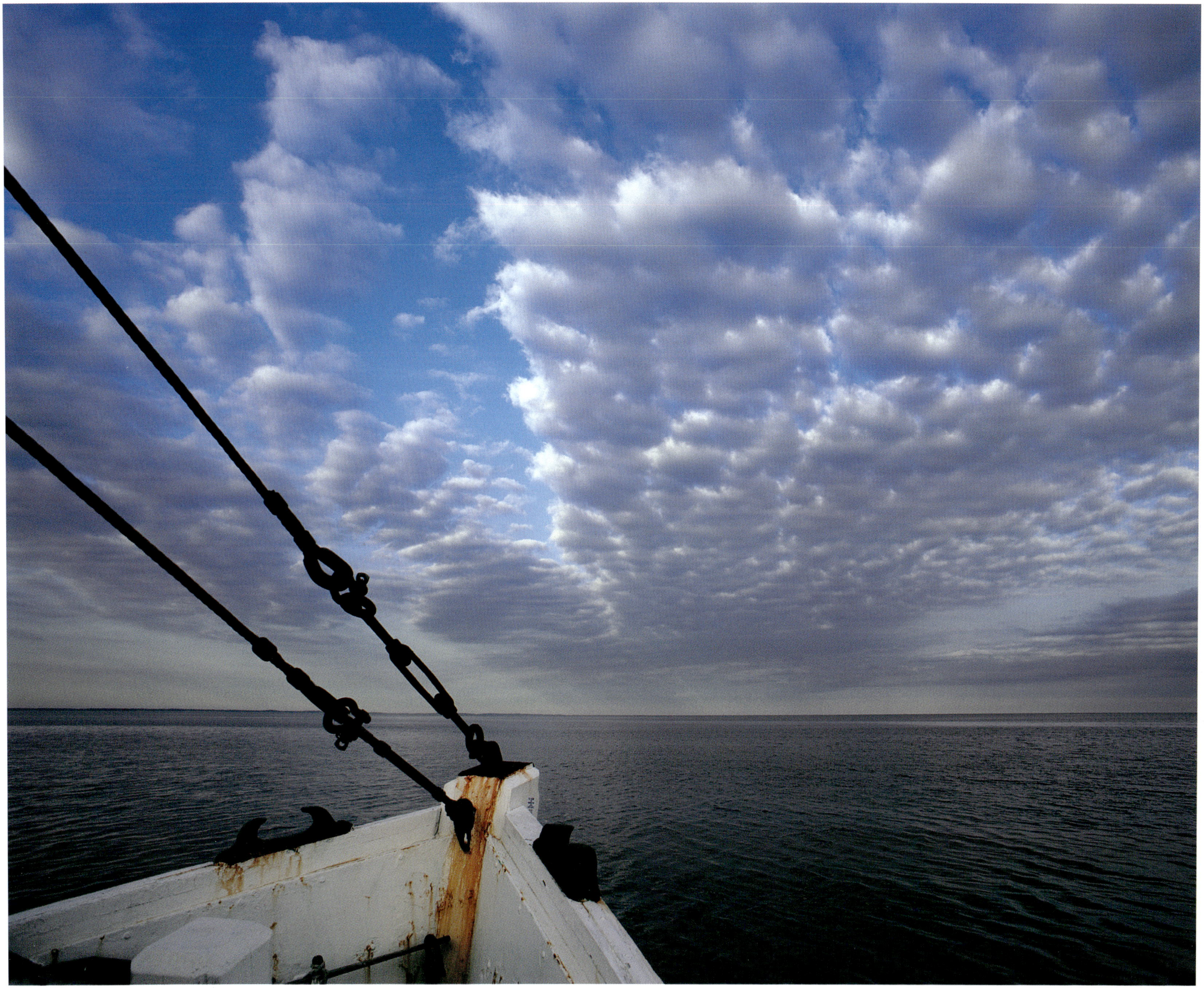

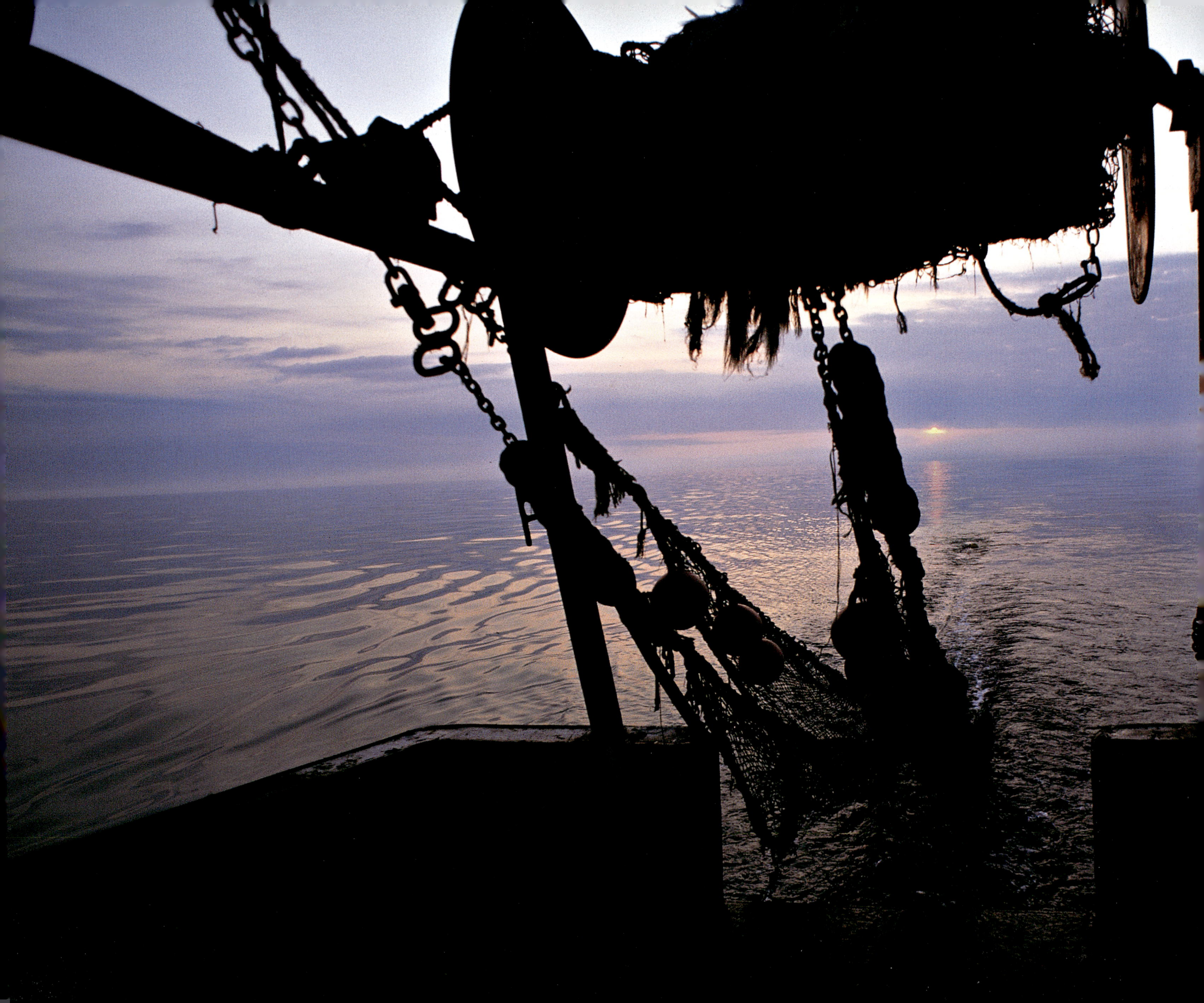

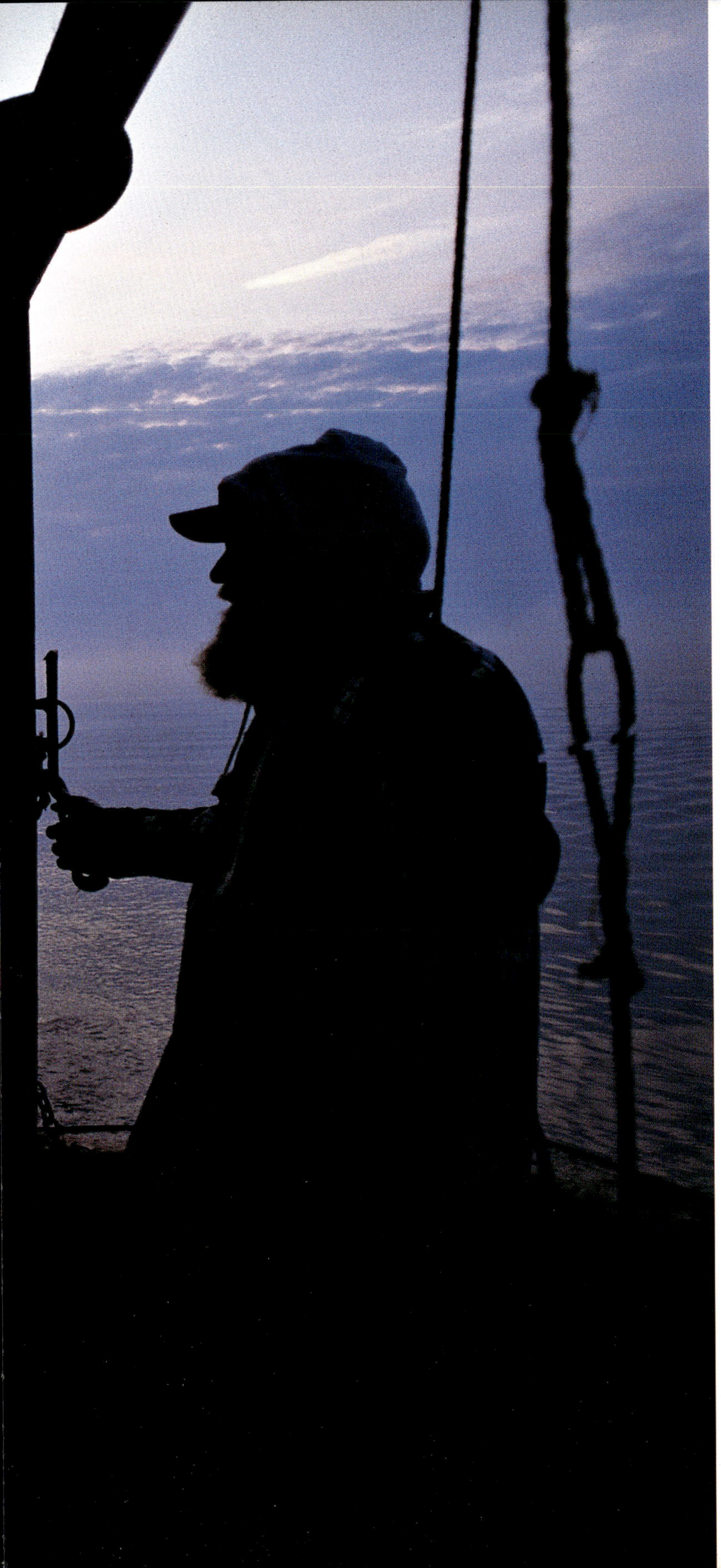

Fisherman at sunset

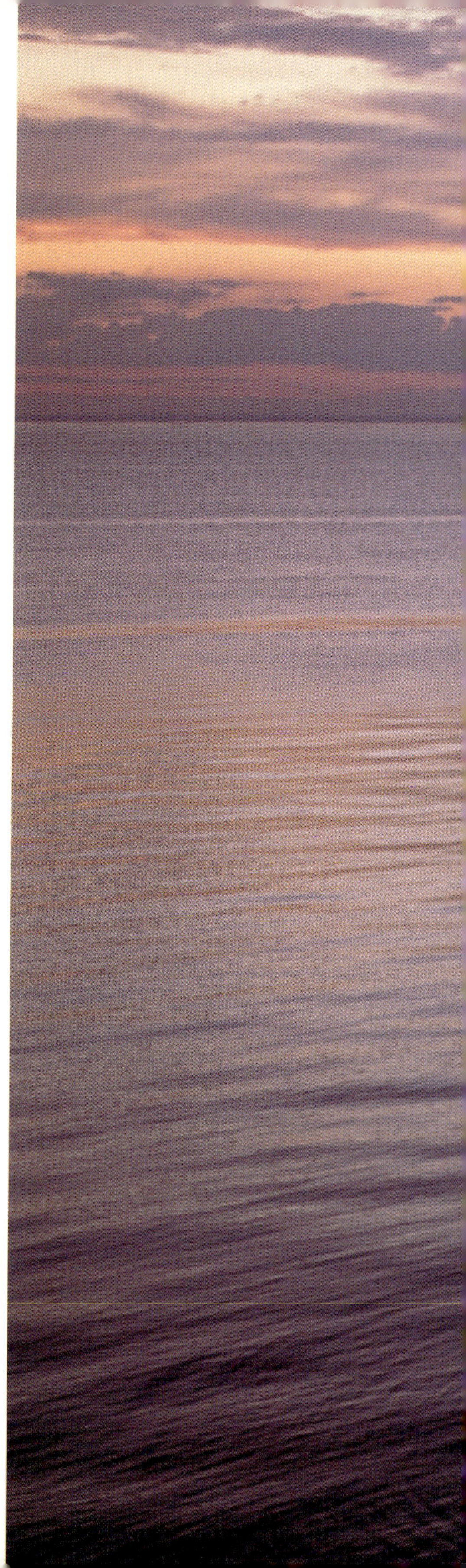

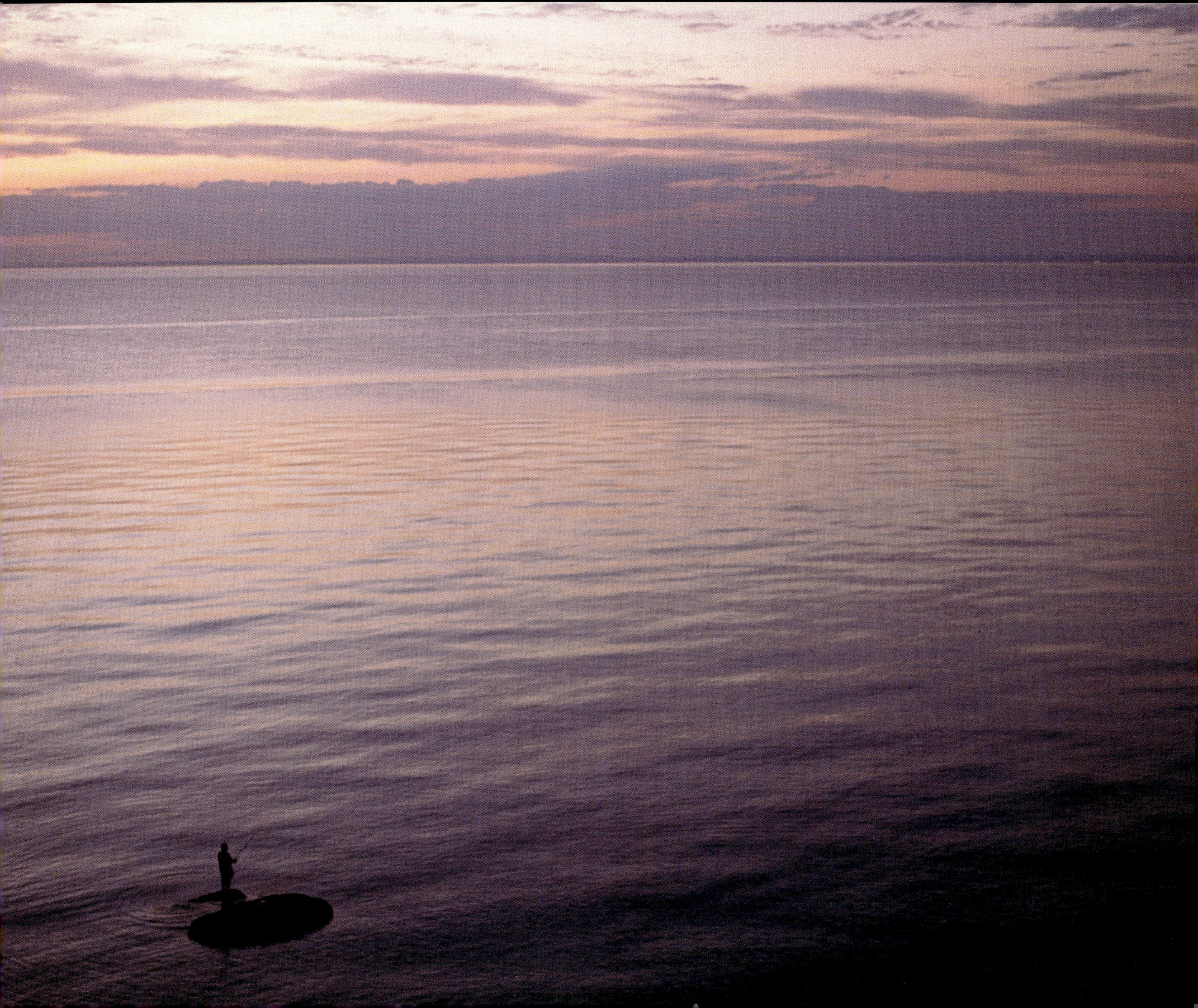

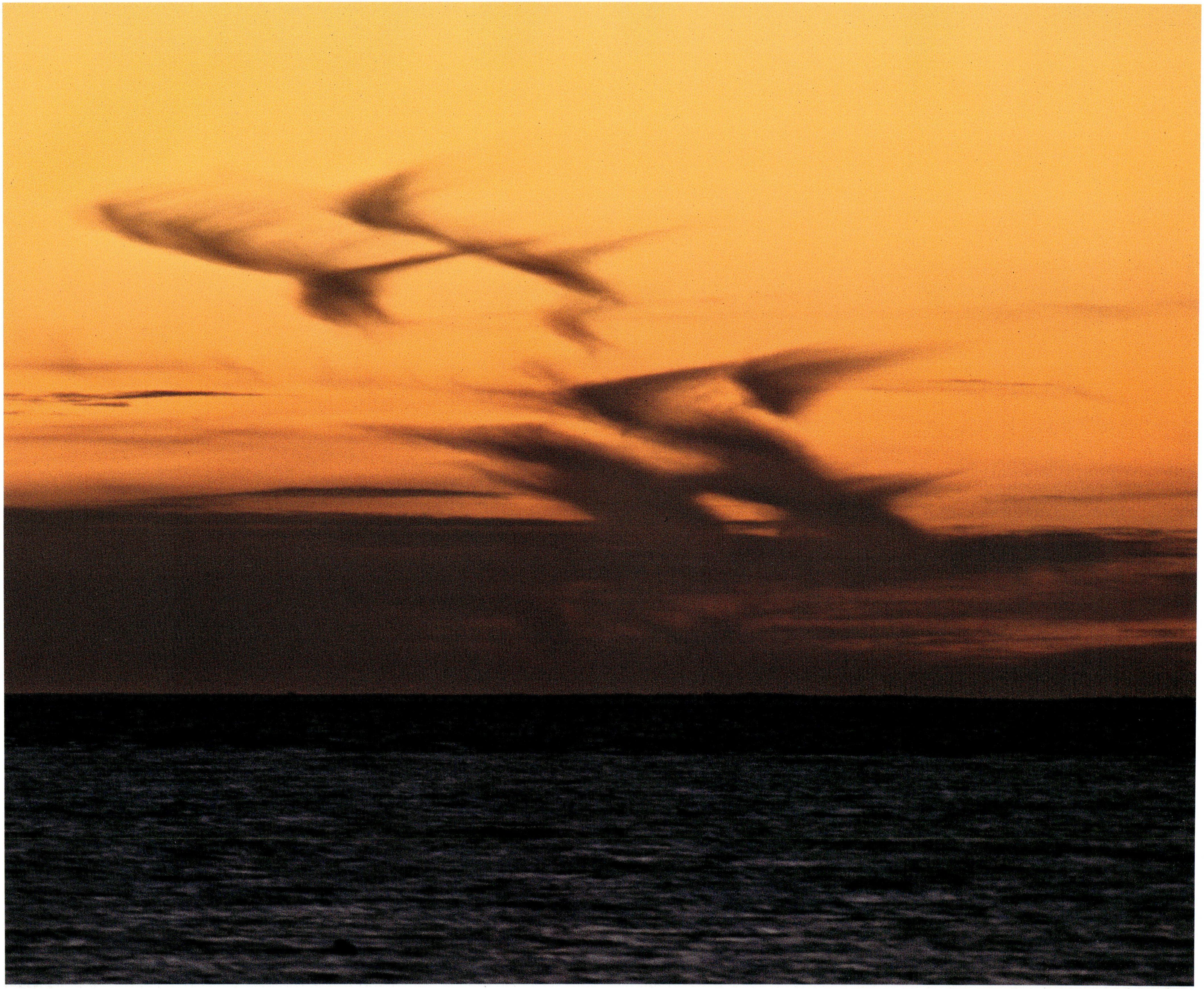

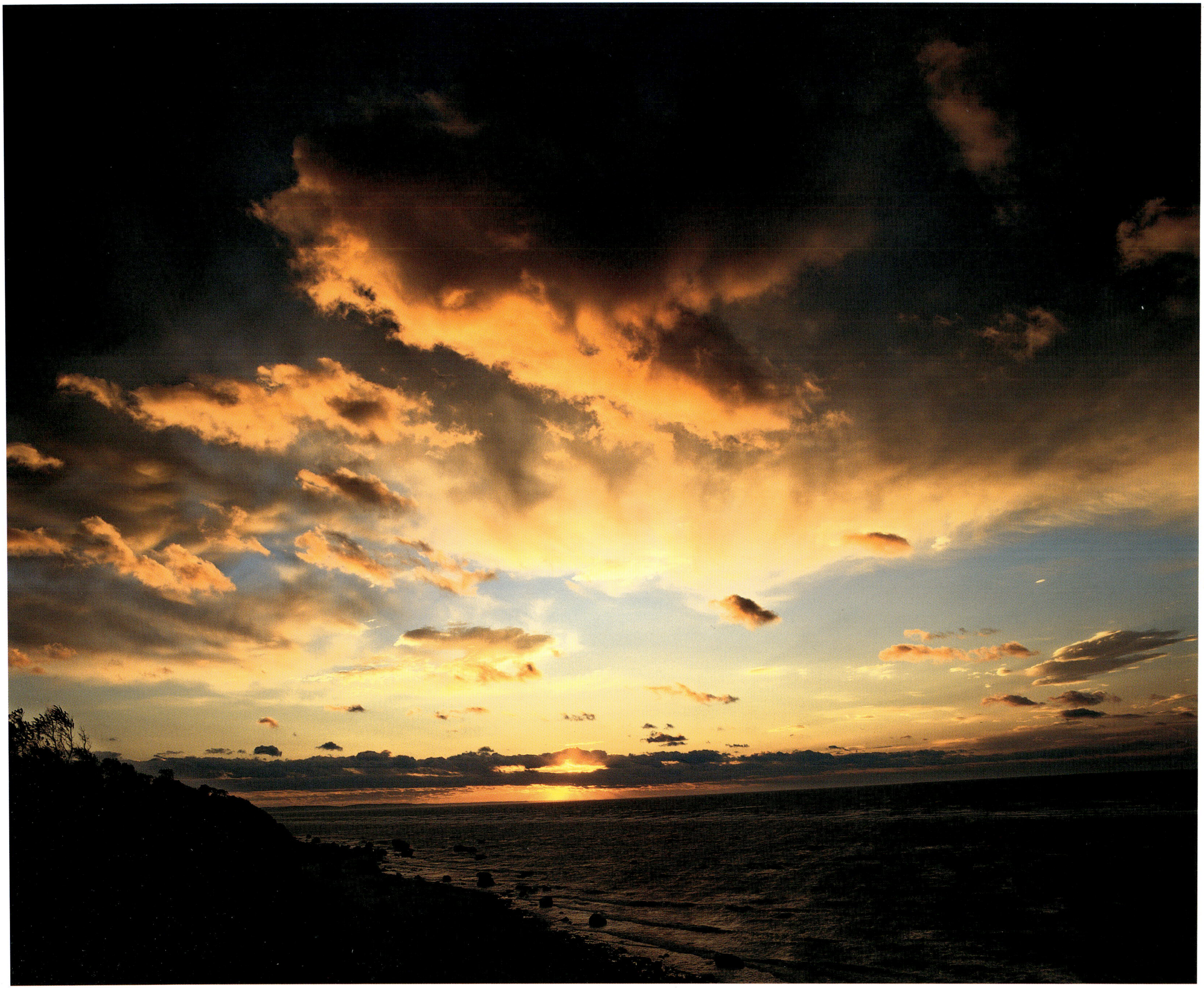

Truman Beach, Orient Park, East Marion

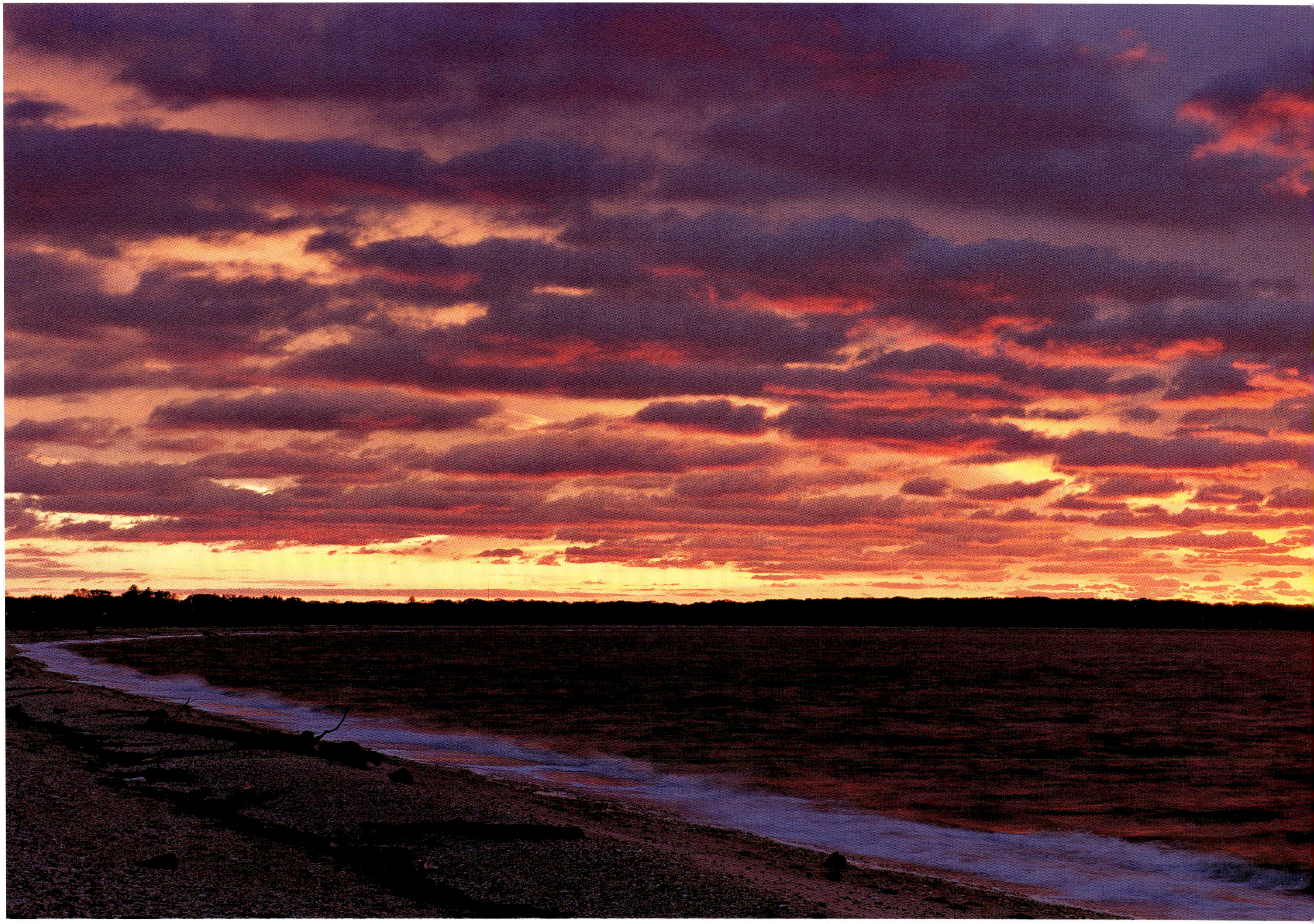

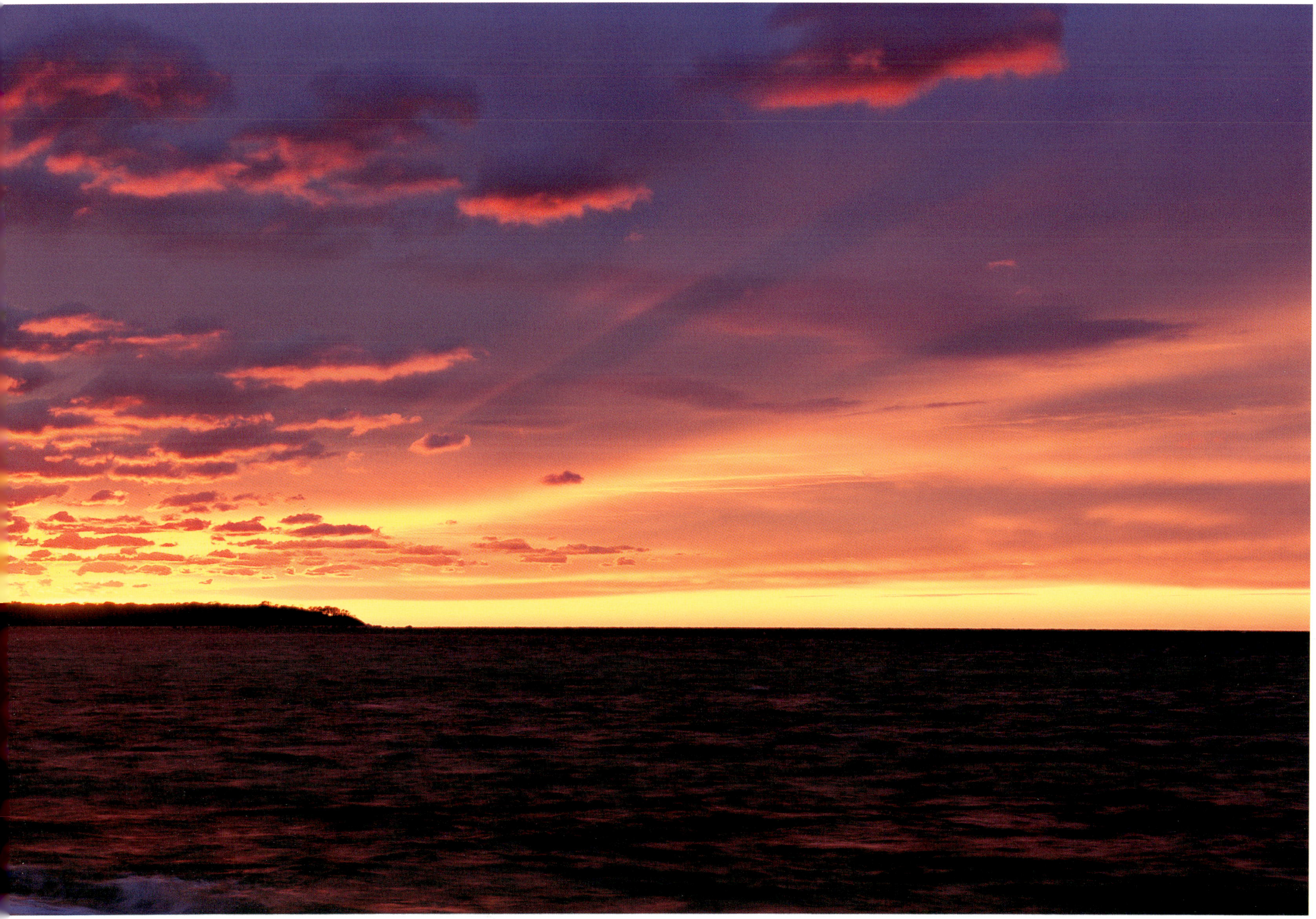

# Harvest

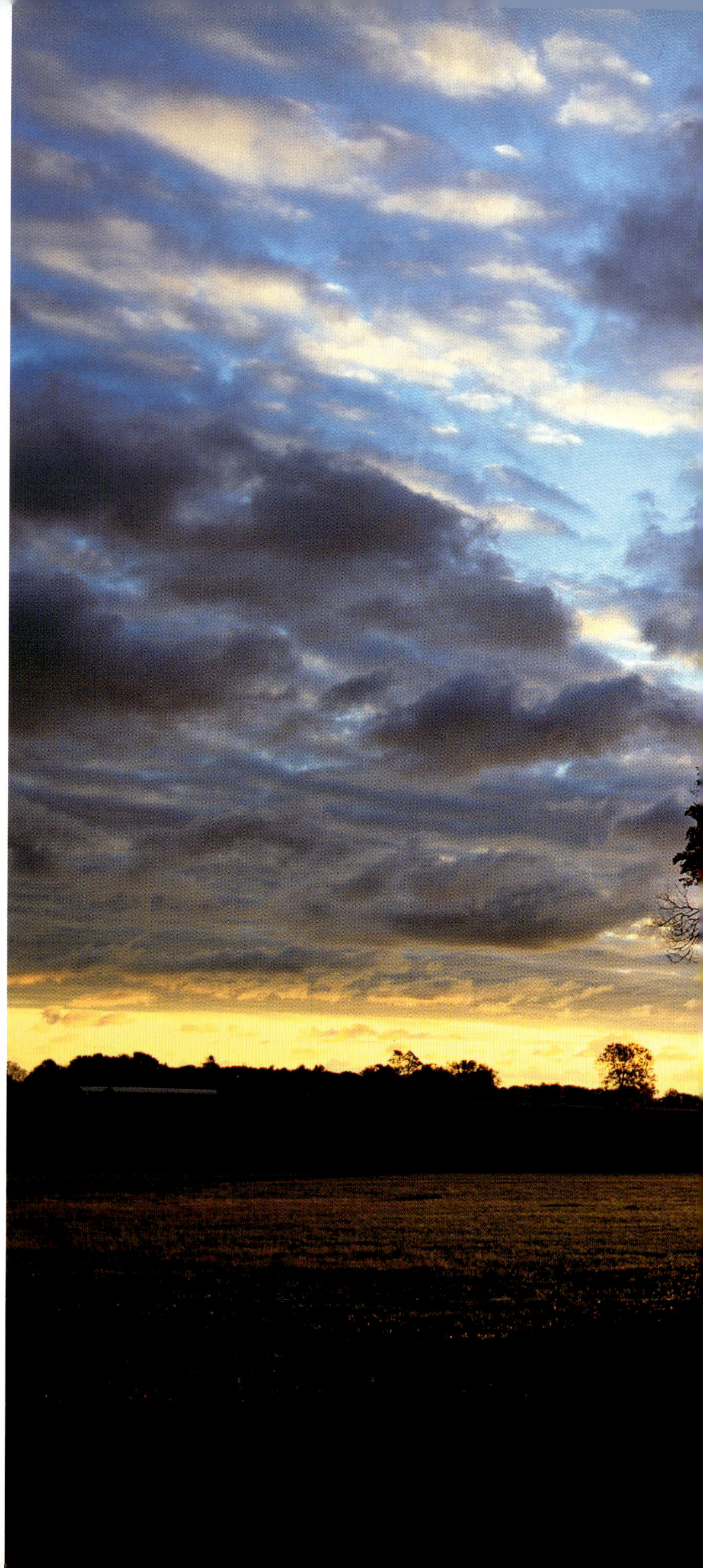

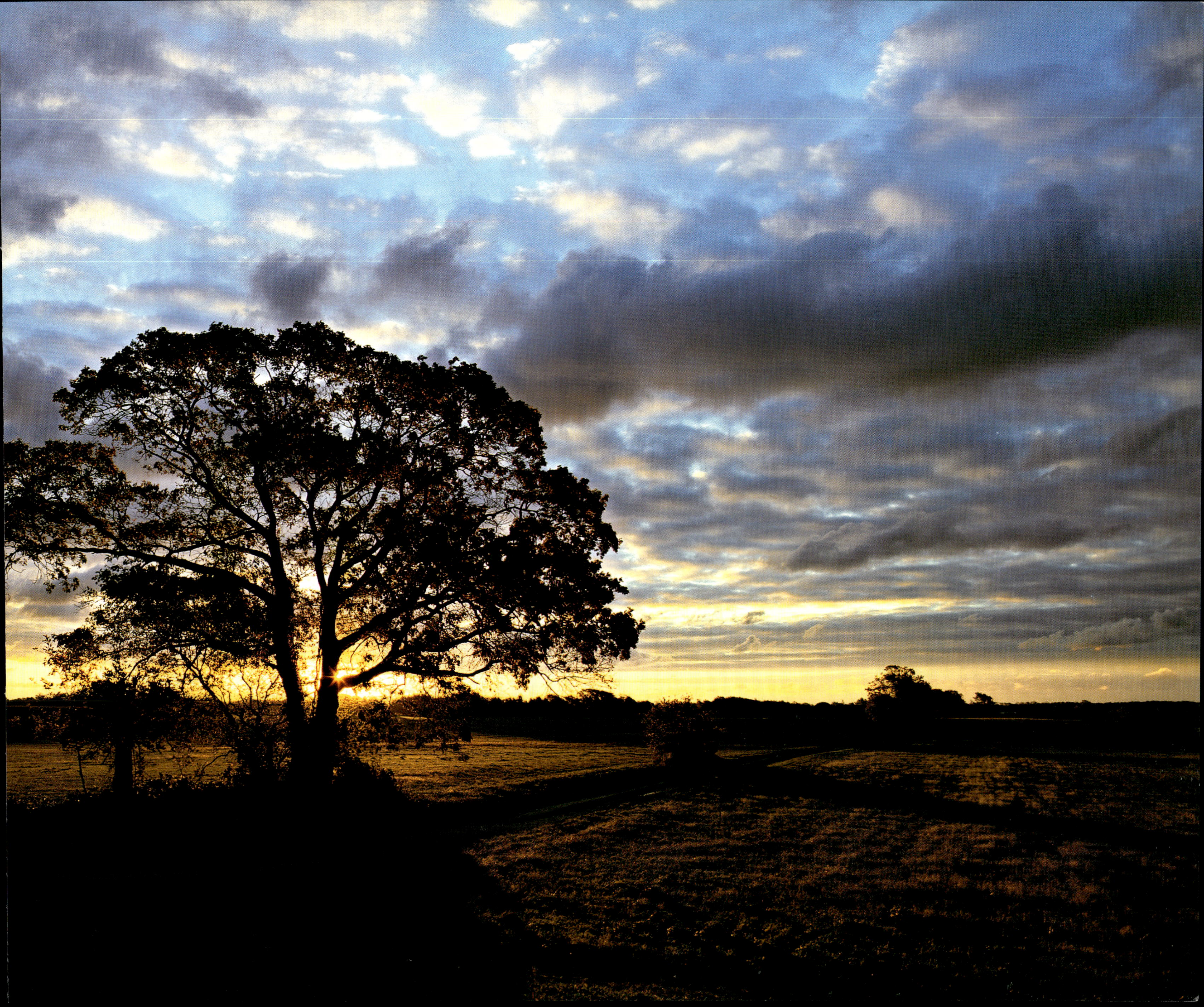

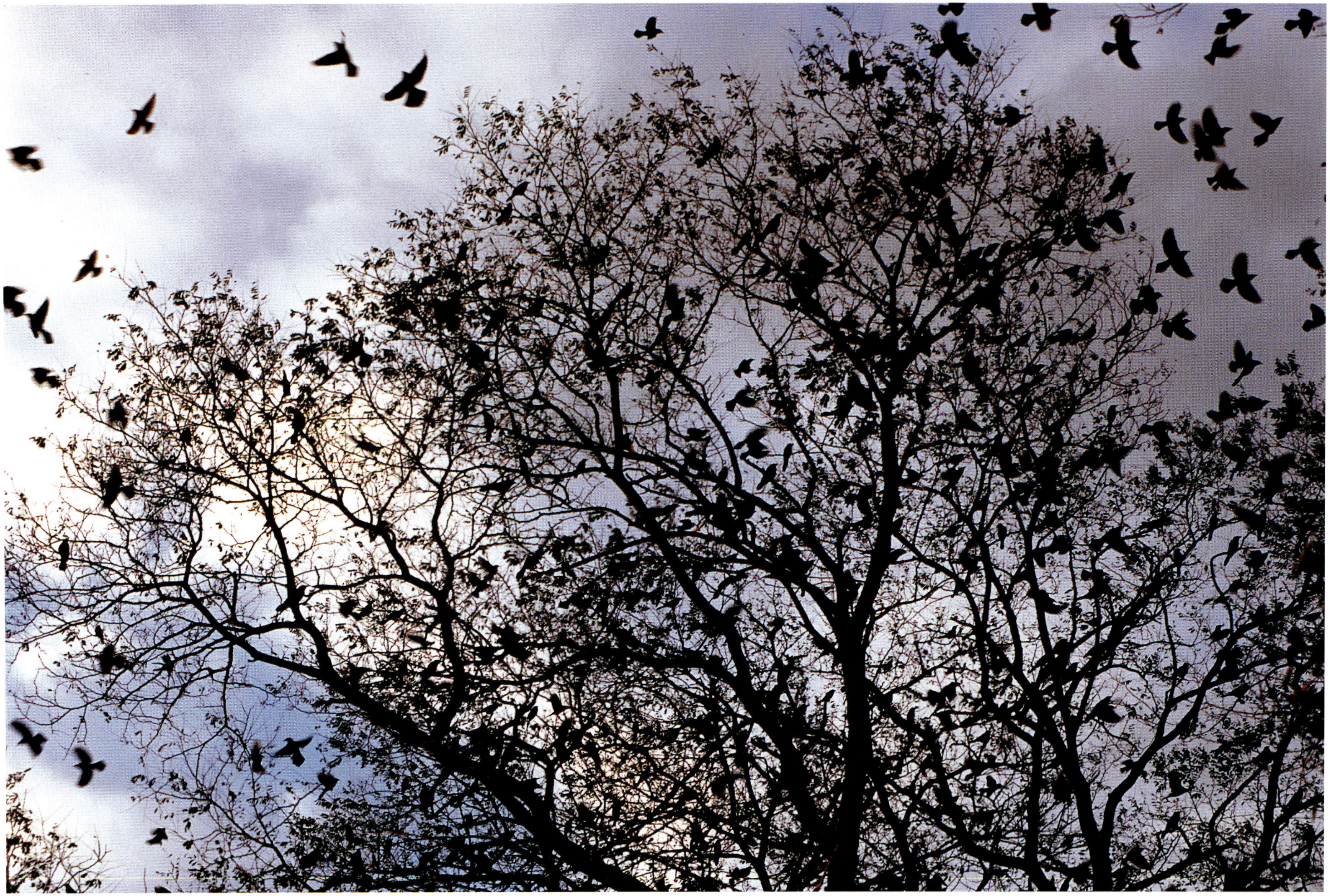

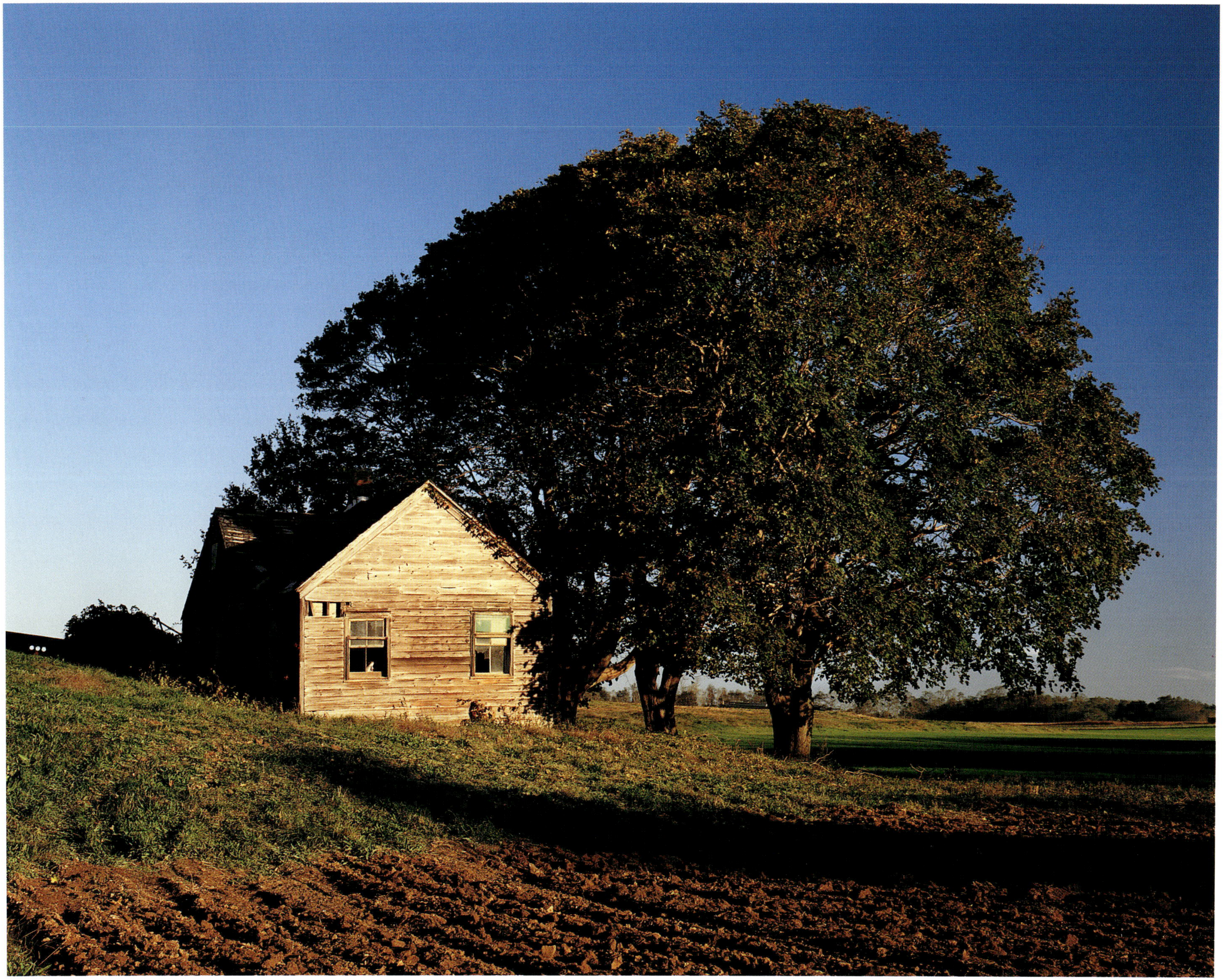

Potato field, Riverhead

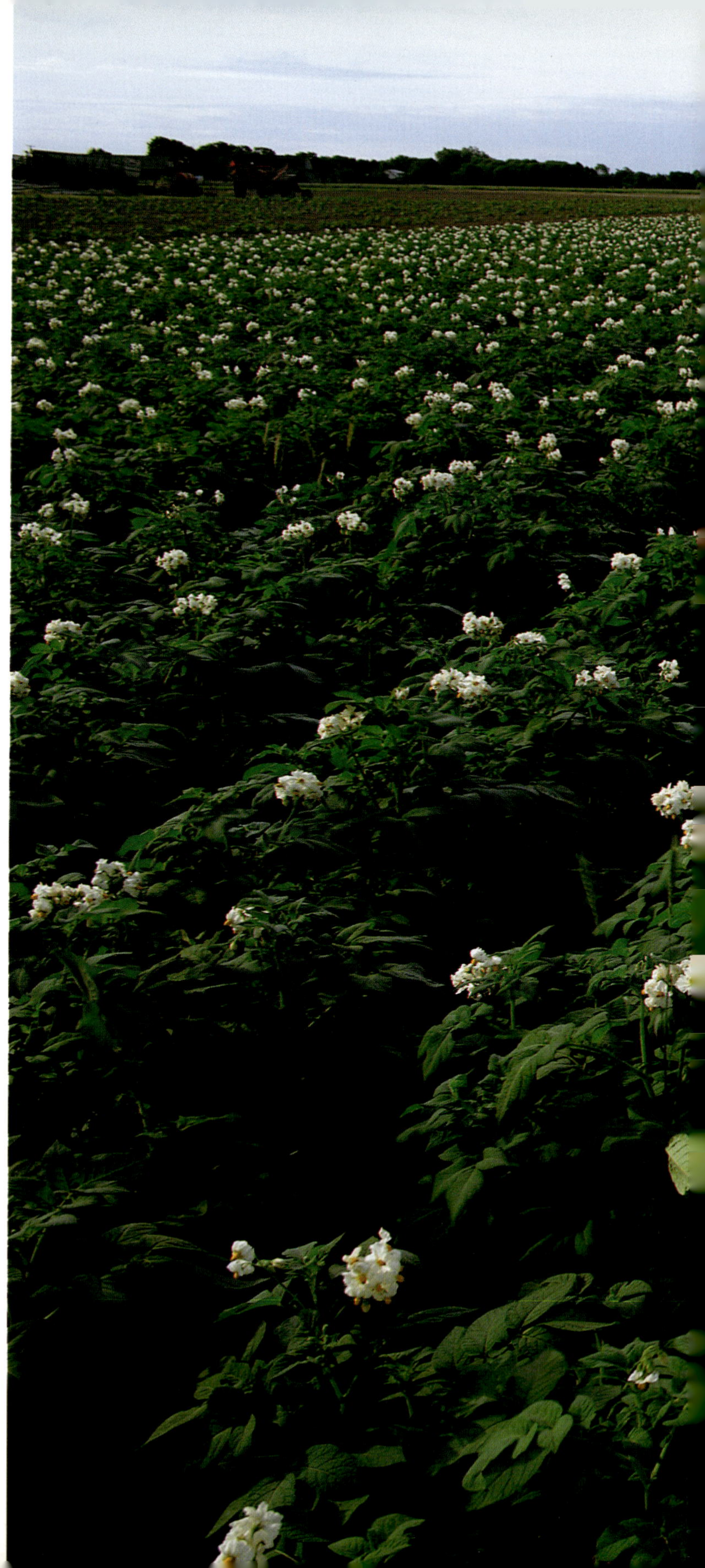

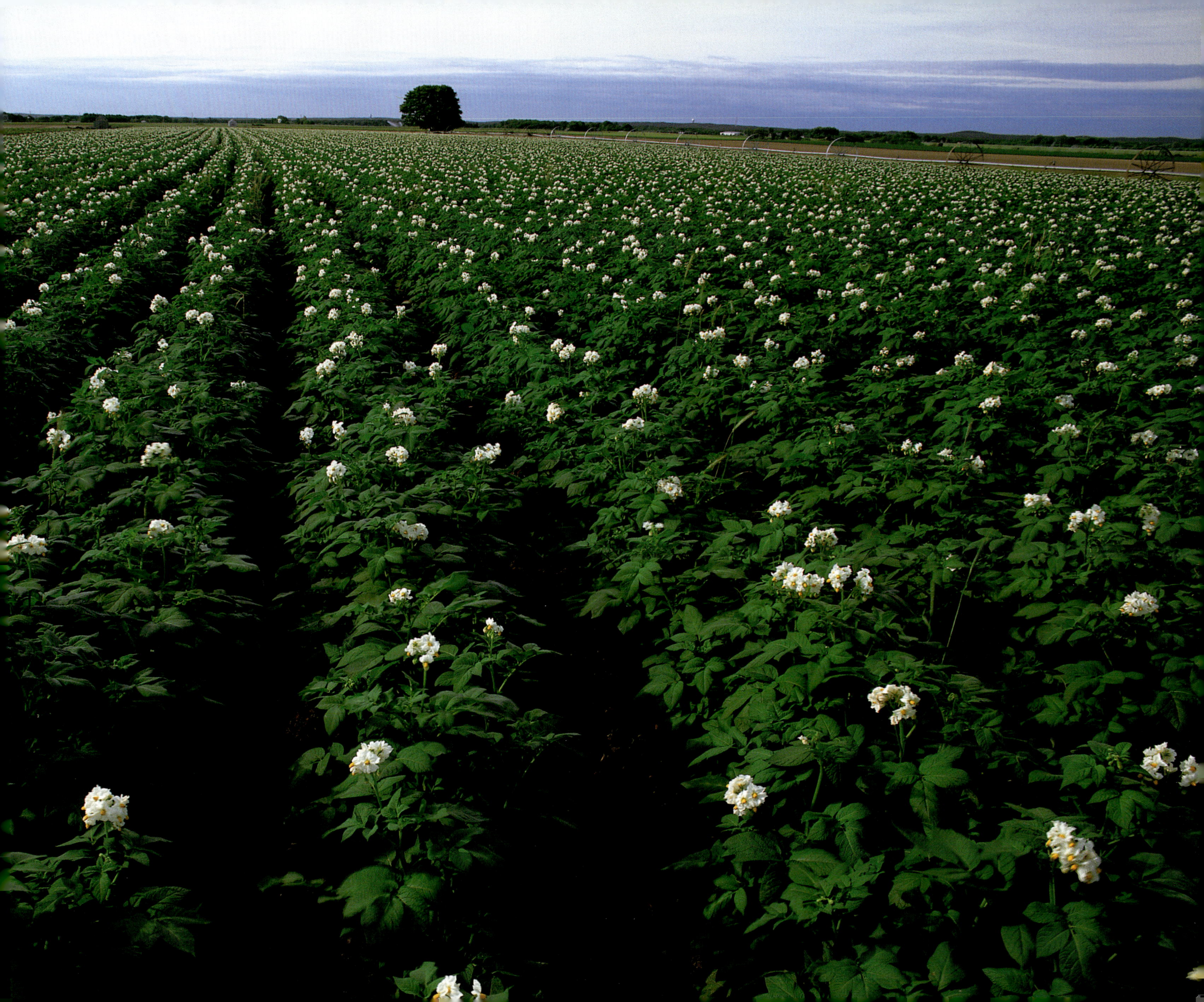

Pellegrini Vineyards, Cutchogue Macari Vineyards, Mattituck Martha Clara Vineyards, Jamesport

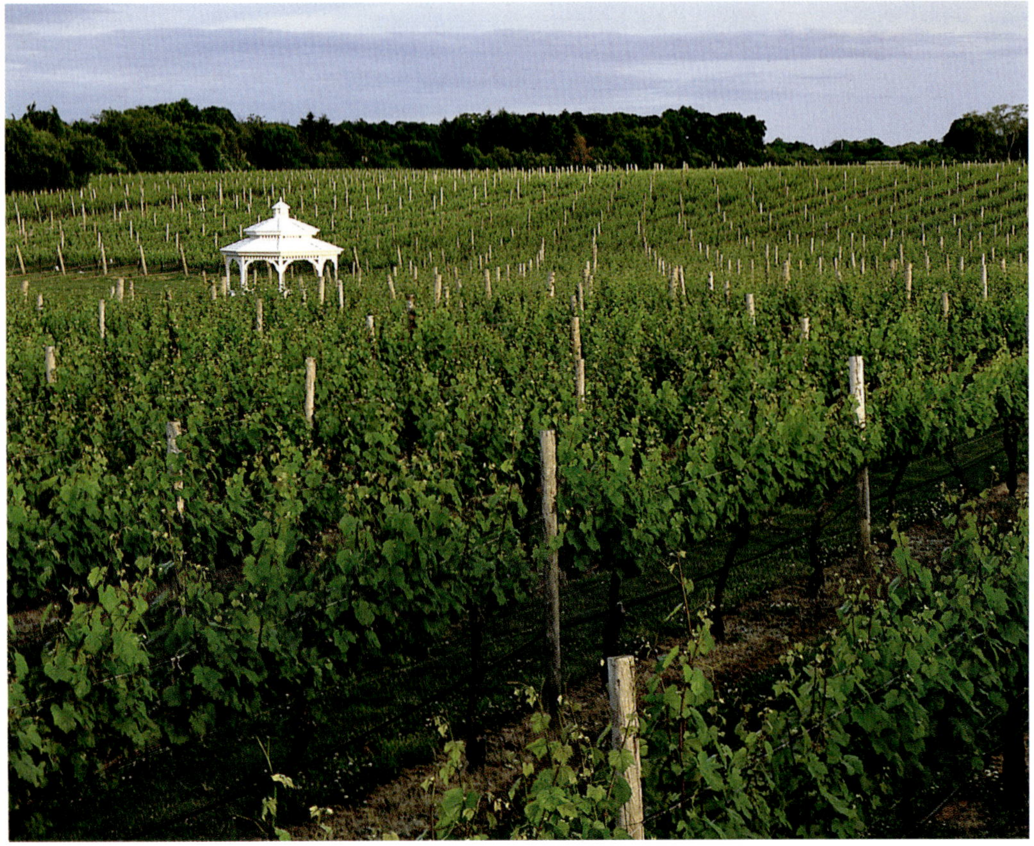

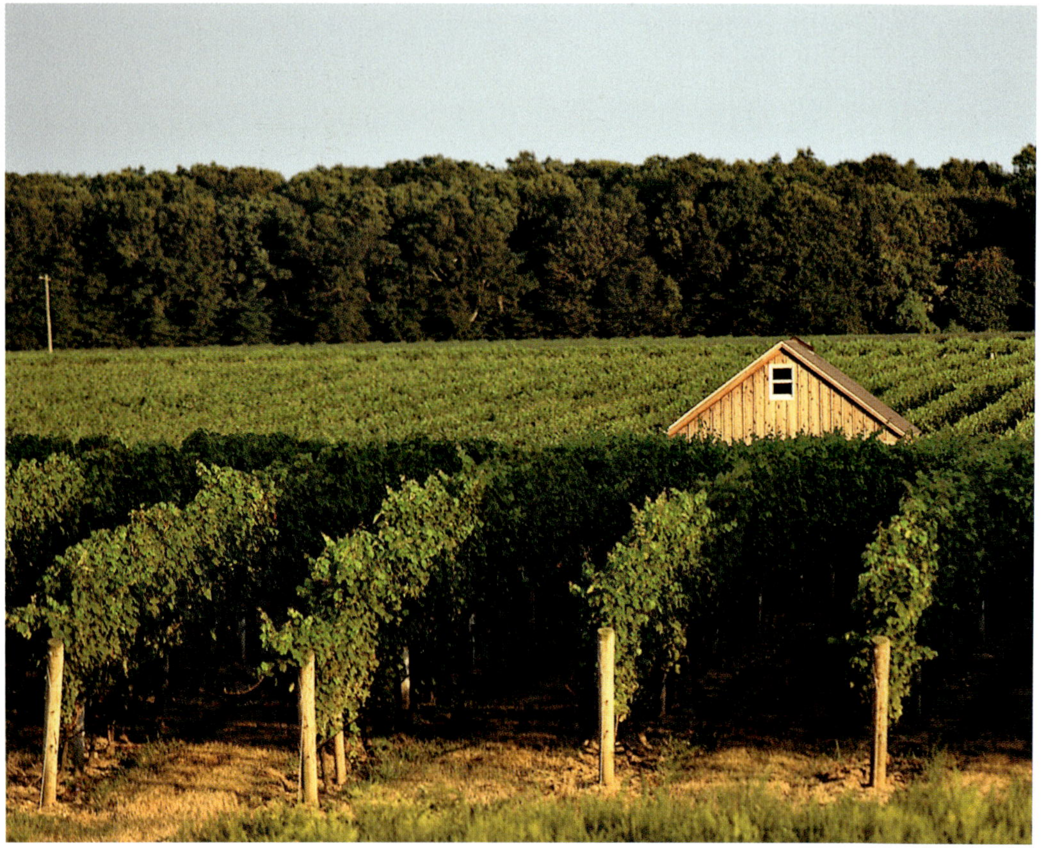

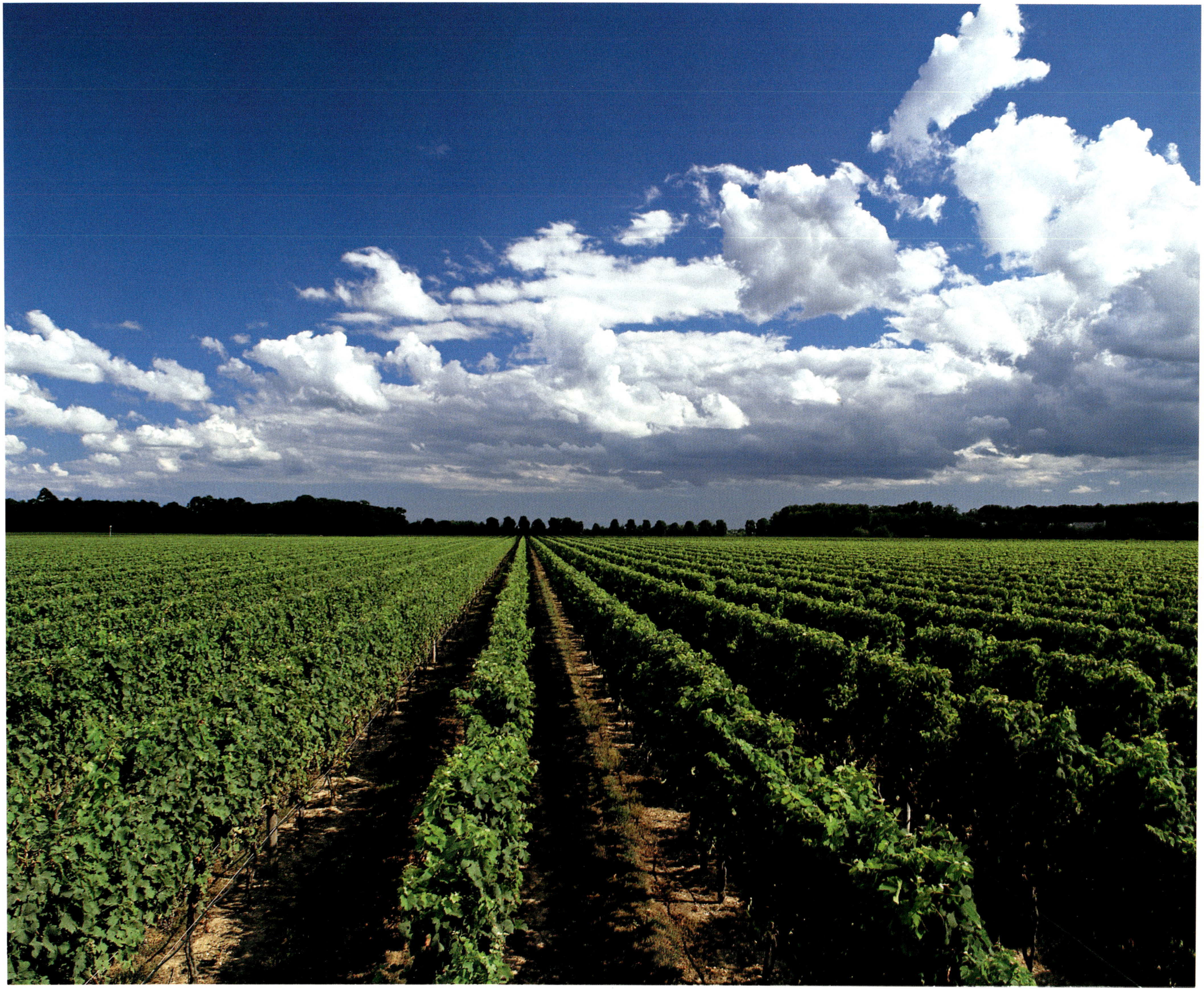

Duck Walk Vineyards, Cutchogue

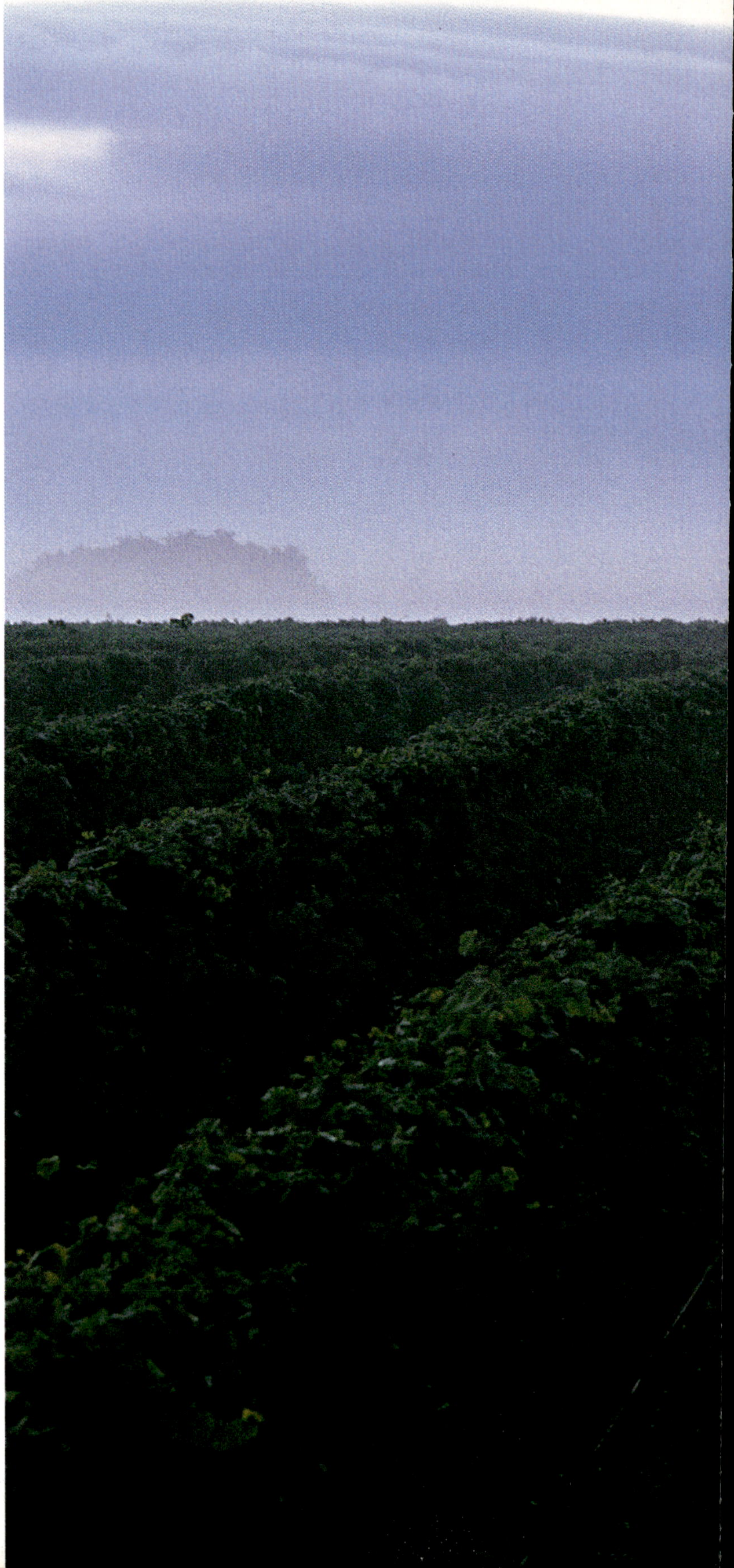

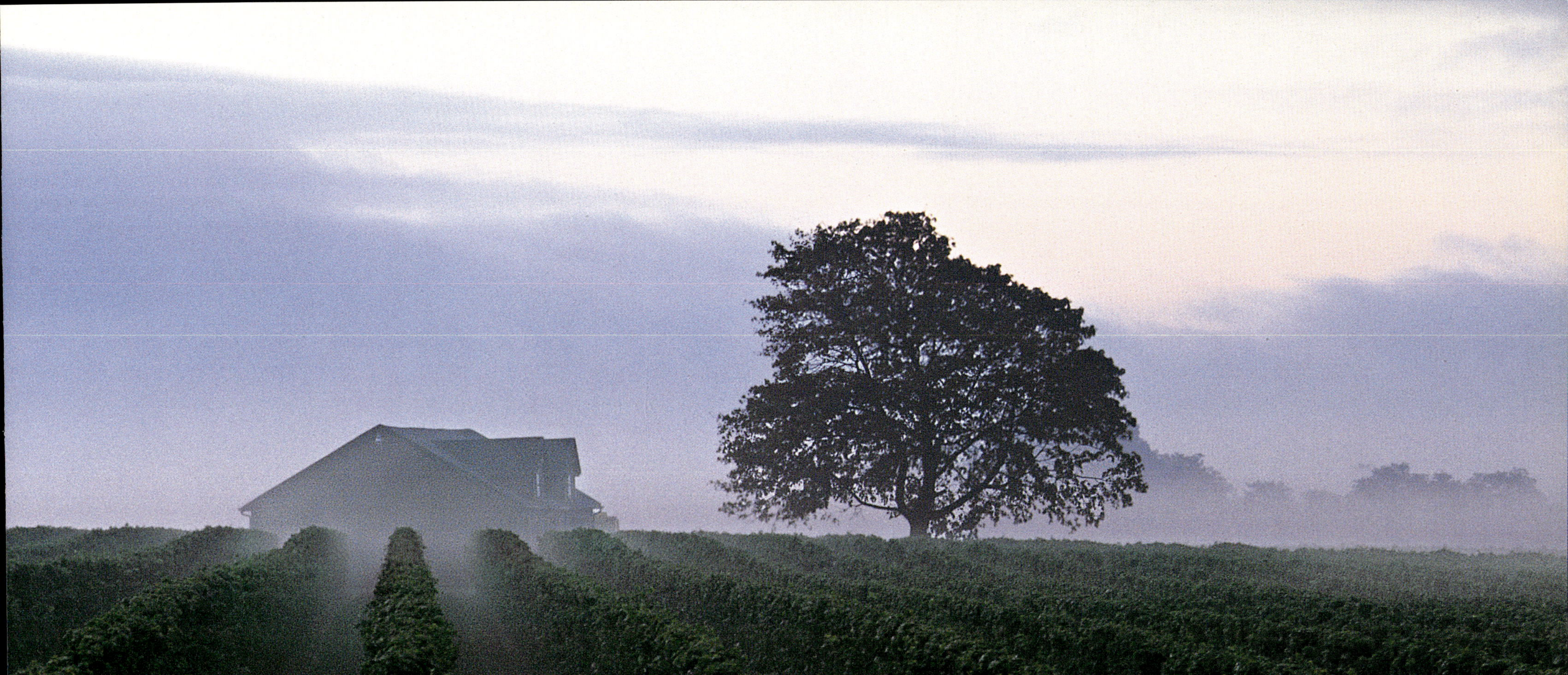

Stakey Farm, Aquebogue

Roanoke Farm, Riverhead

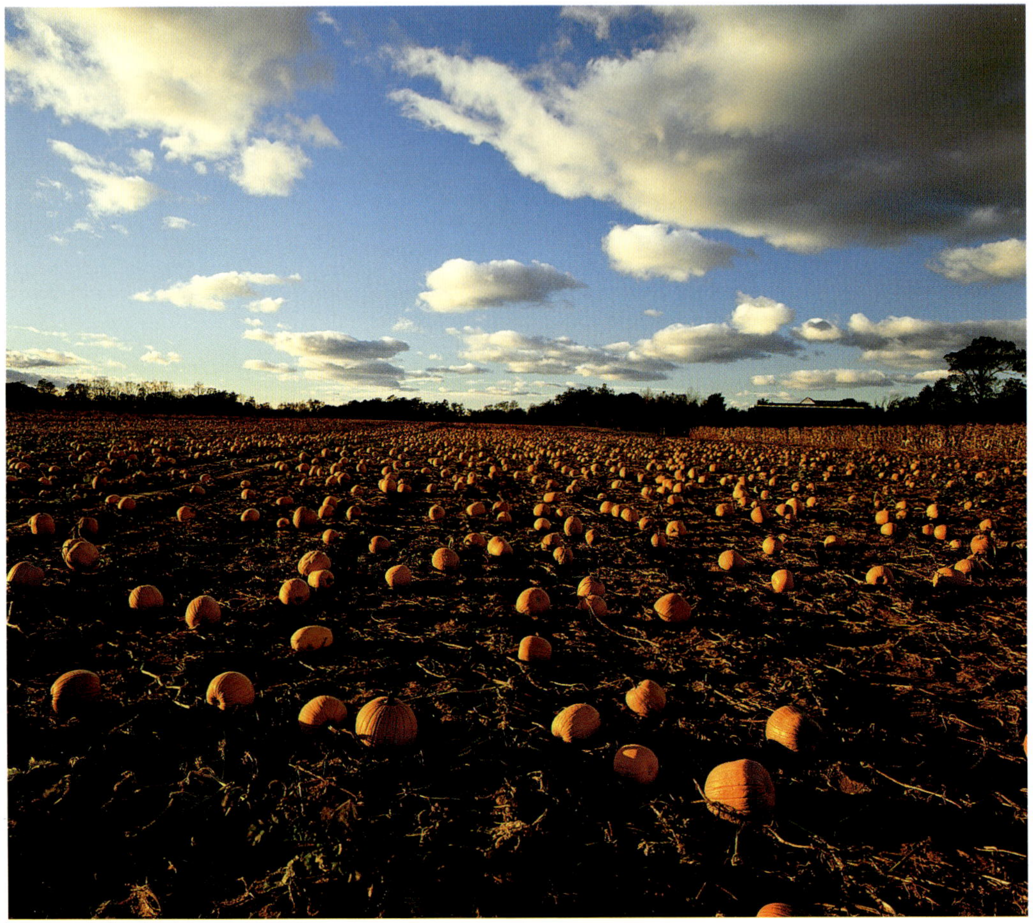

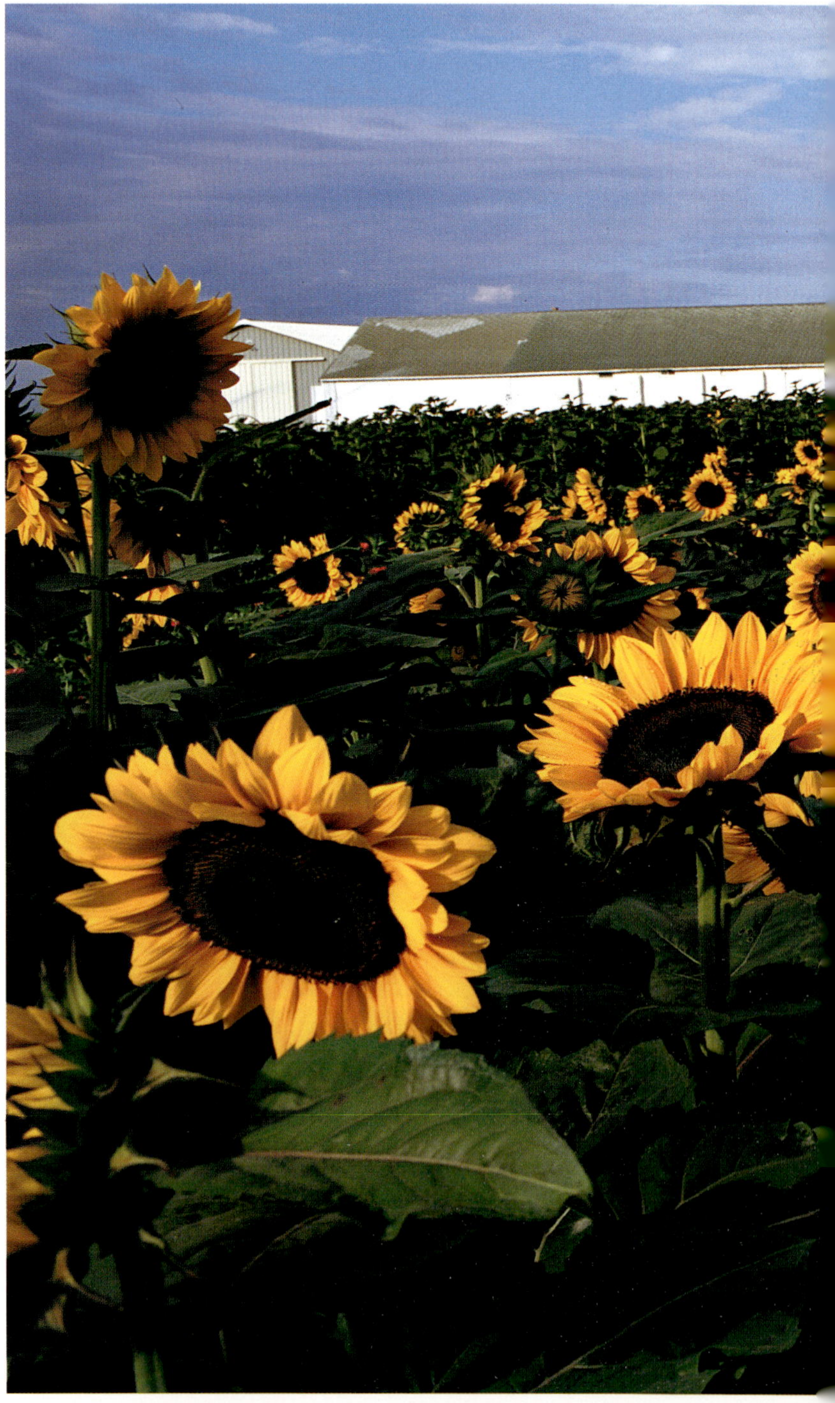

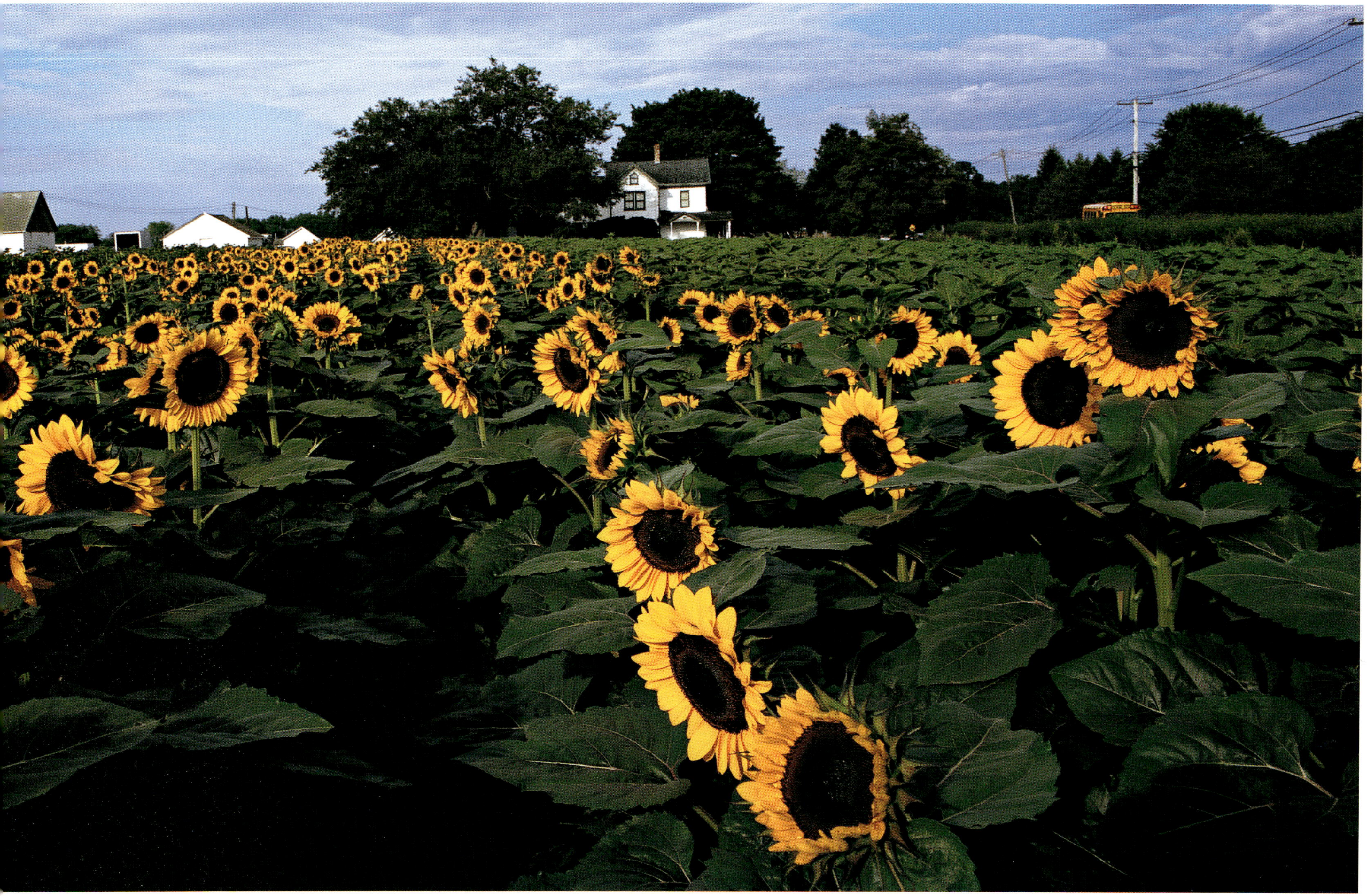

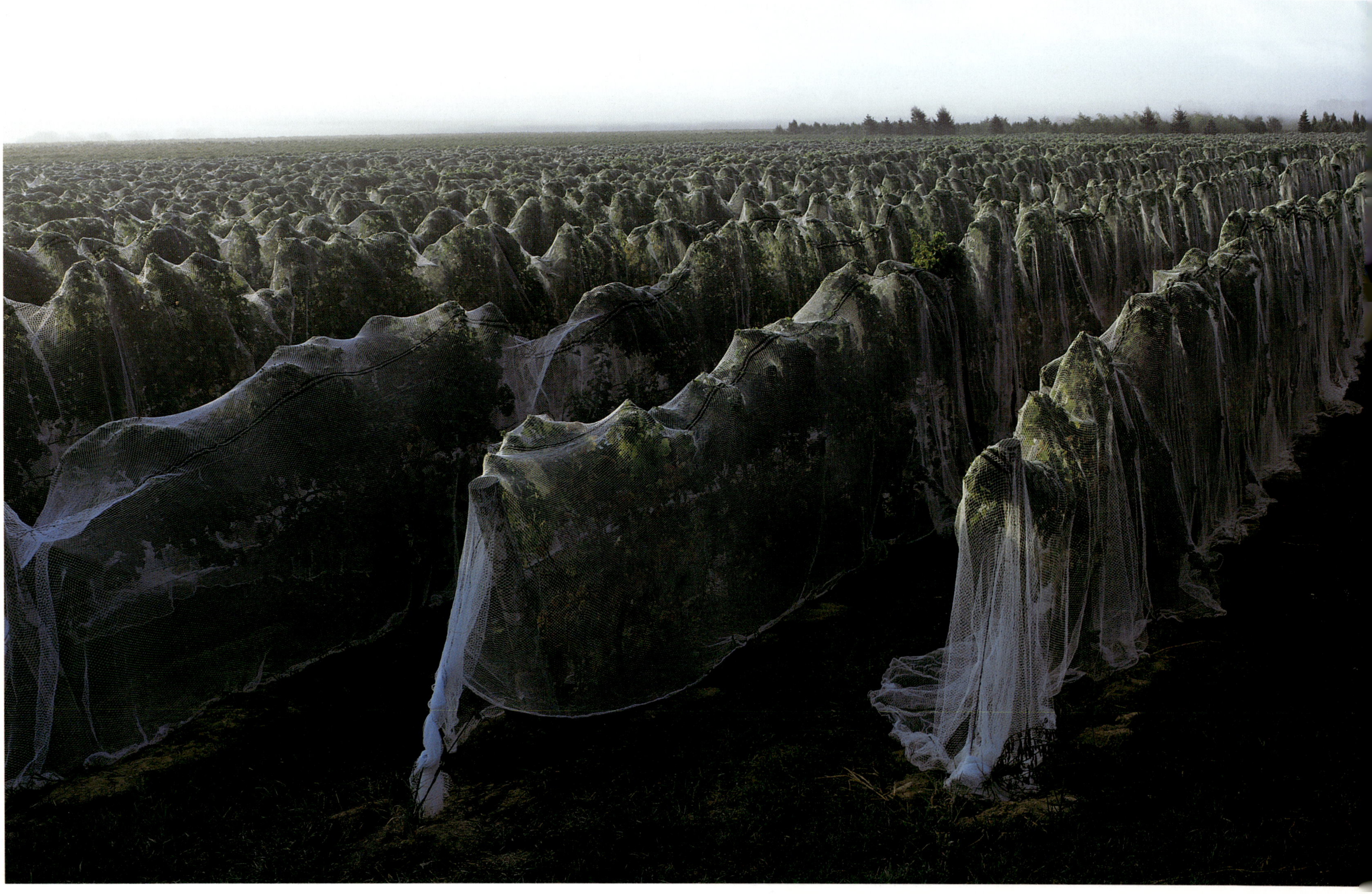

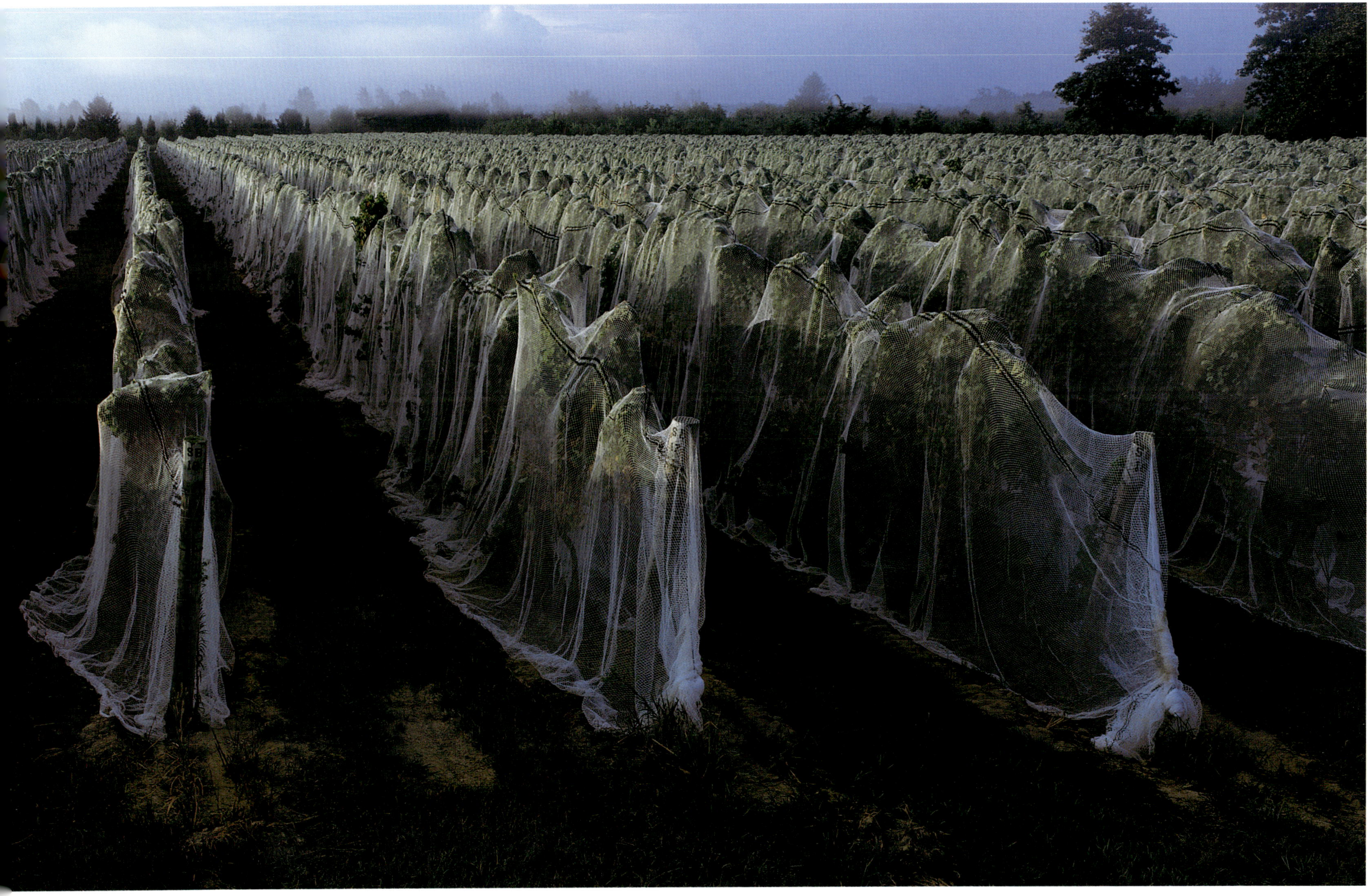

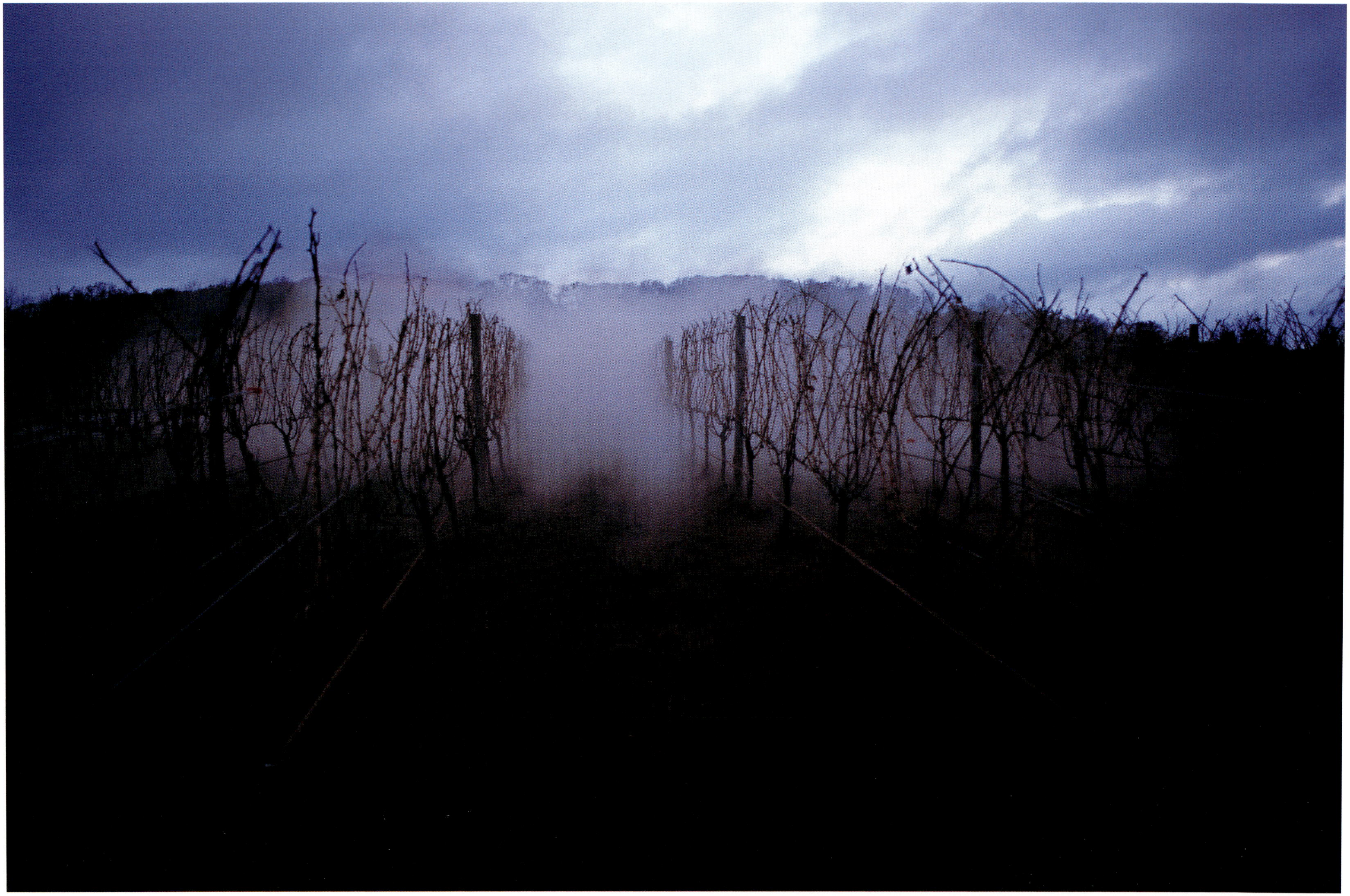

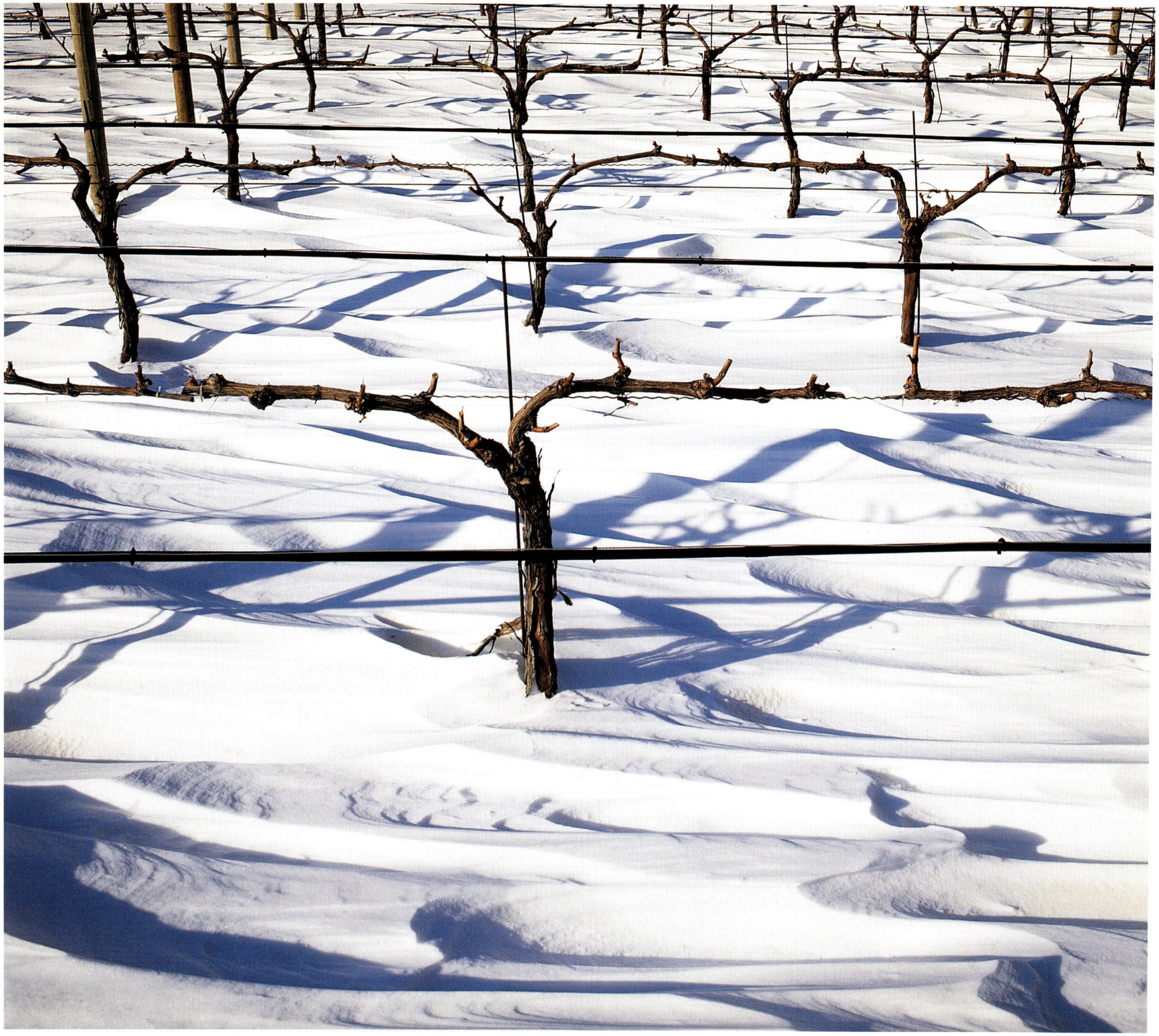

Peconic Bay Winery, Cutchogue

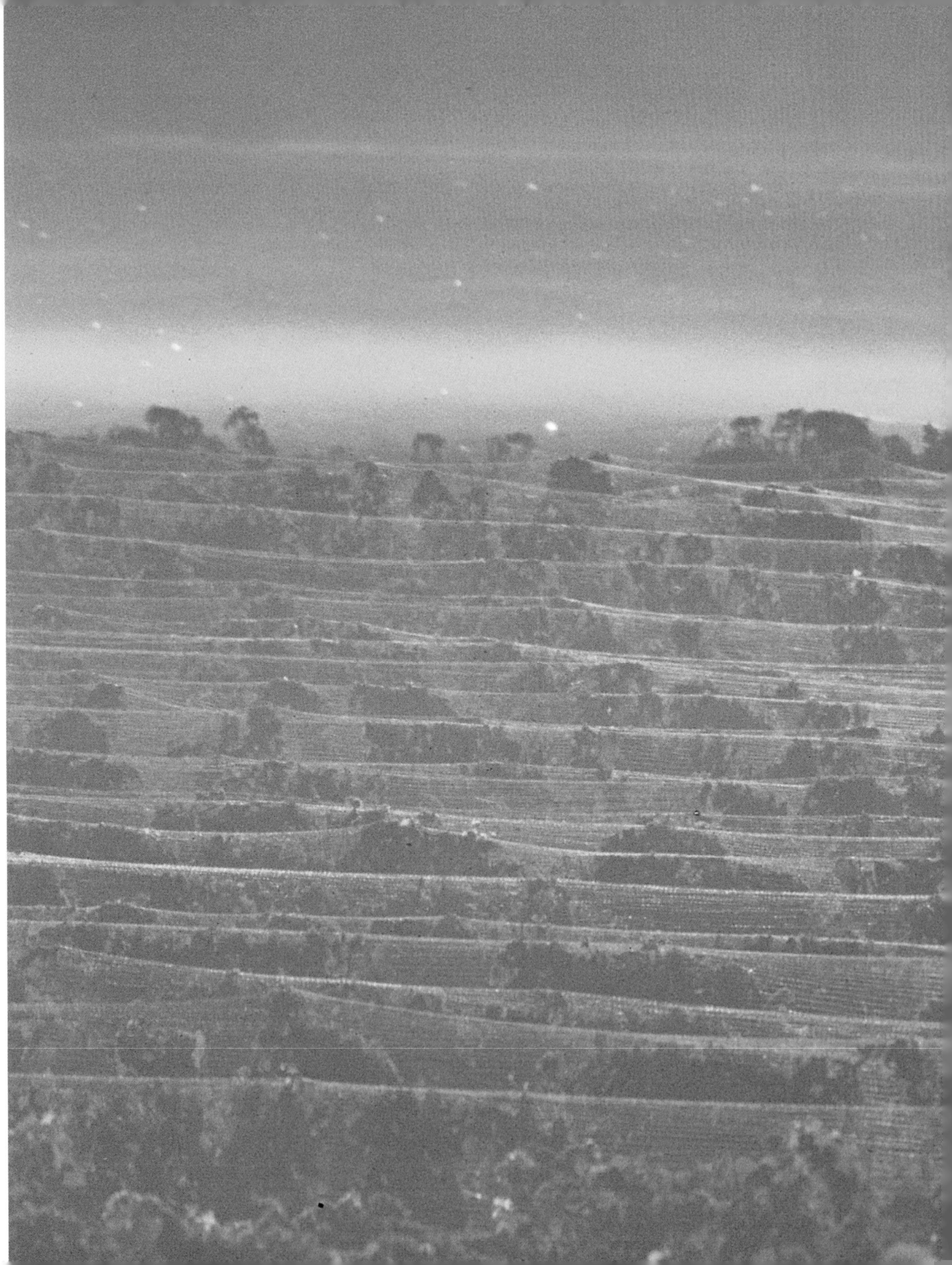

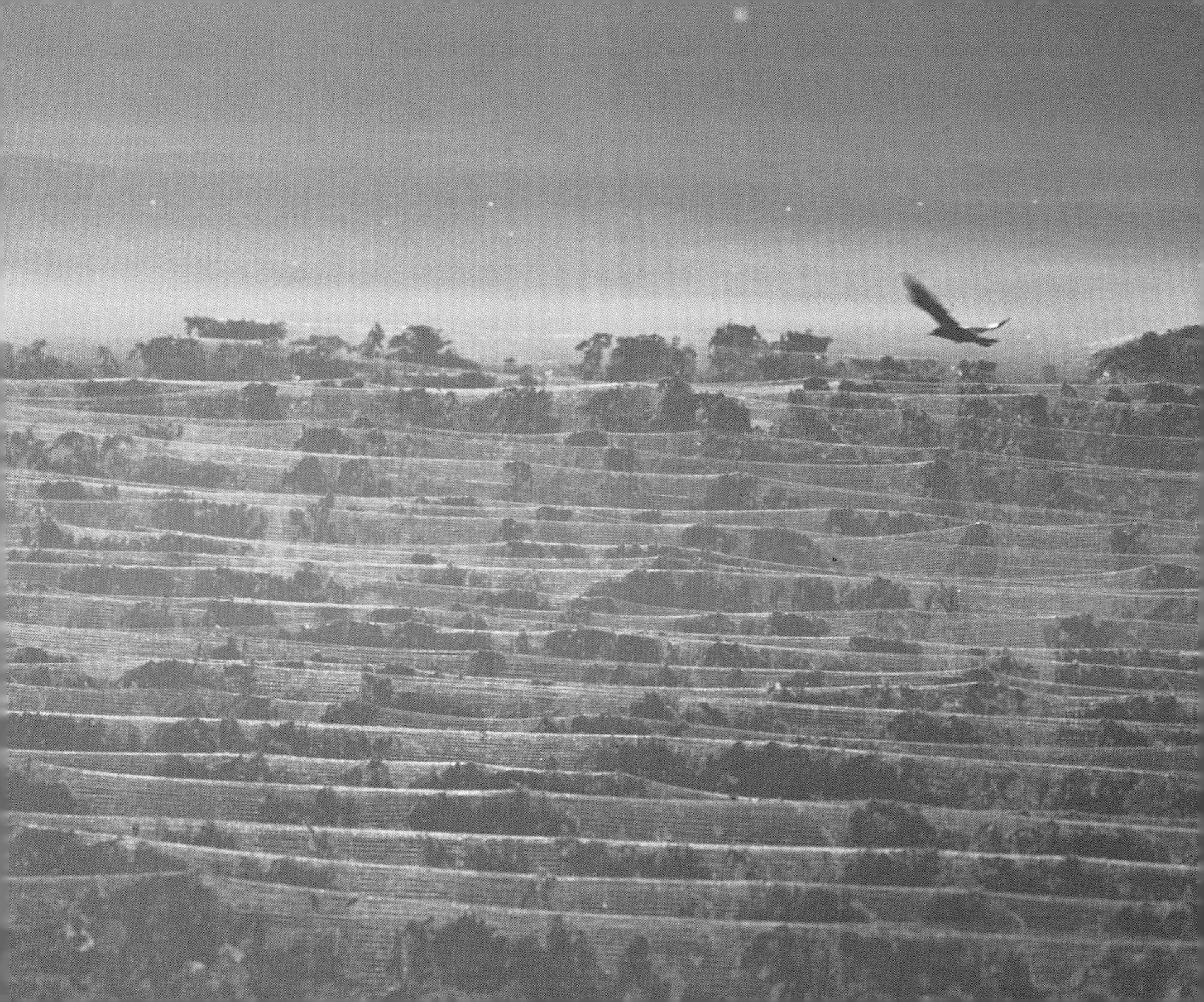

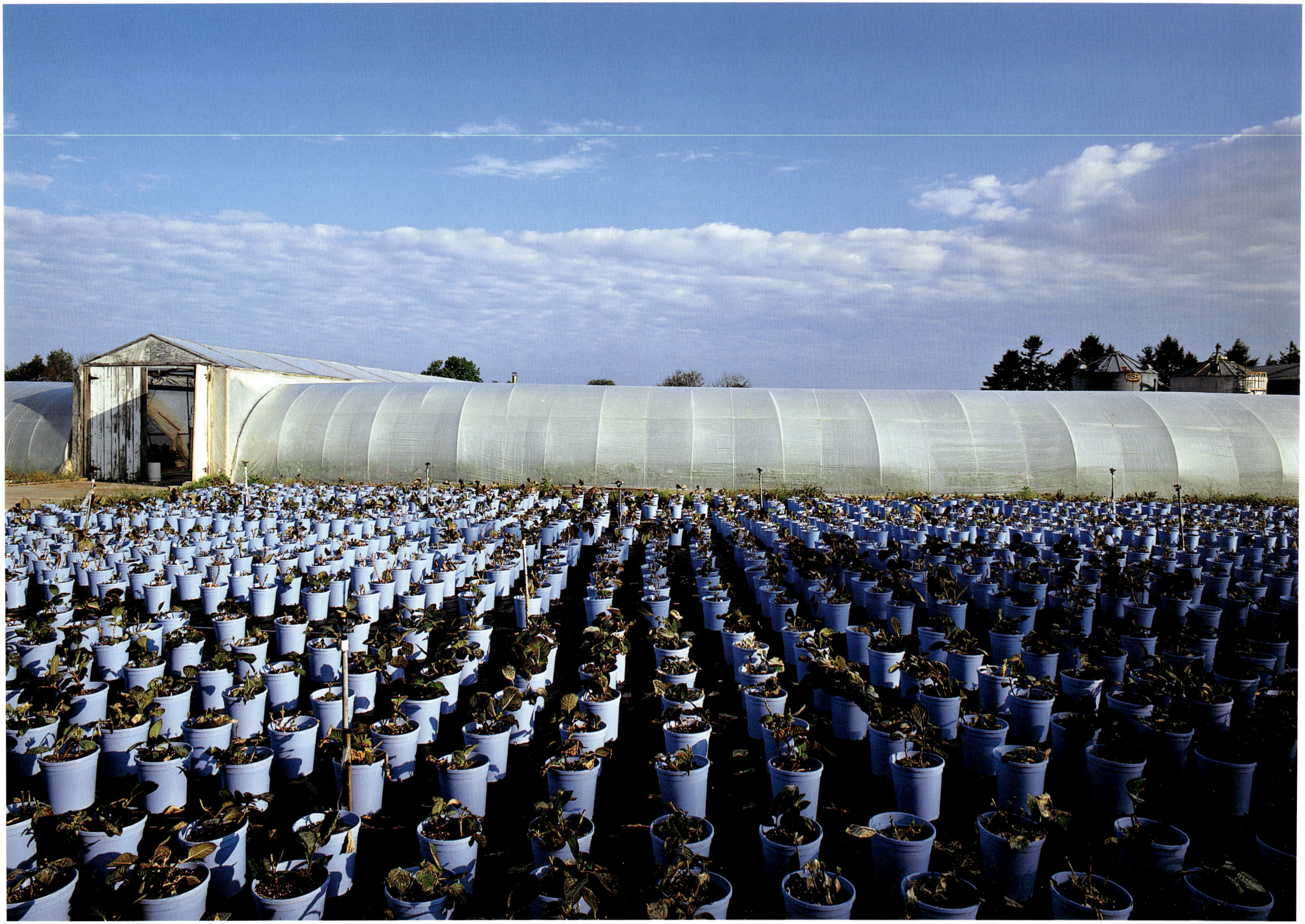

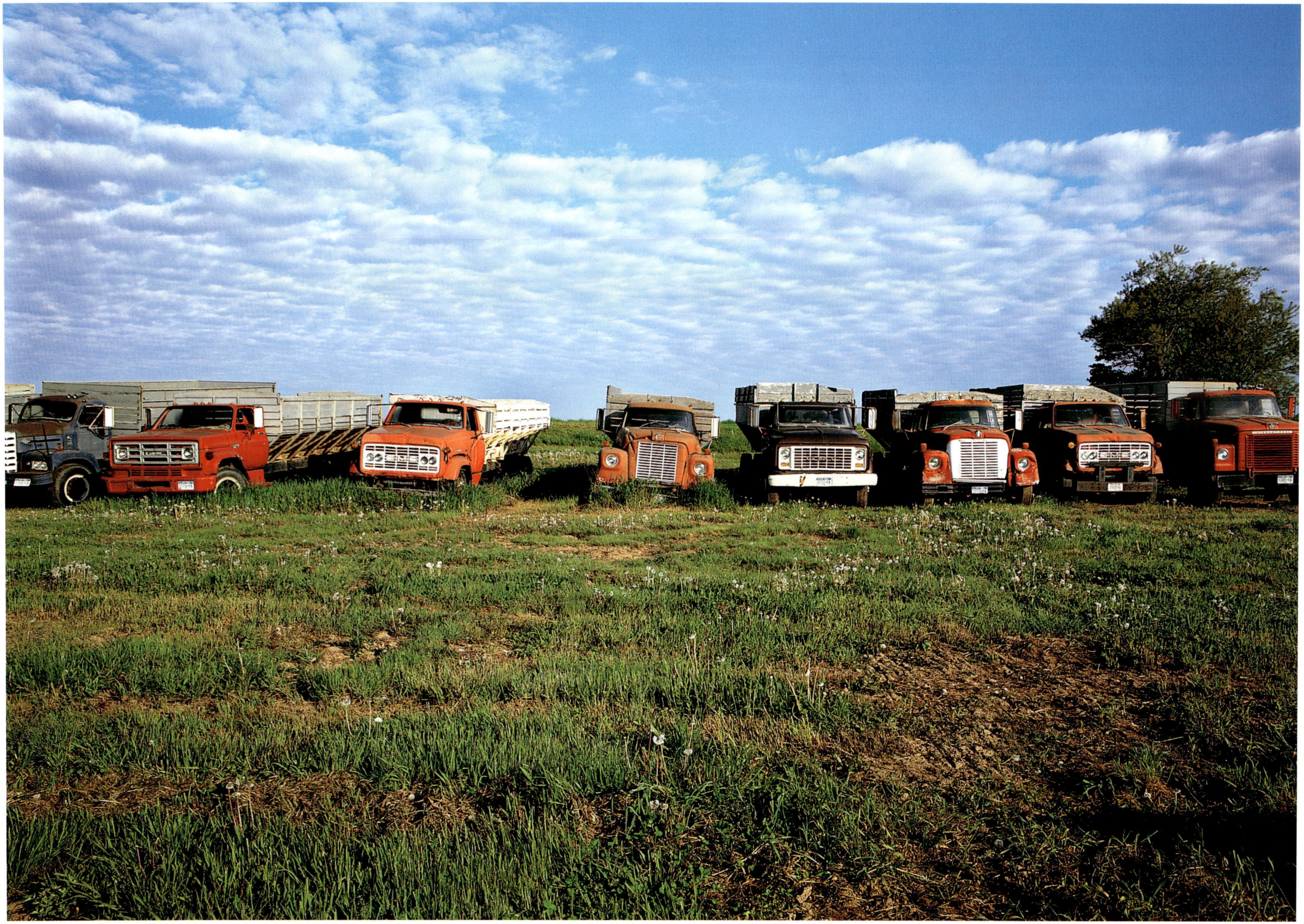

Oregon Road, Cutchogue

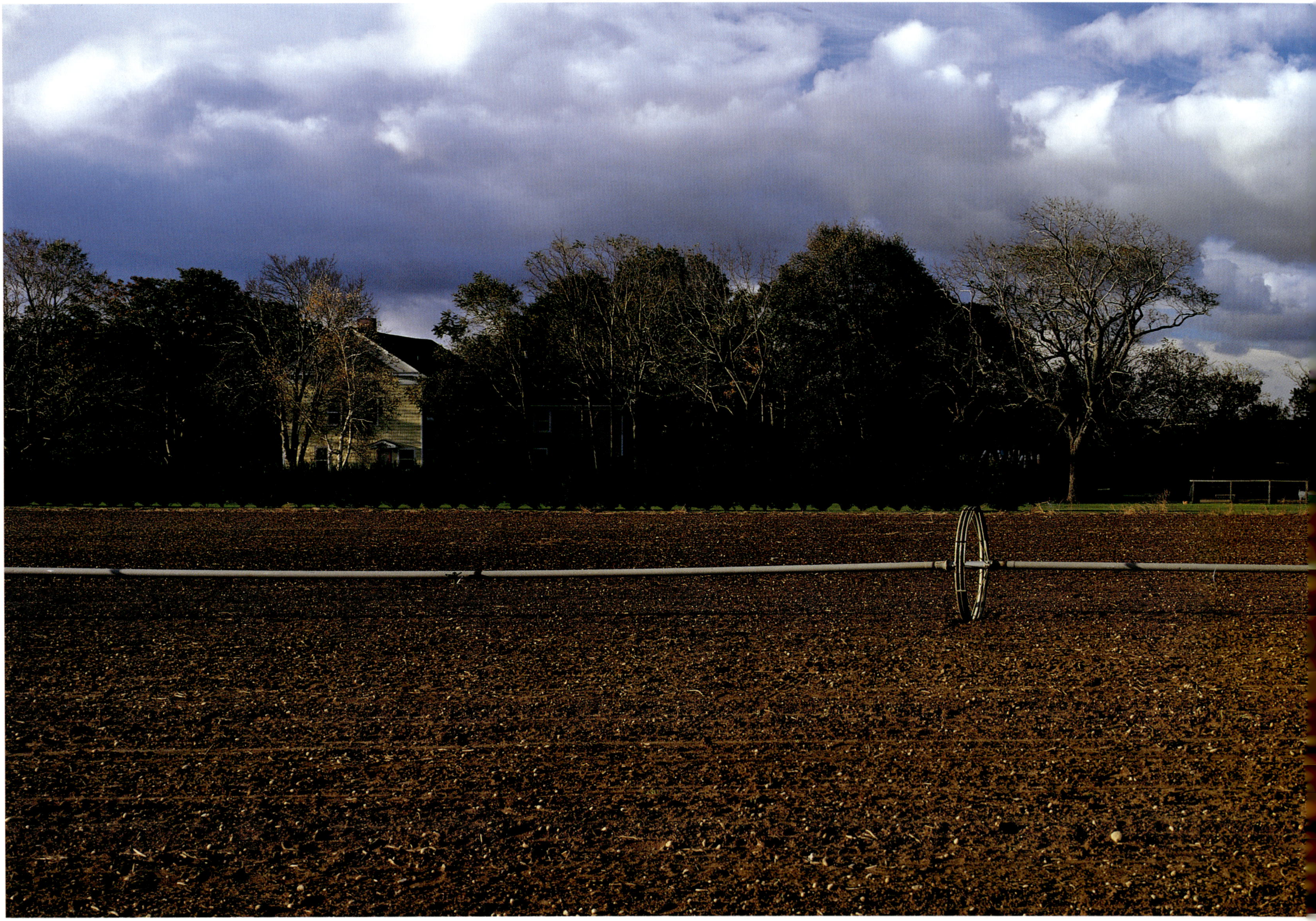

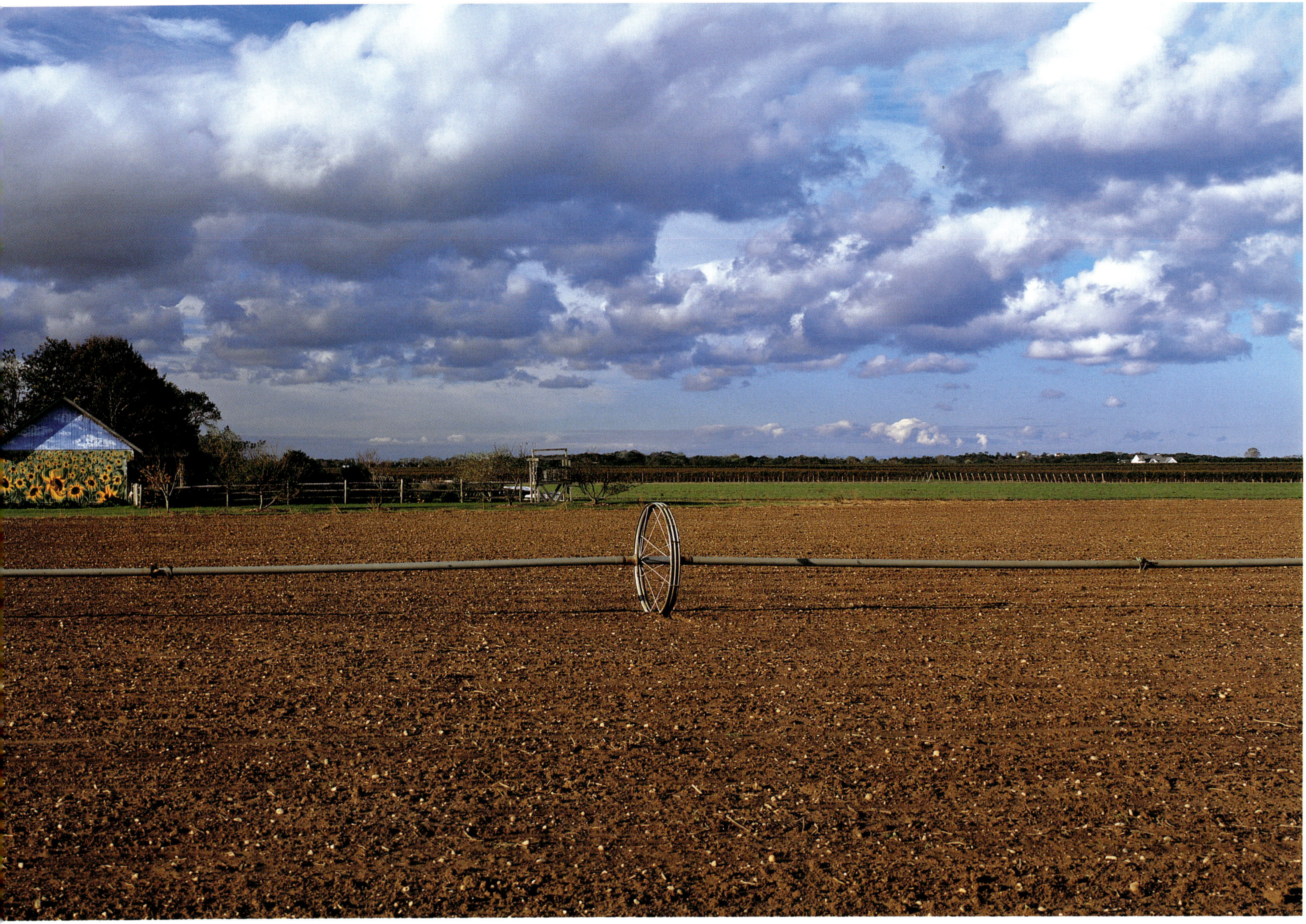

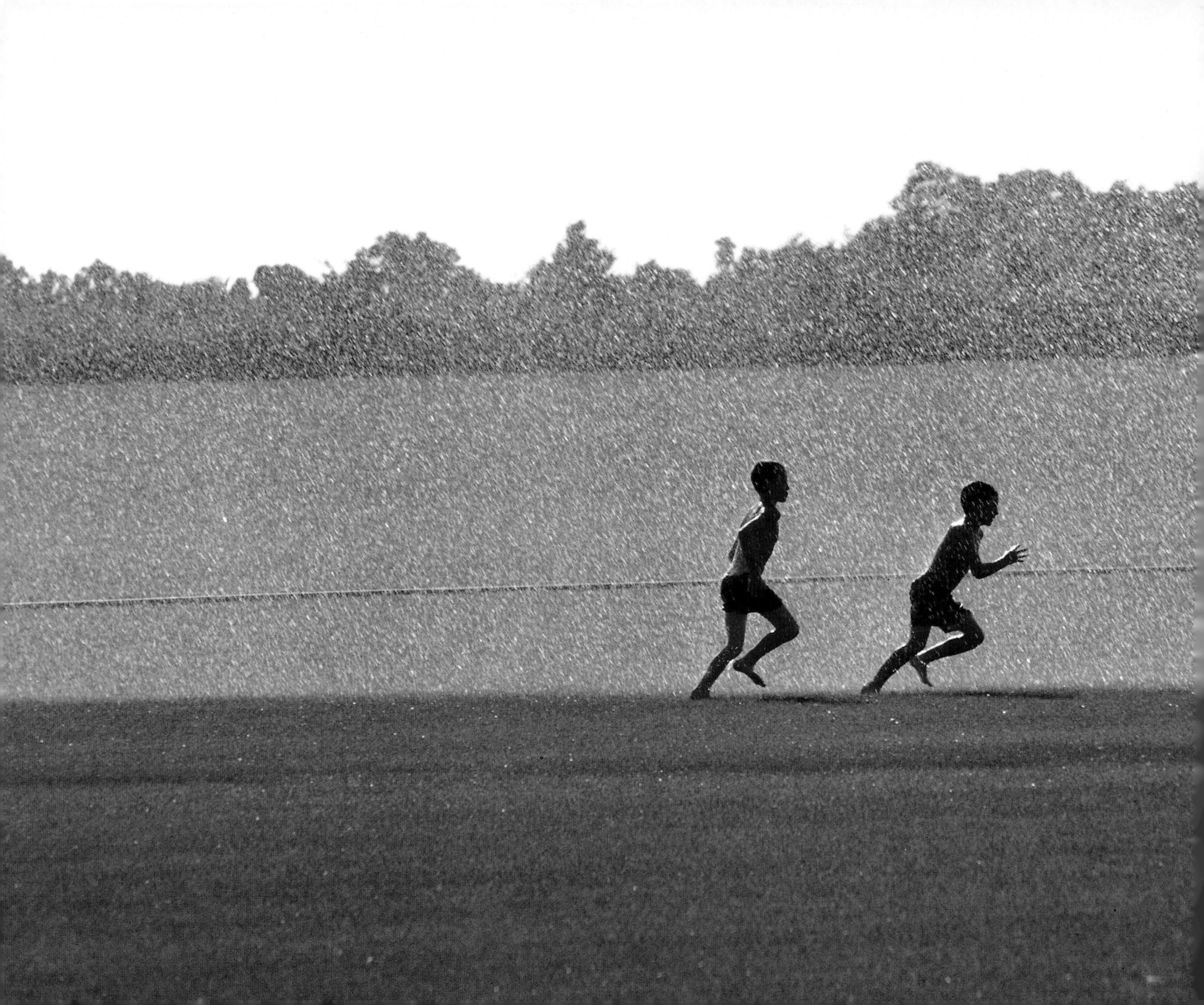

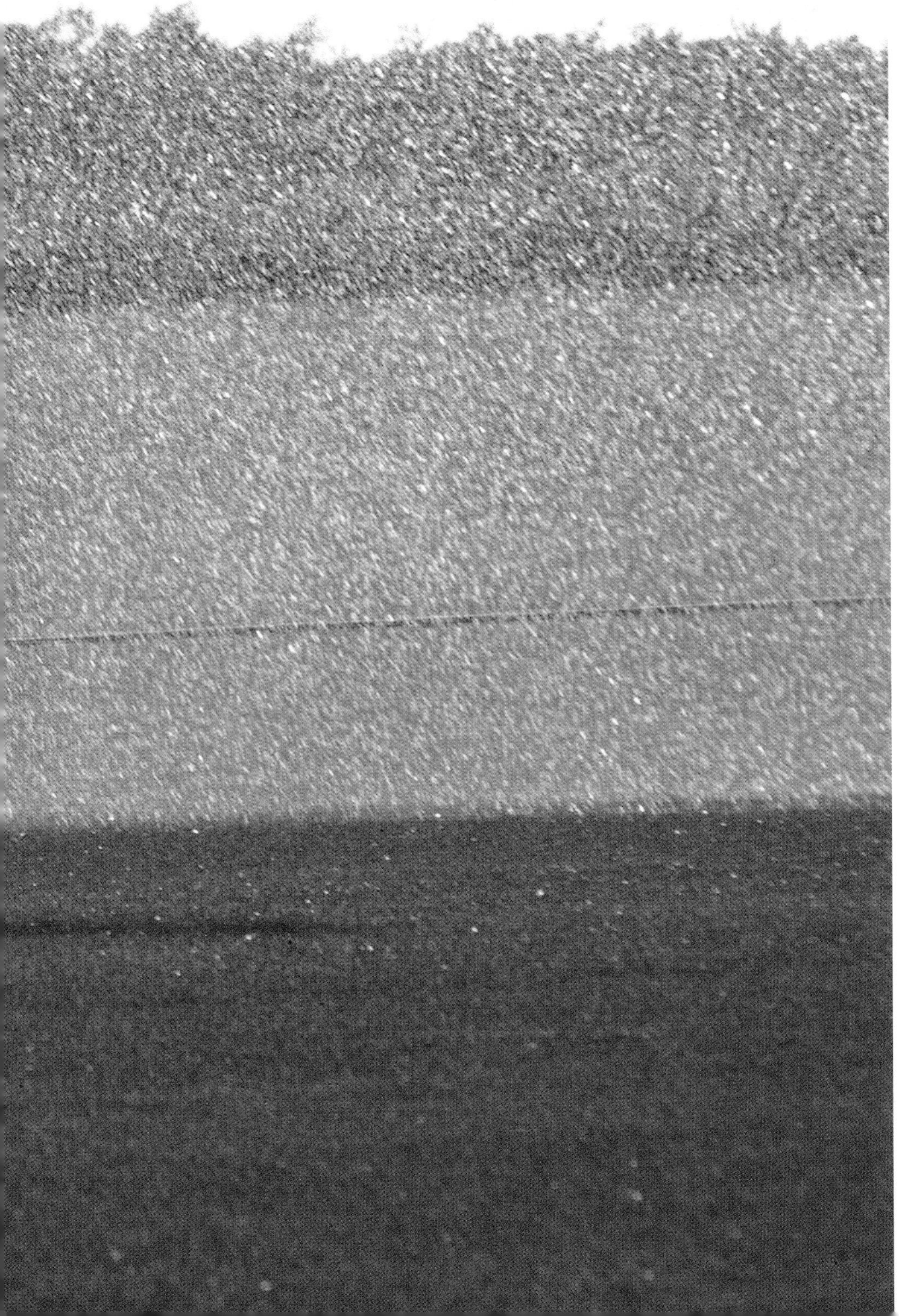

Delea Sod Farm, Cutchogue

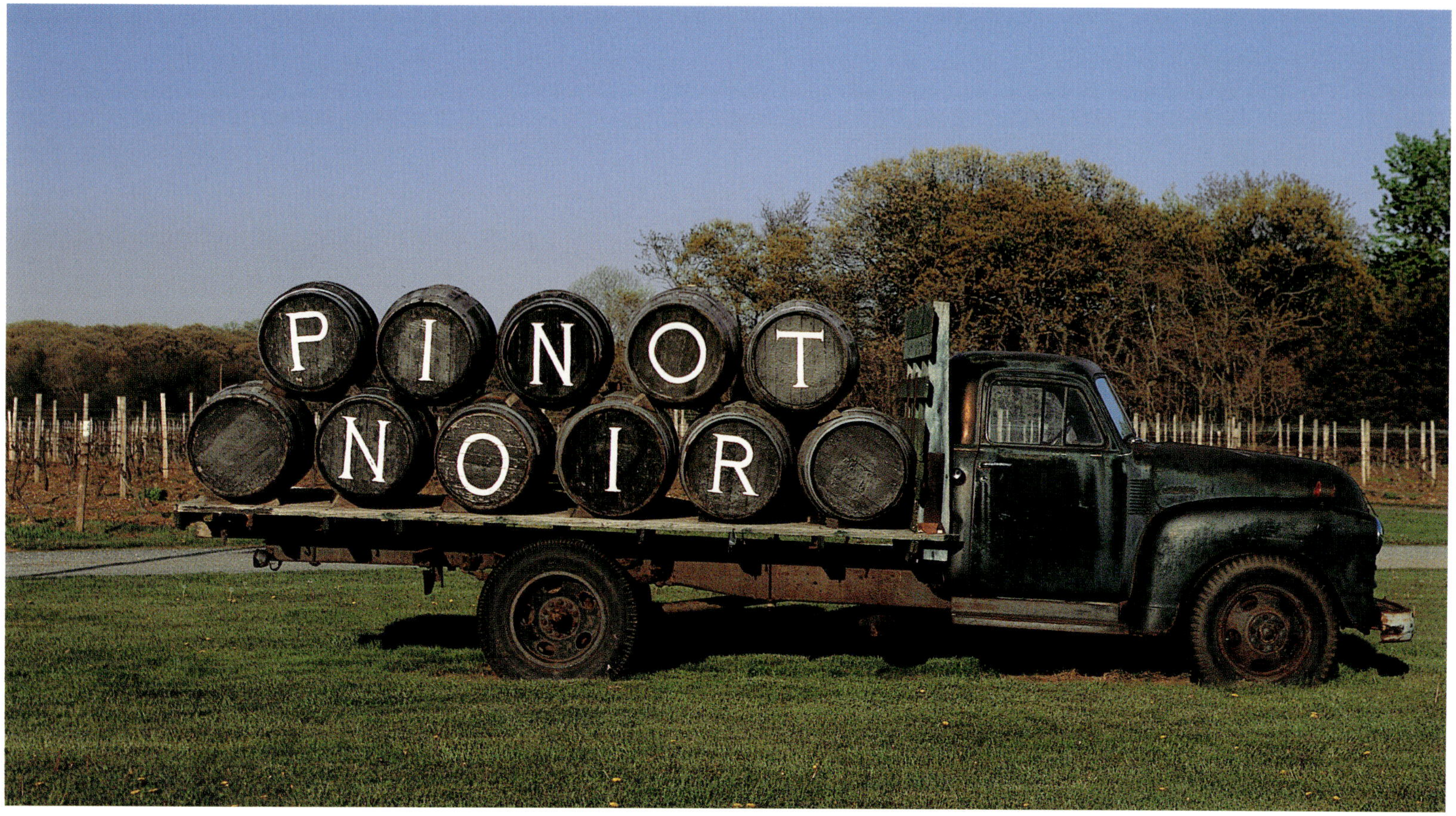
PINOT
NOIR

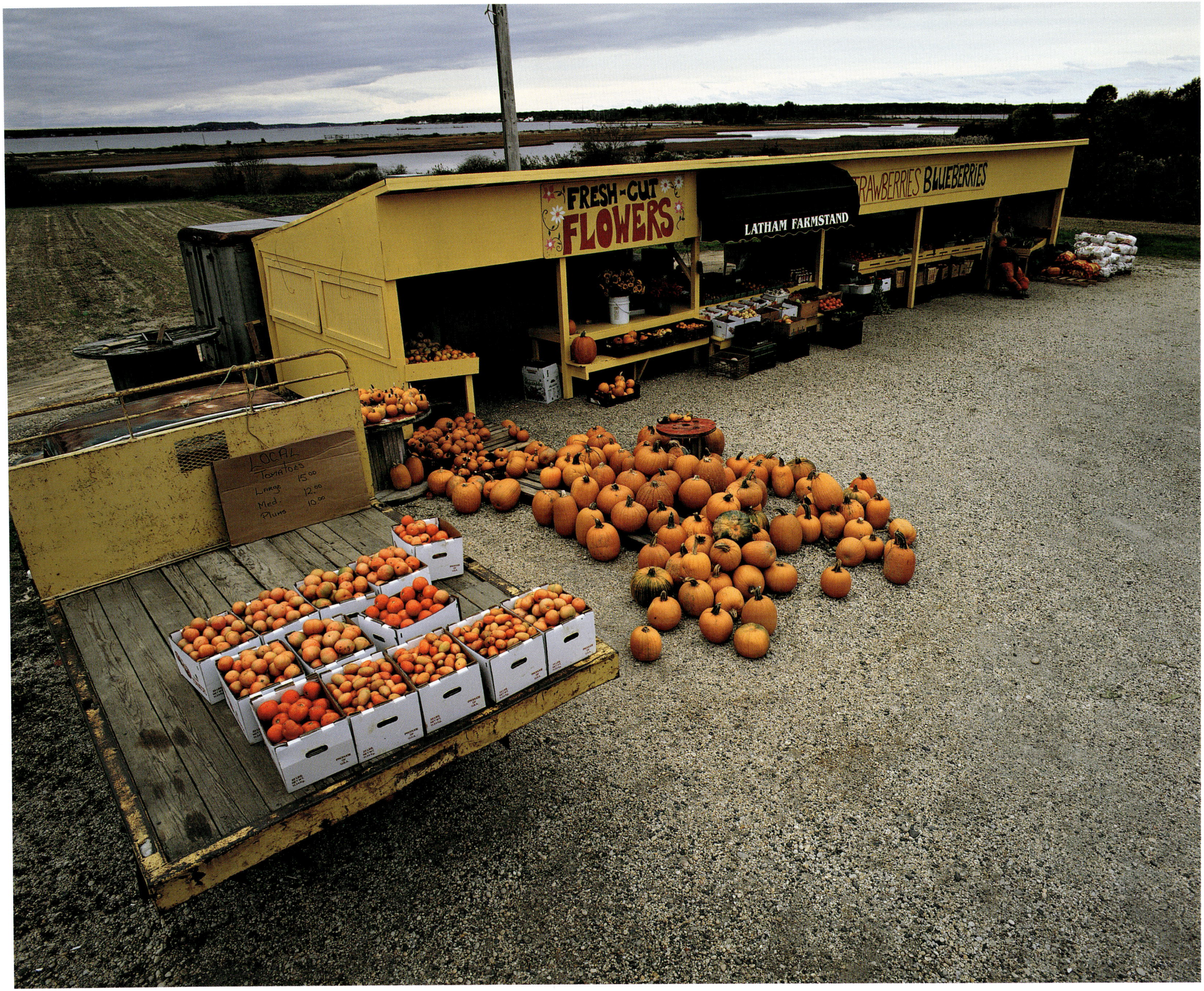
FRESH-CUT
FLOWERS
BLUEBERRIES
LATHAM FARMSTAND
LOCAL
Tomatoes
15.00
Large
12.00
Med.
10.00
Plums

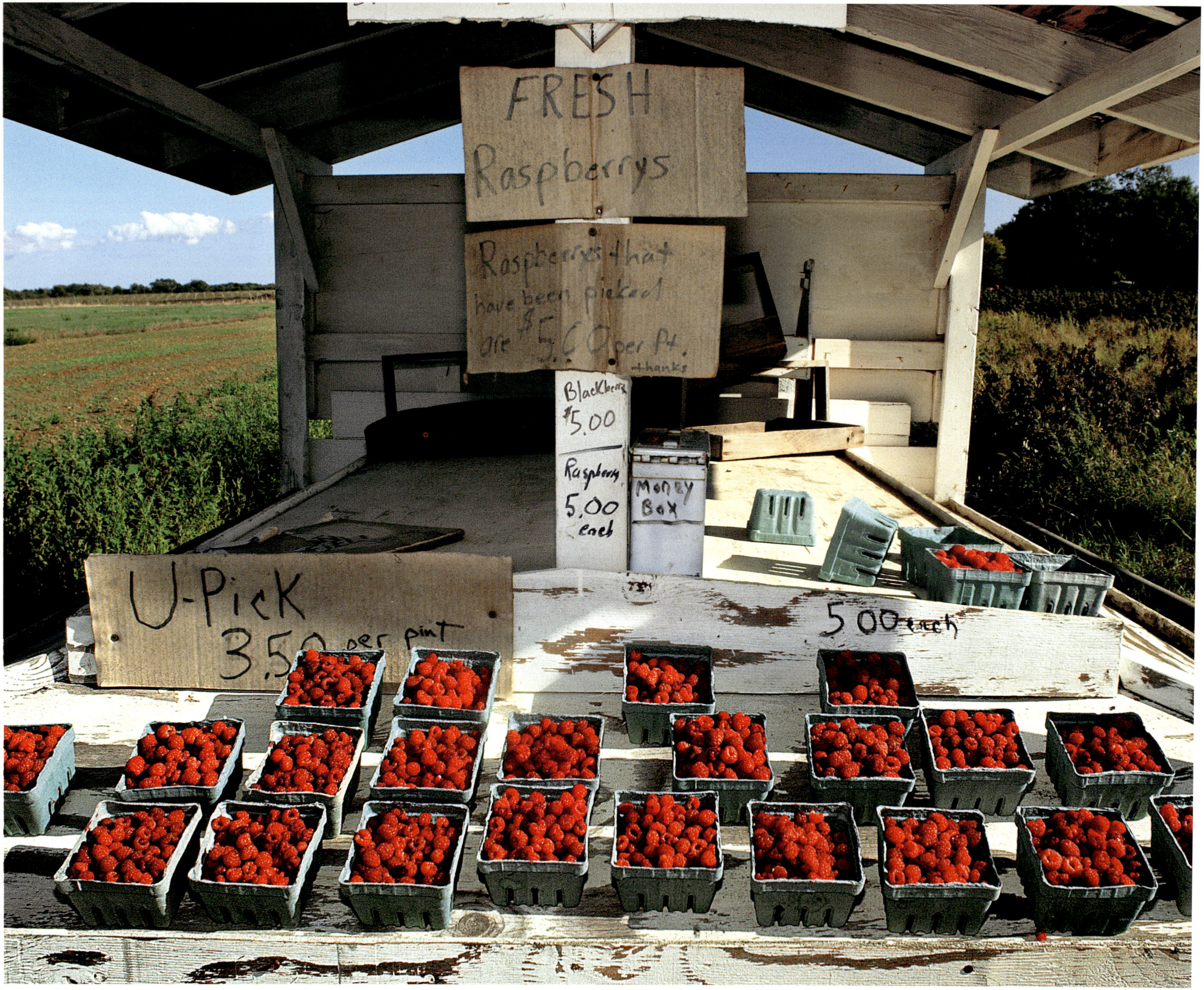
FRESH
Raspberrys
Raspberrys that
have been picked
are $5.00 per Pt.
thanks
Blackberry
$5.00
Raspberry
5.00
each
Money
Box
U-Pick
3.50 per pint
500 each

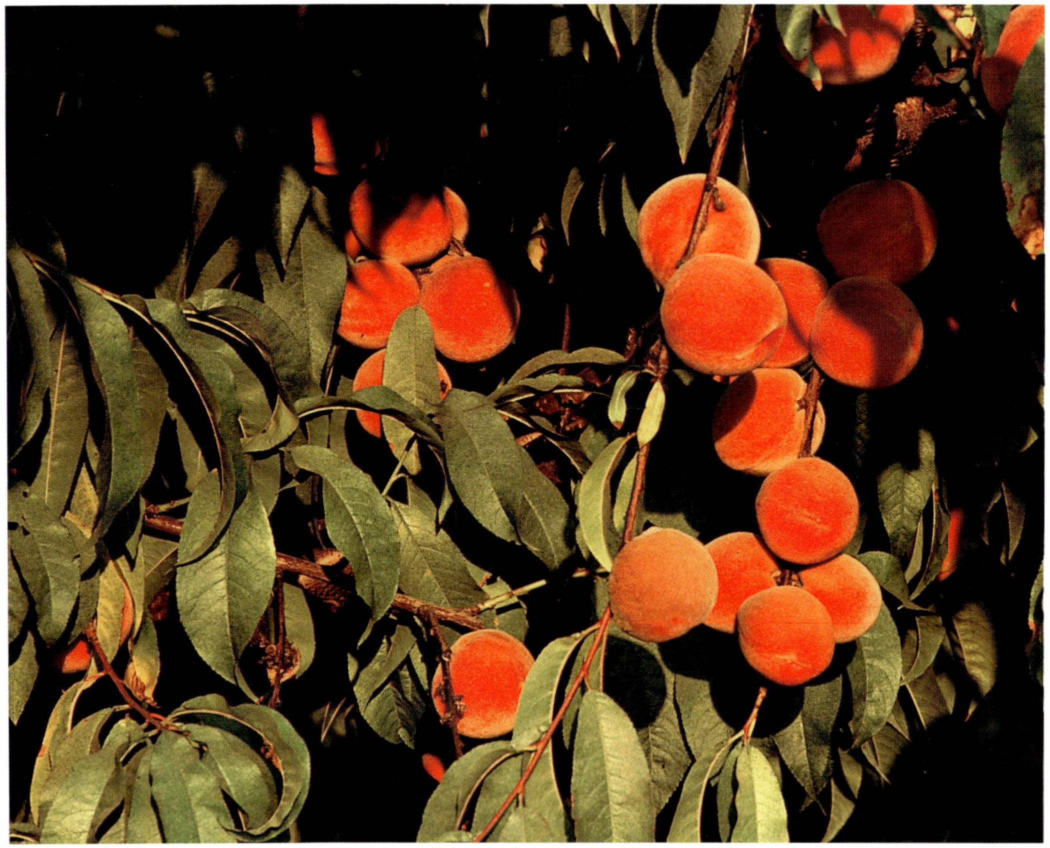

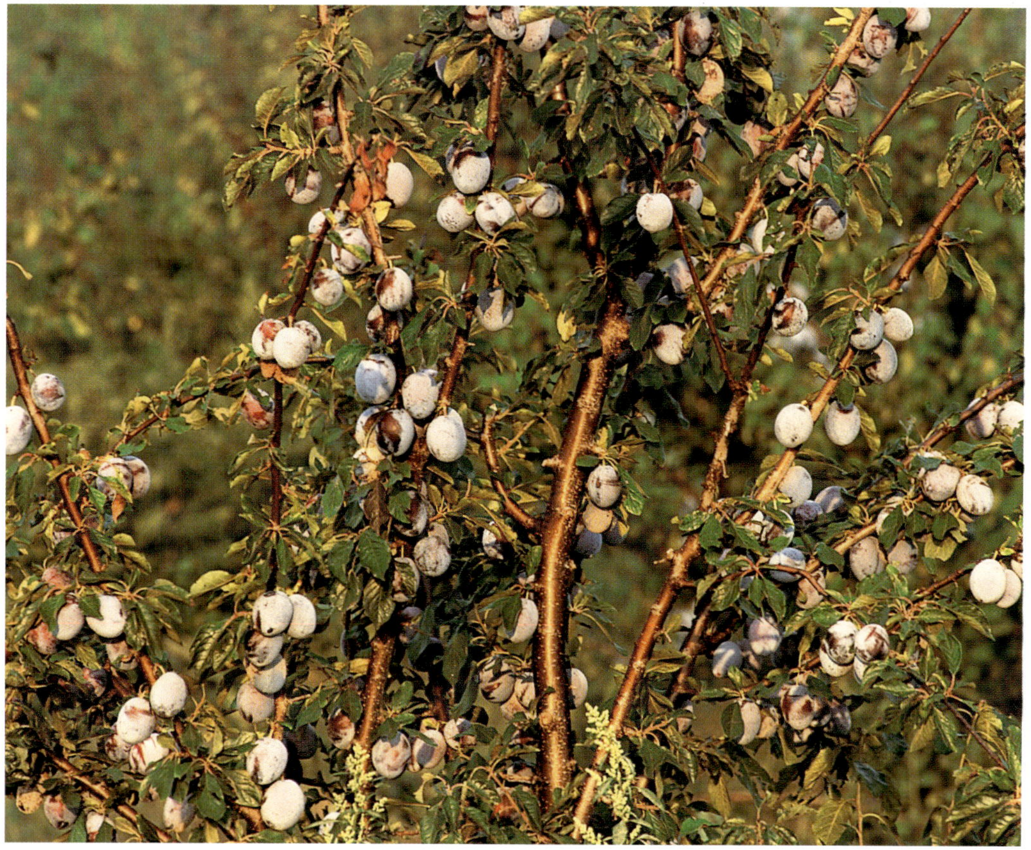

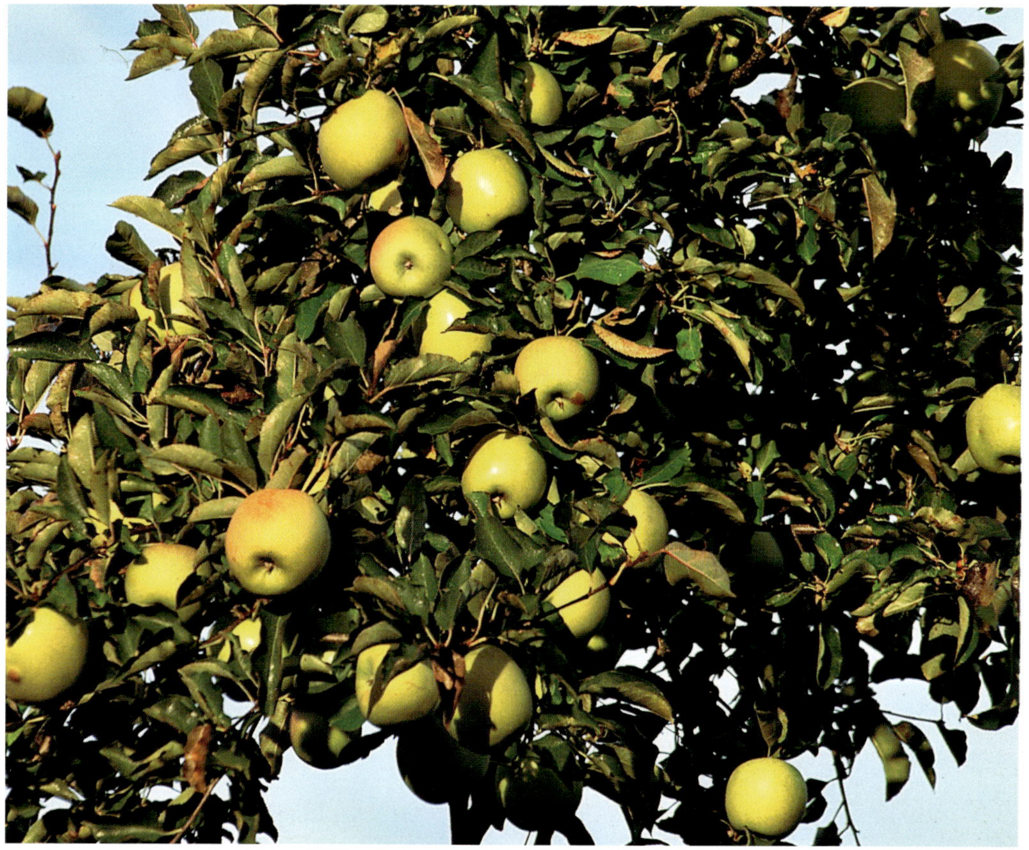

Steele Farm, Cutchogue    Wickham's Fruit Farm, Cutchogue

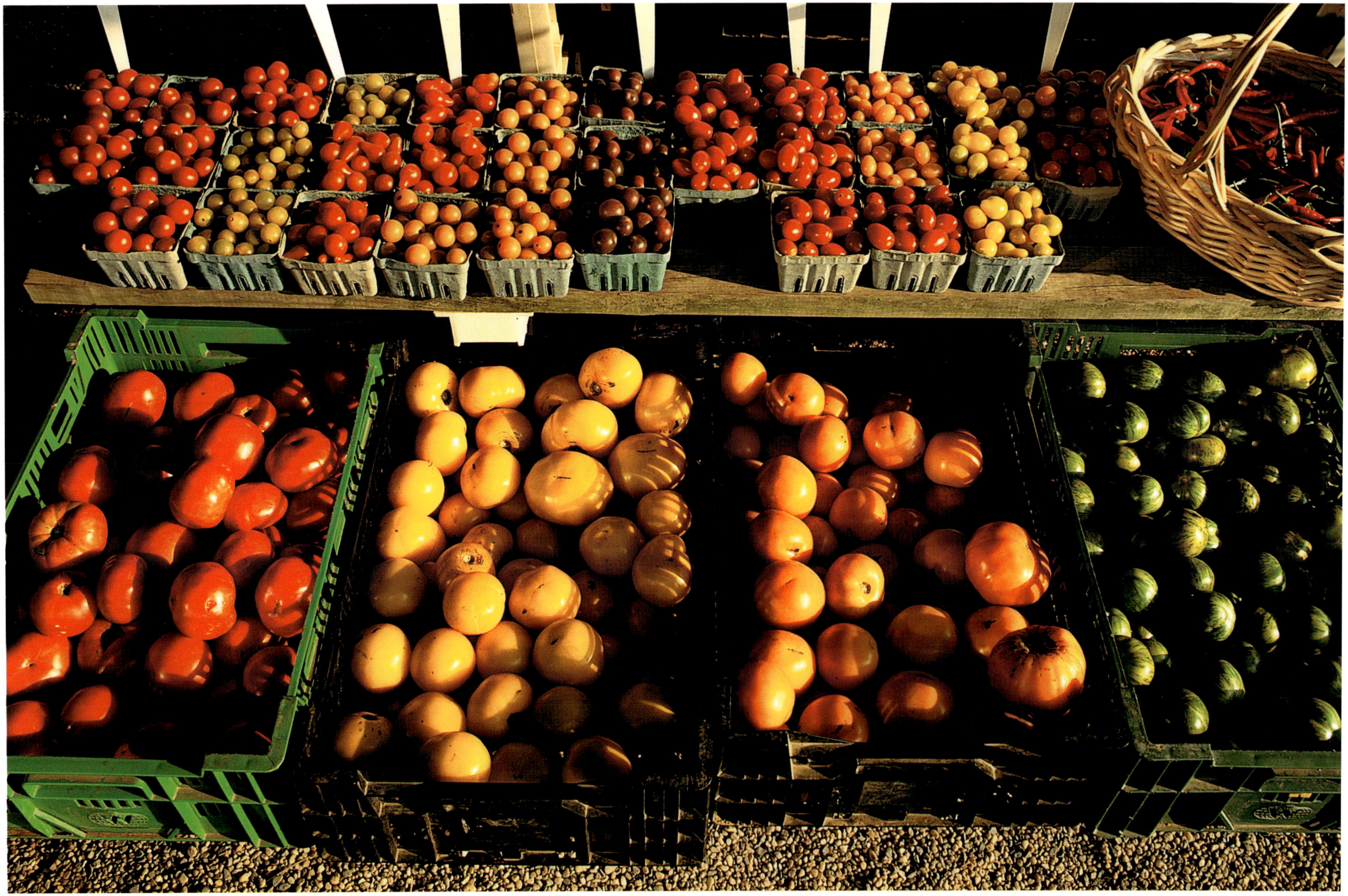

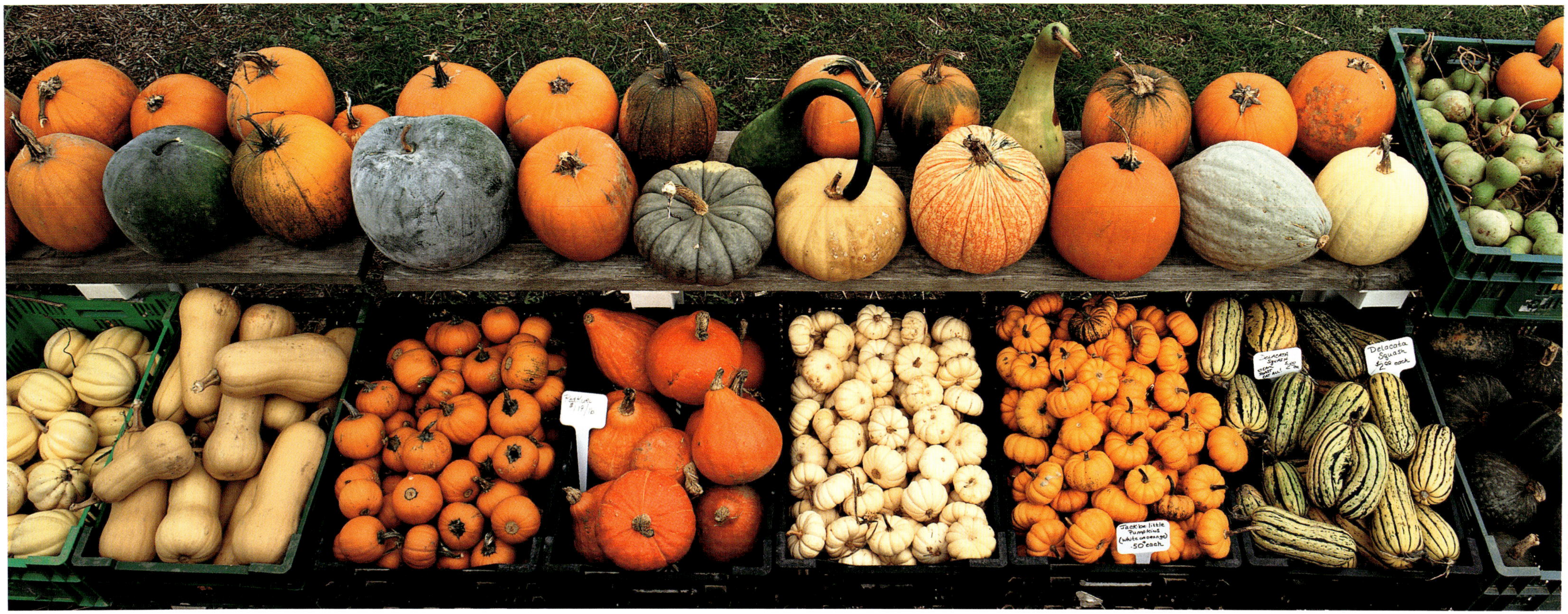
Jack-be-little Pumpkins (white or orange) .50¢ each
Delacata Squash
Delacata Squash $2.00 each

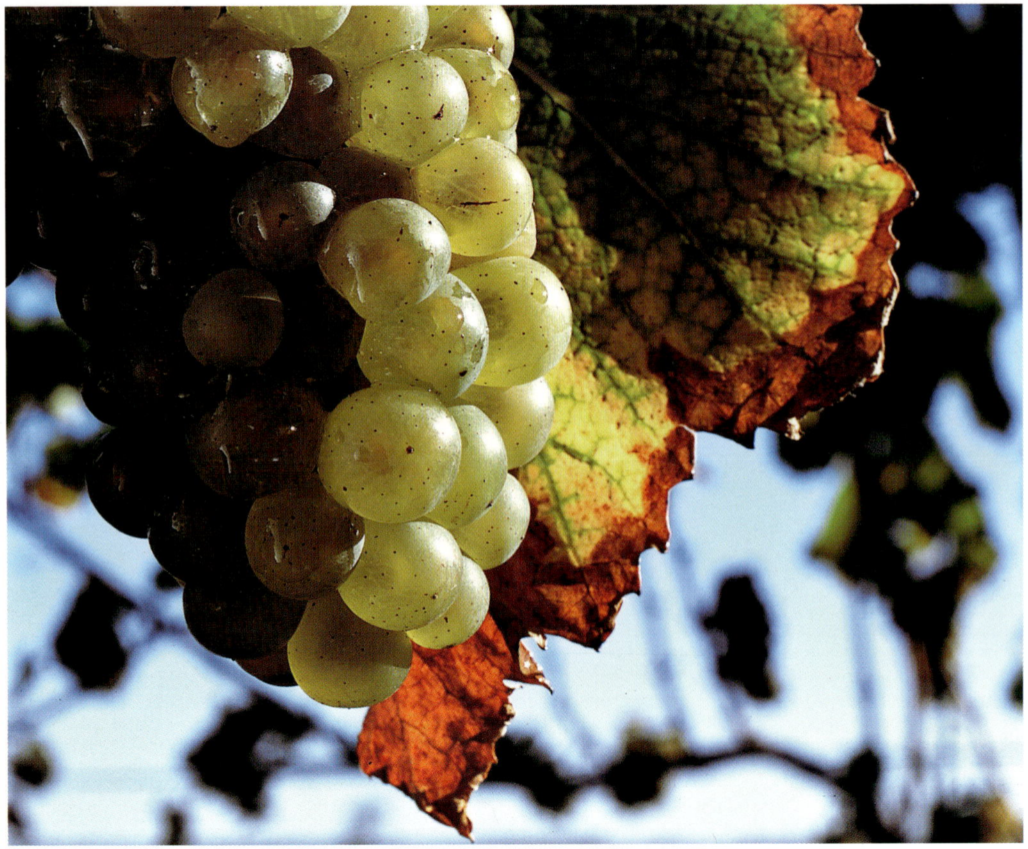

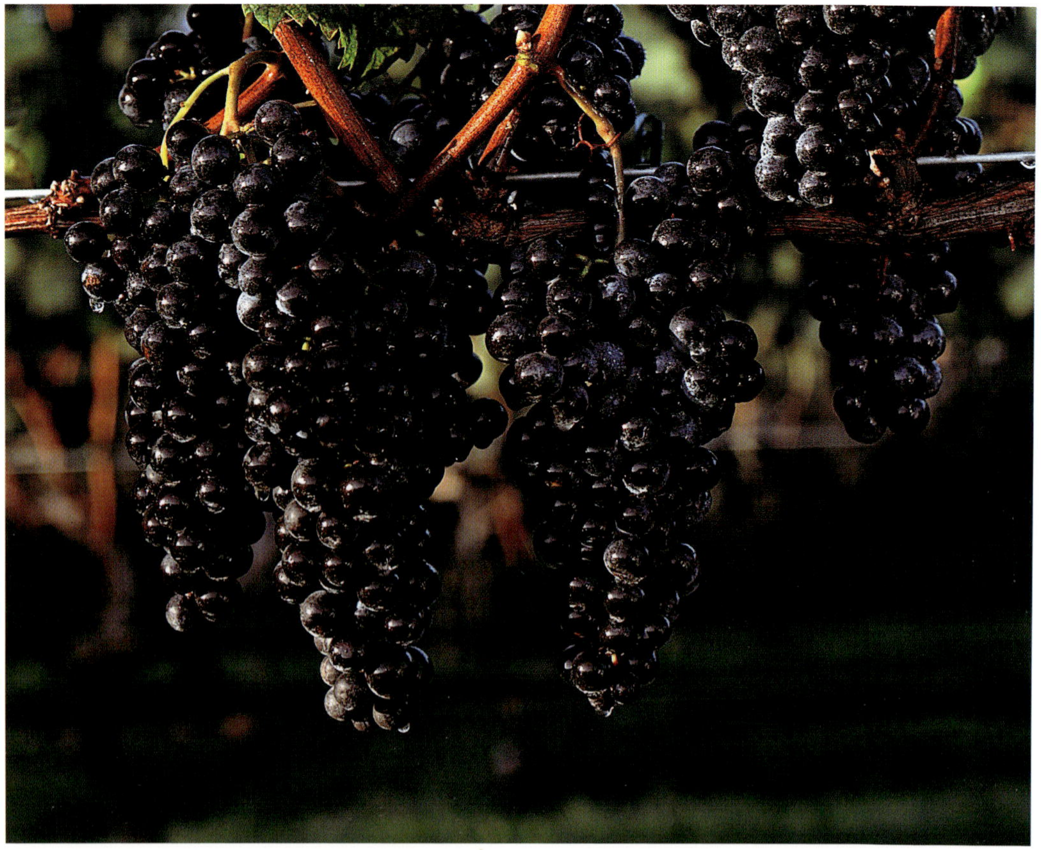

Lieb Family Cellars, Mattituck    Duck Walk Vineyards, Cutchogue    Peconic Bay Winery, Cutchogue

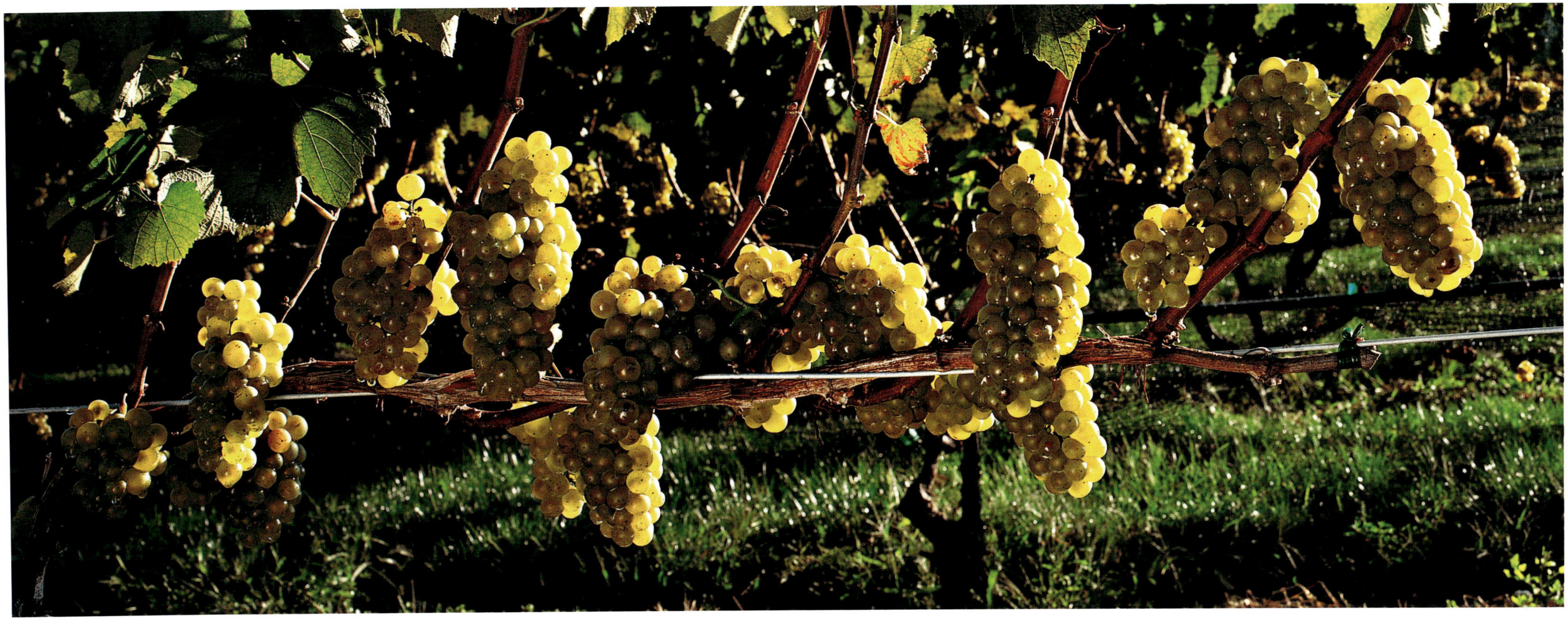

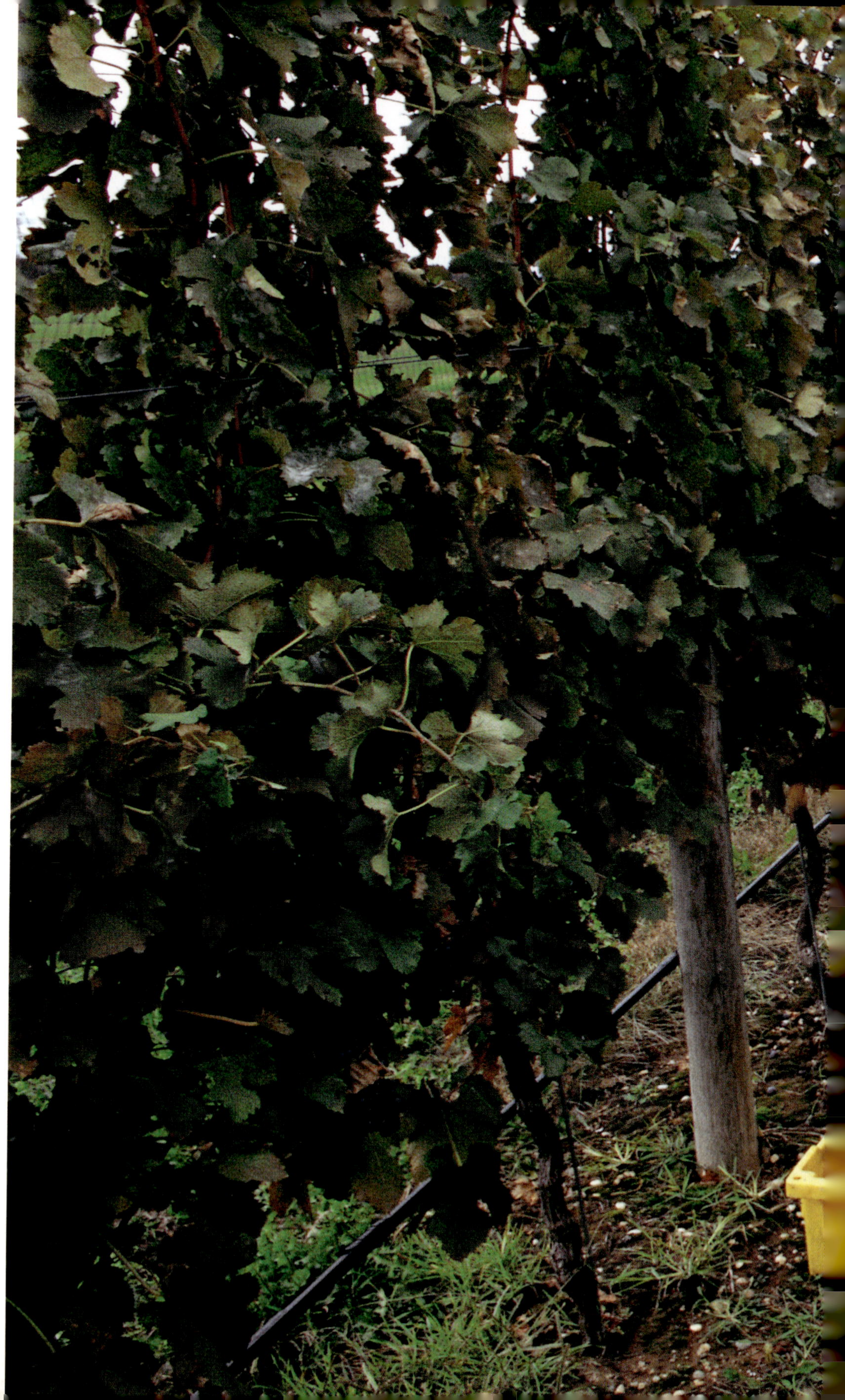

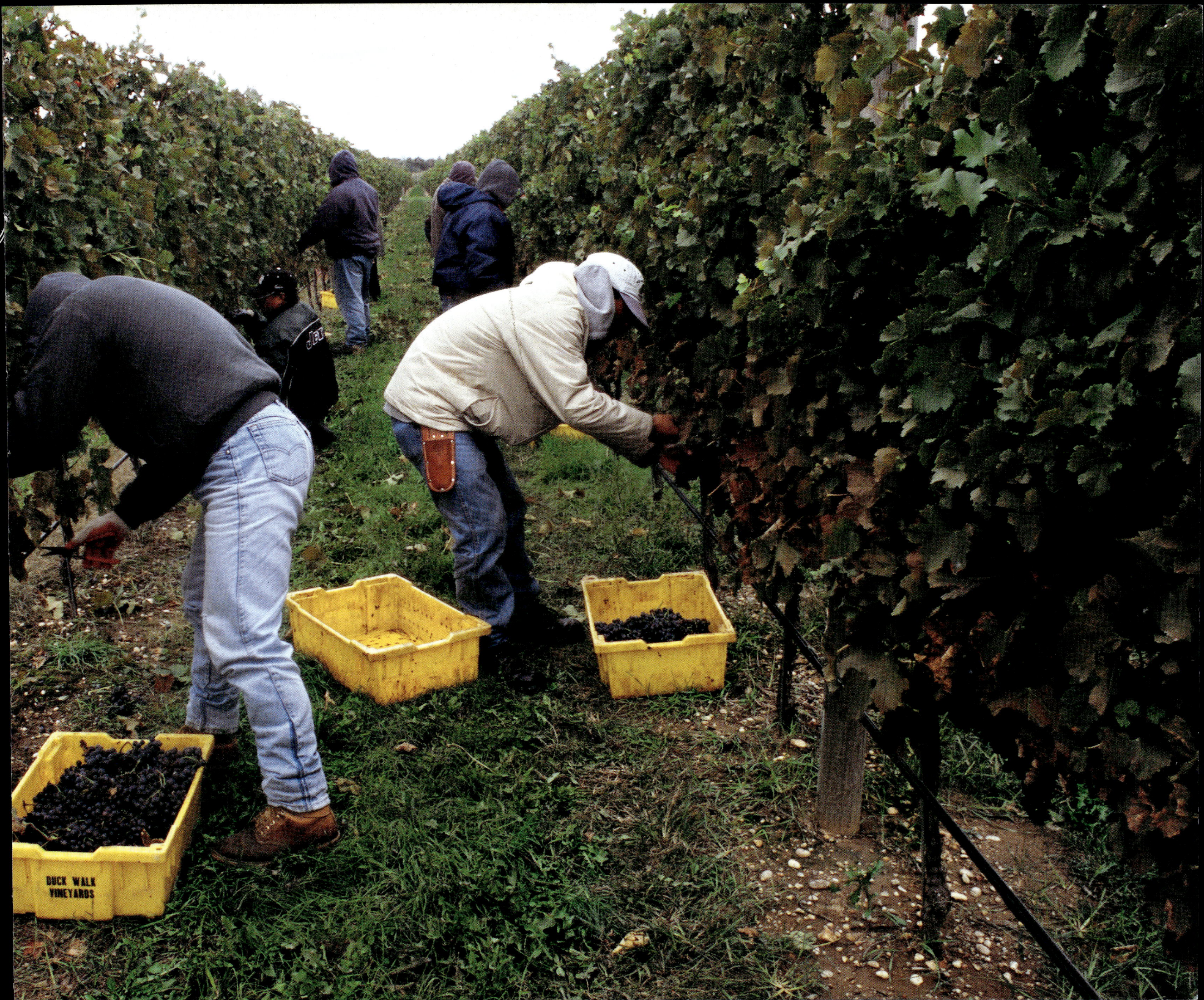
DUCK WALK
VINEYARDS

Phil Schmidt Farm, Riverhead

Van Bourgondien greenhouse, Peconic

Riverhead

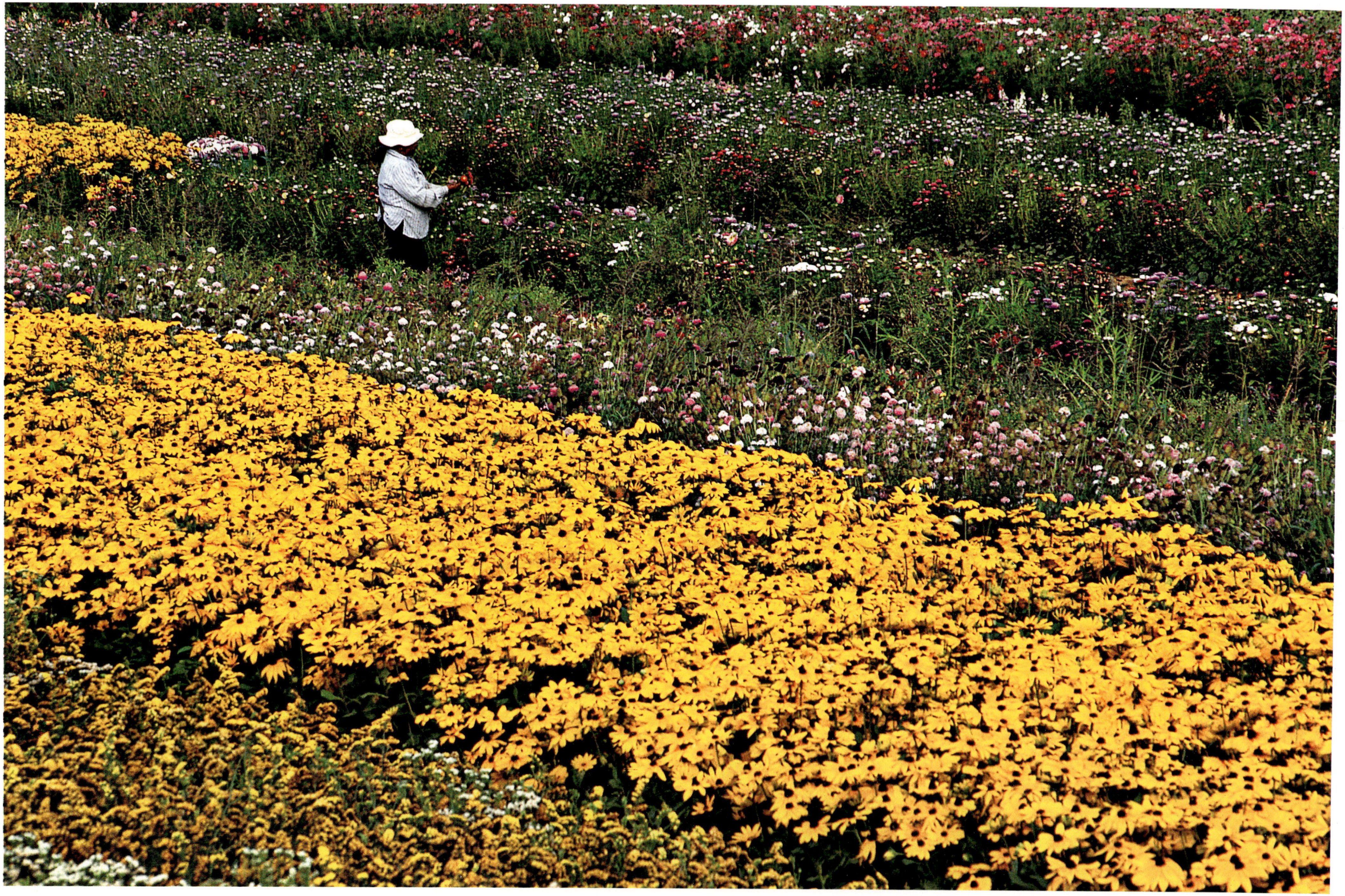

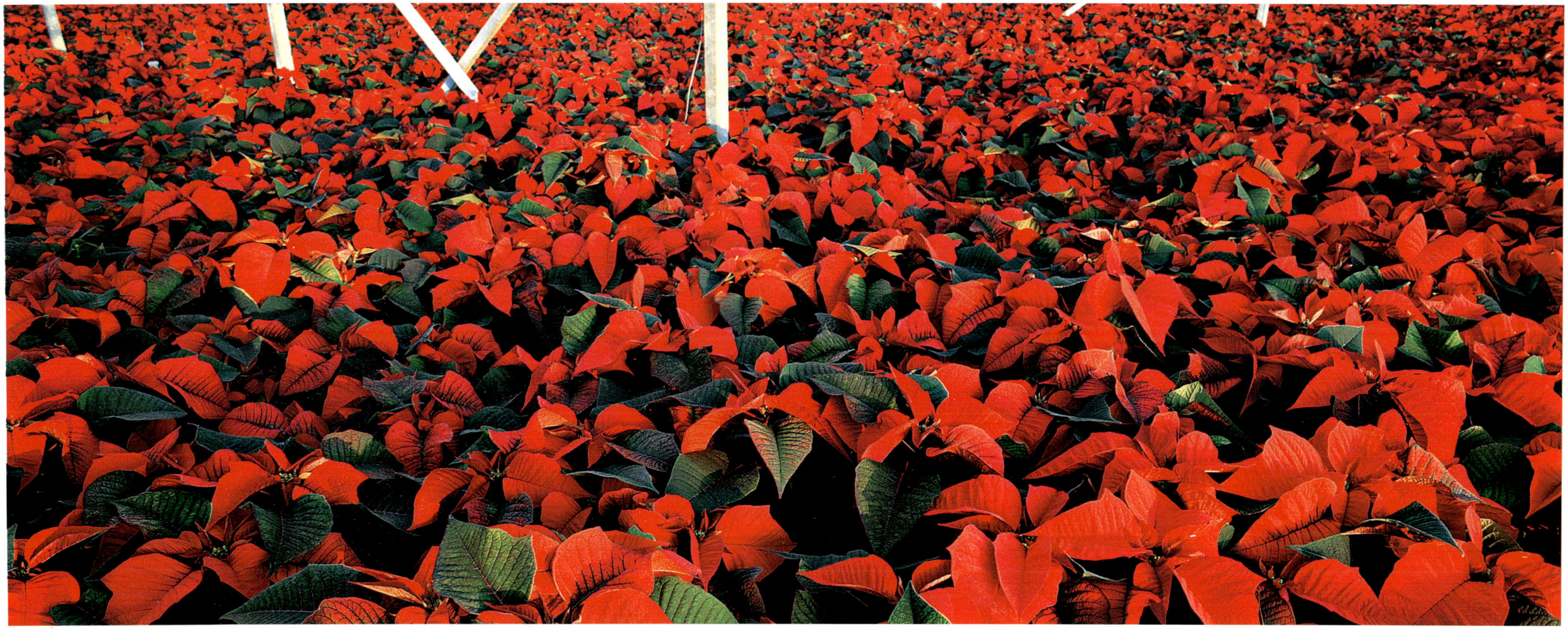

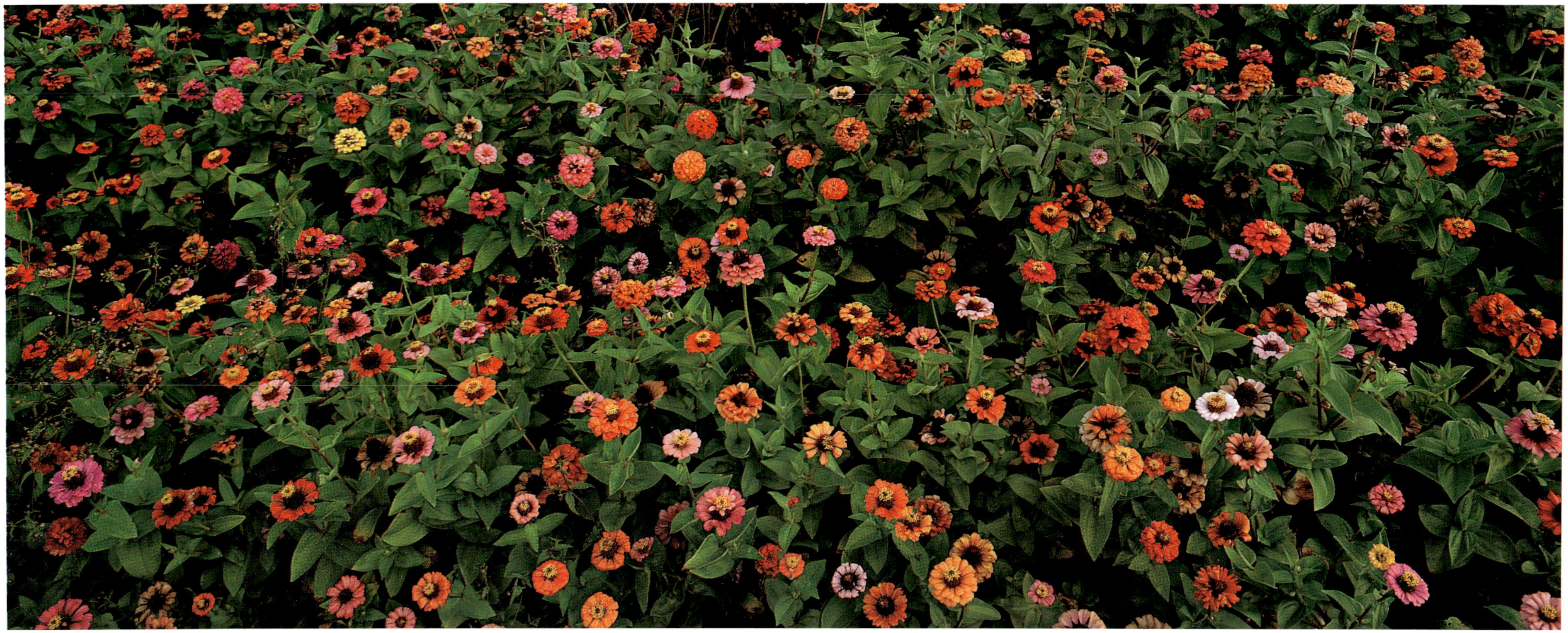

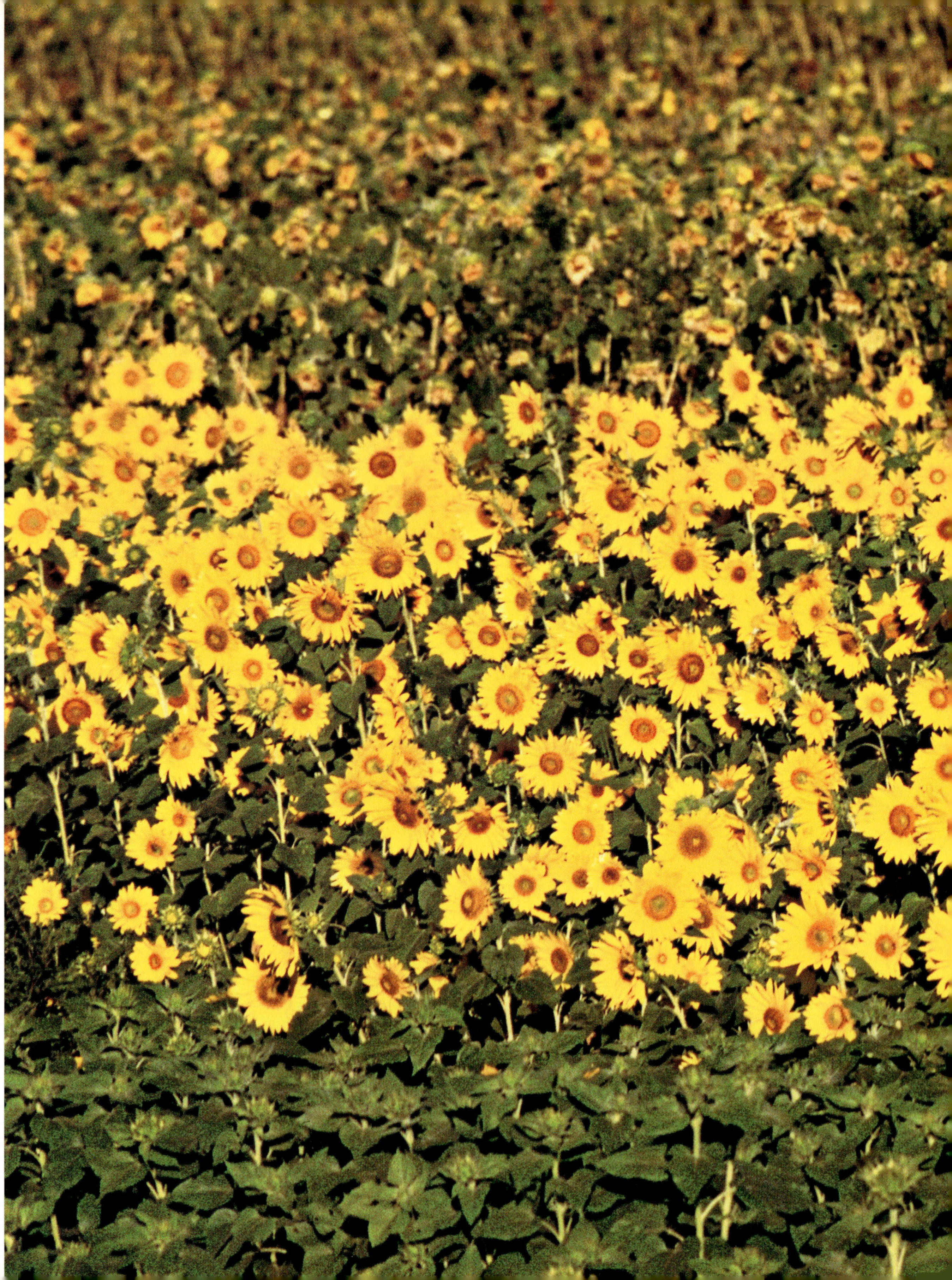

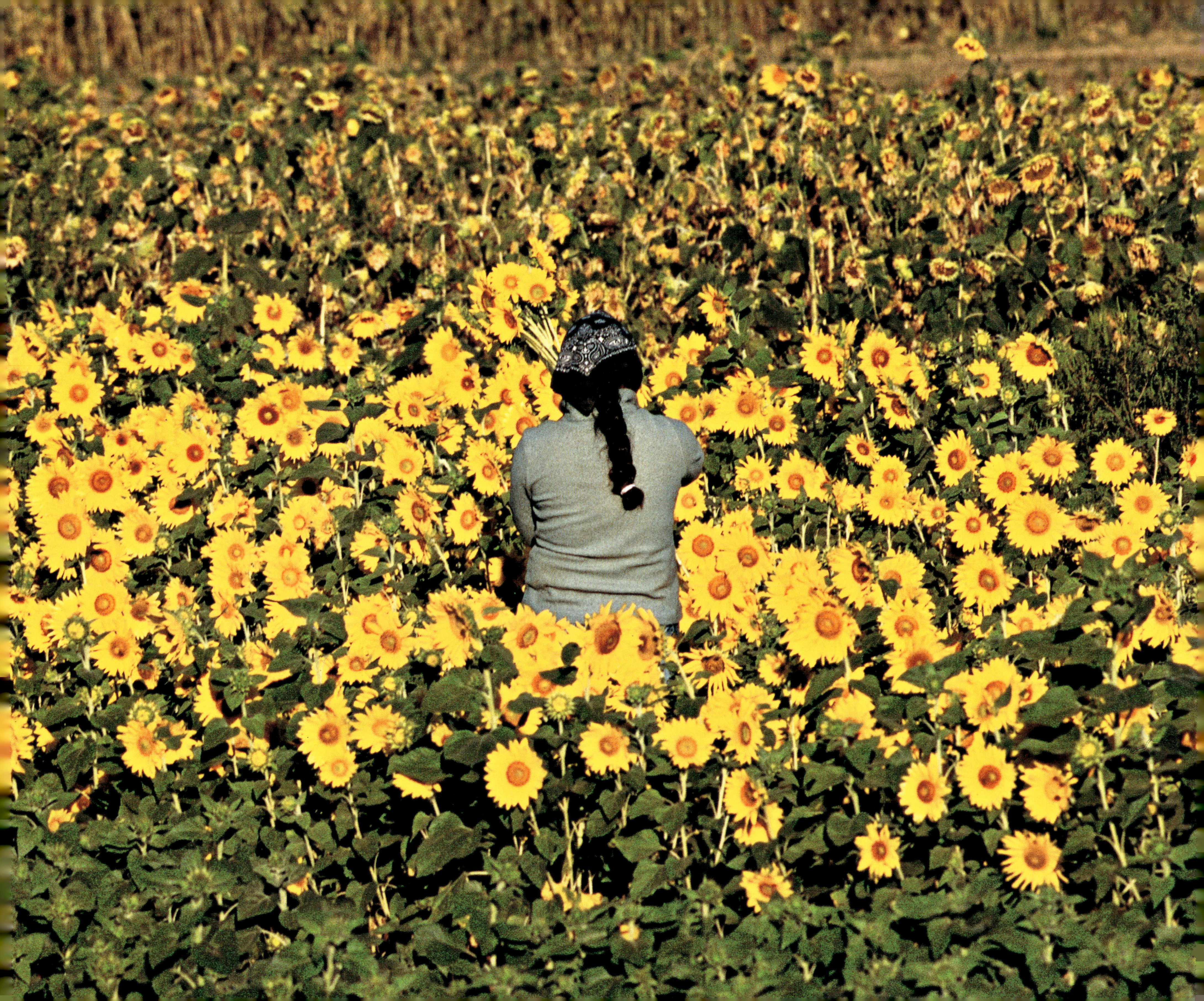

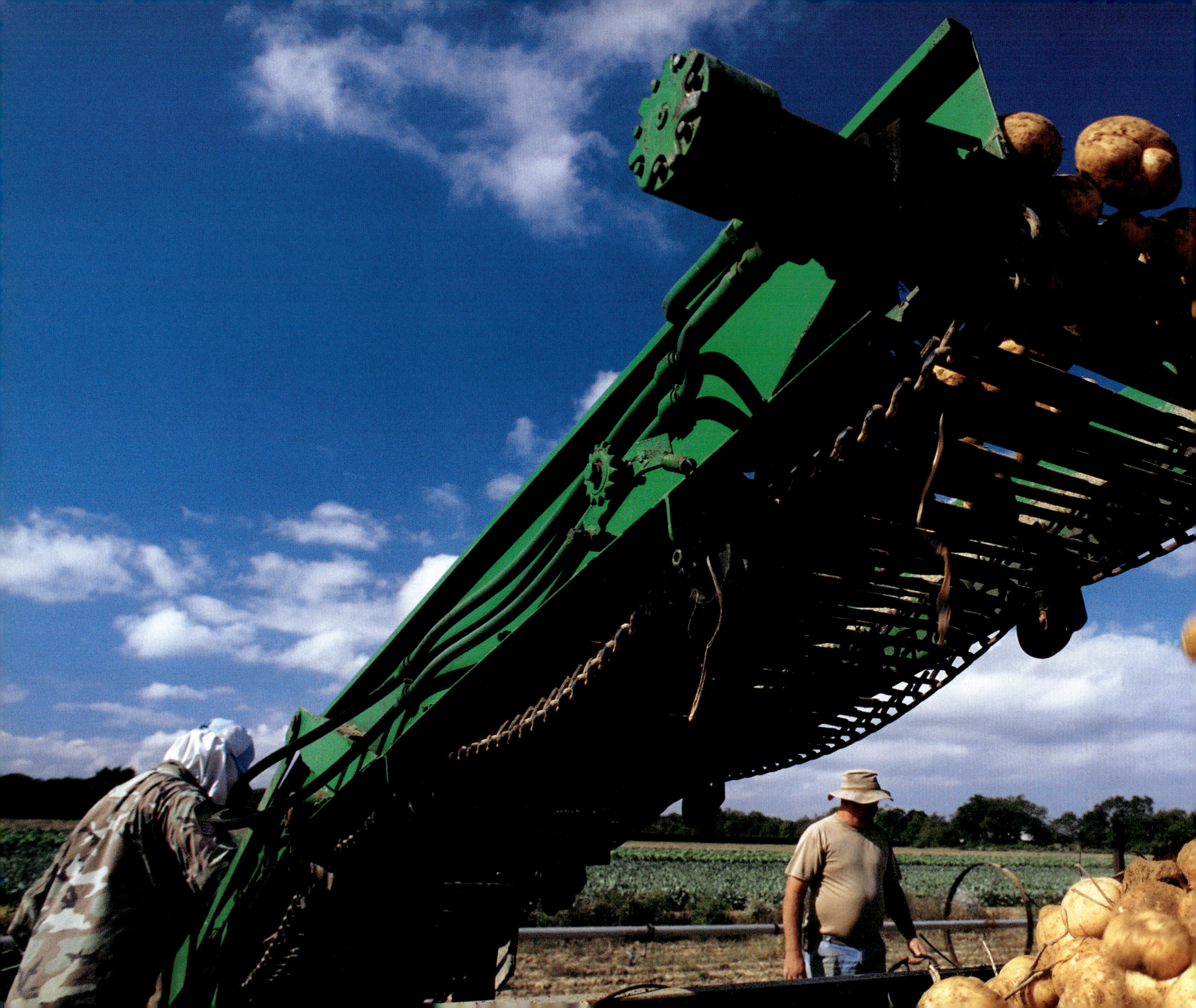

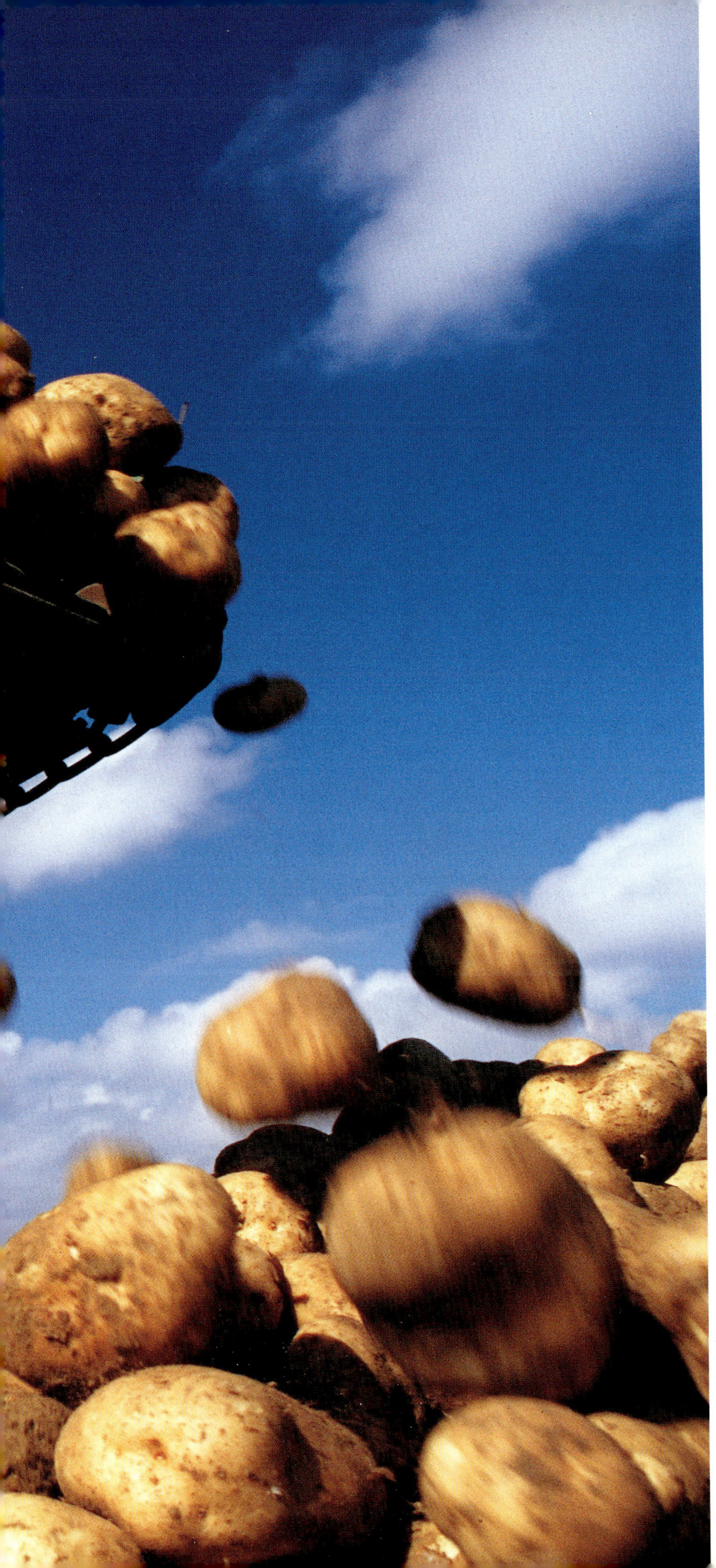

Steele Farm, Cutchogue

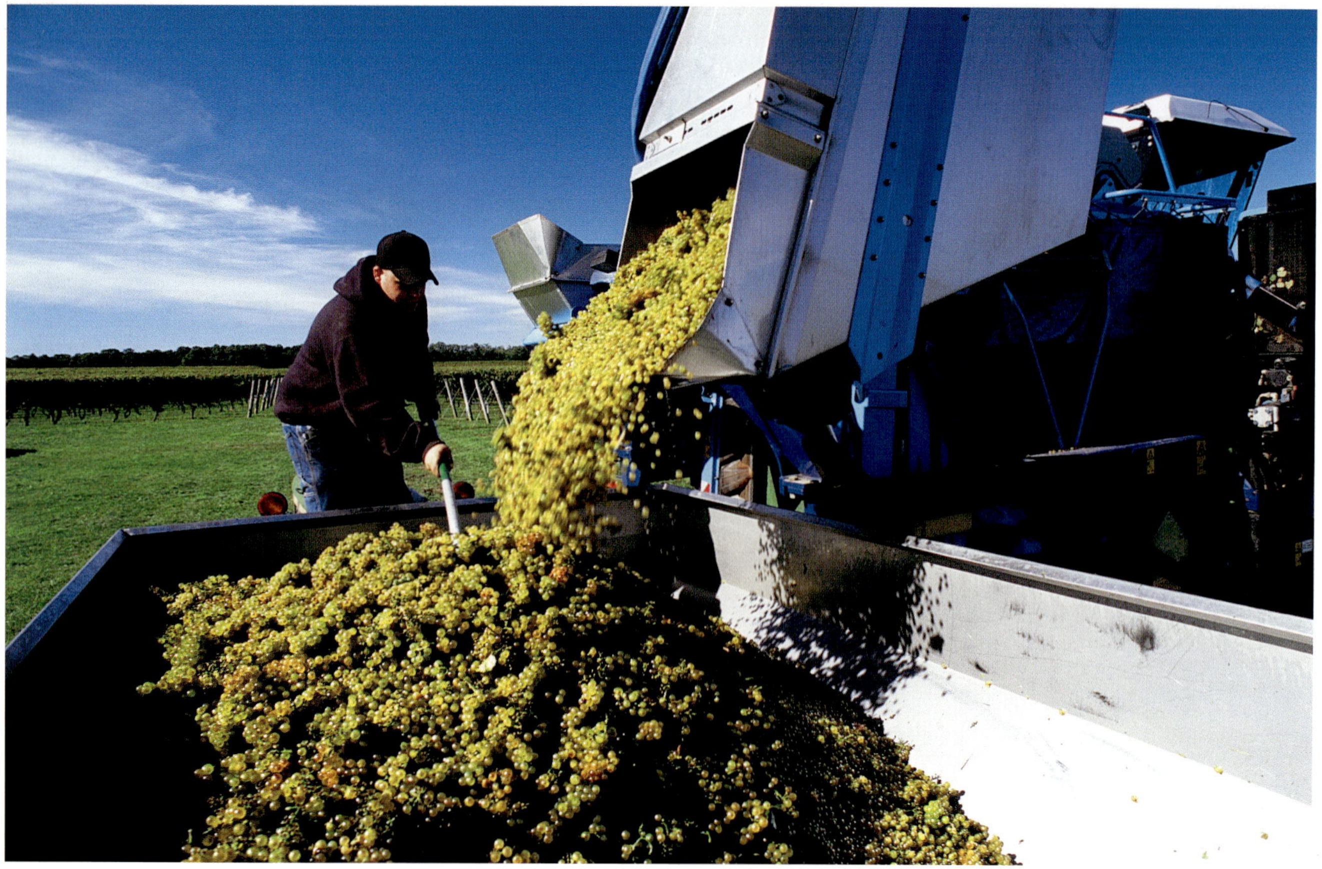

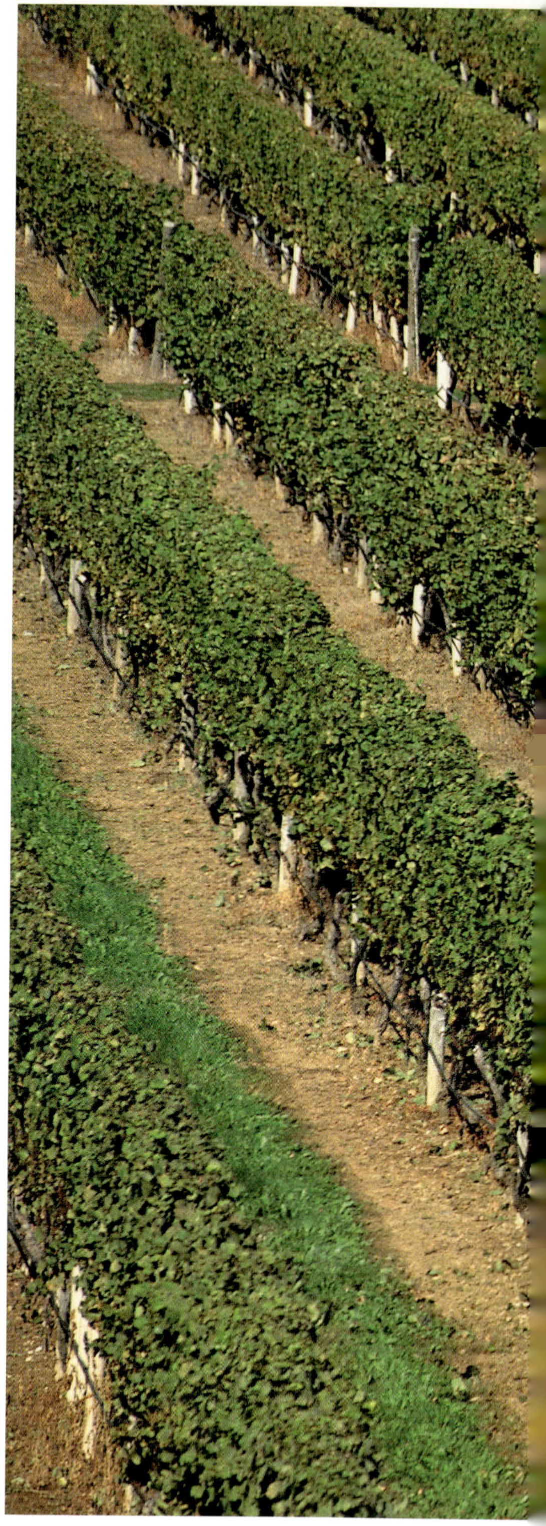

Lieb Family Cellars, Mattituck

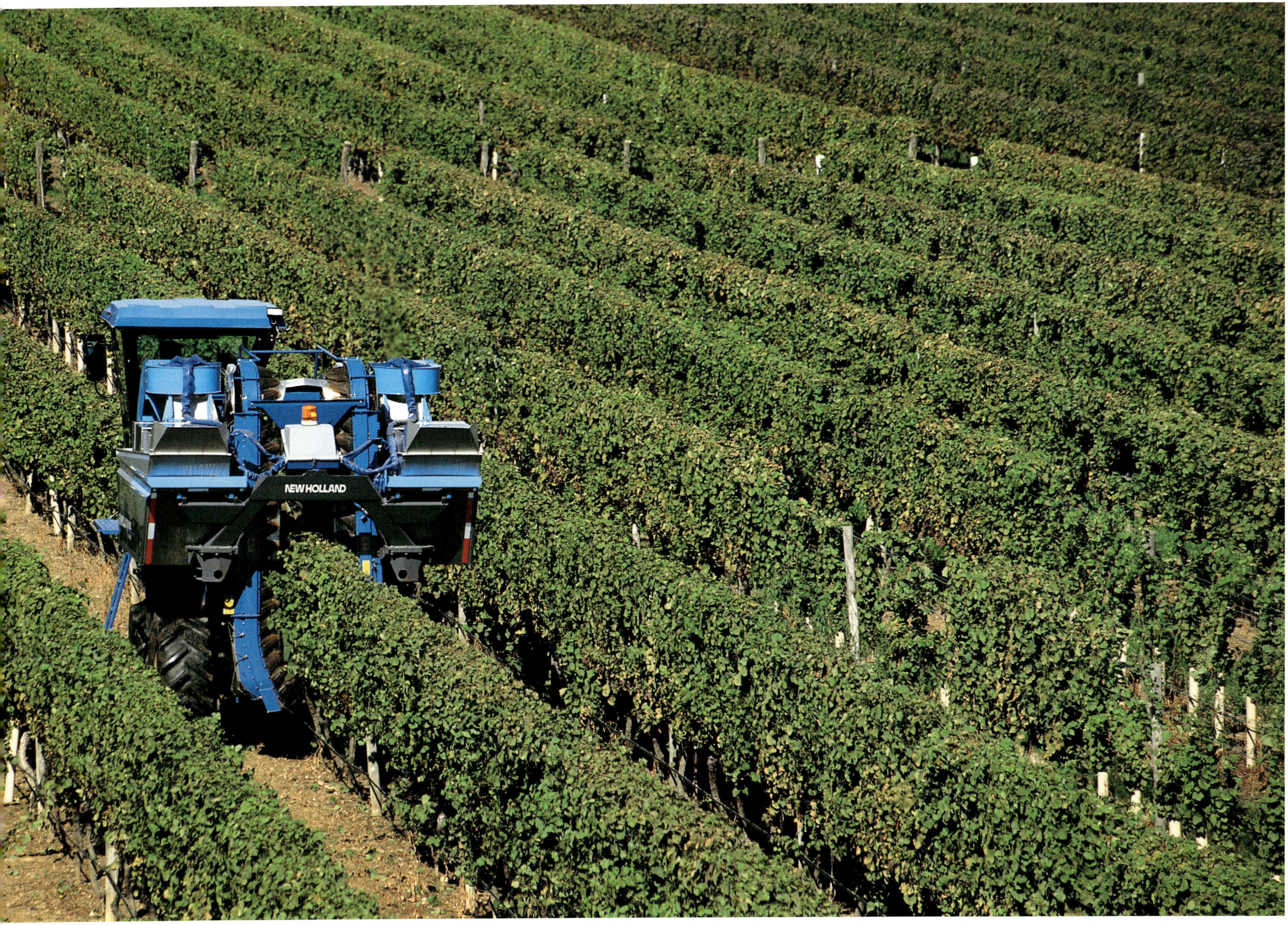
NEW HOLLAND

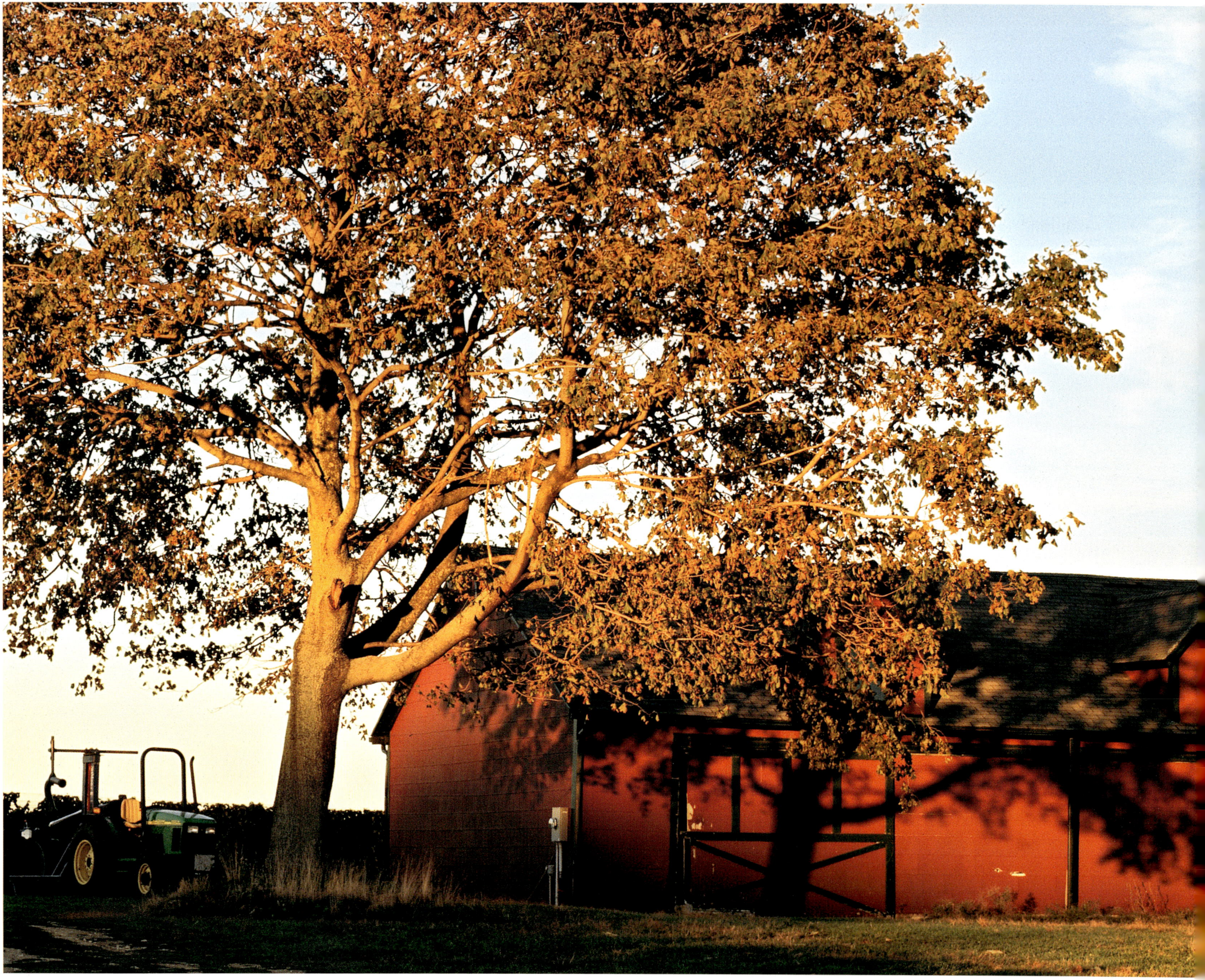

Duck Walk Vineyards, Cutchogue    Depot Lane, Cutchogue

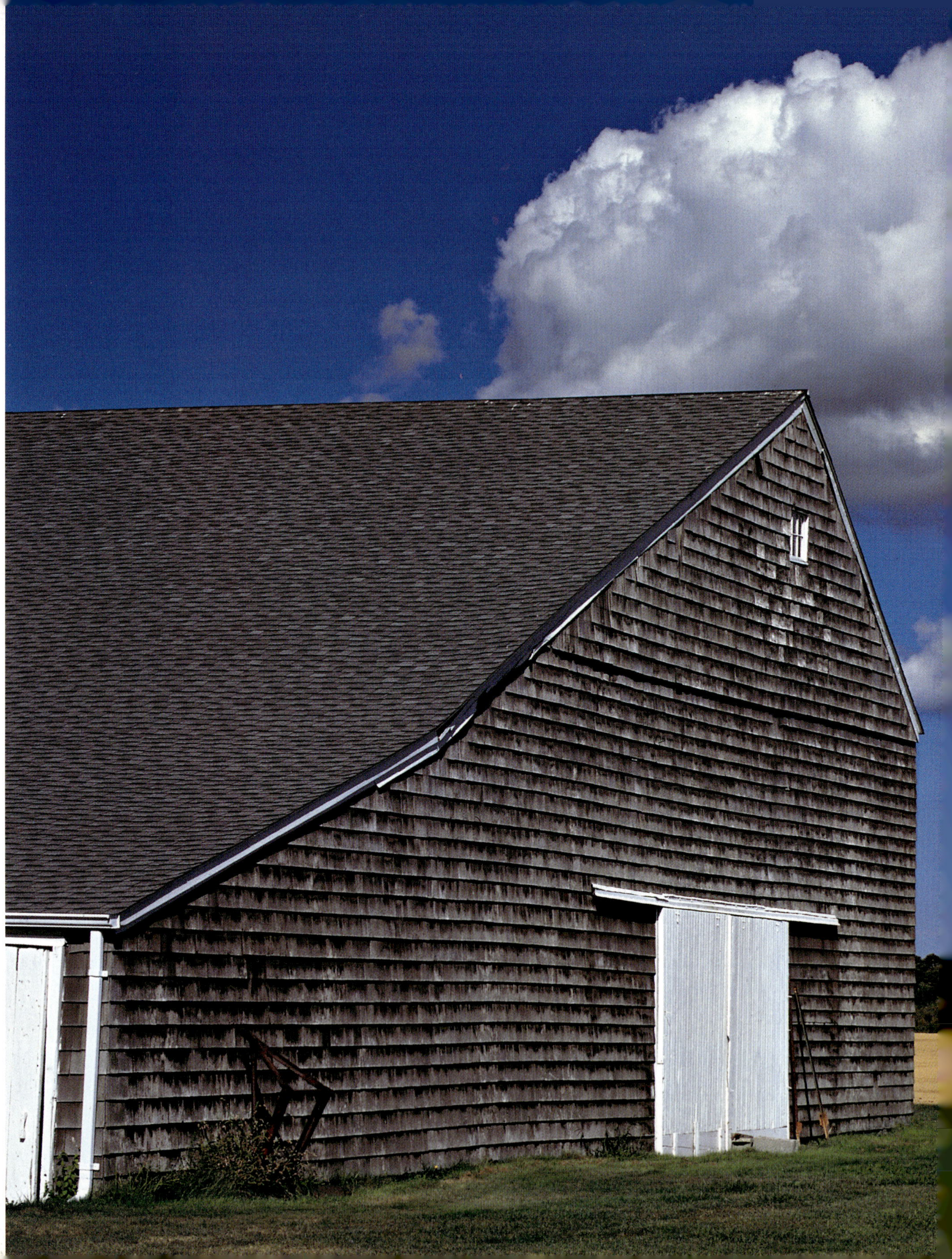

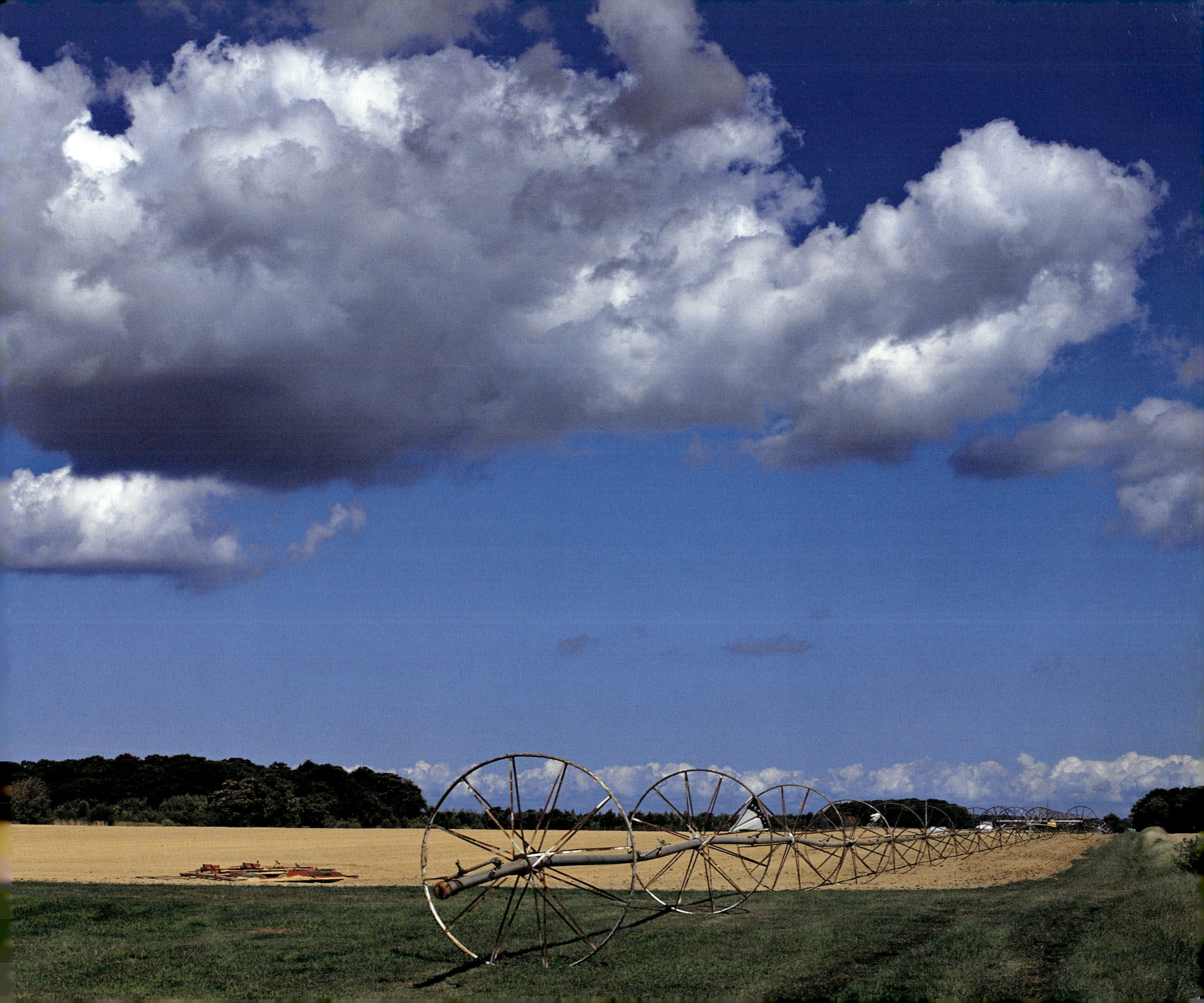

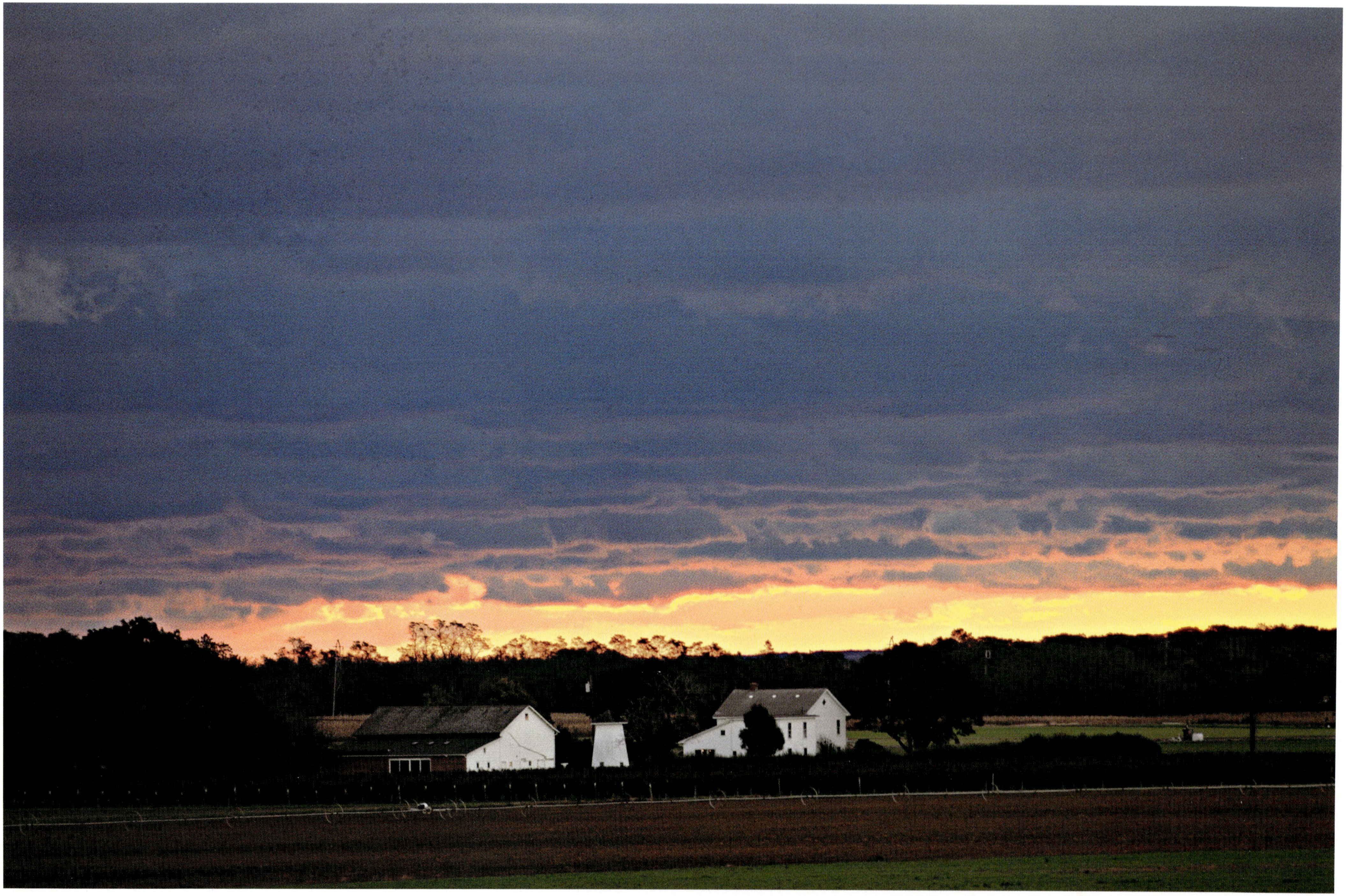

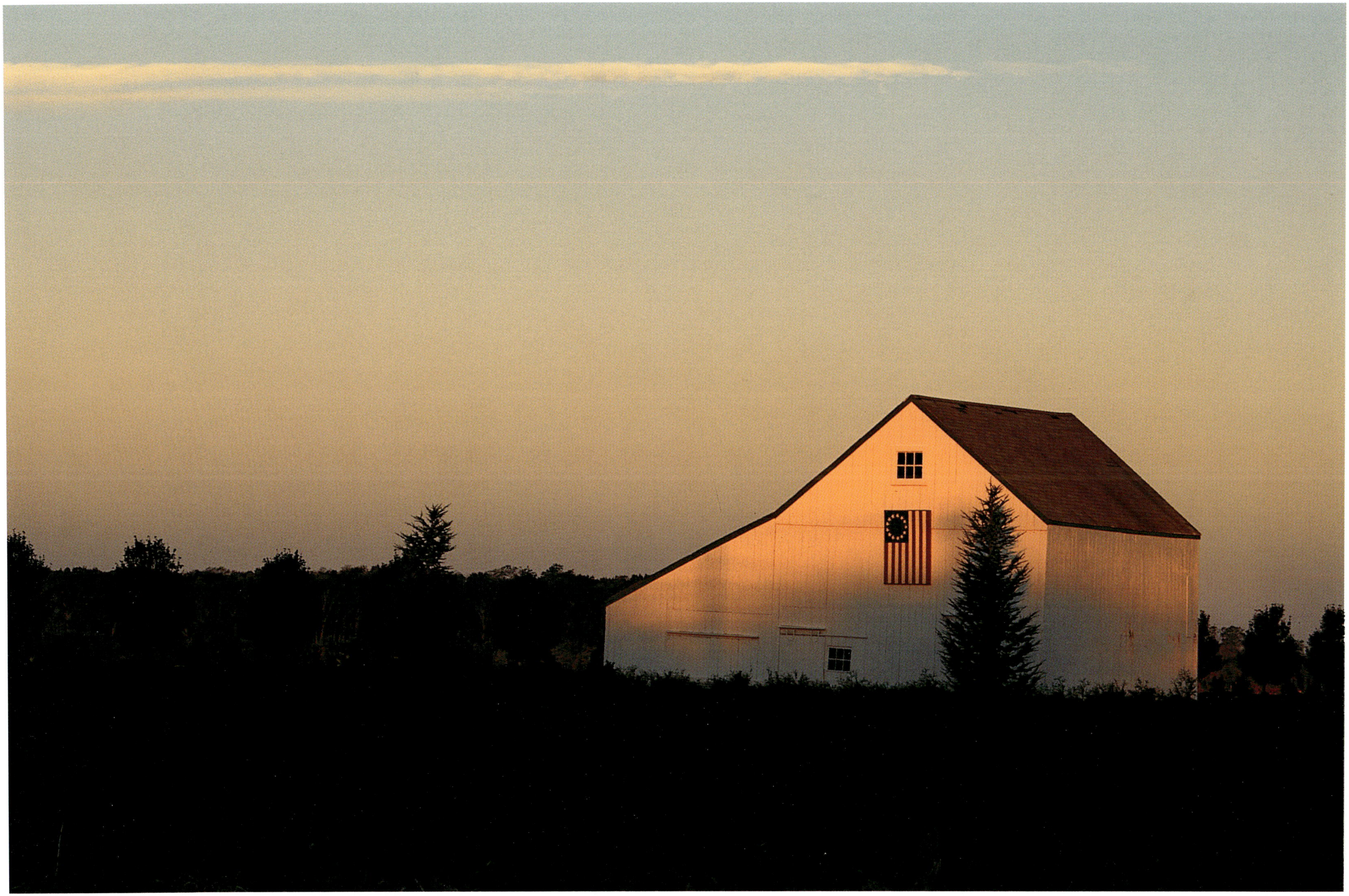

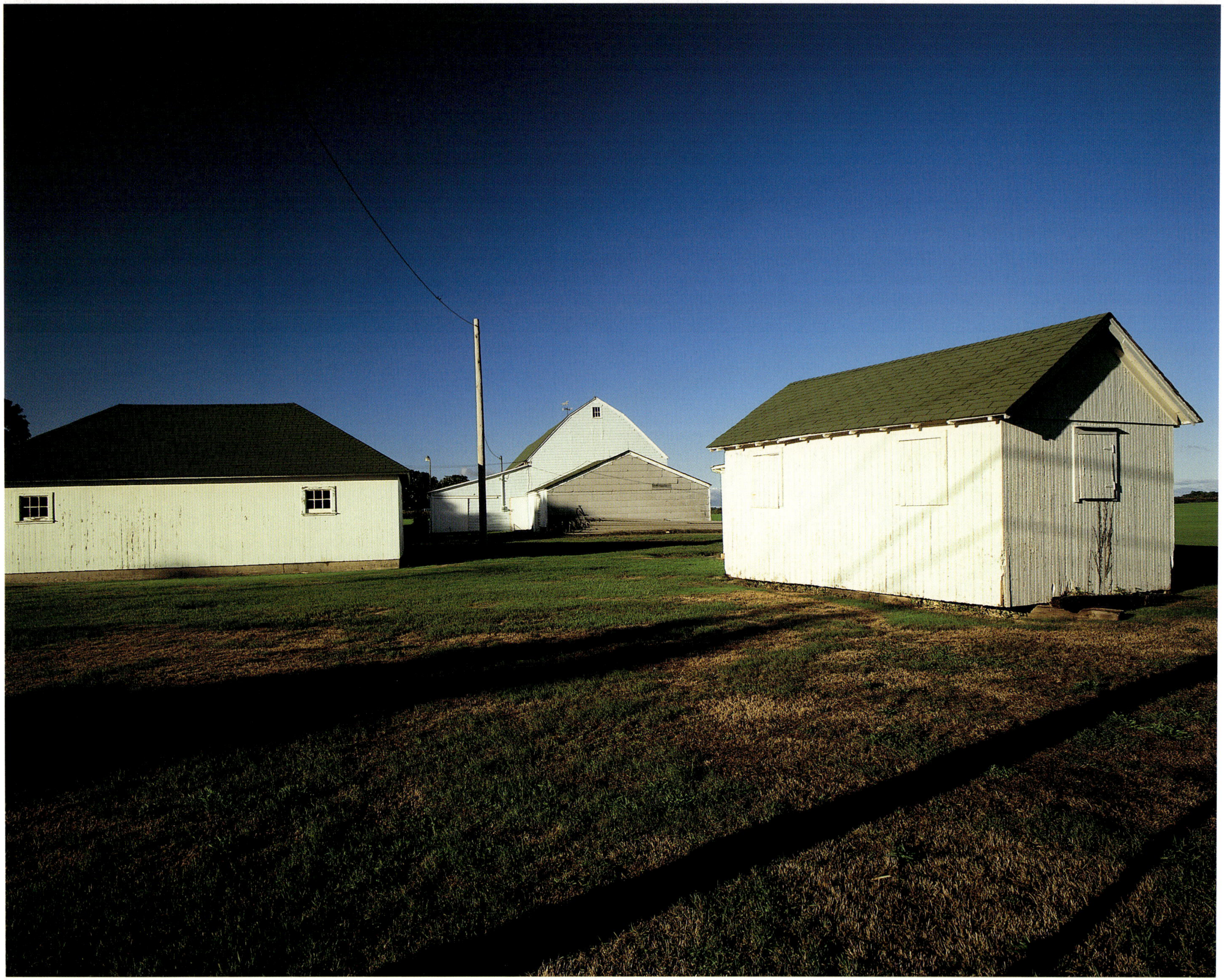

Oregon Road, Cutchogue    Schreiber Farm, Oregon Road, Cutchogue

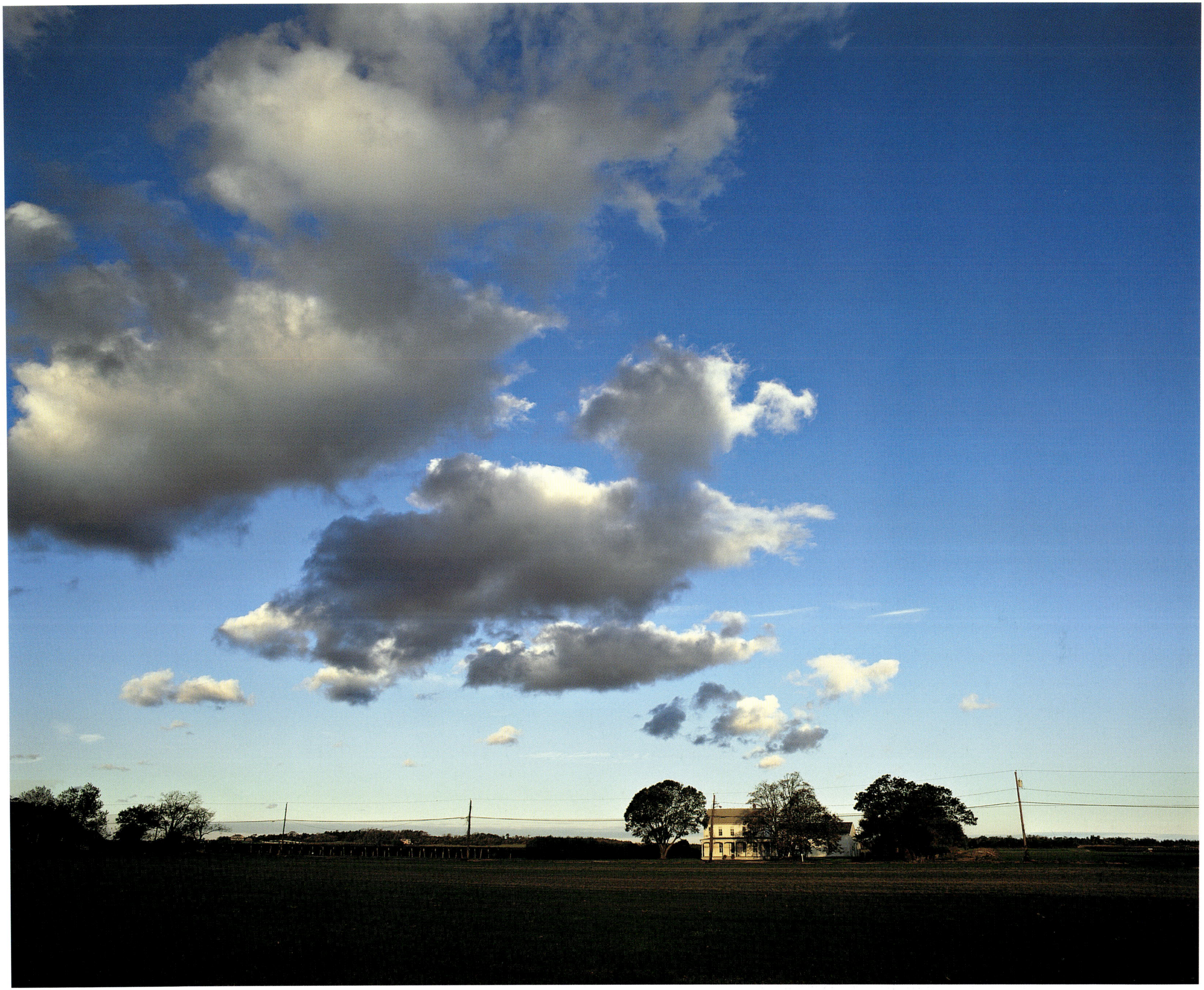

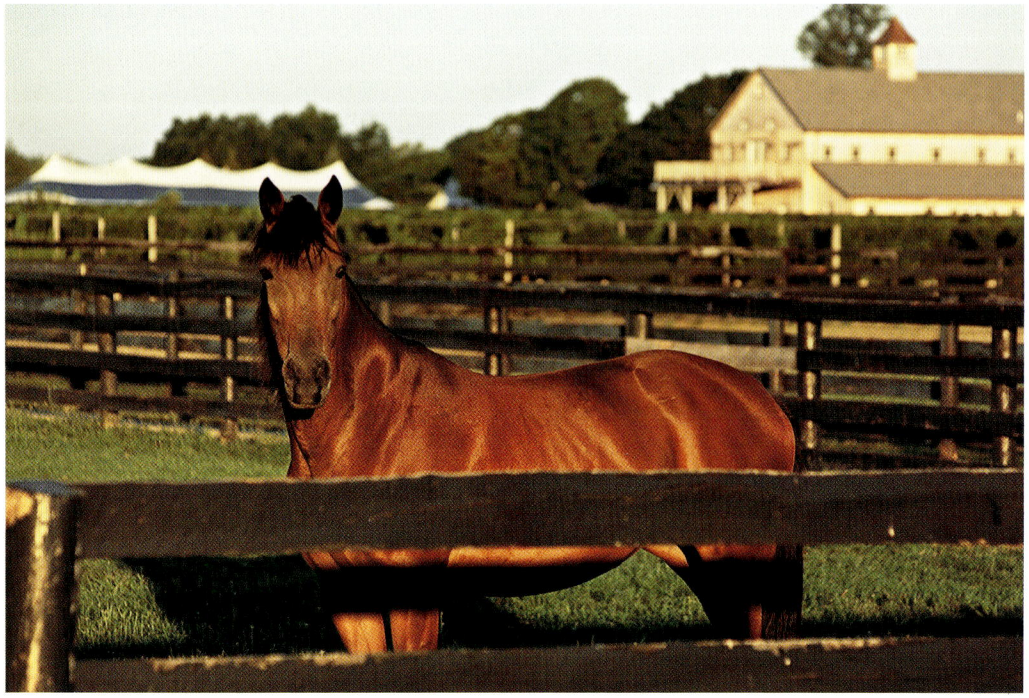

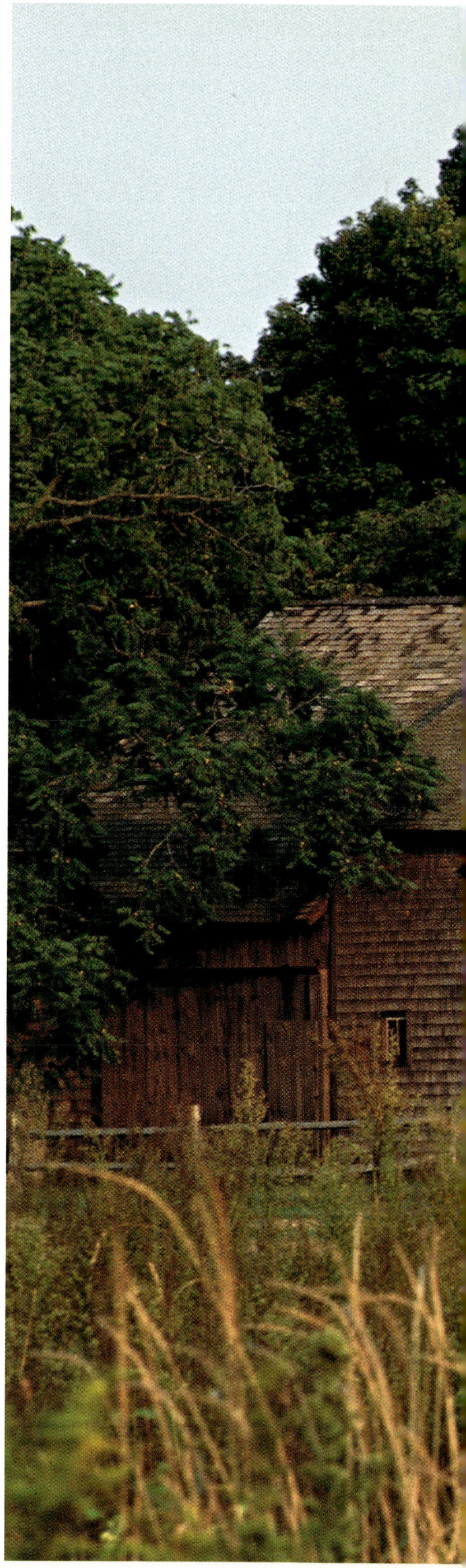

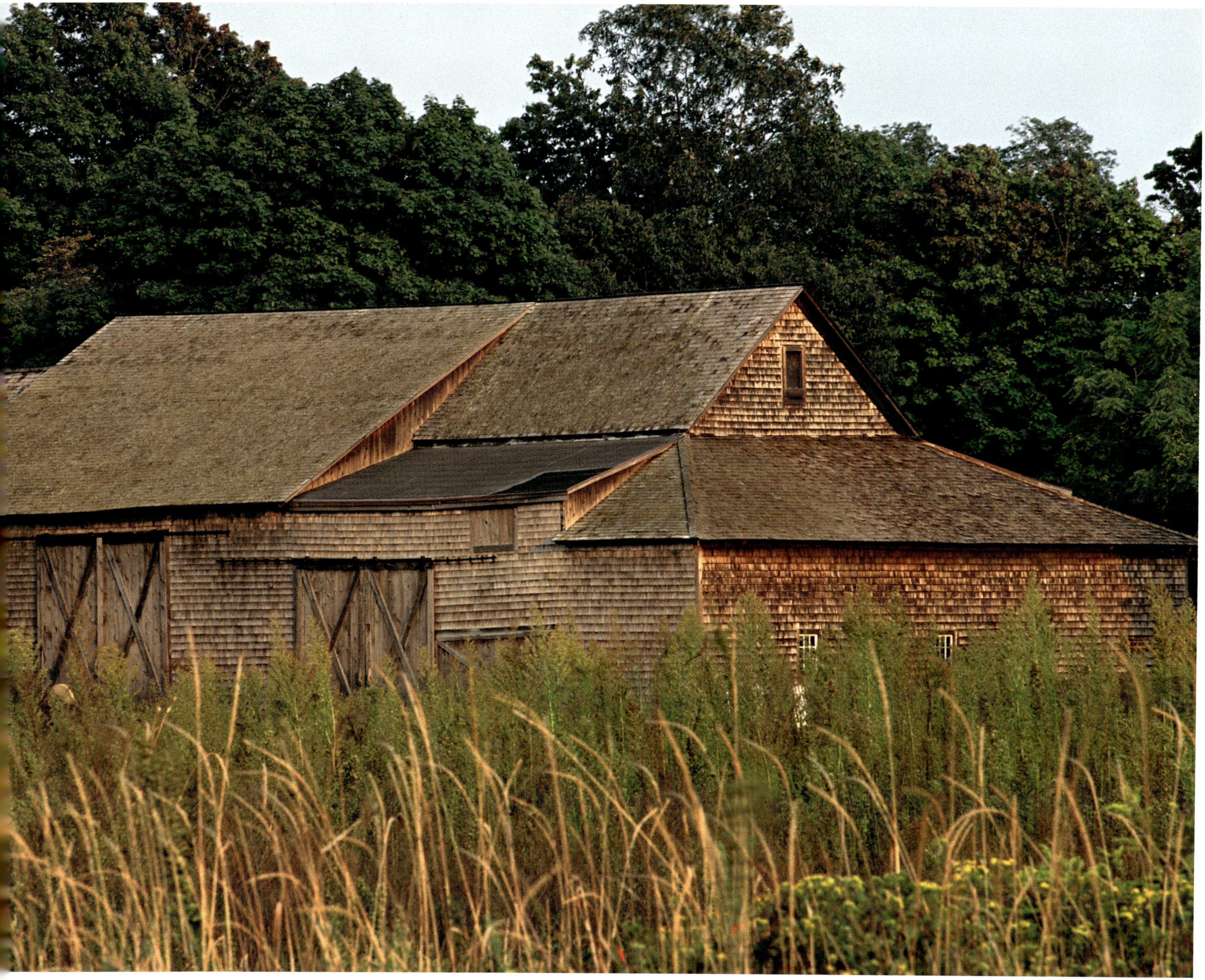

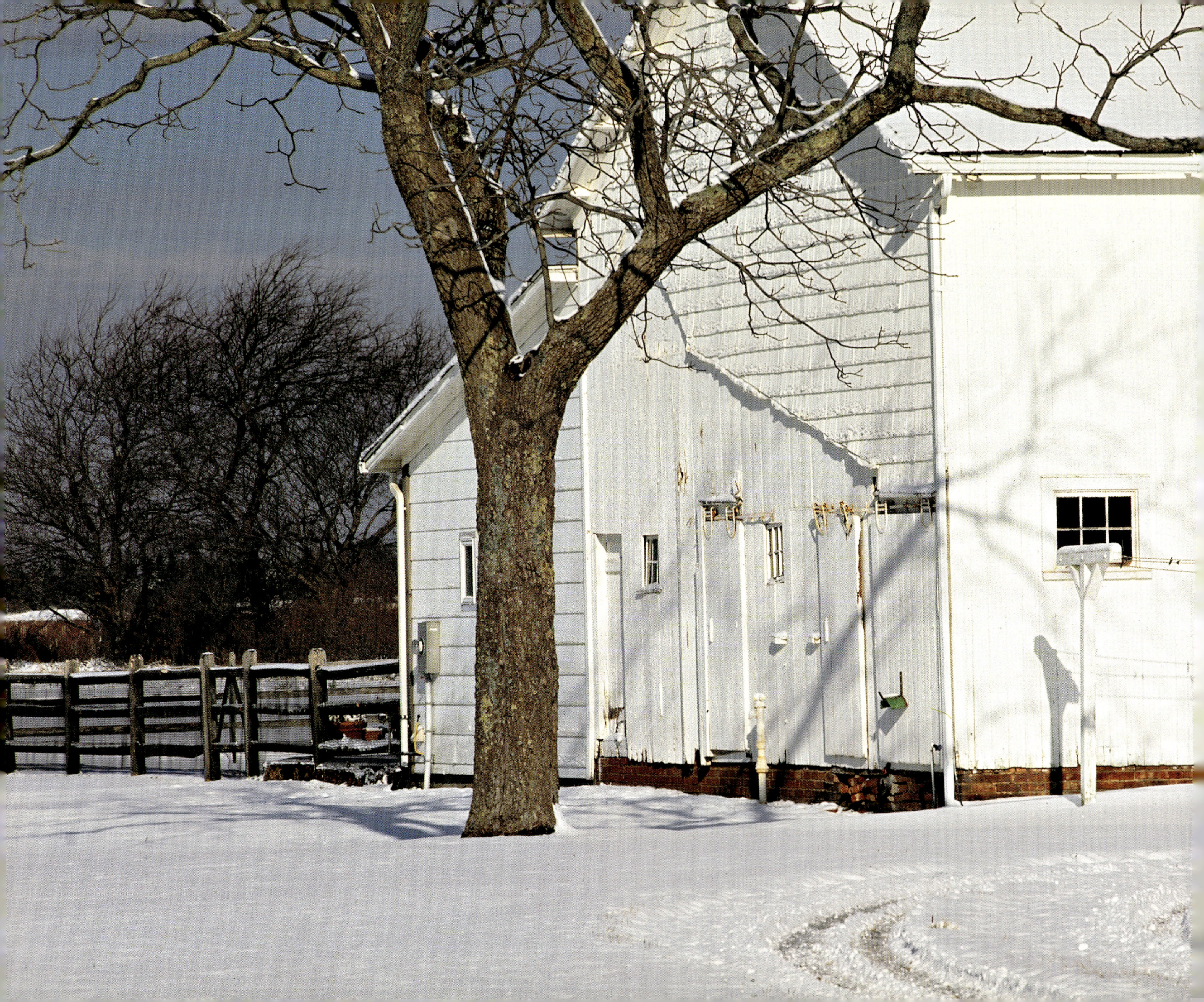

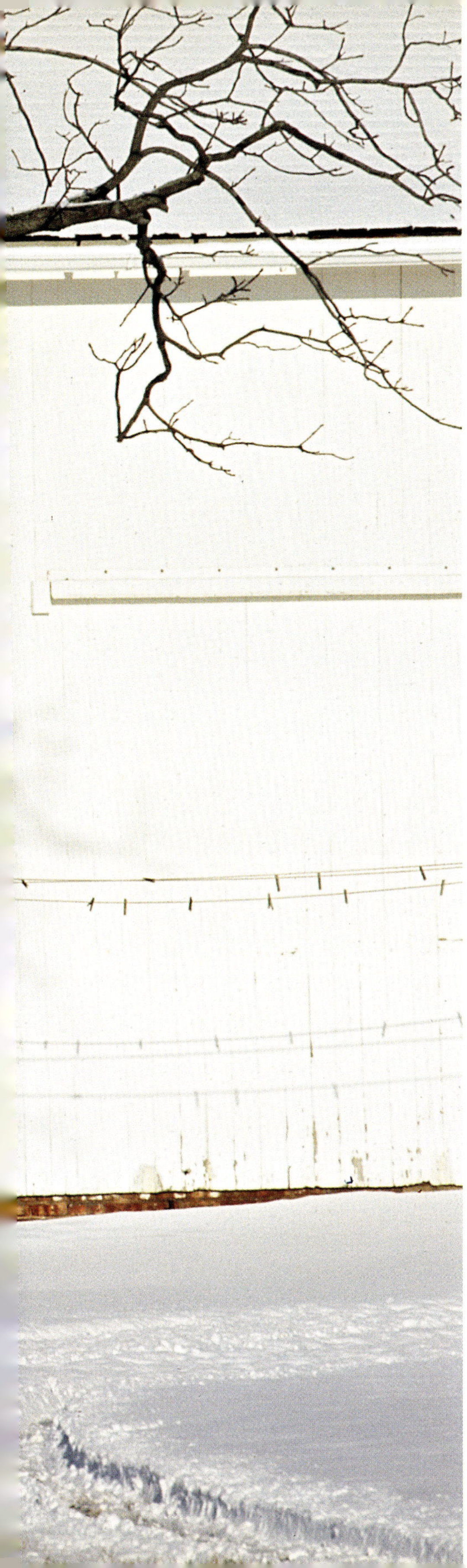

Schreiber Farm, Oregon Road, Cutchogue → Mount Beulah Road, Southold → East Marion

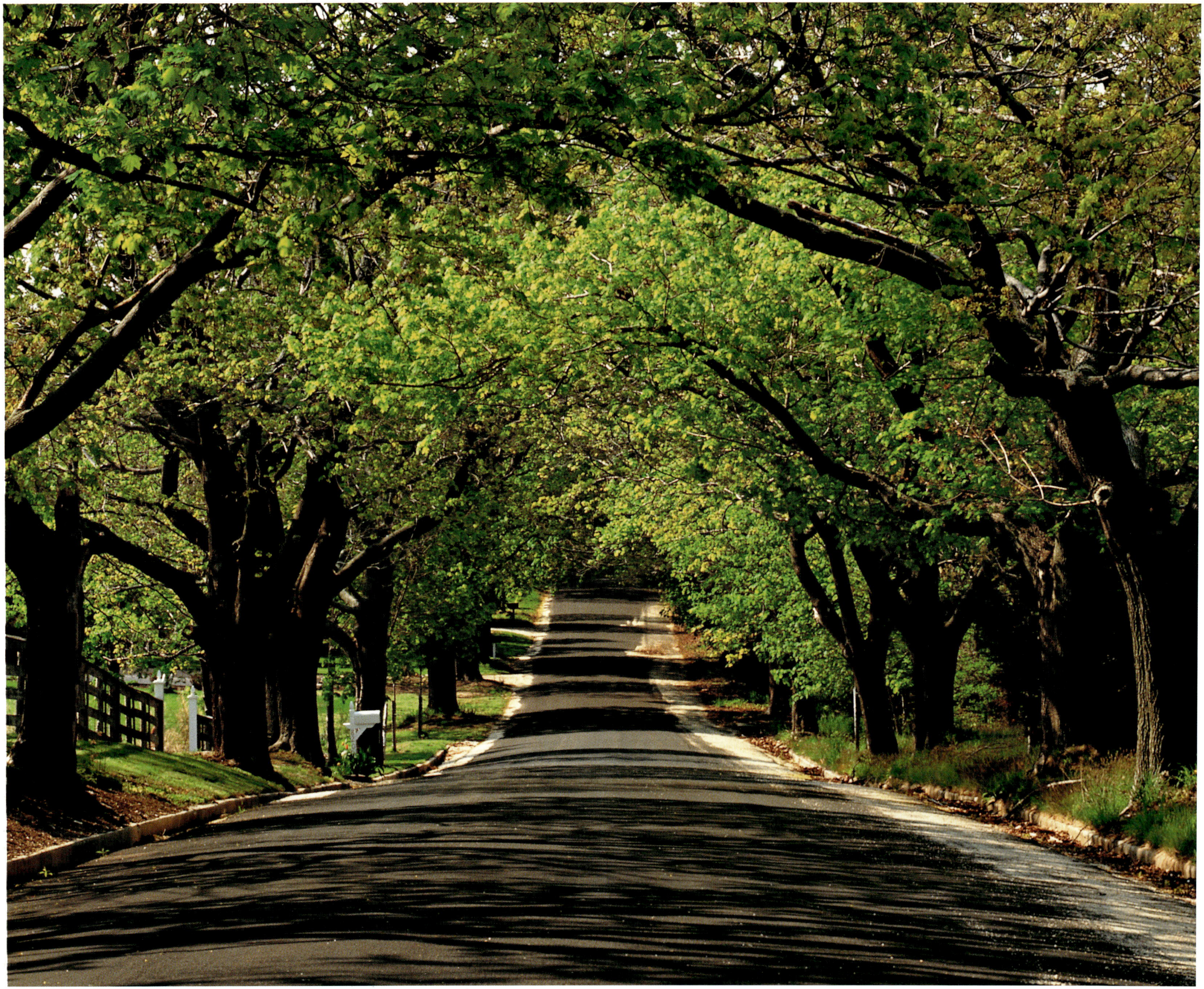

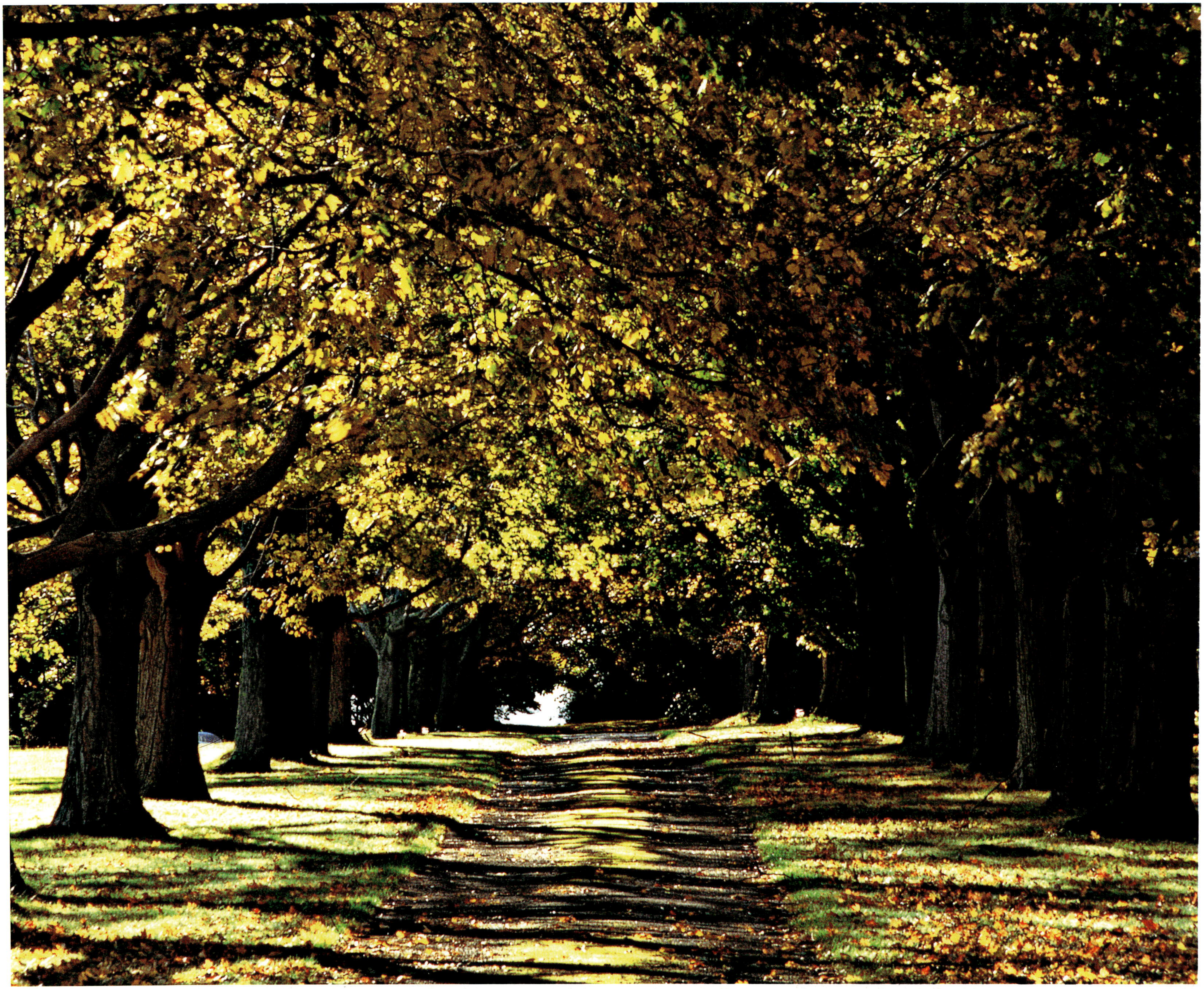

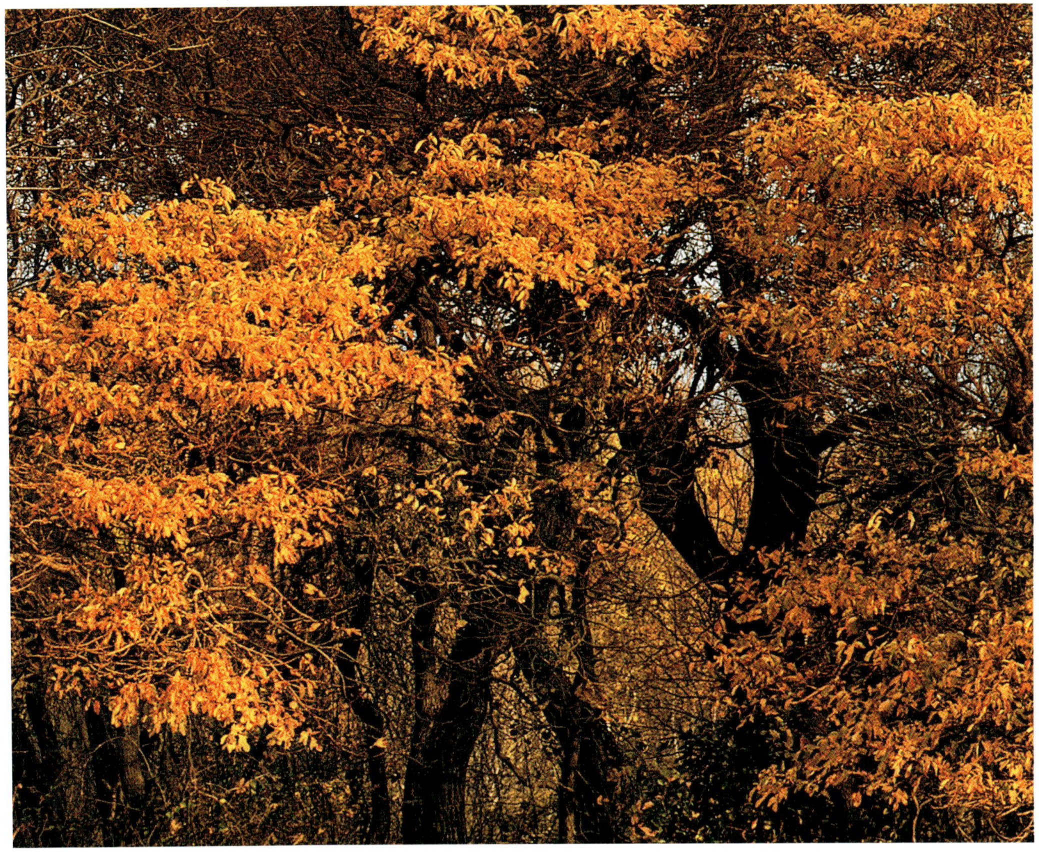
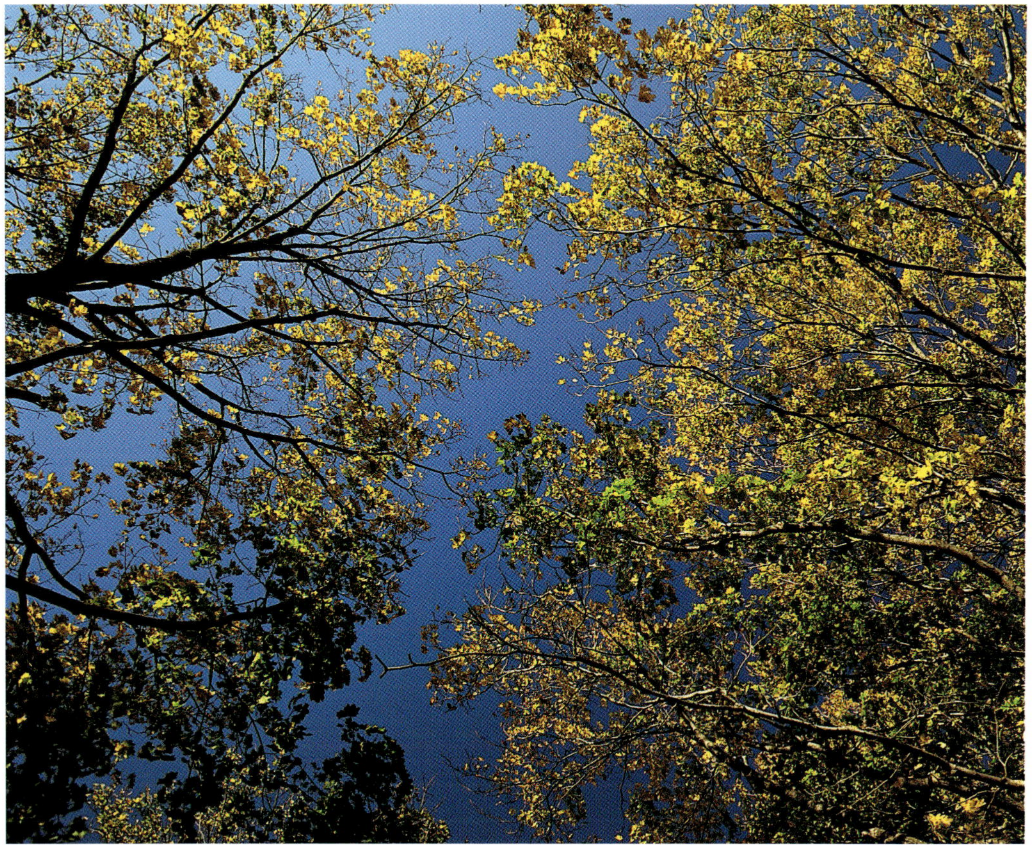
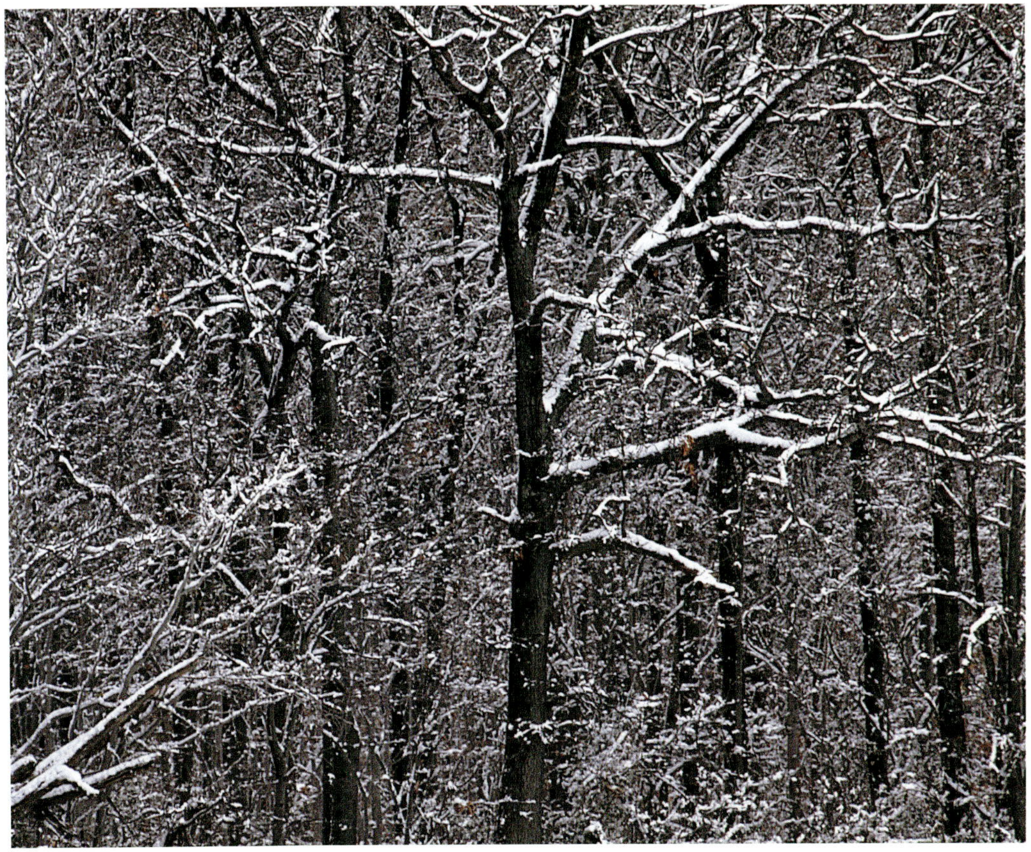
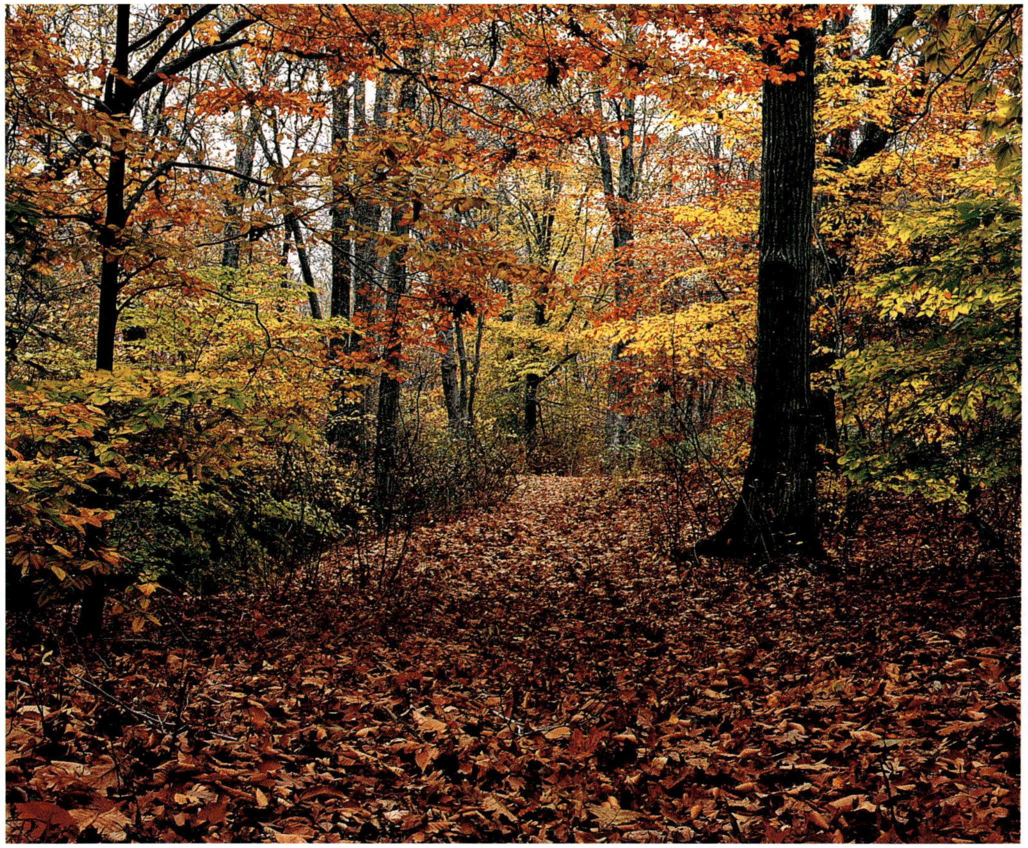

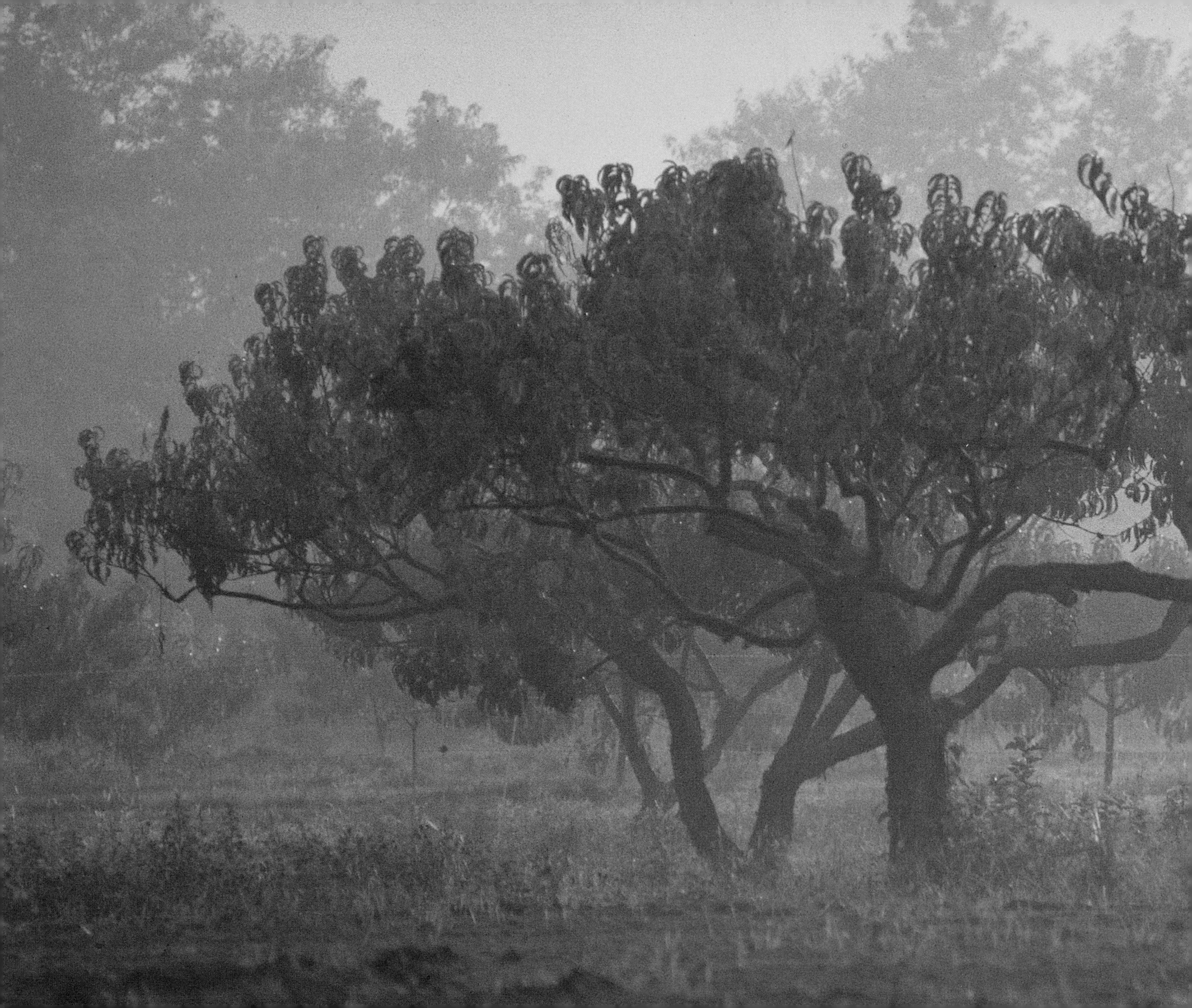

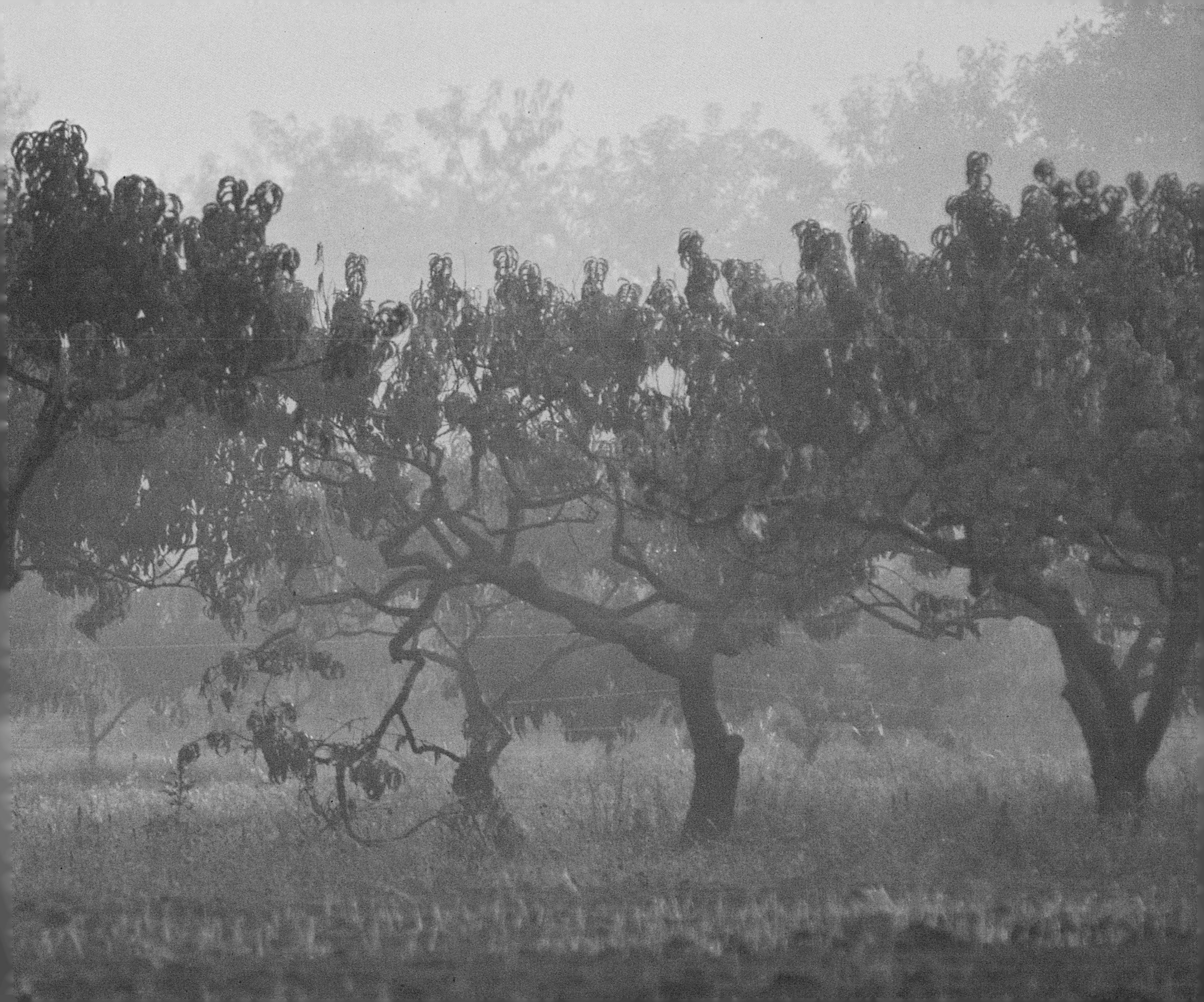

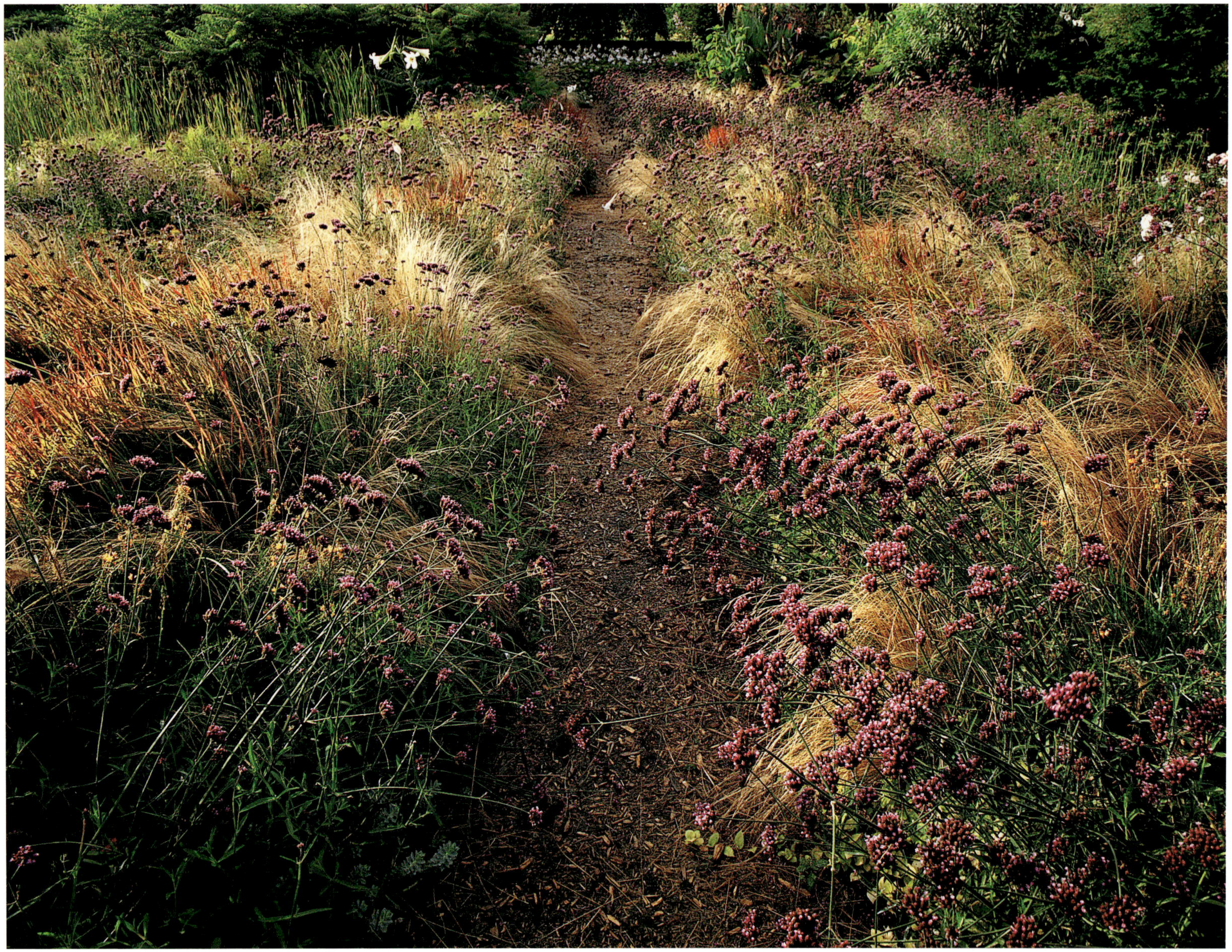

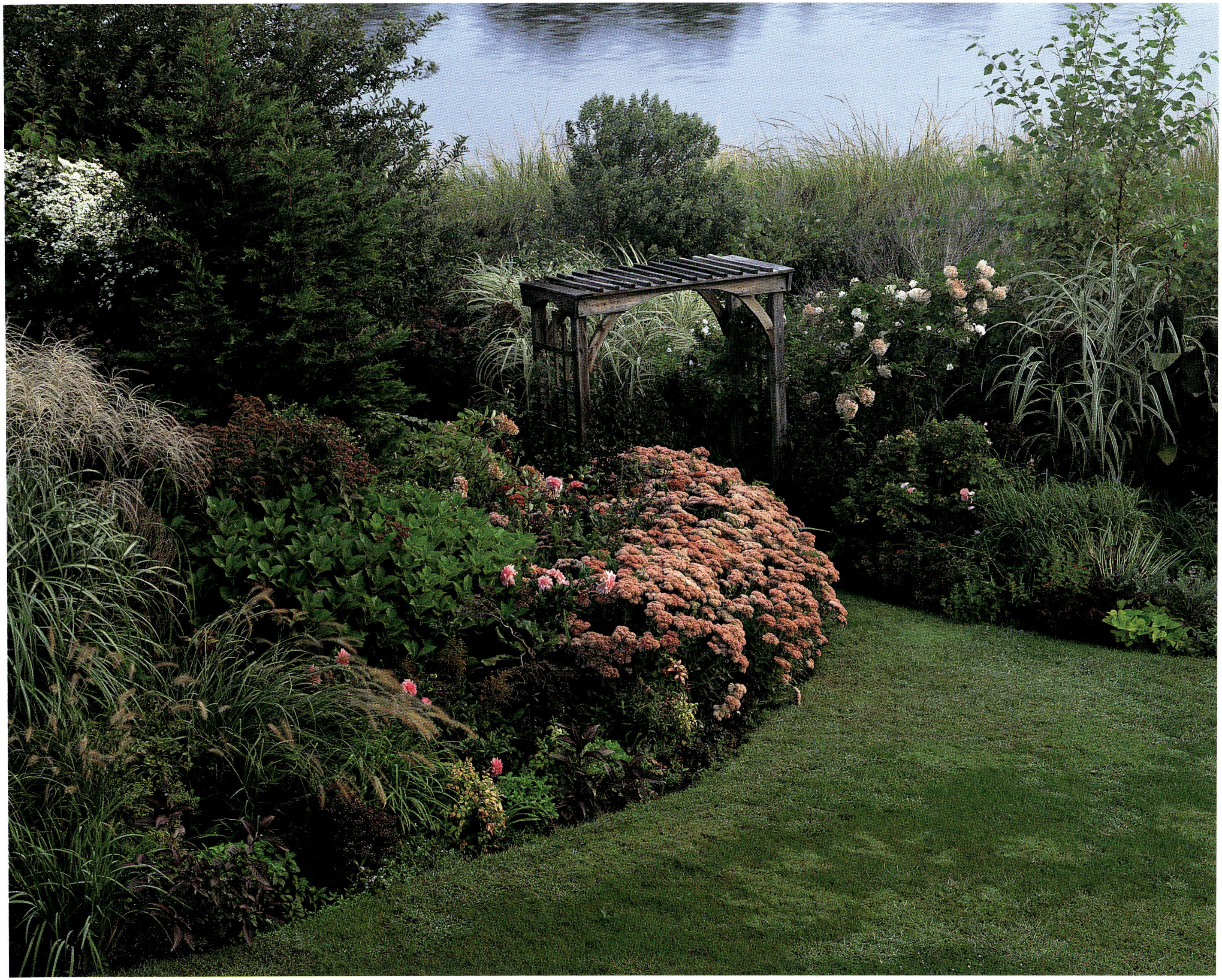

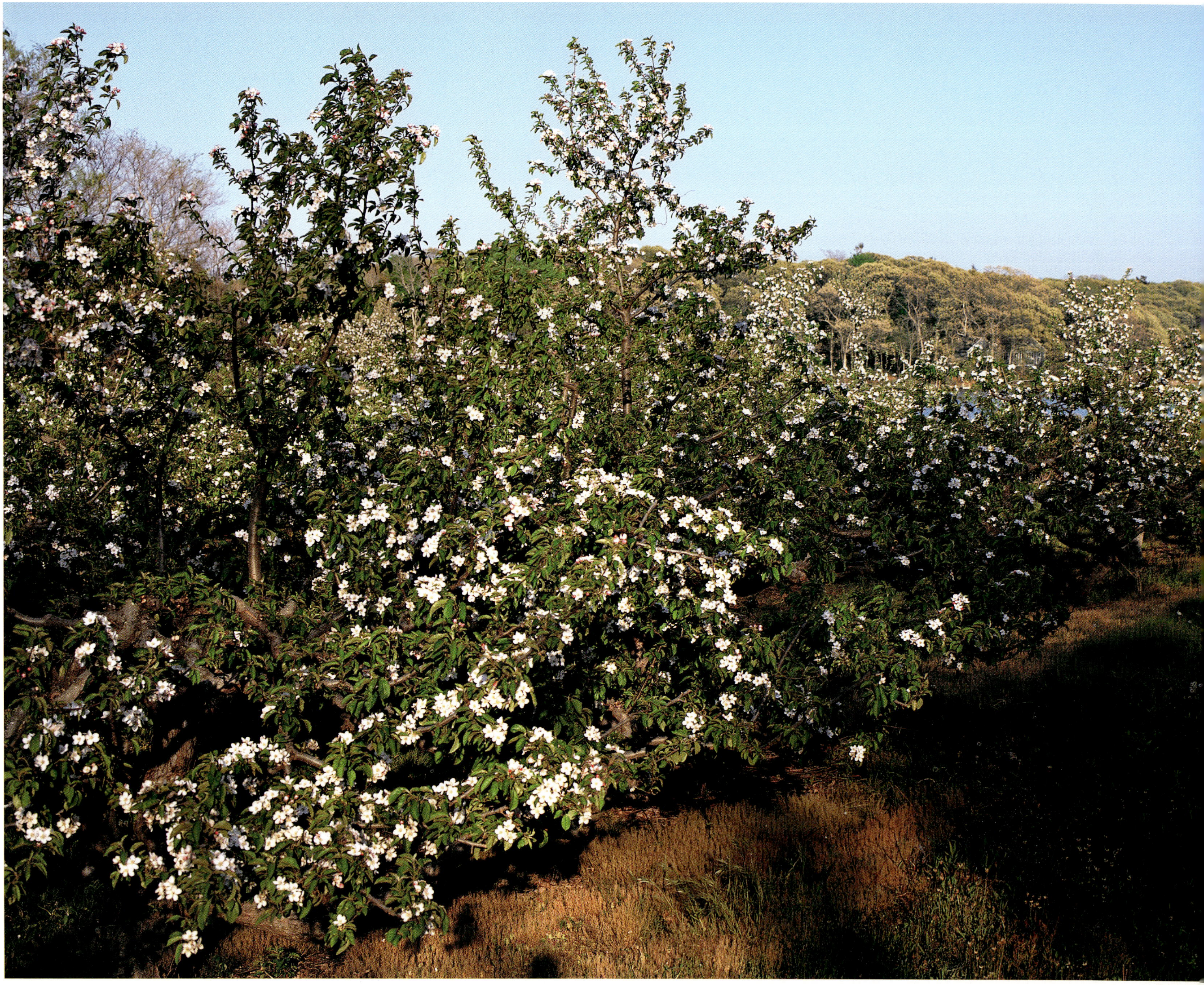

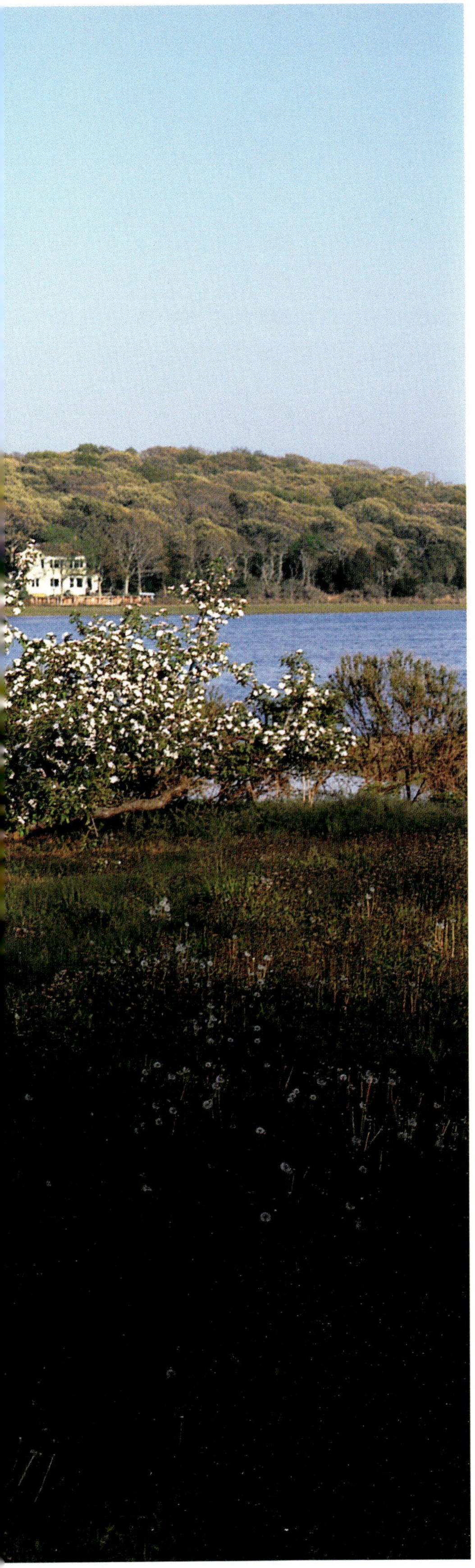

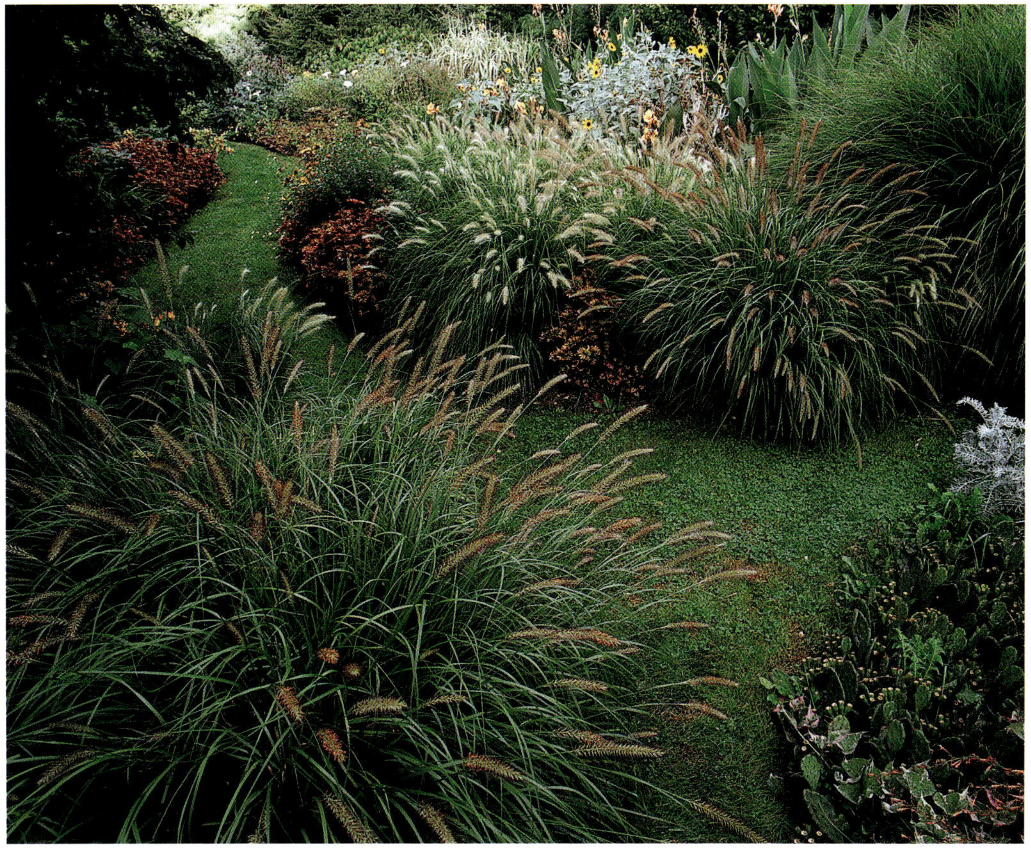

Wickham's Fruit Farm, Cutchogue

Landcraft Environments, Mattituck

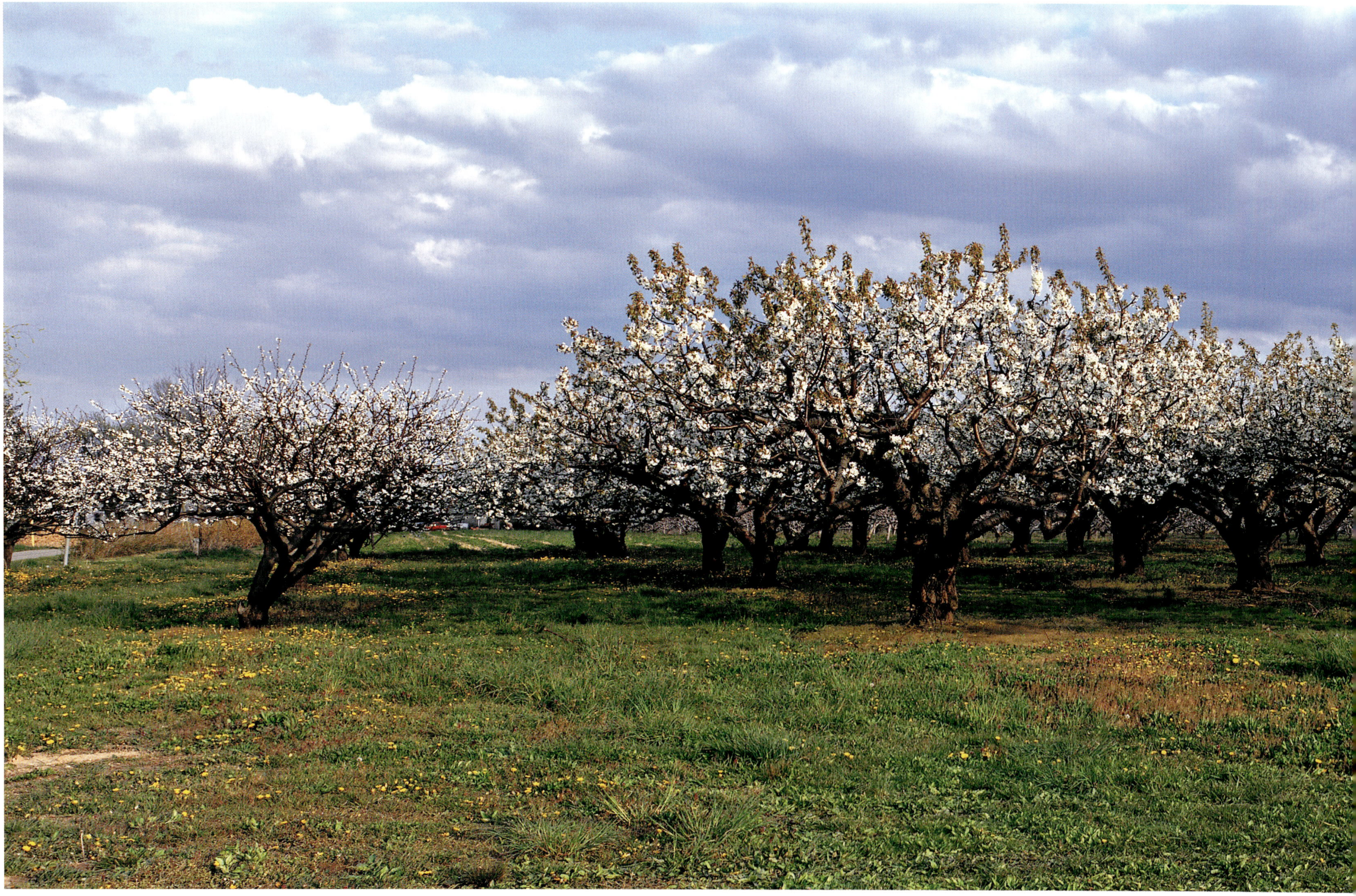

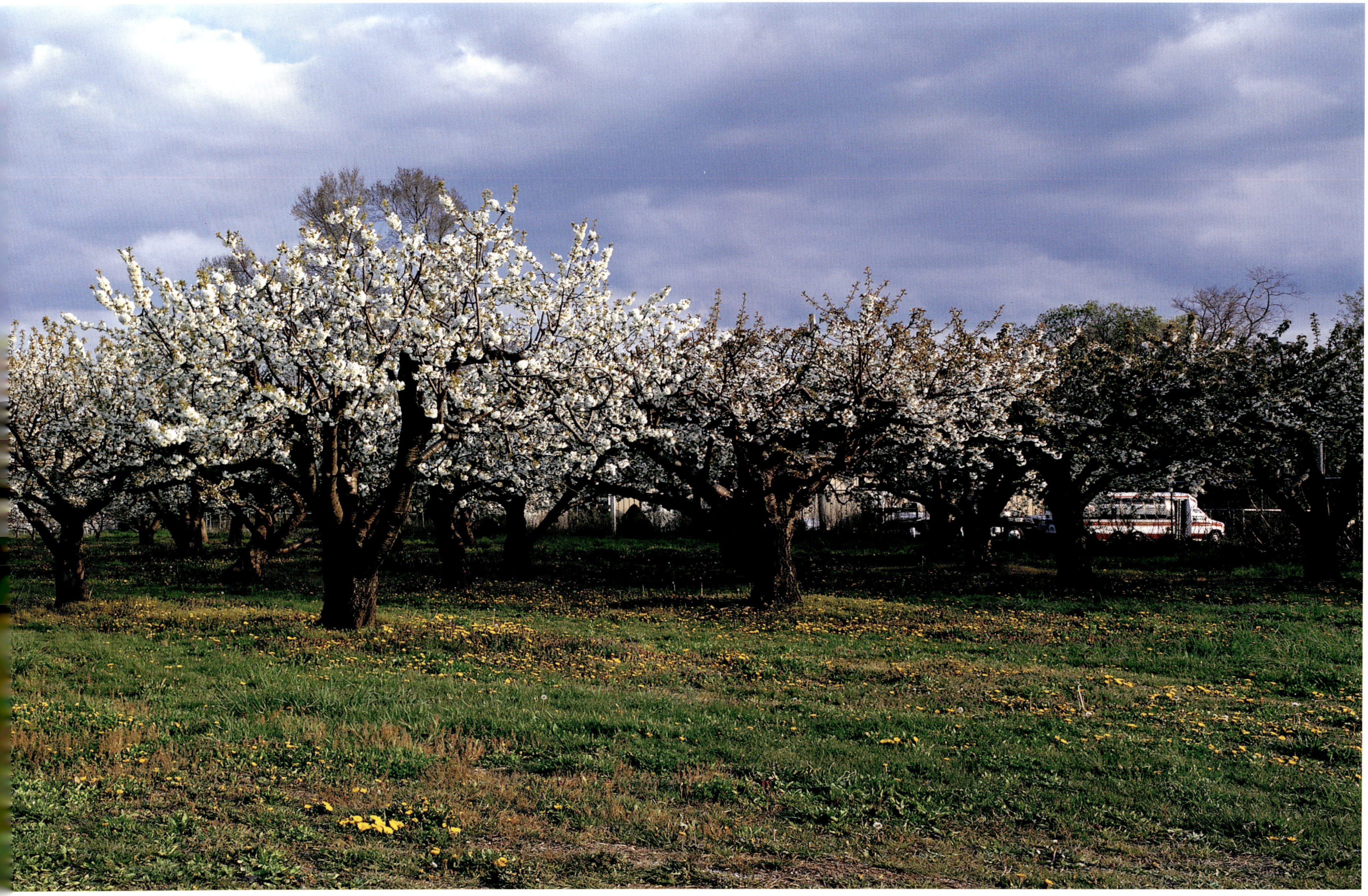

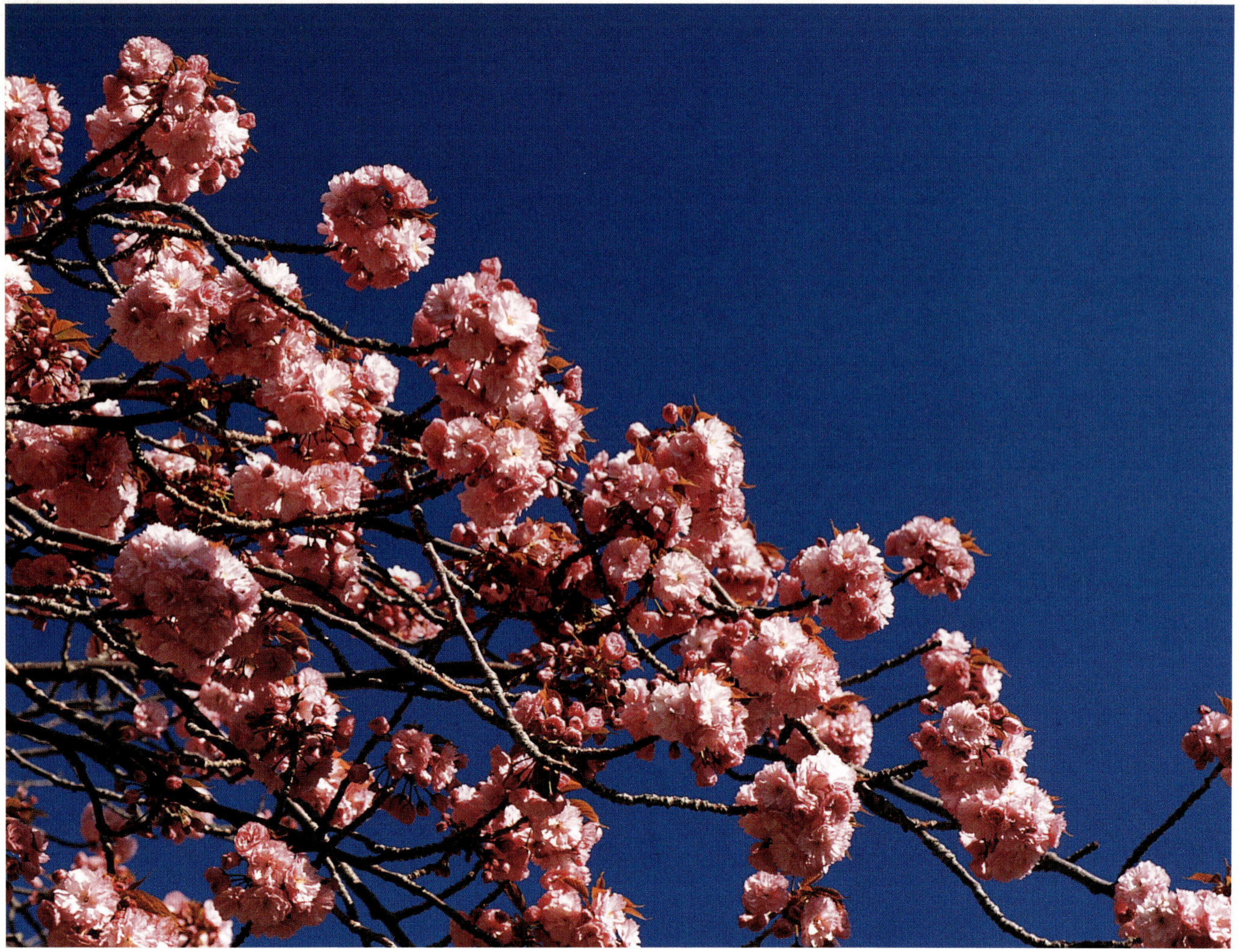

Greenport

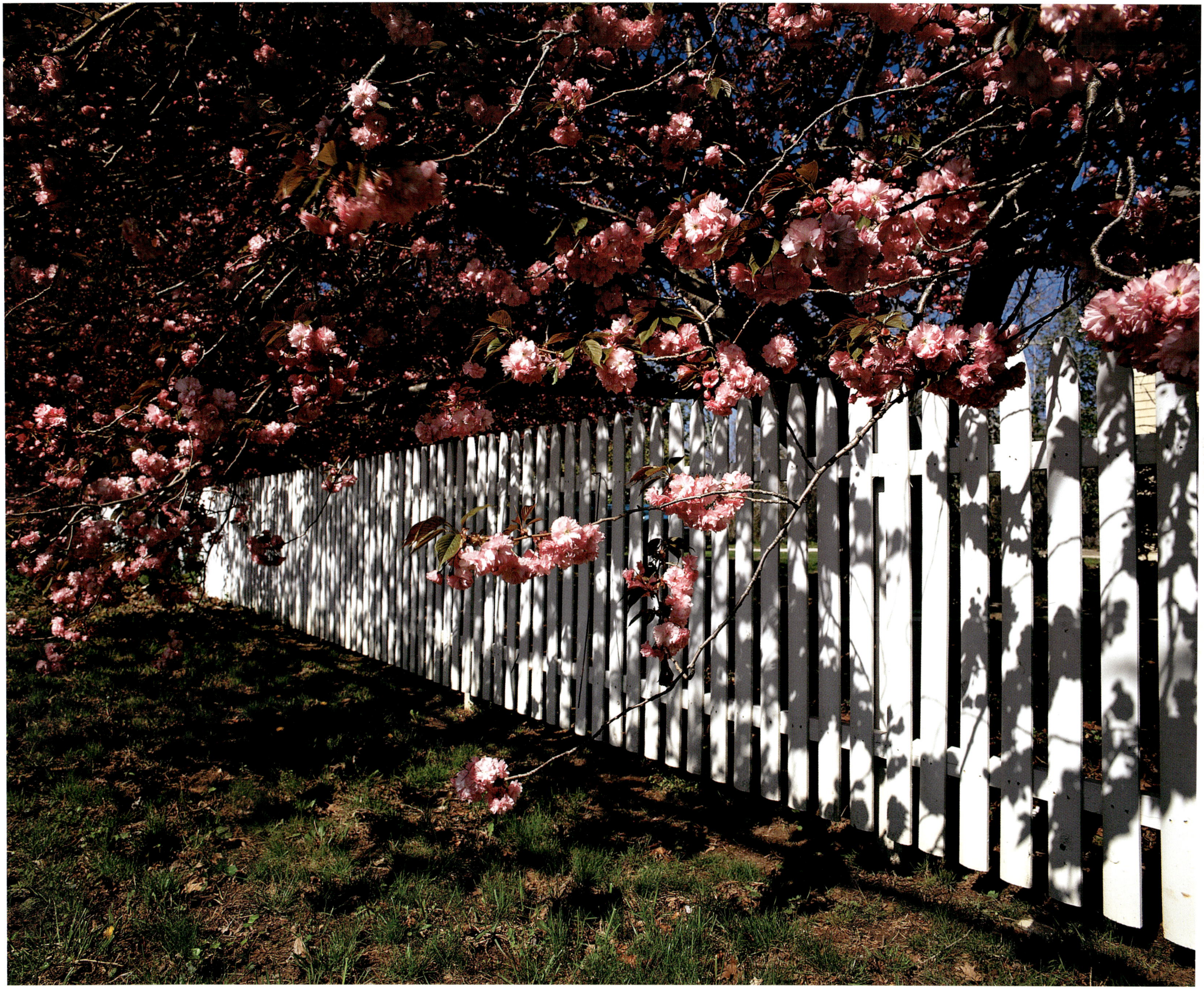

Oregon Road, Mattituck Route 48, Mattituck

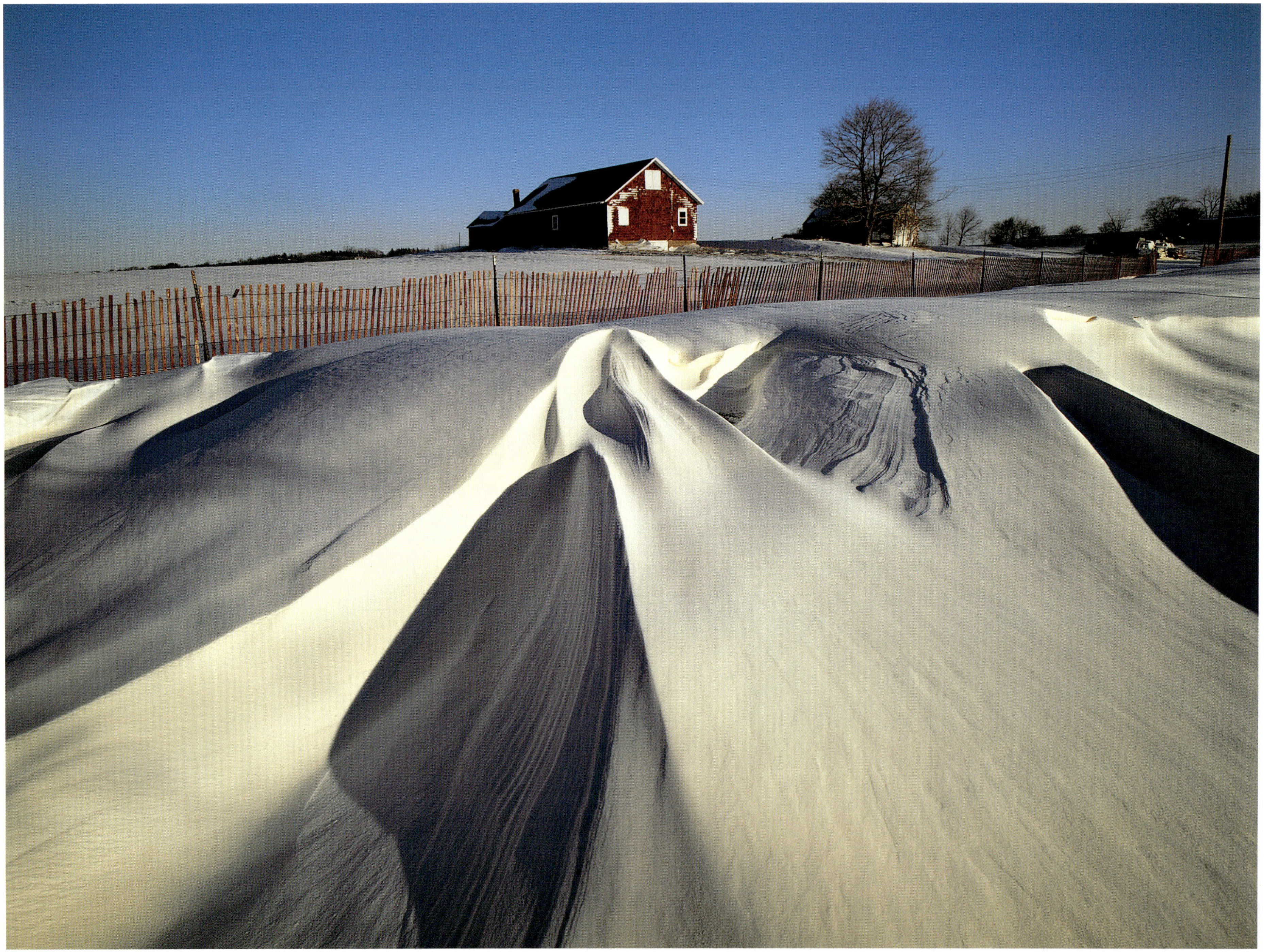

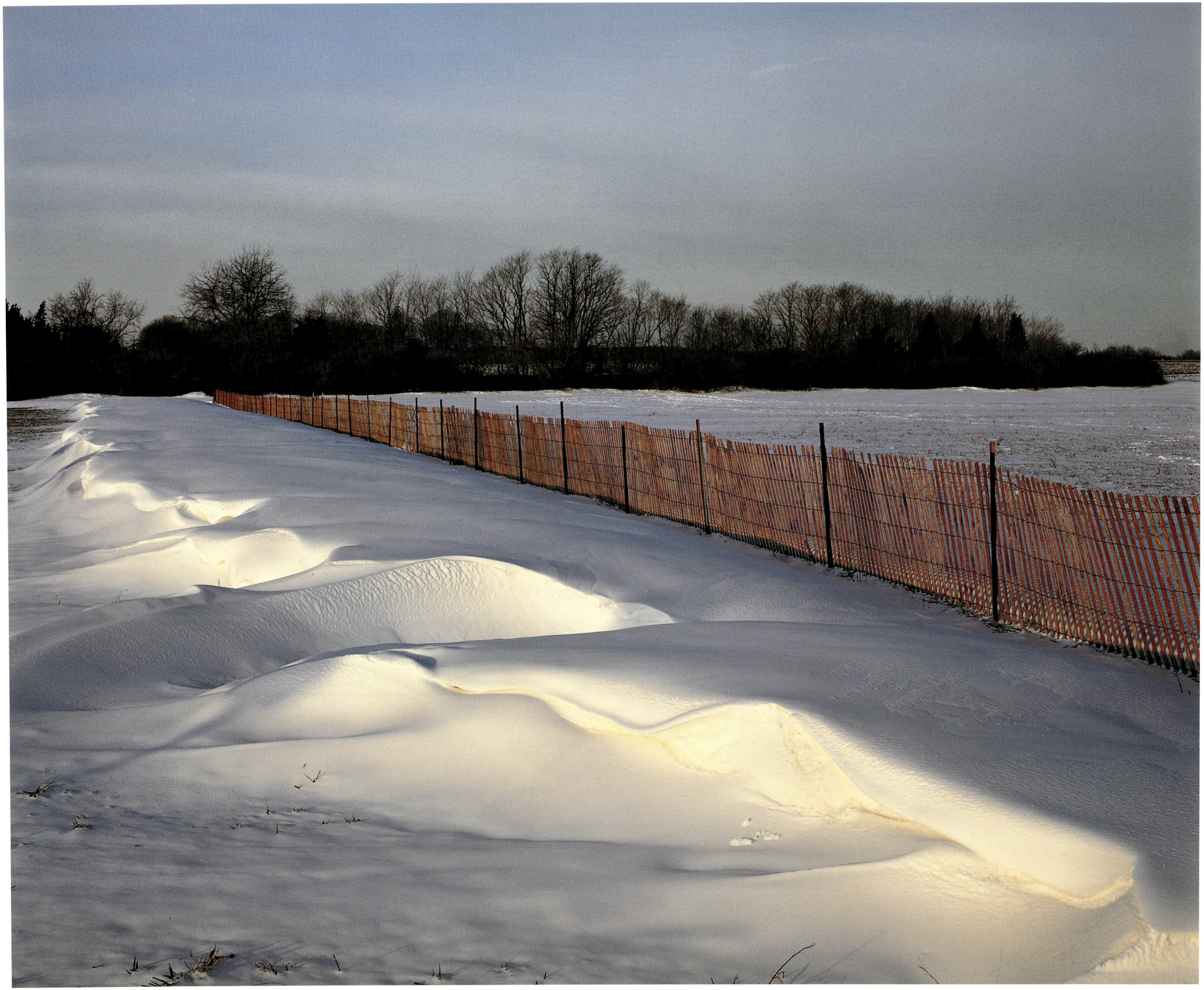

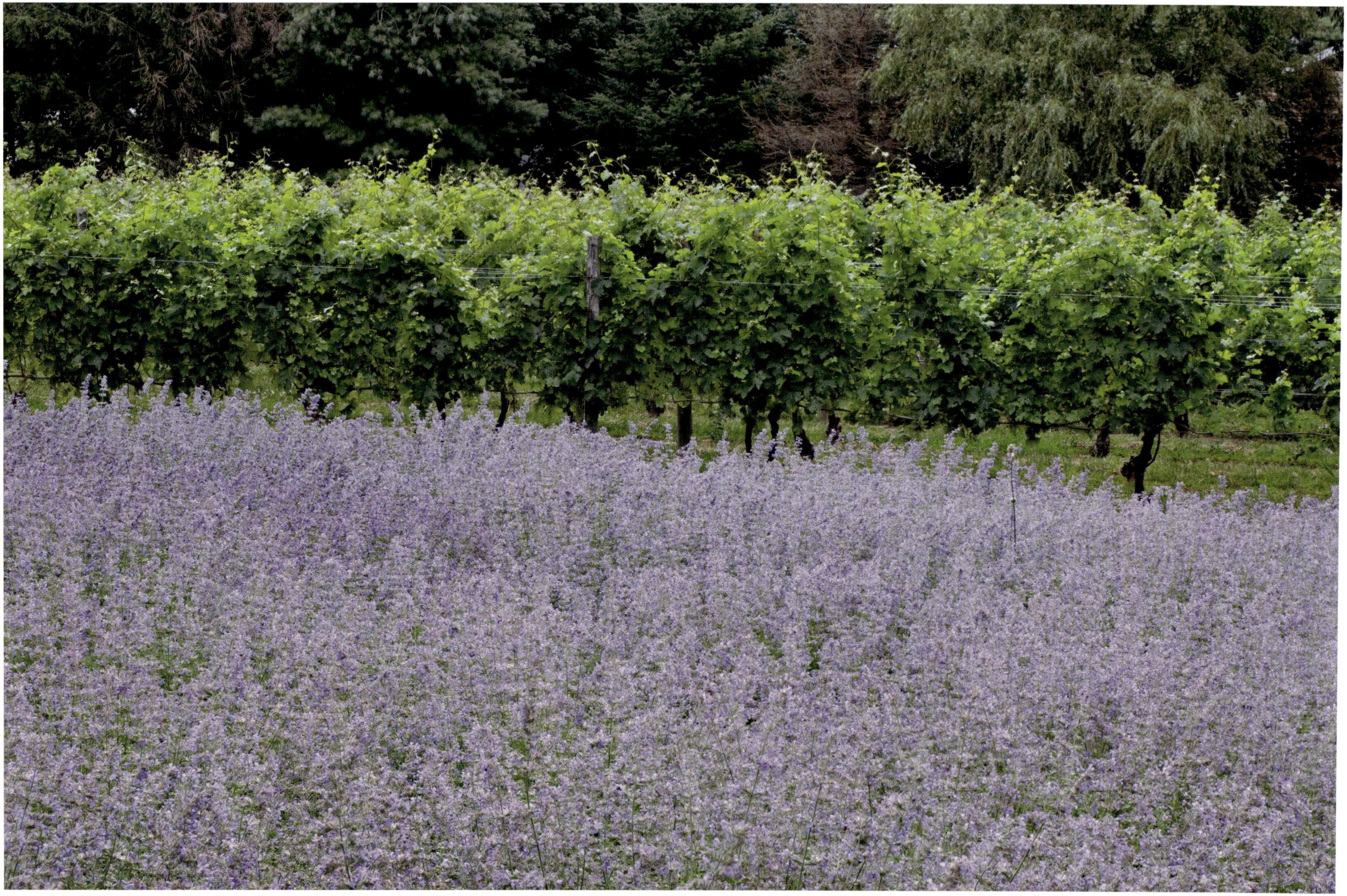

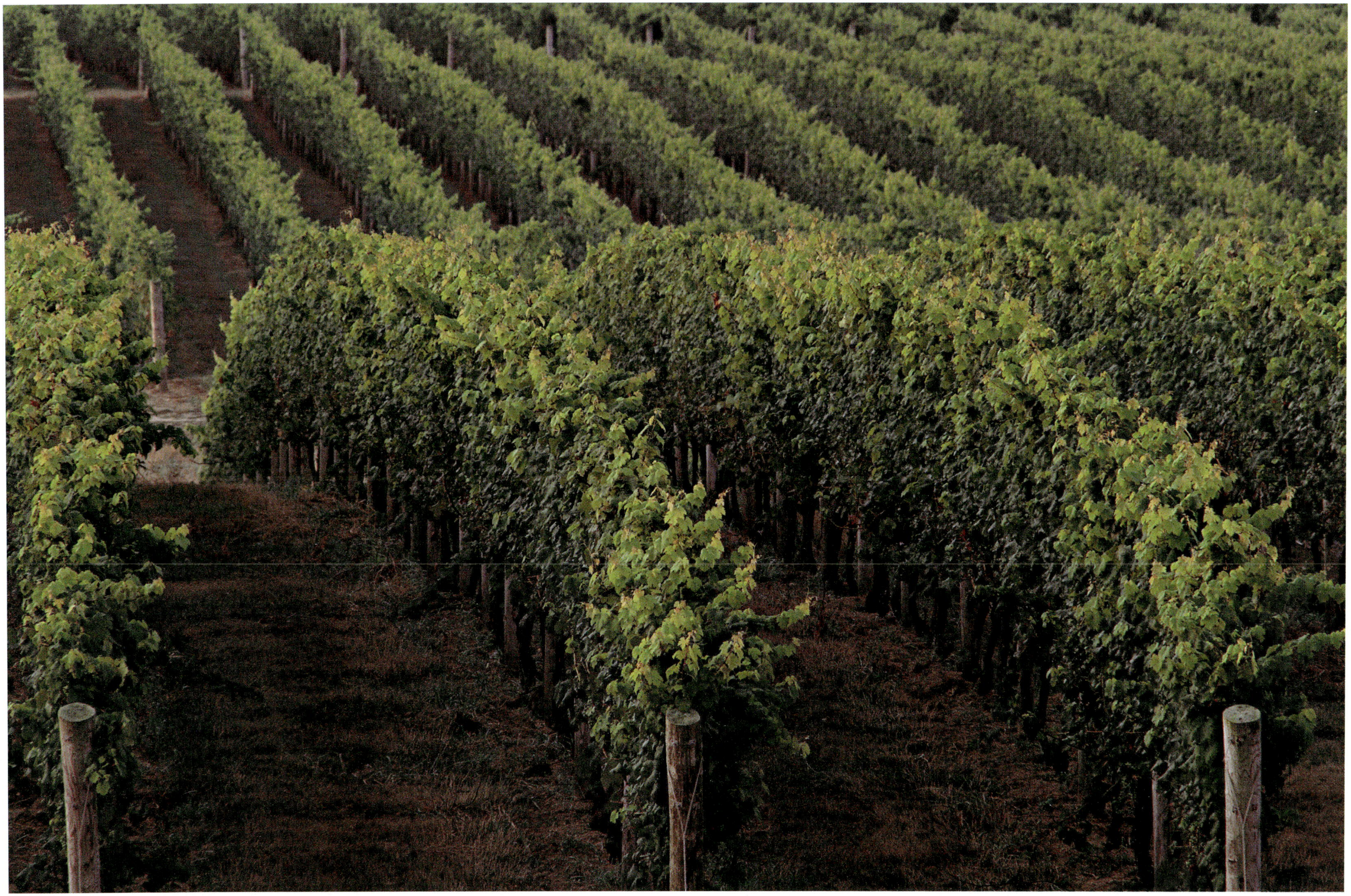

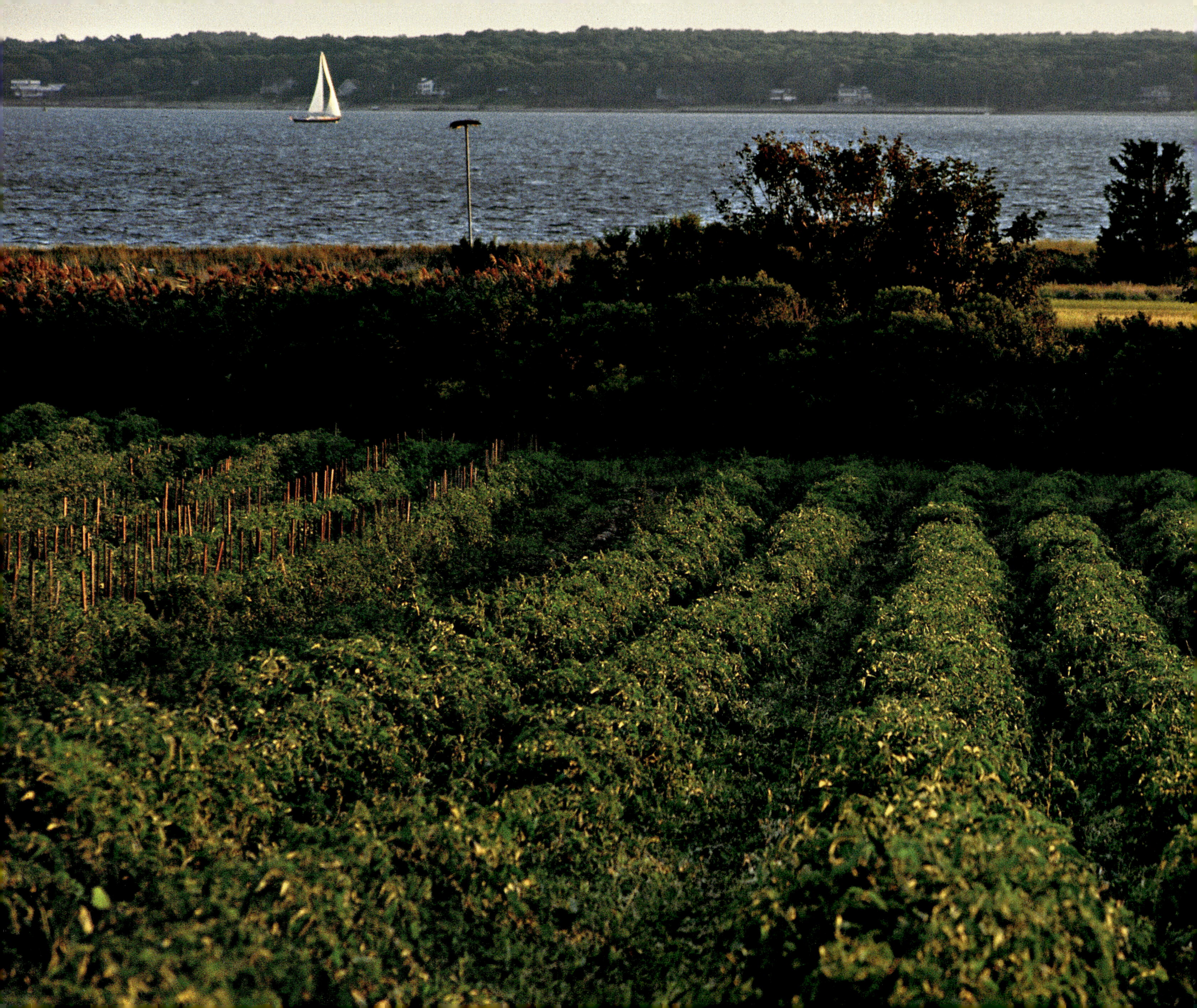

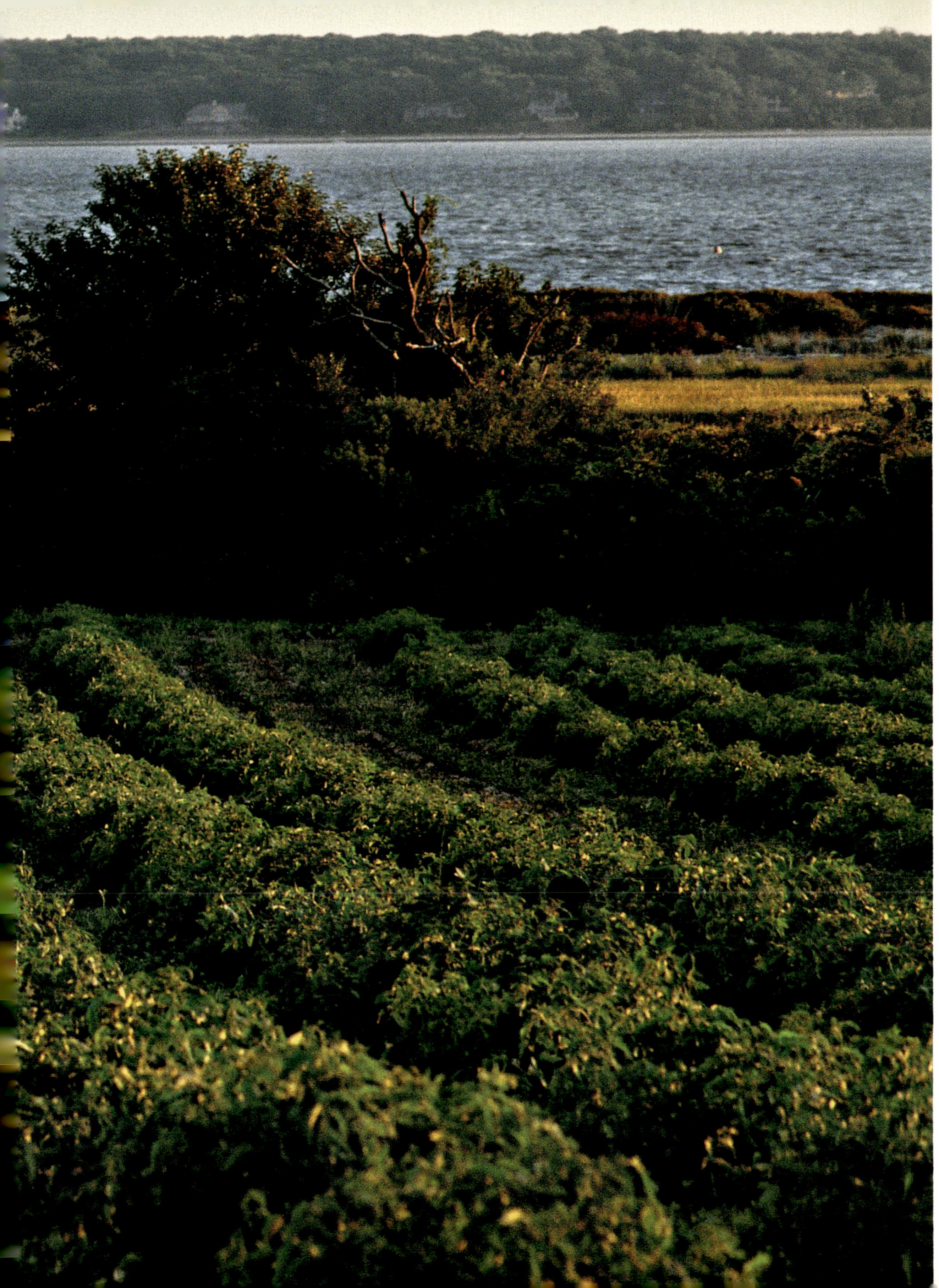

Latham's Farm, Orient

# Bay

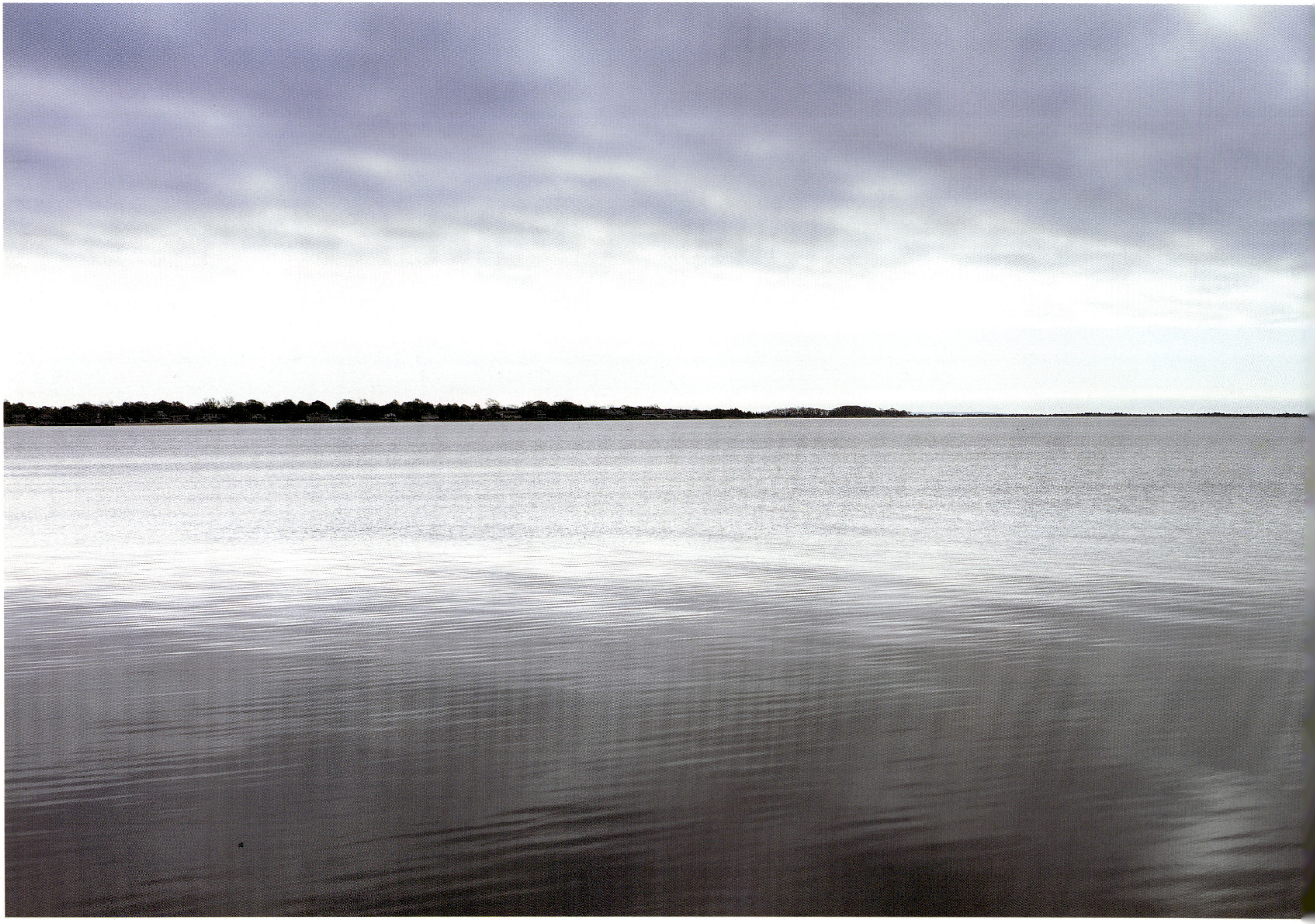

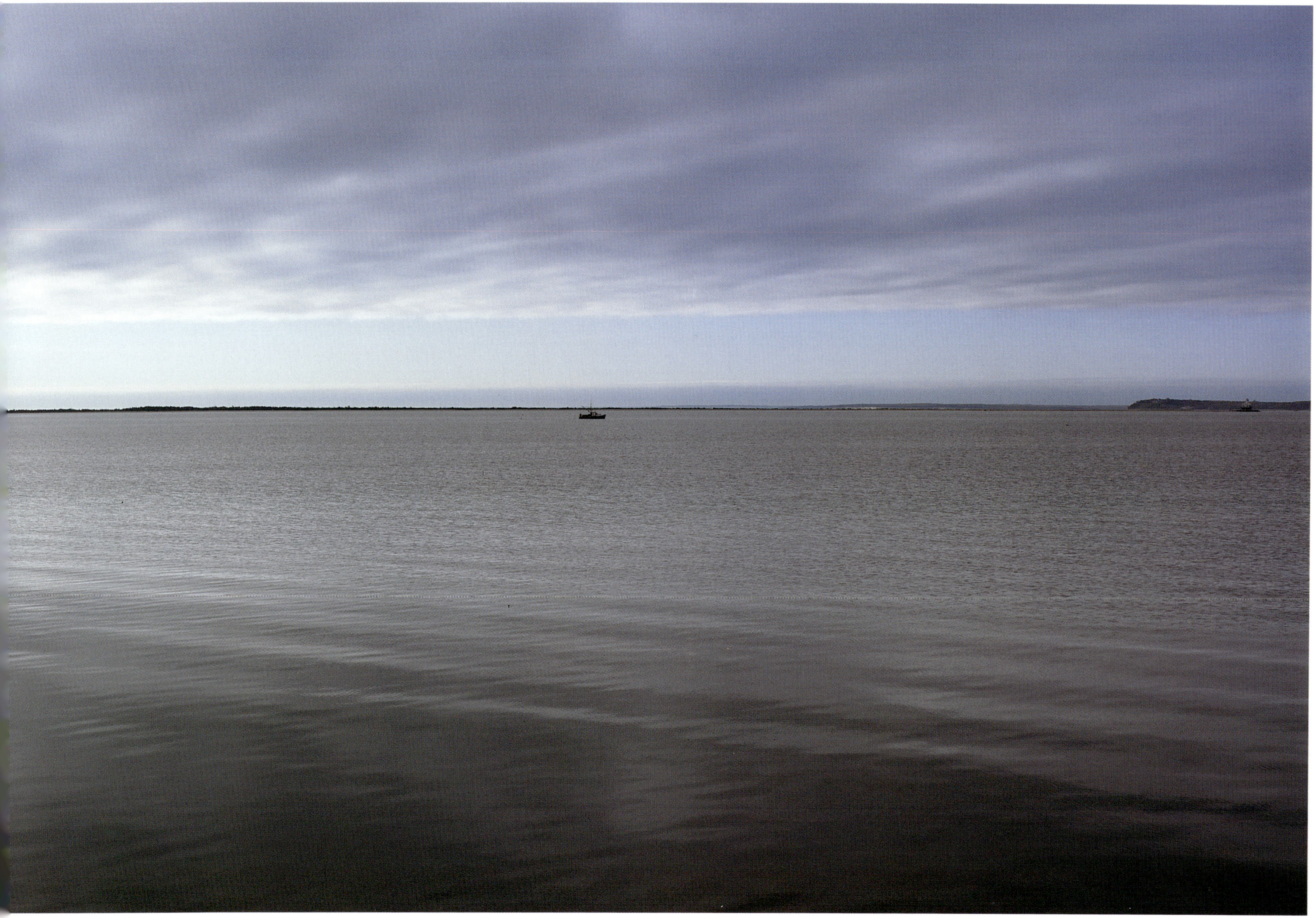

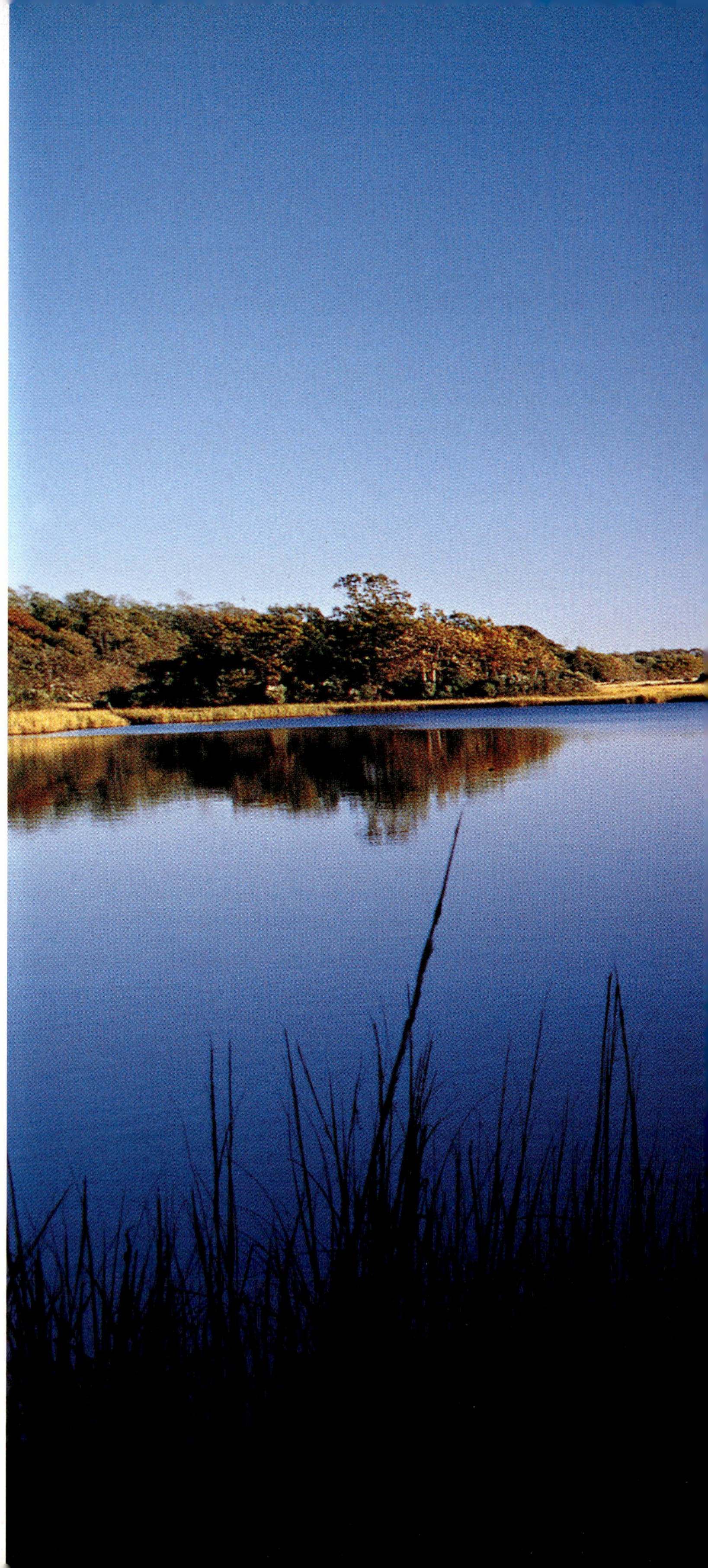

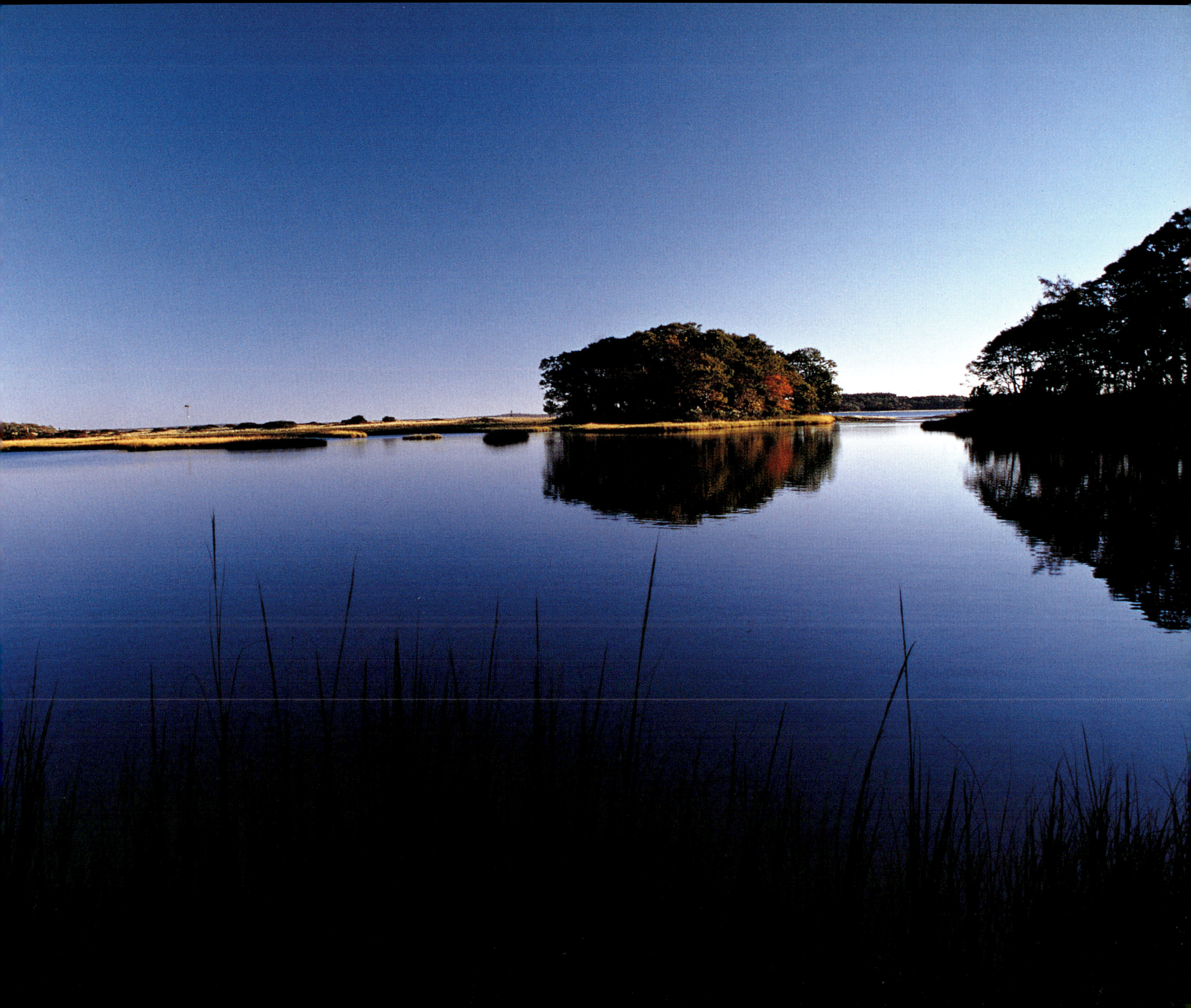

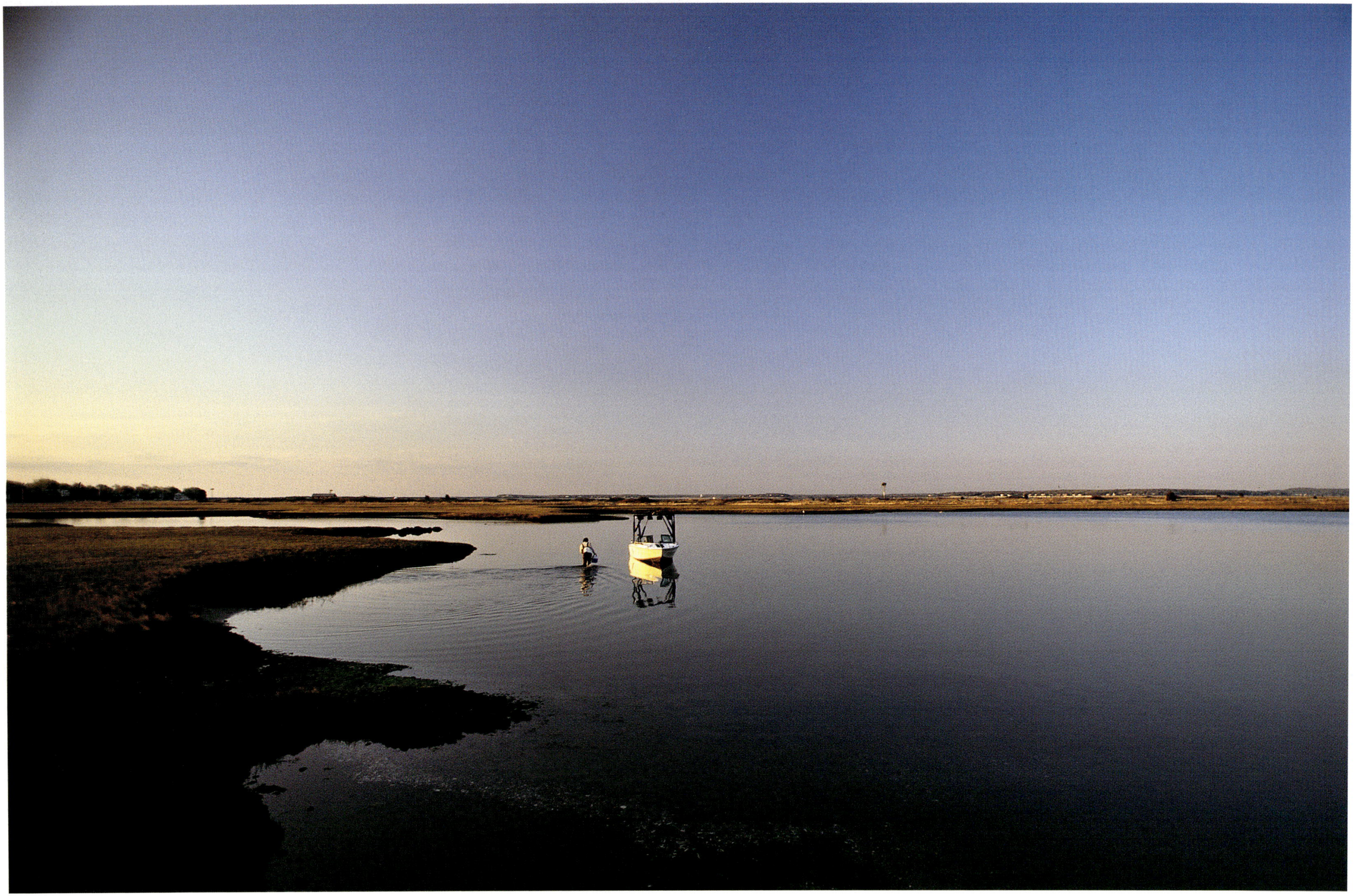

Orient Clam Shack, Orient

→ Heron, Southold → Dering Harbor, Shelter Island

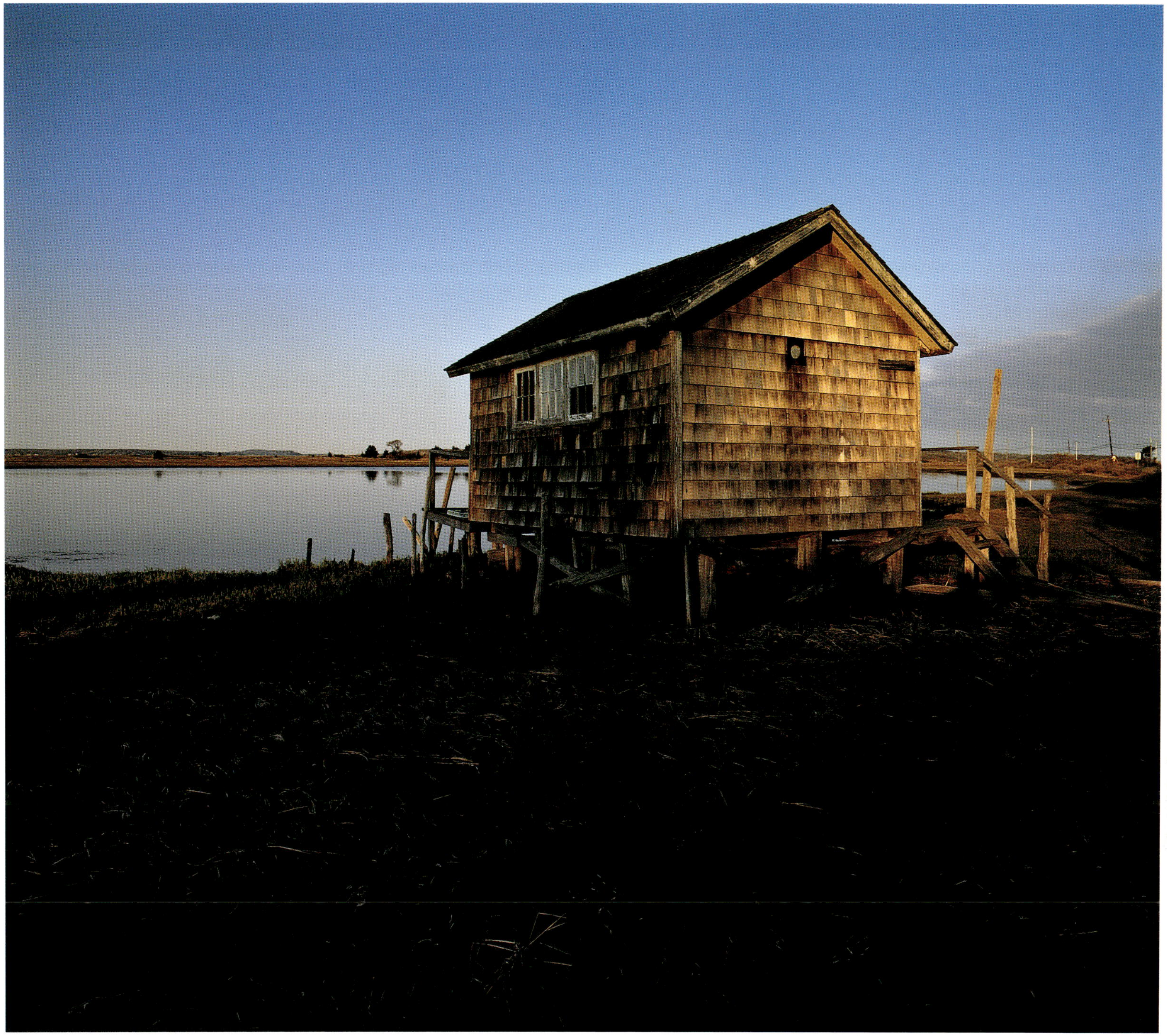

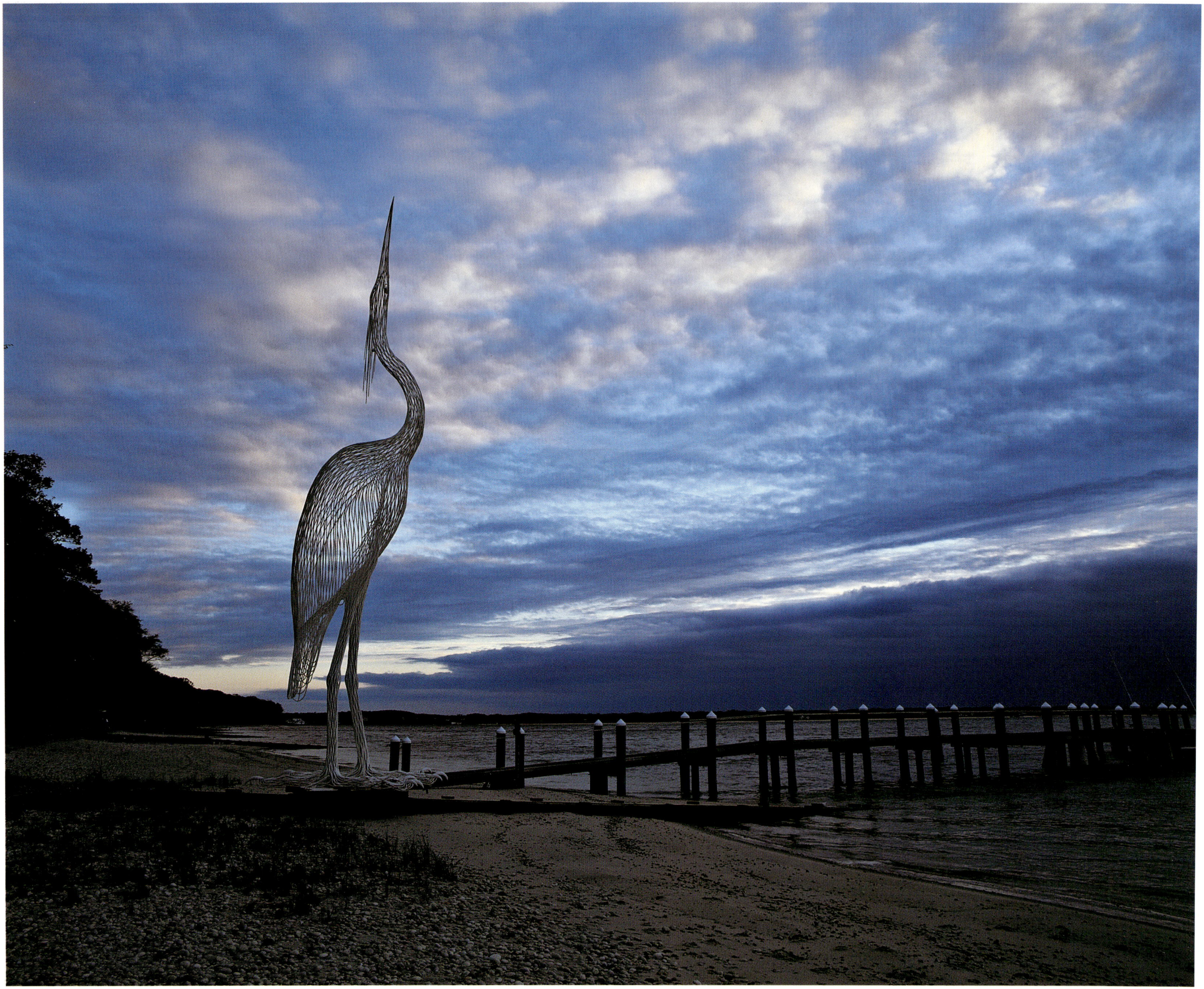

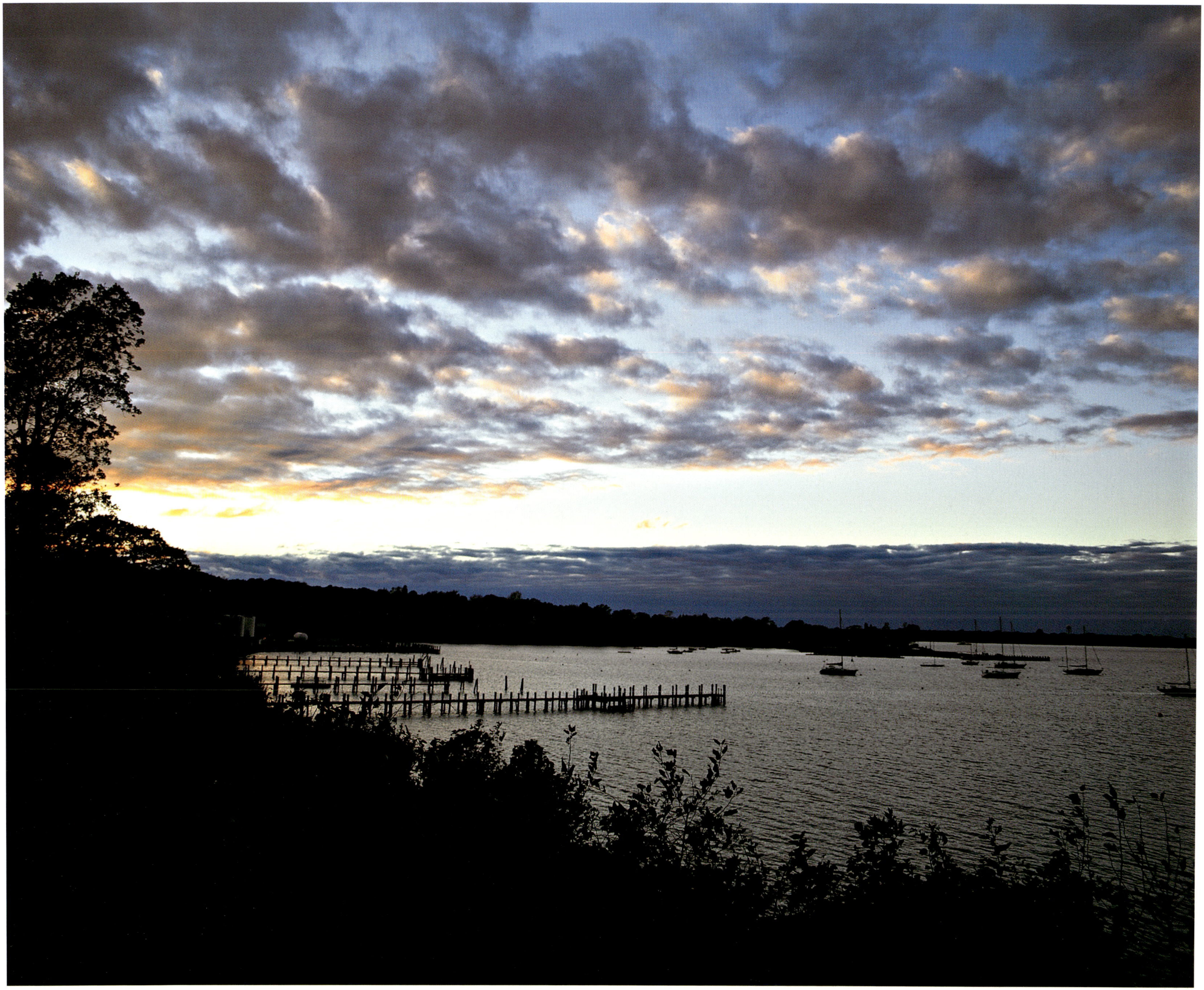

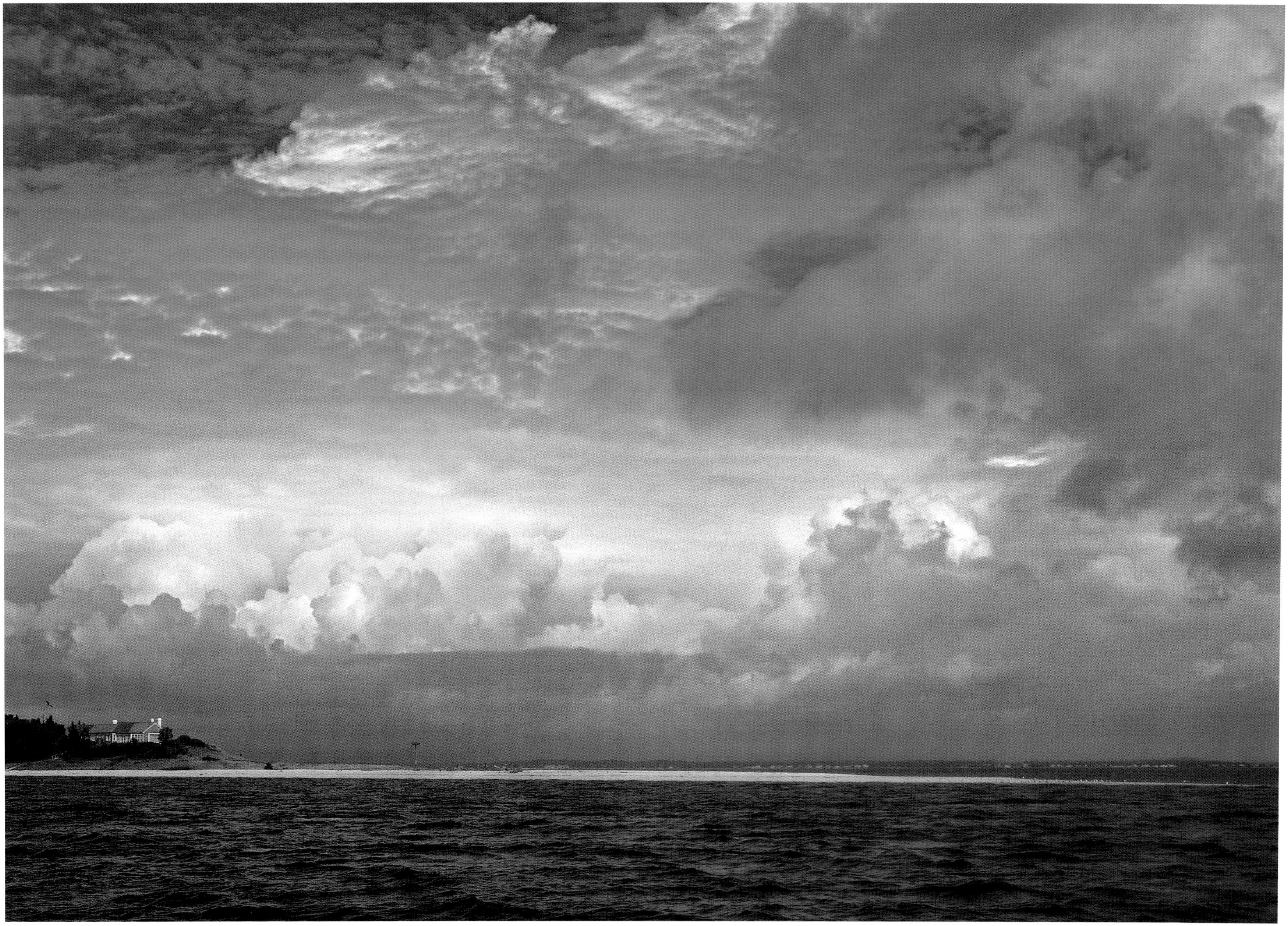

Nassau Point, Cutchogue     Peconic River, Riverhead

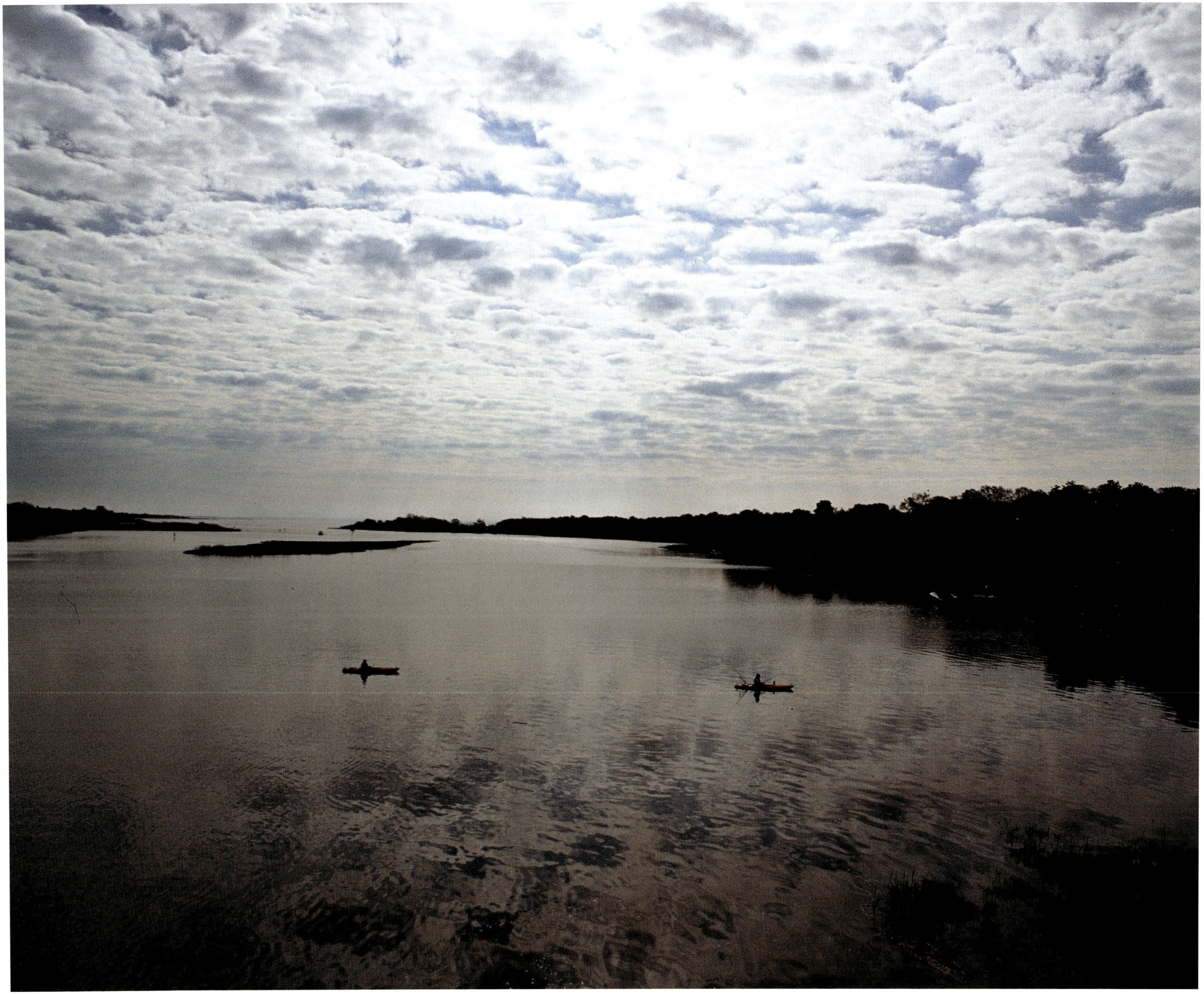

Cutchogue Harbor, New Suffolk

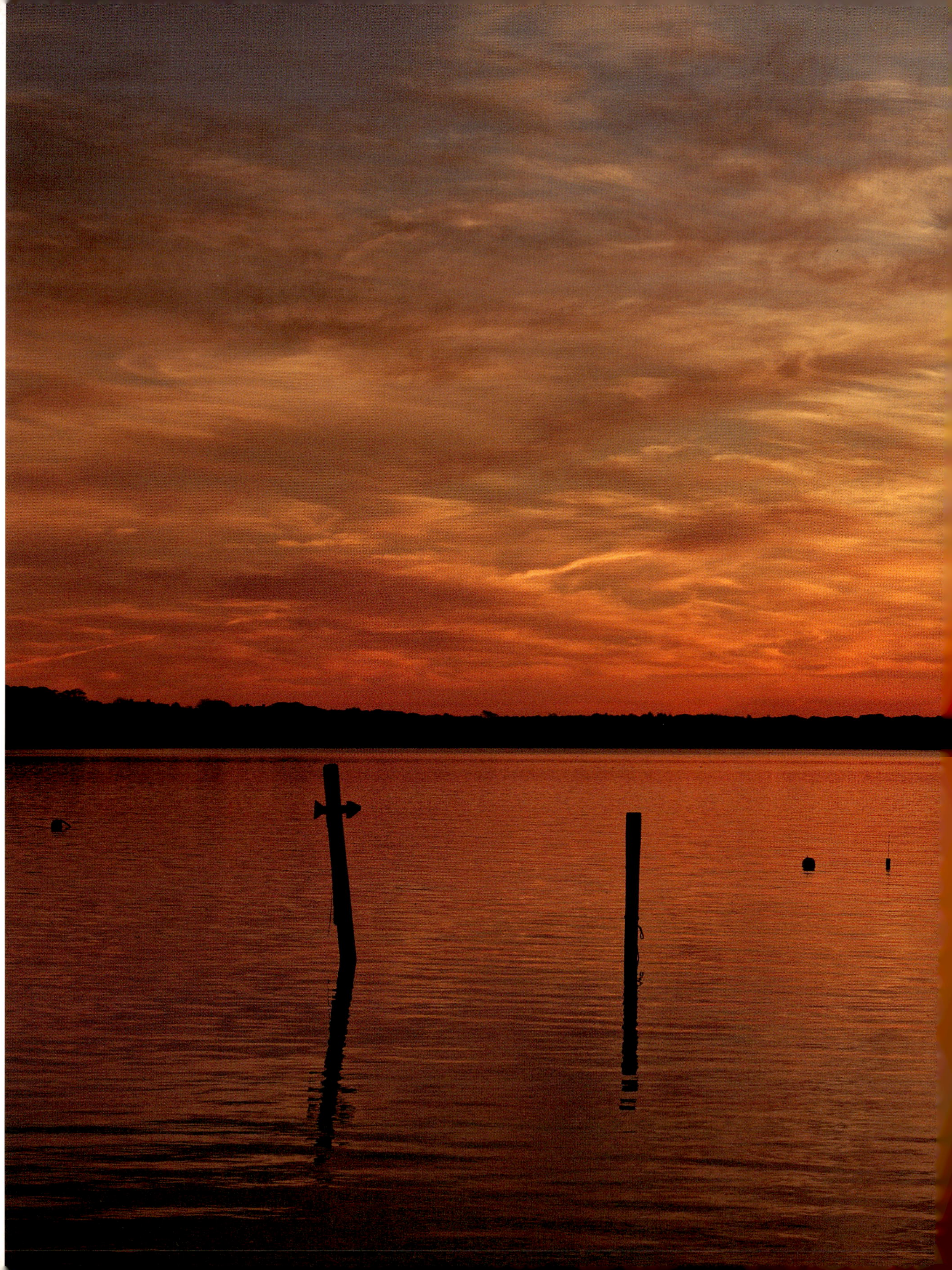

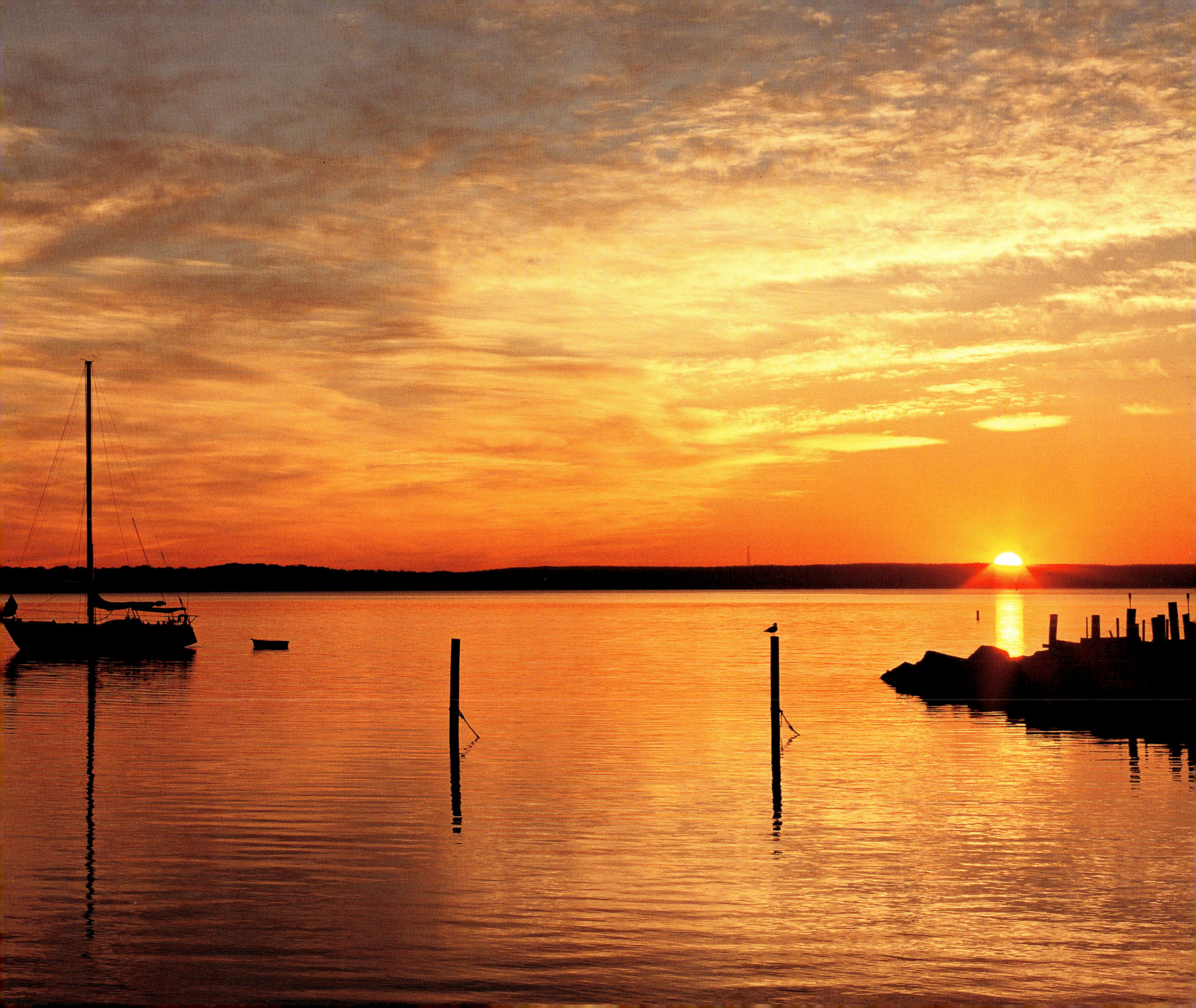

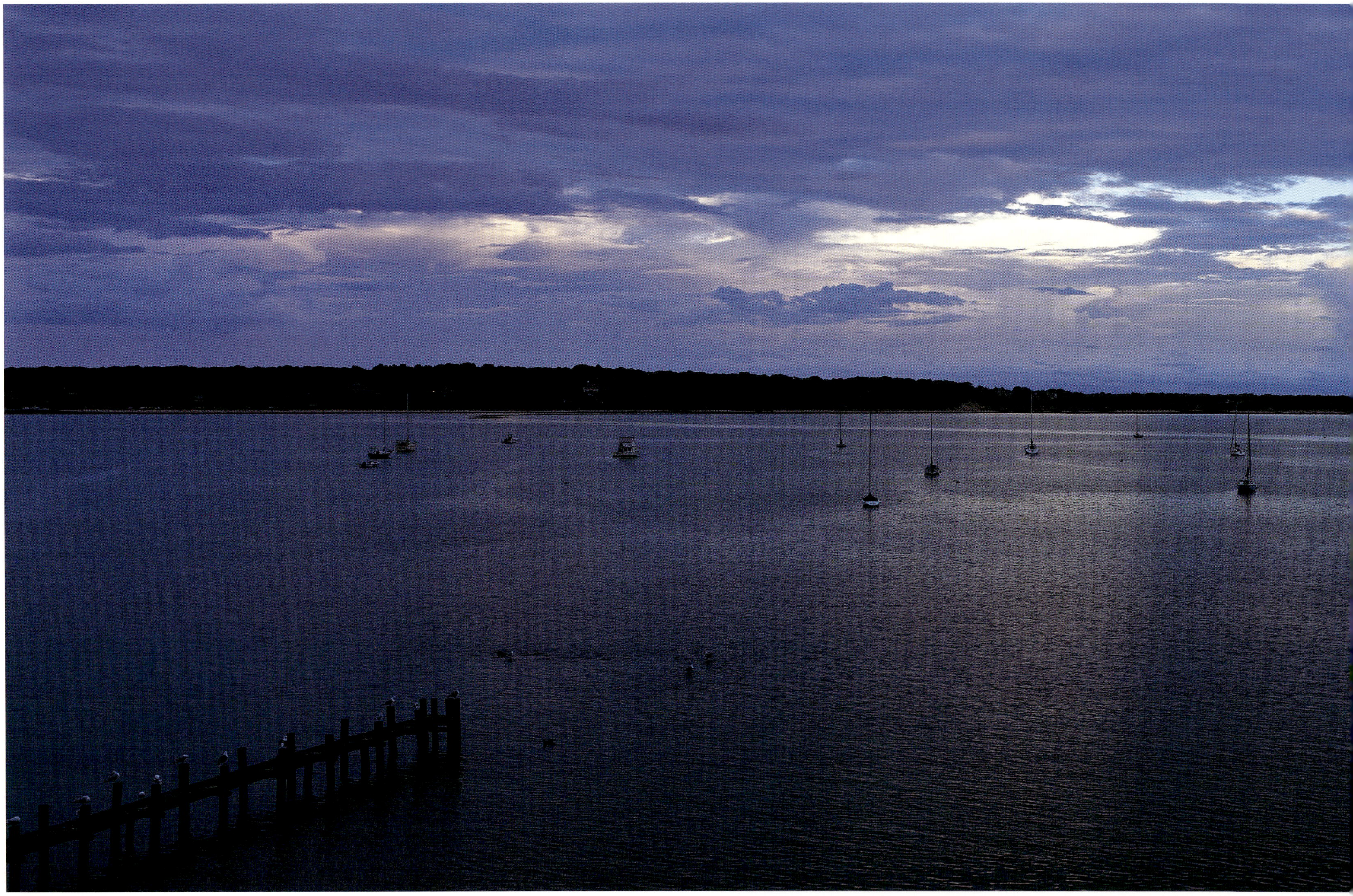

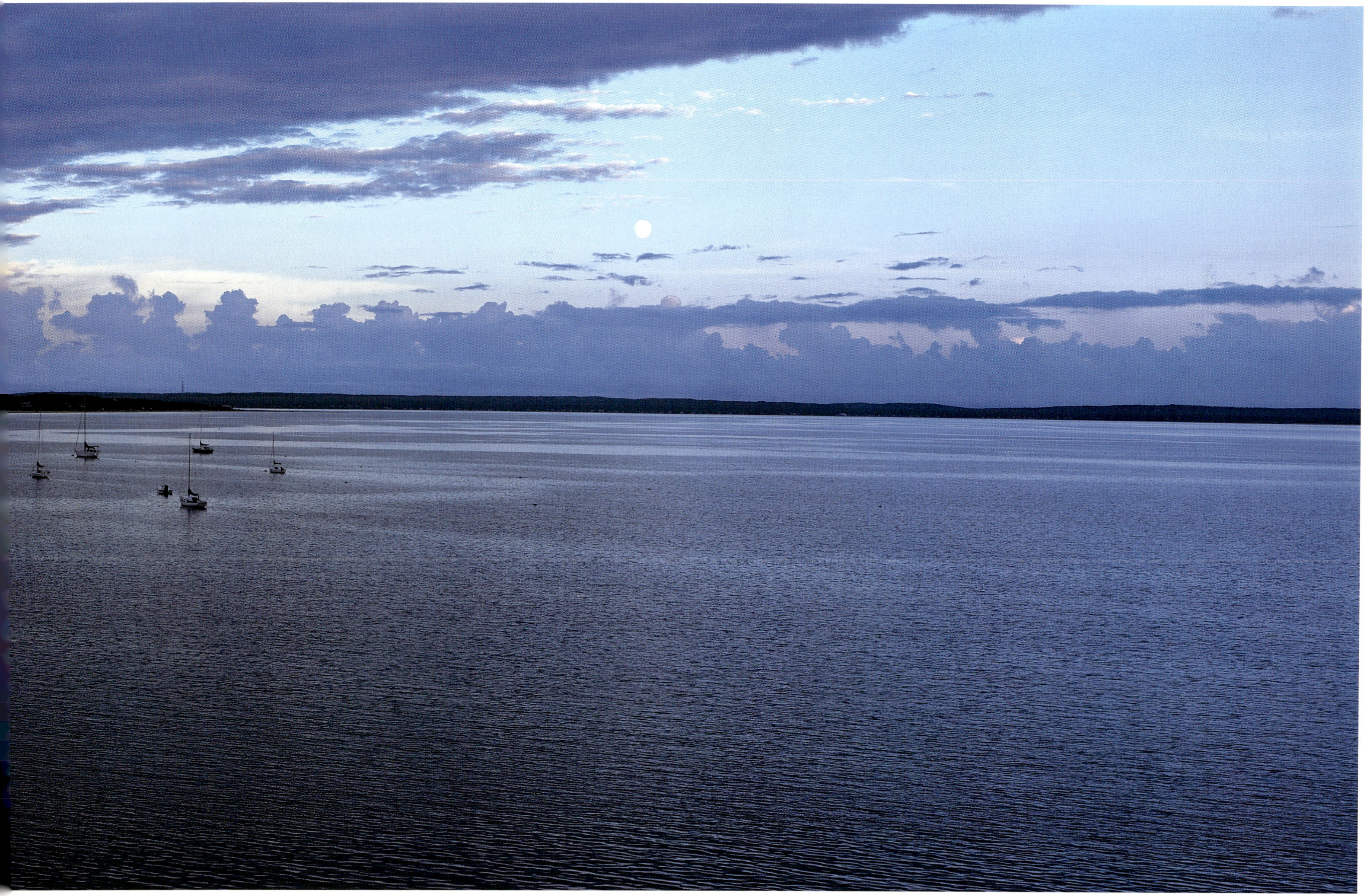

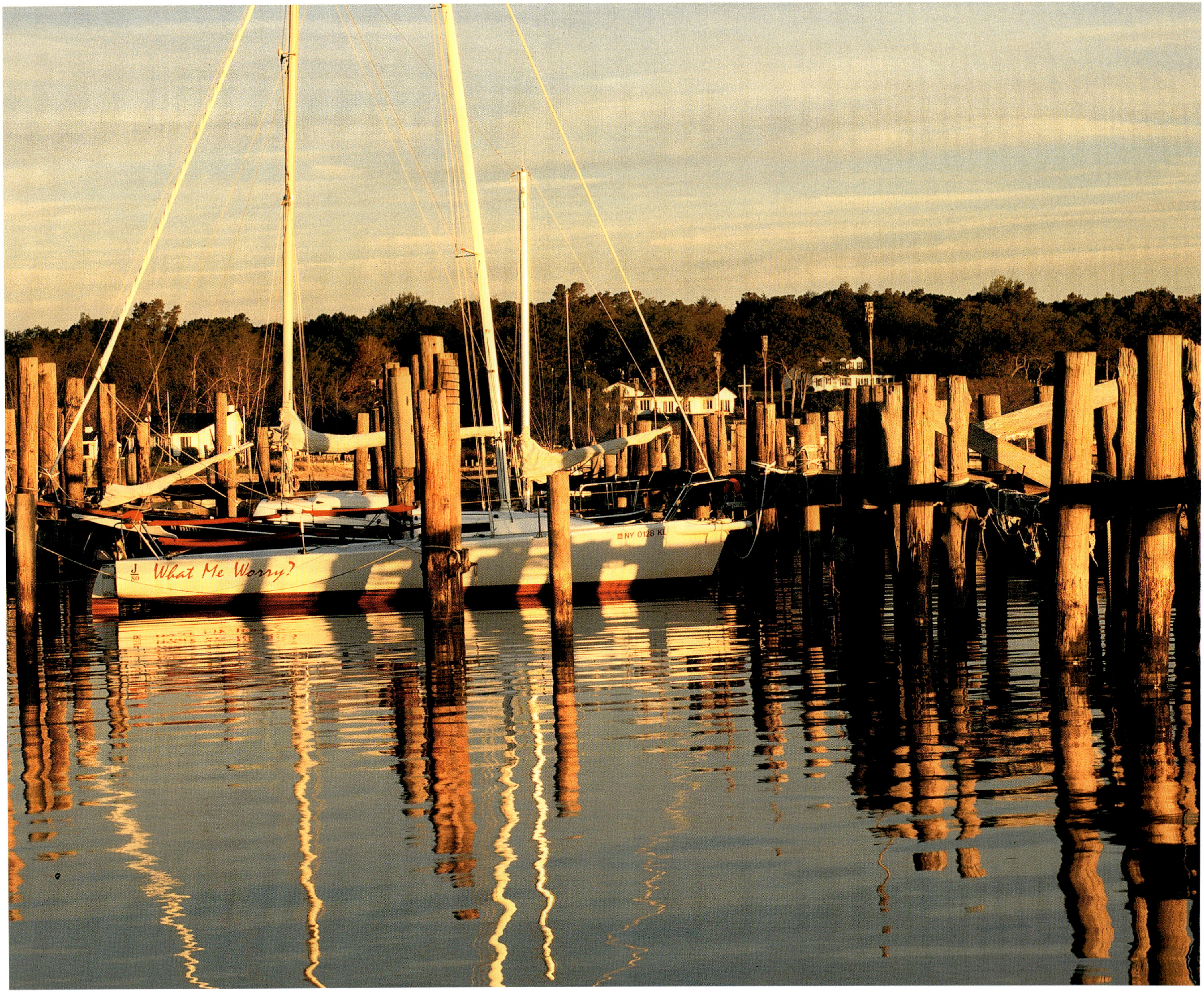
What Me Worry?
NY 0128 KL

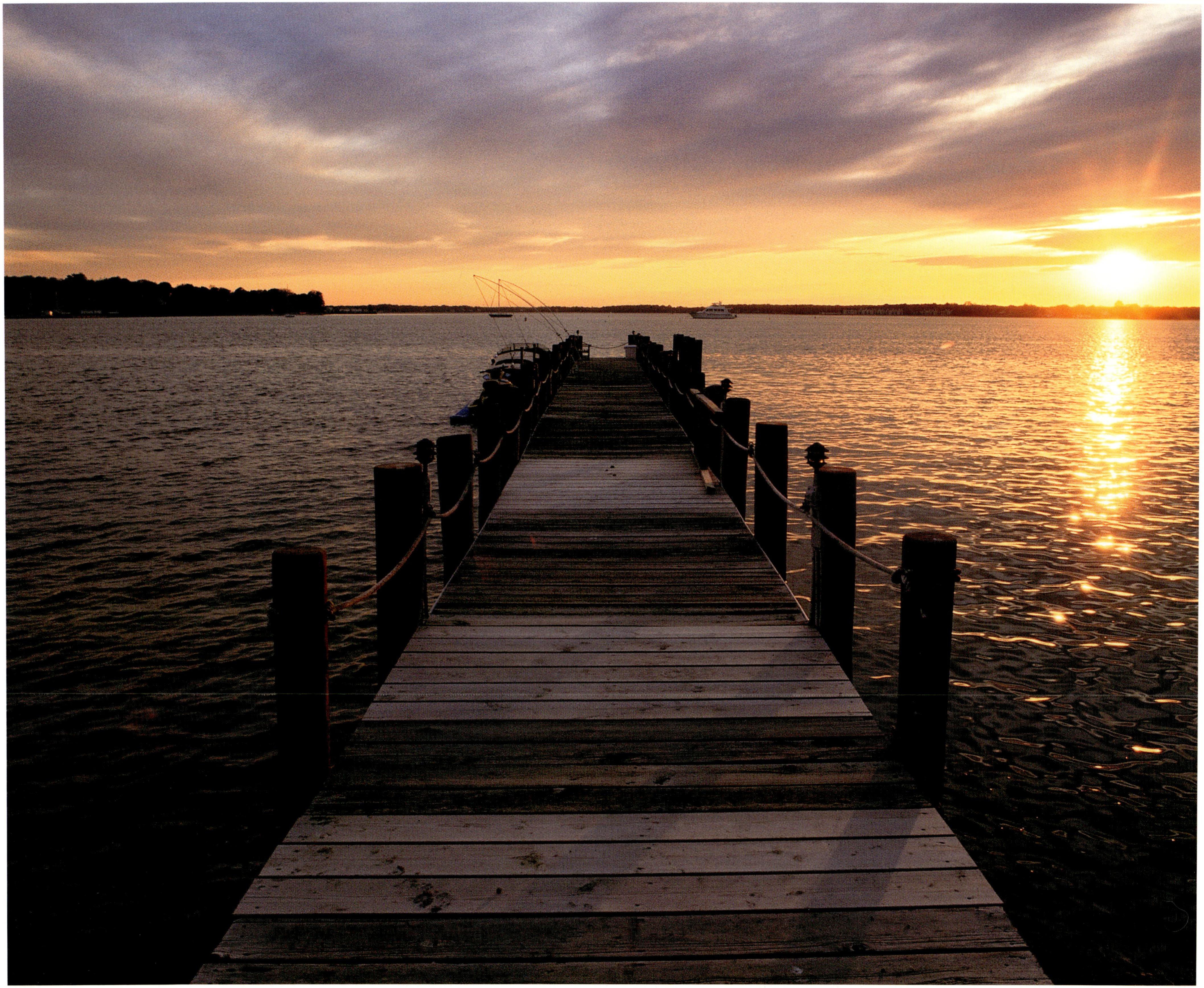

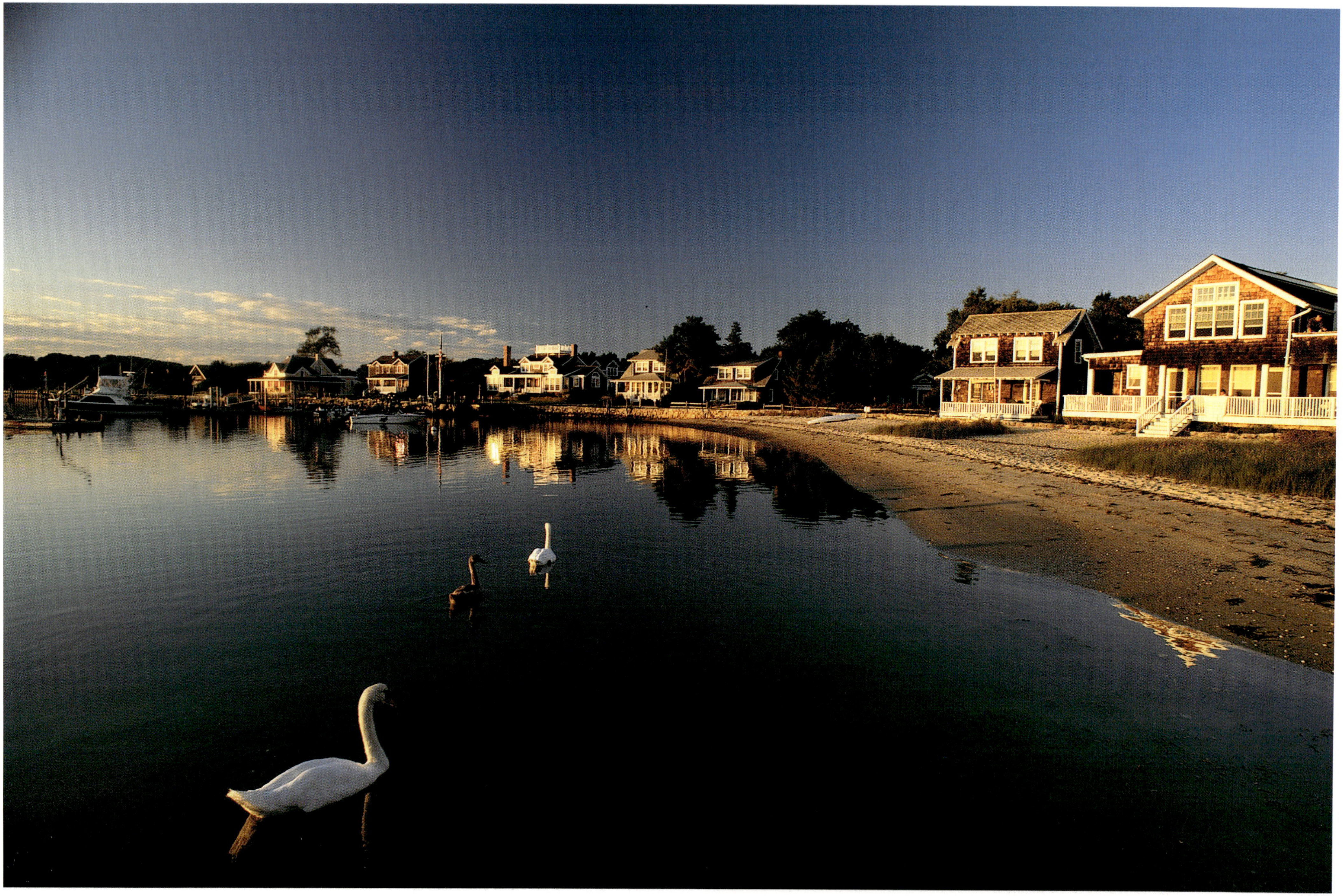

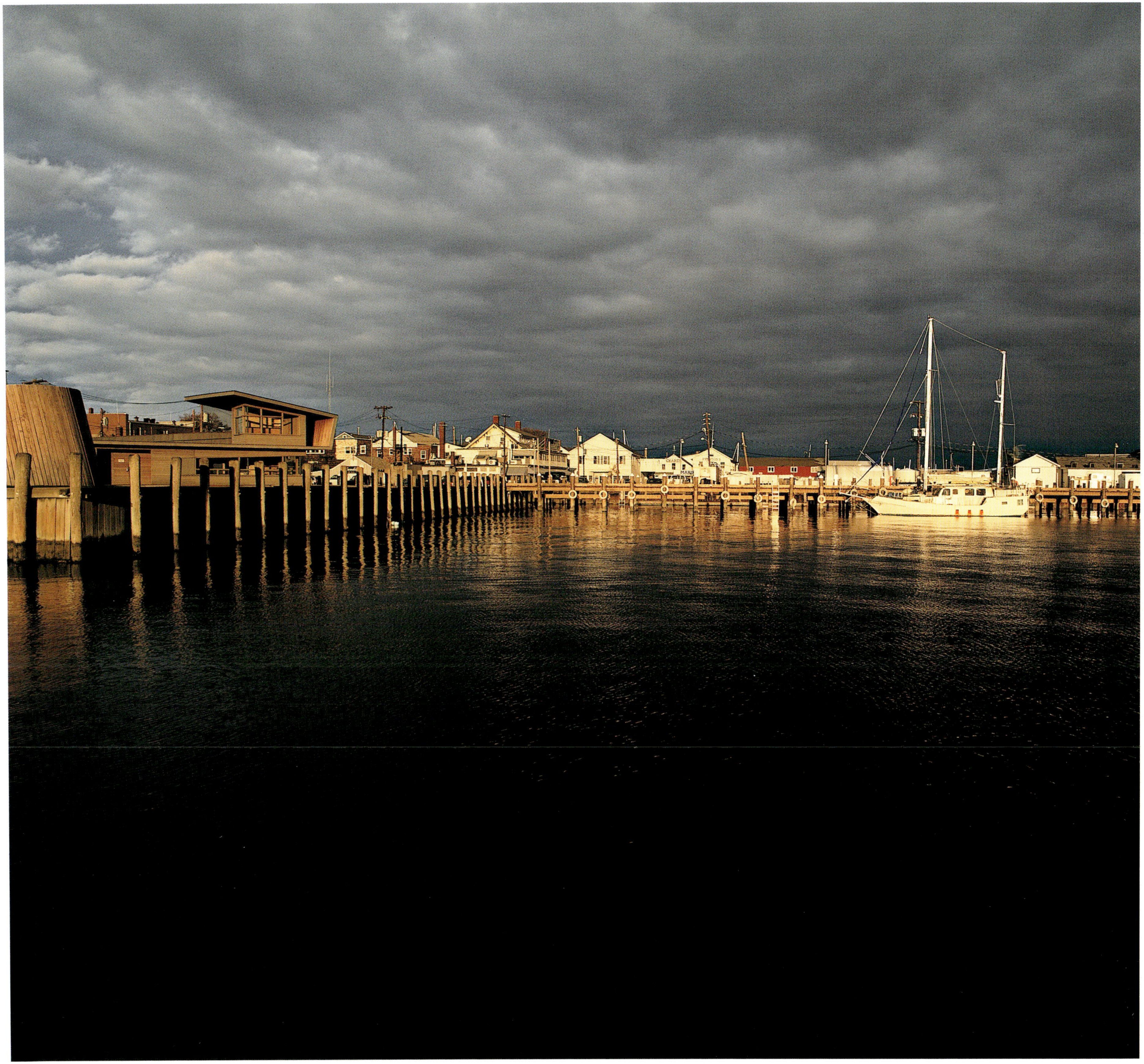

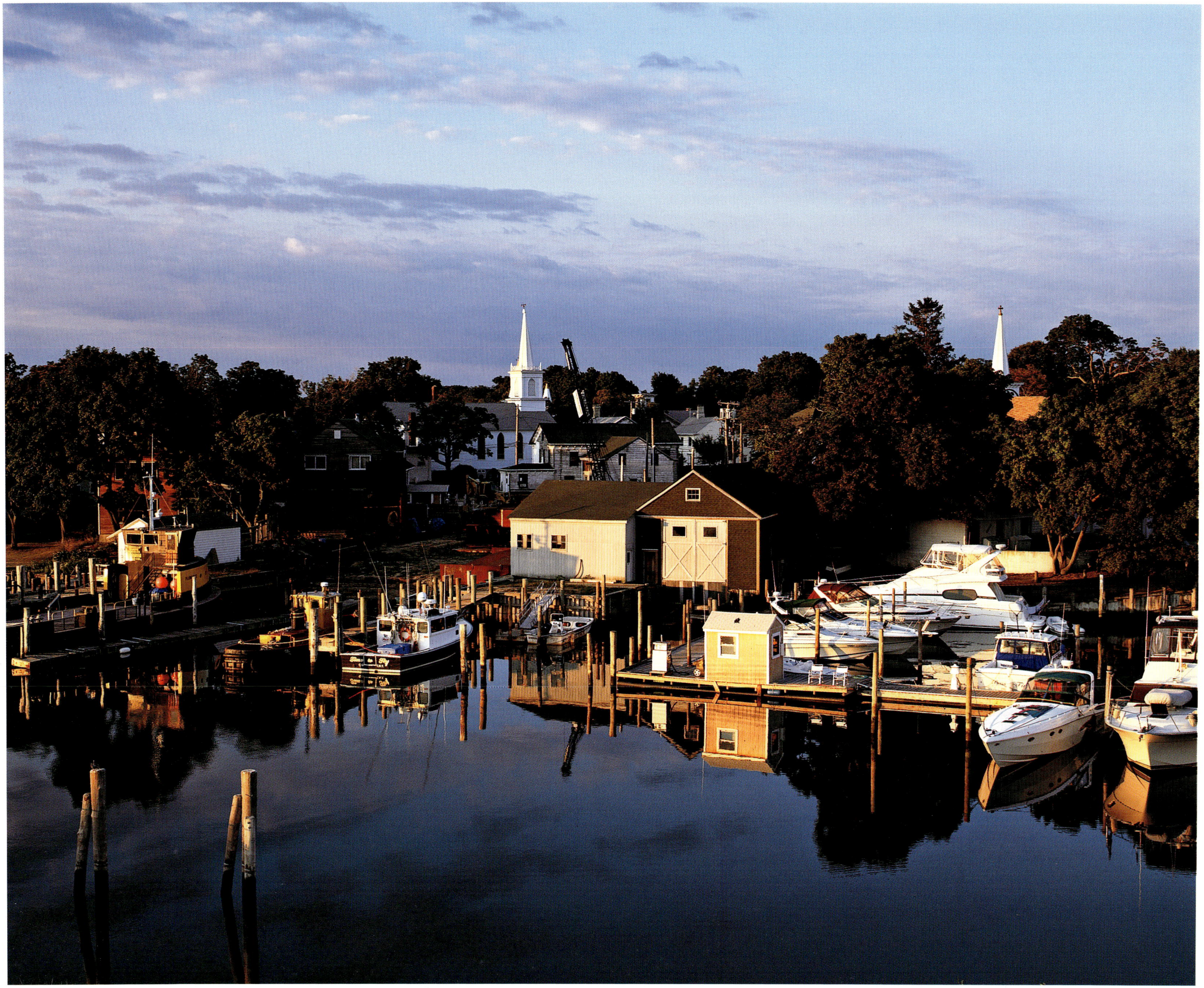

→ Breezy Shores, Southold → Greenport

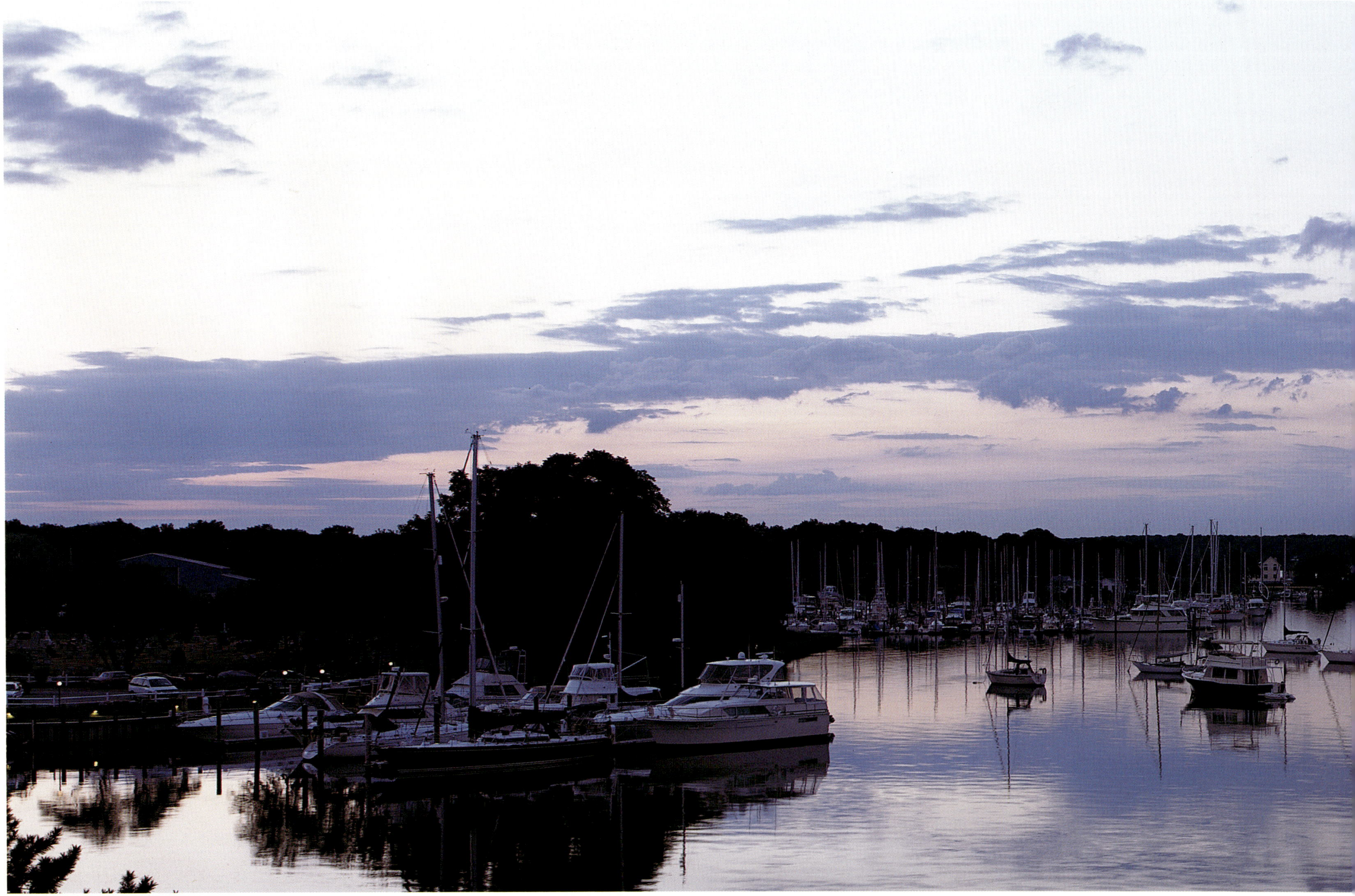

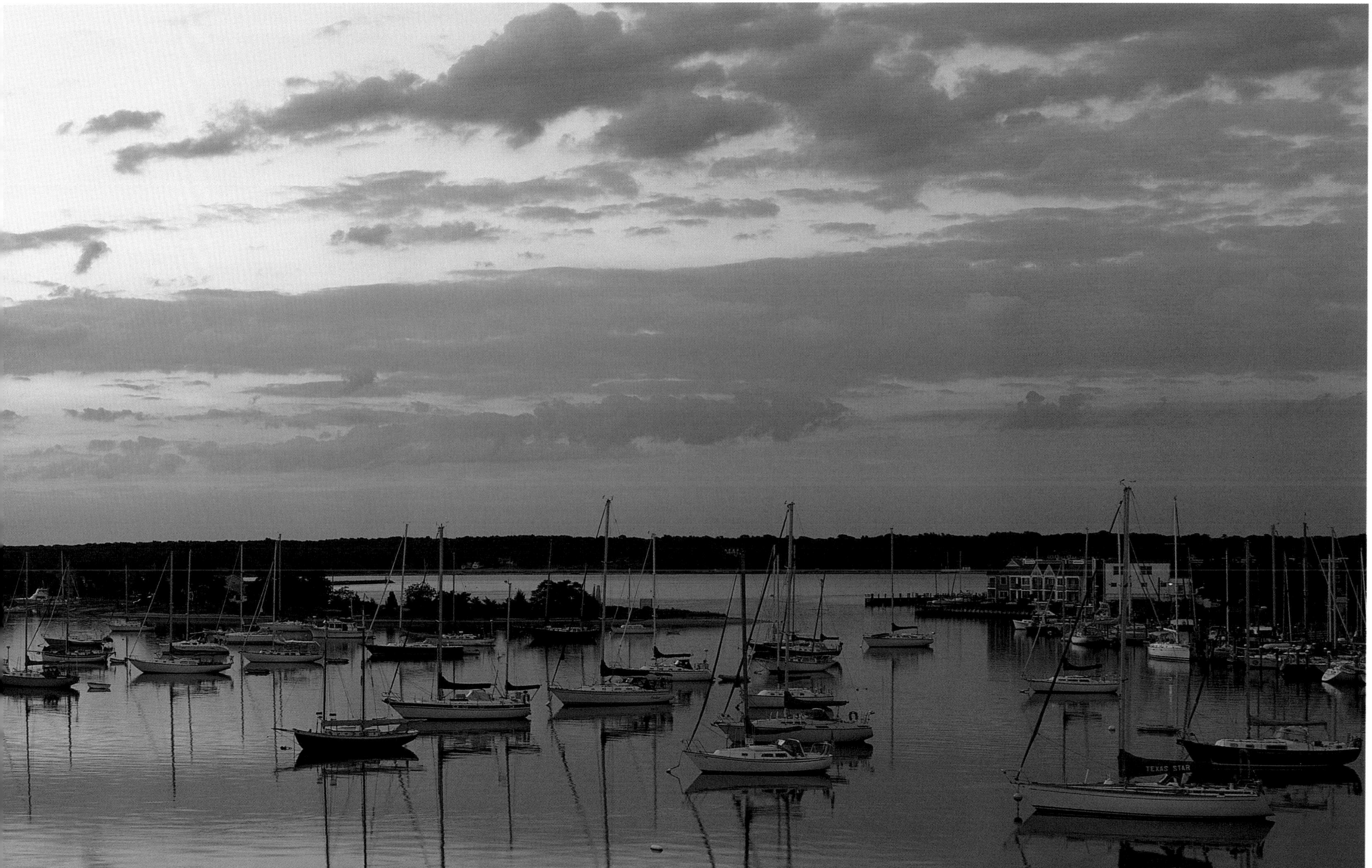
TEXAS STAR

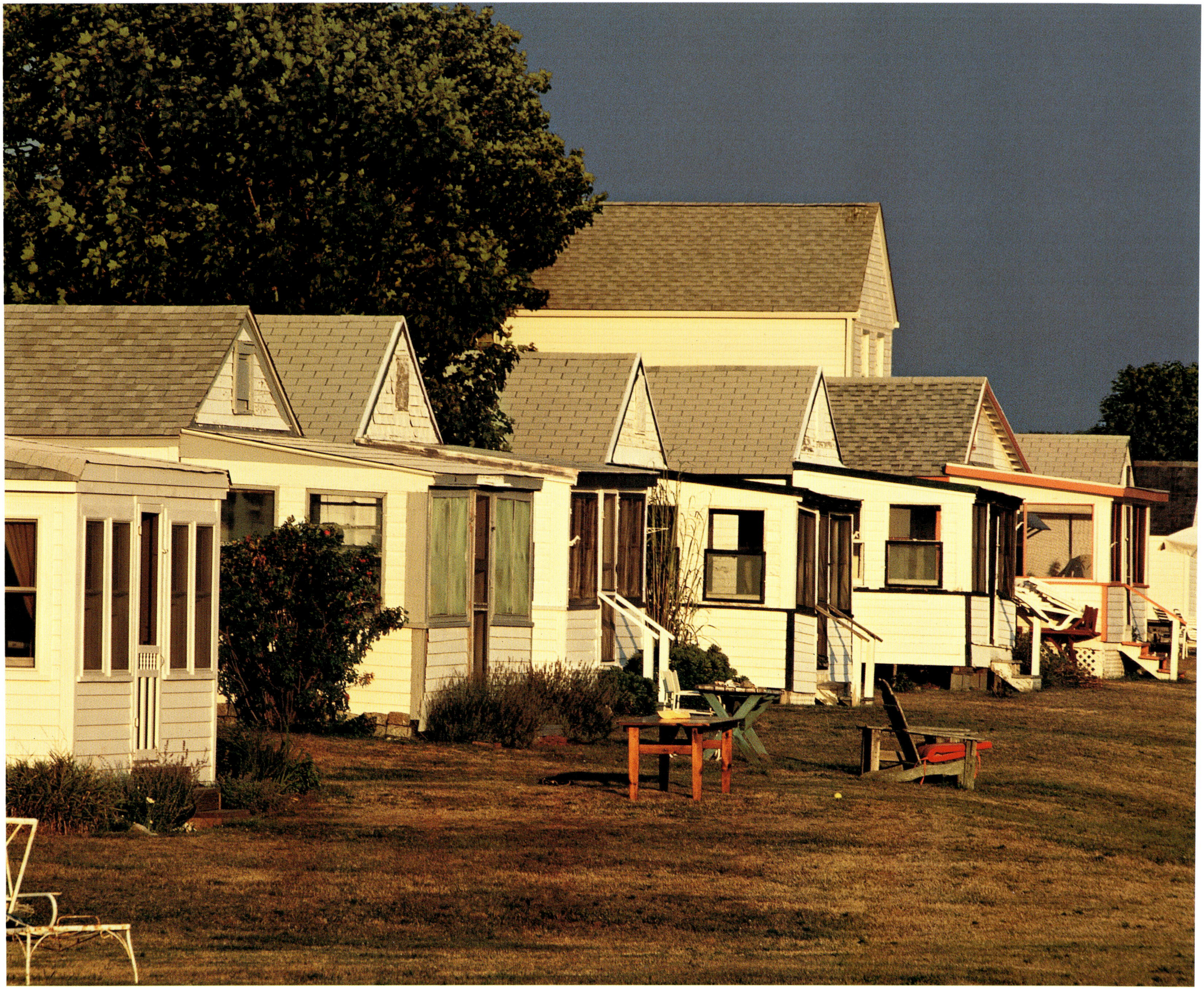

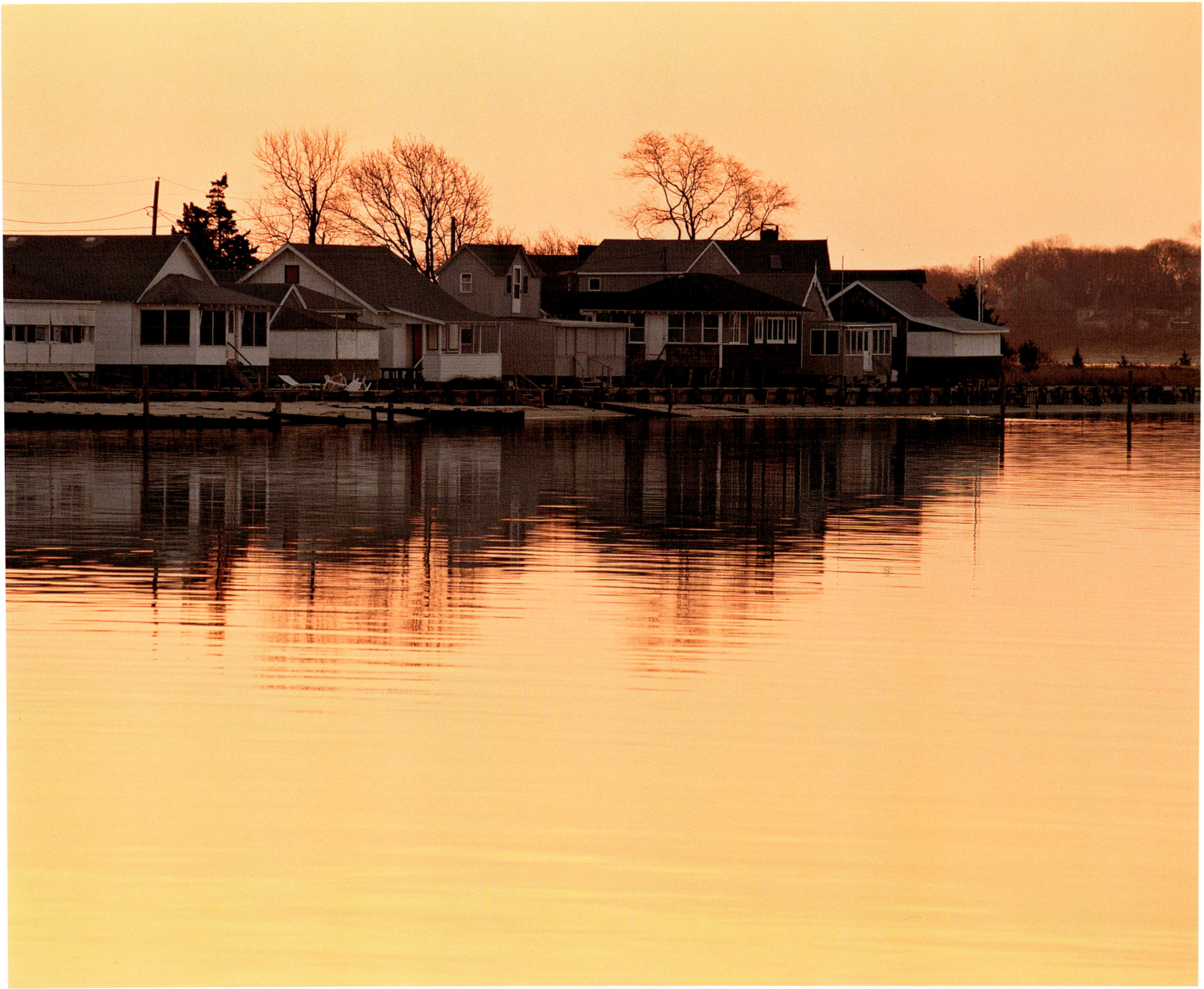

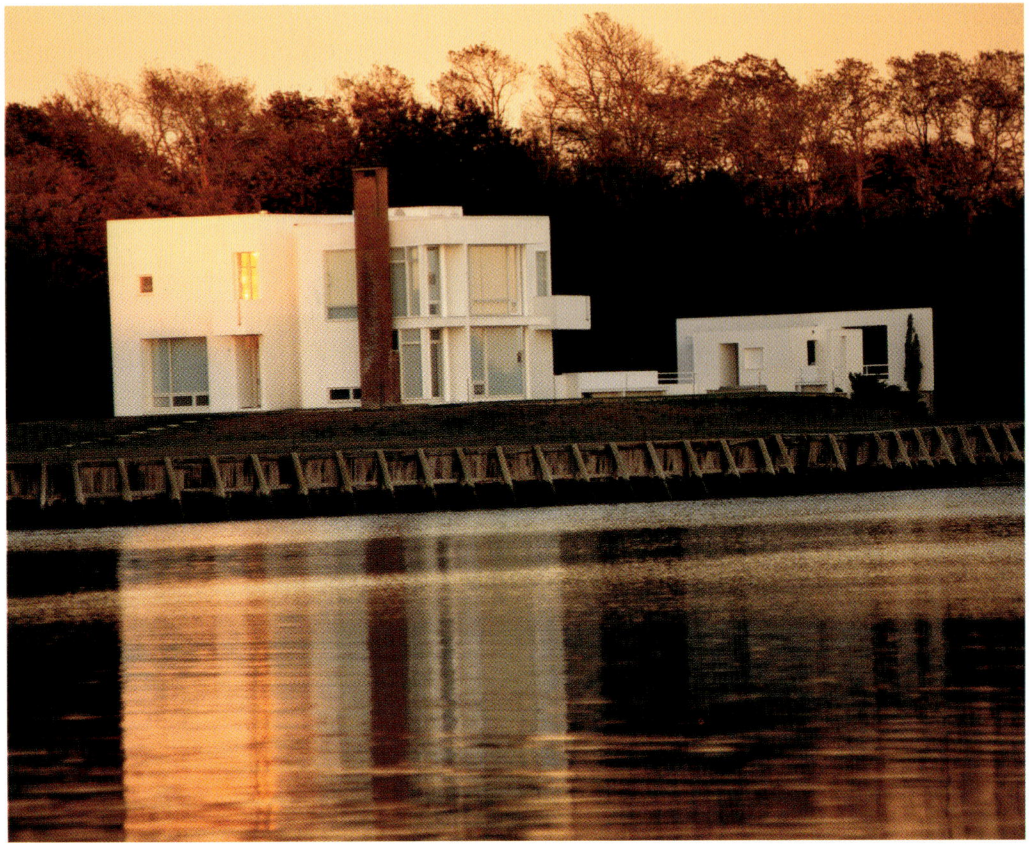

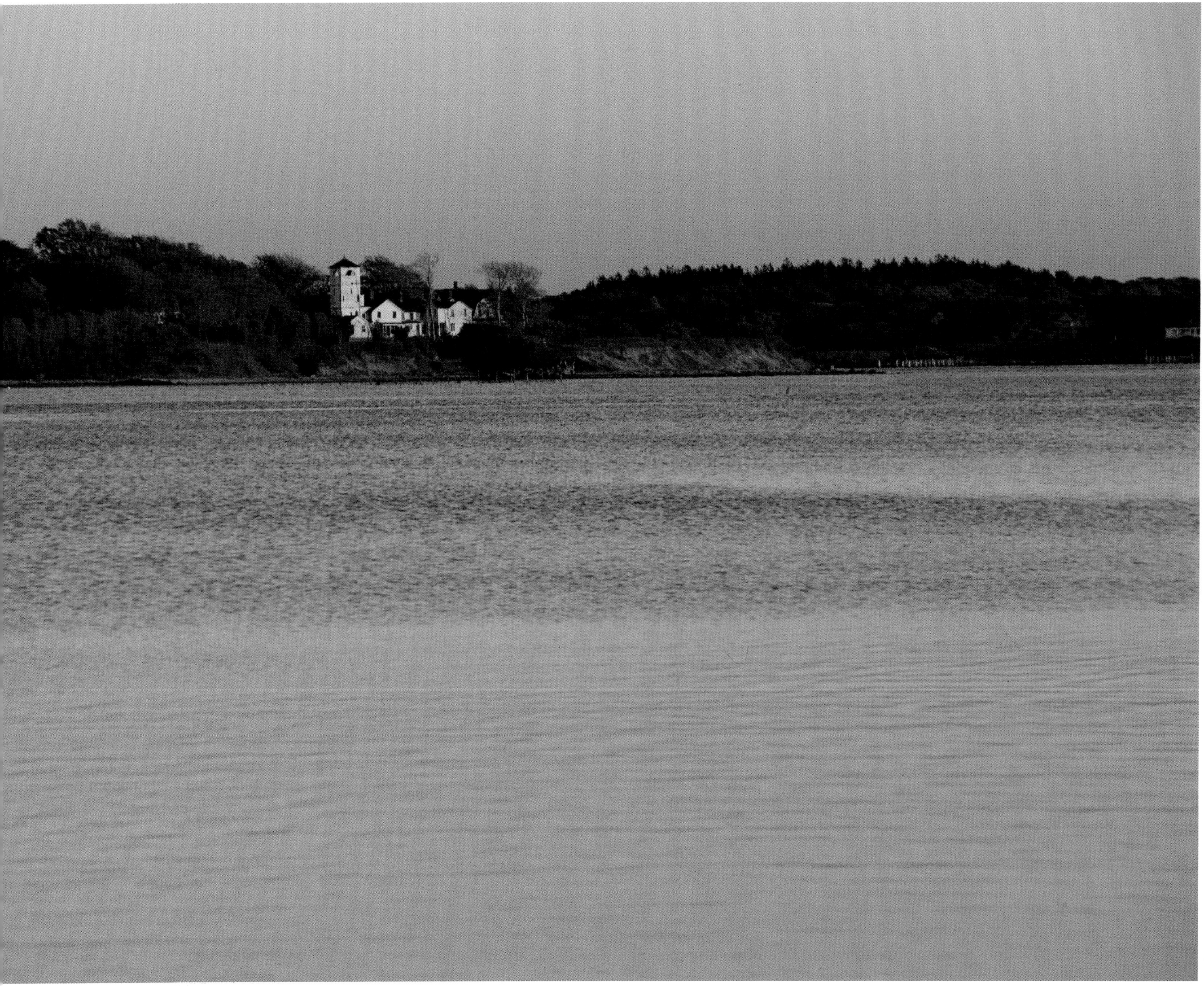

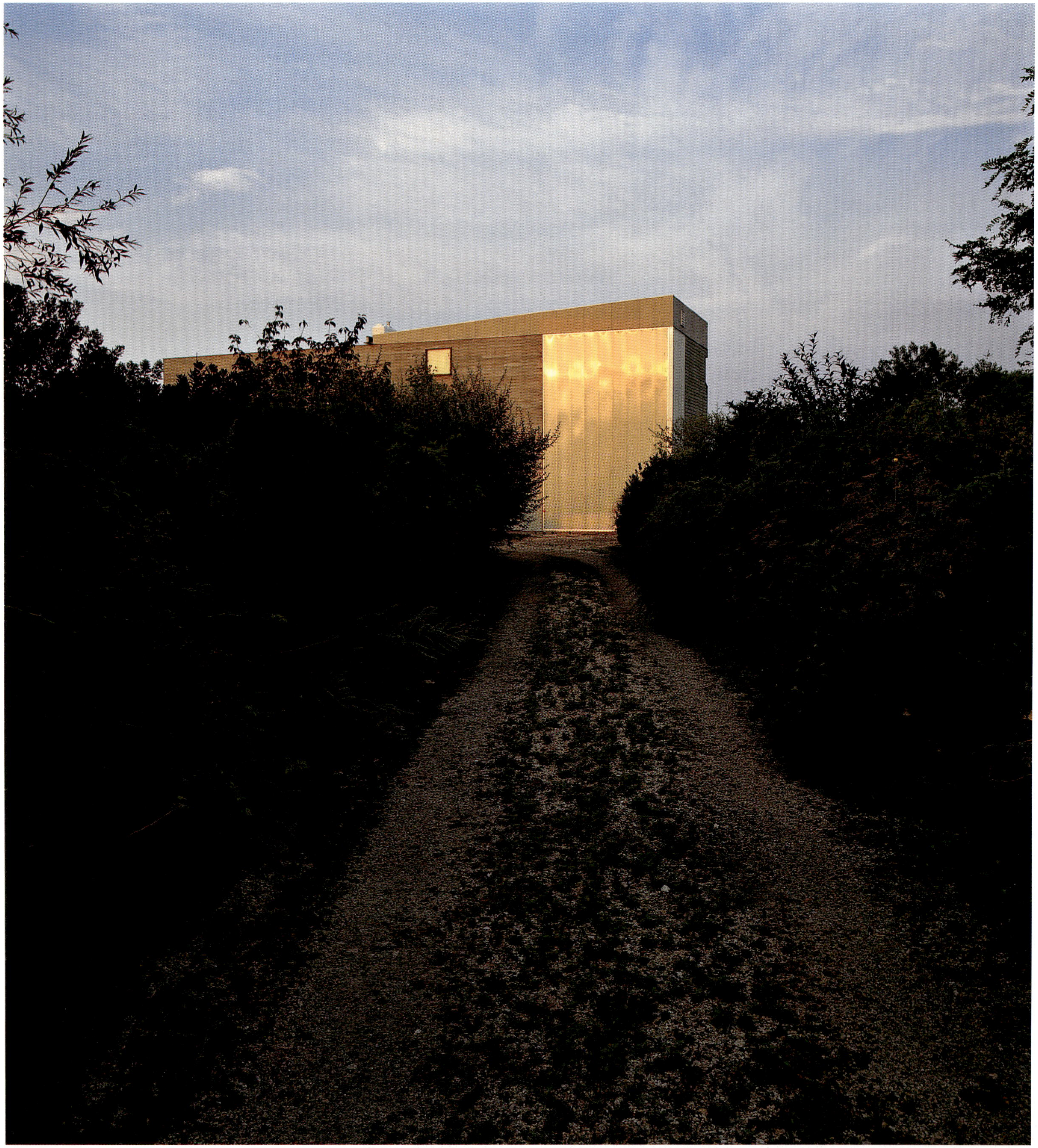

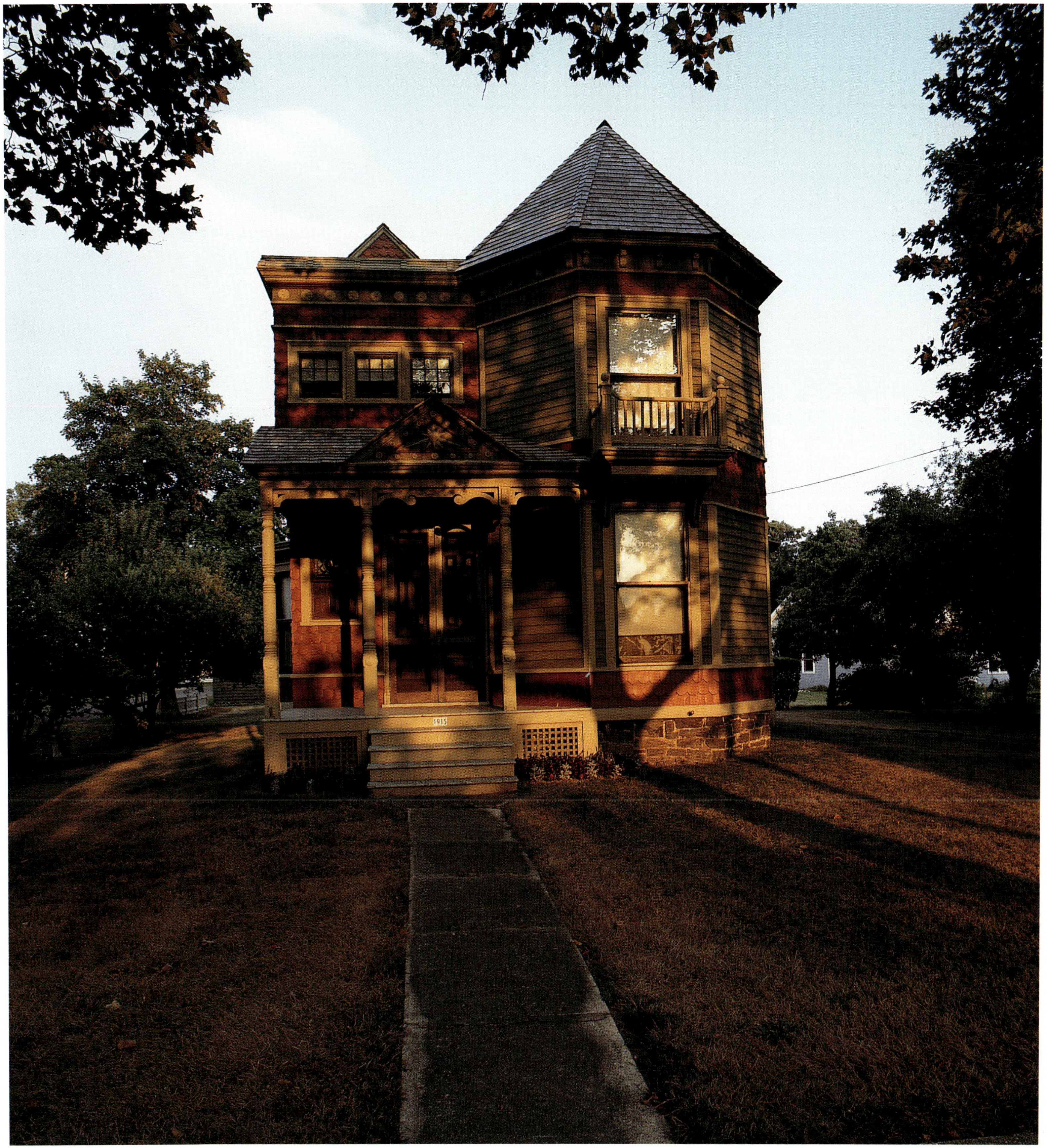
1915

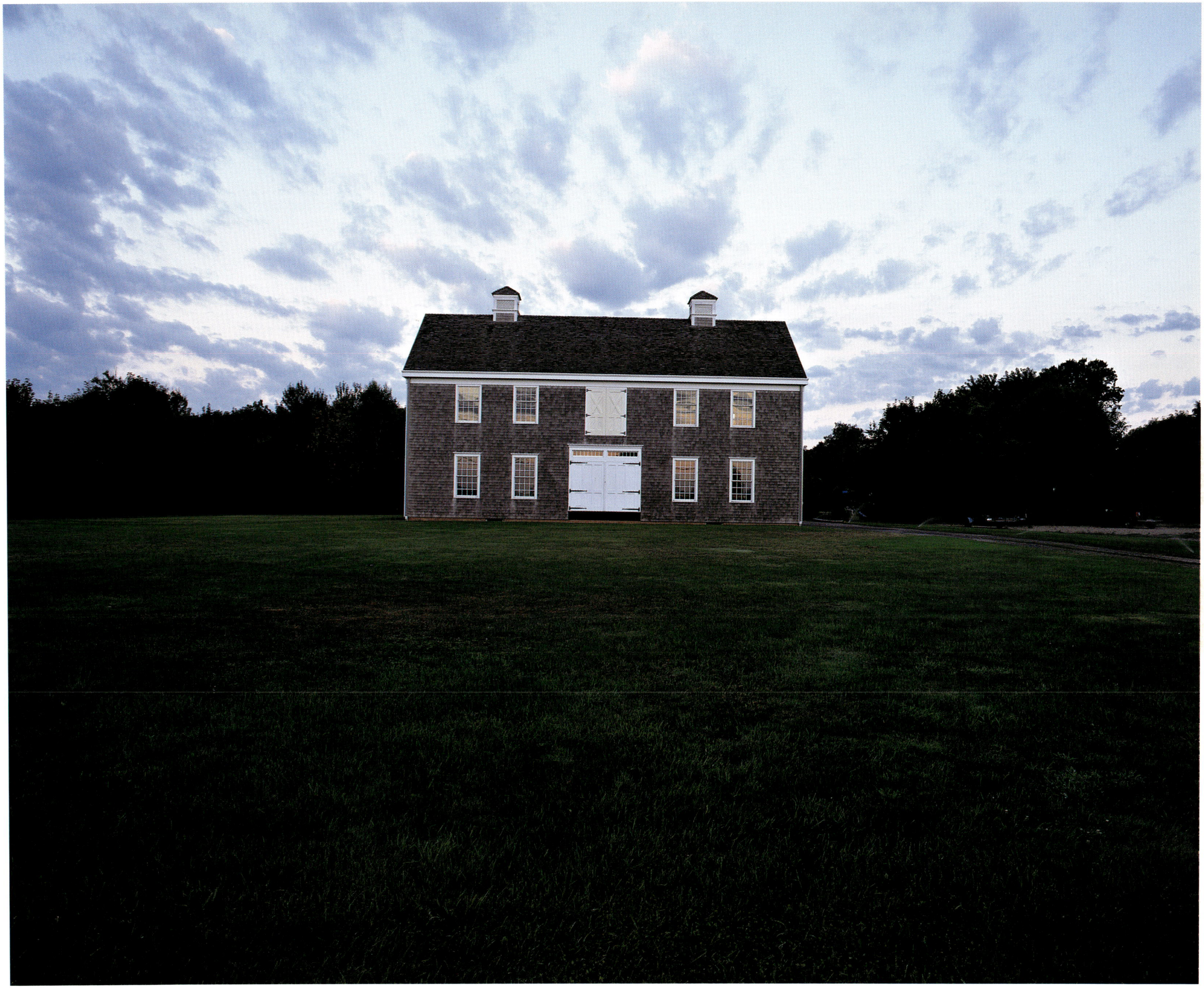

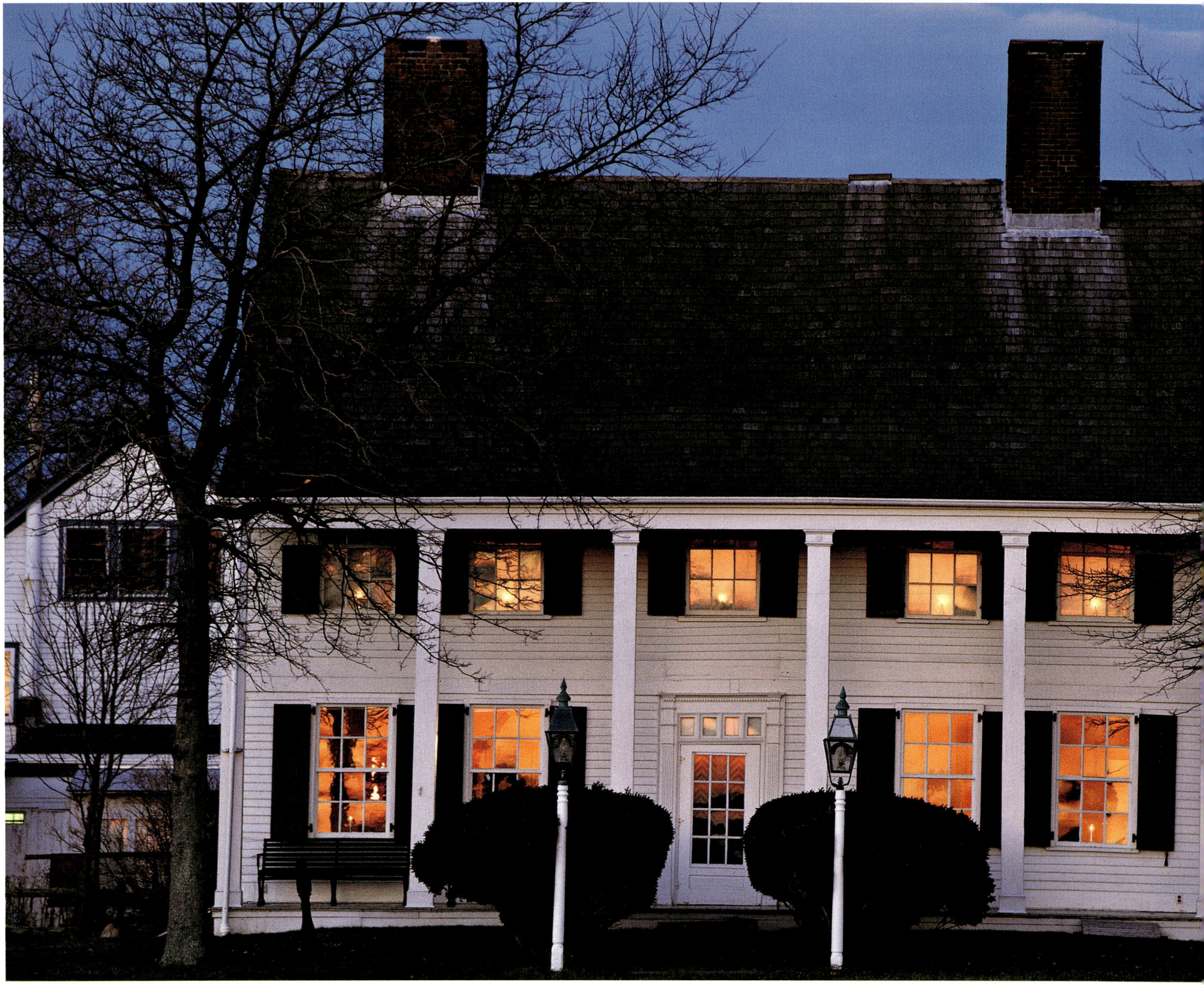

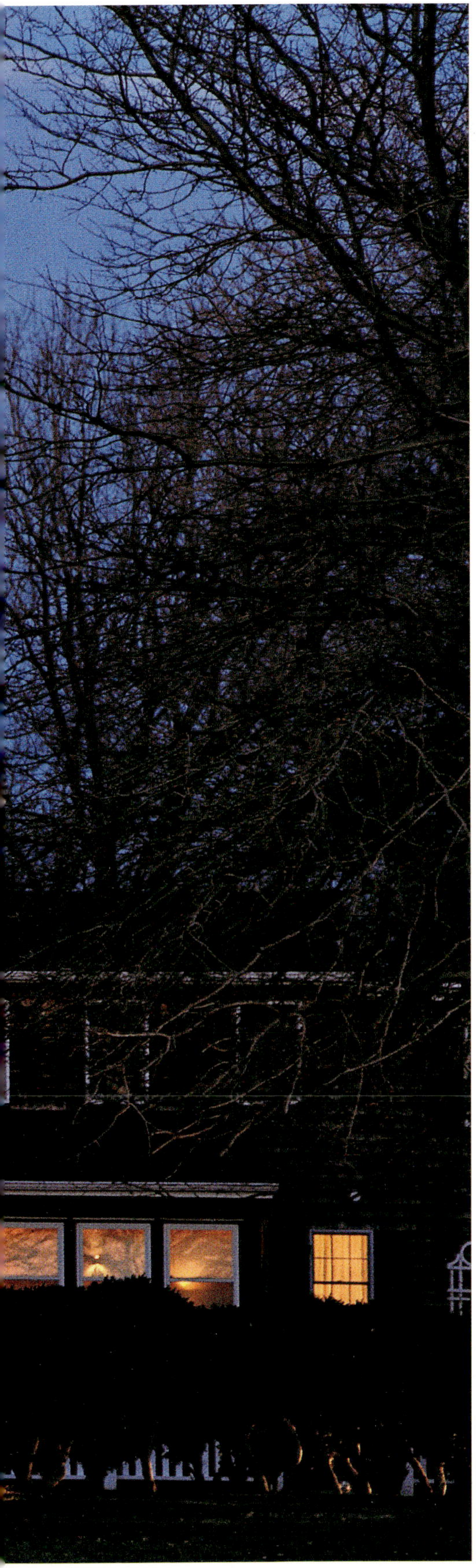

Webb House, Orient

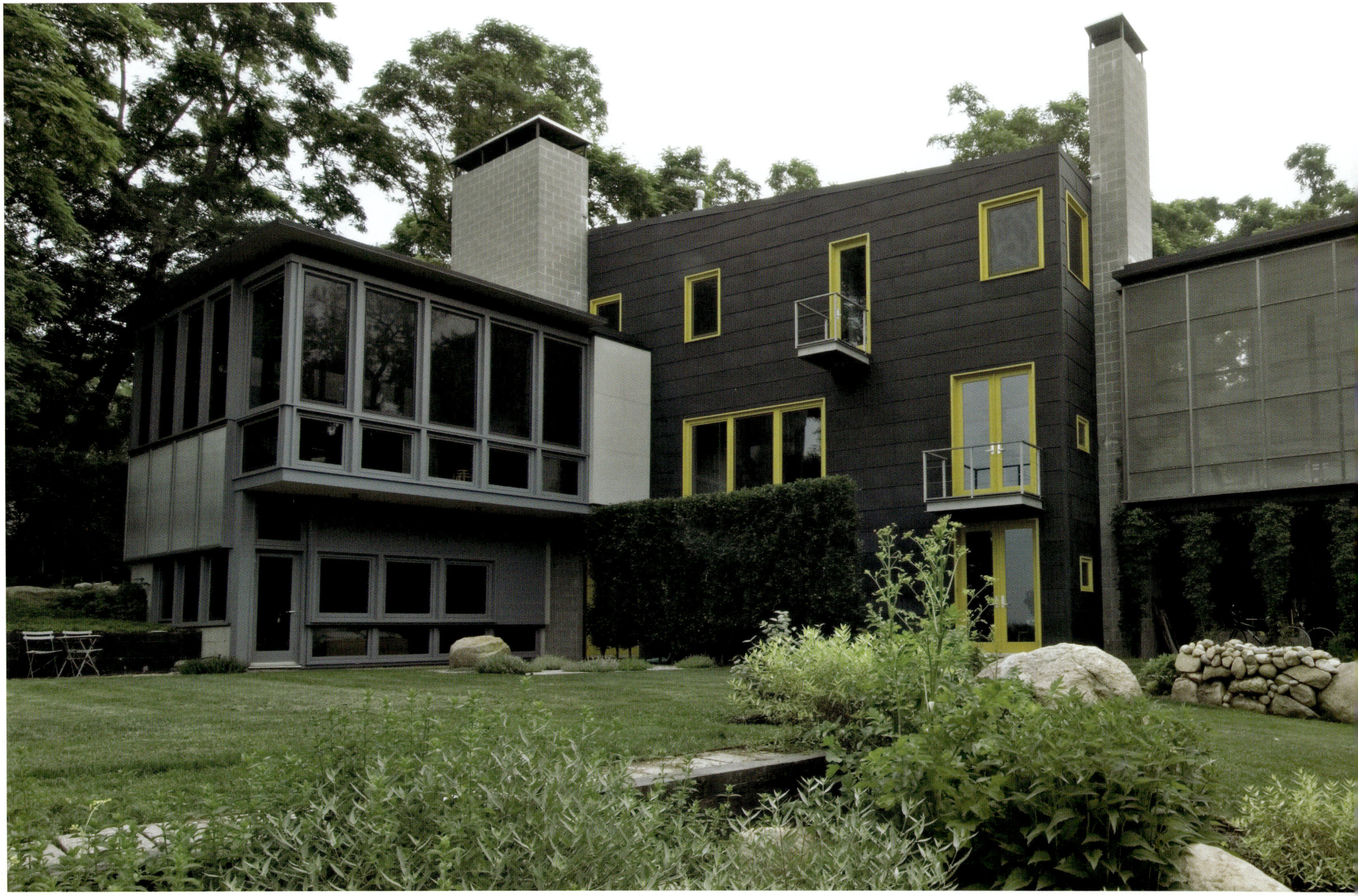

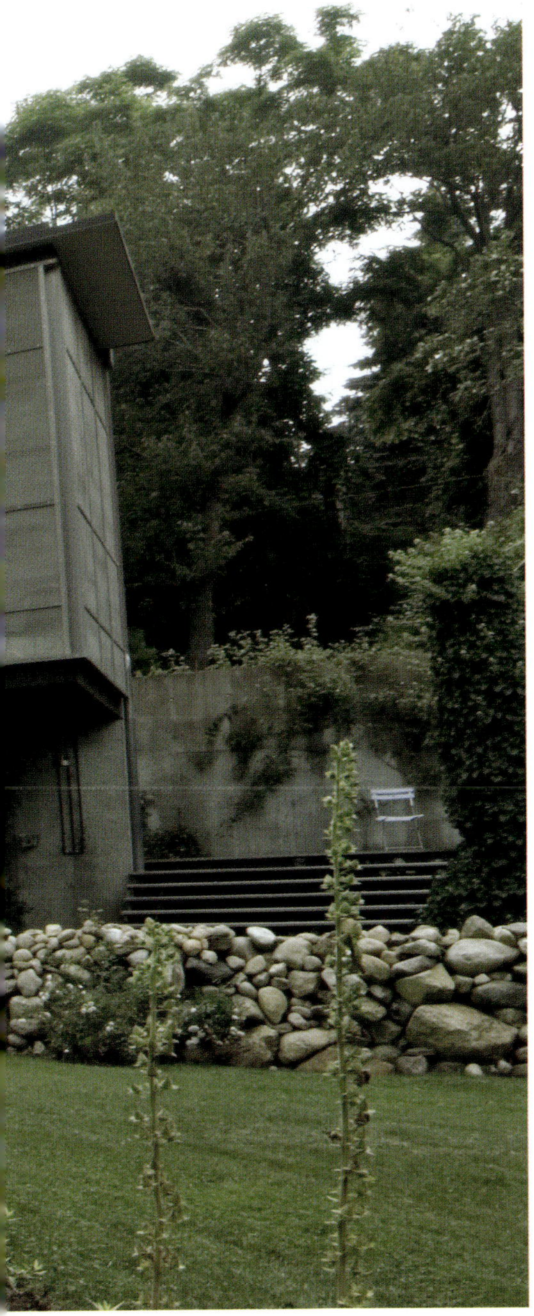
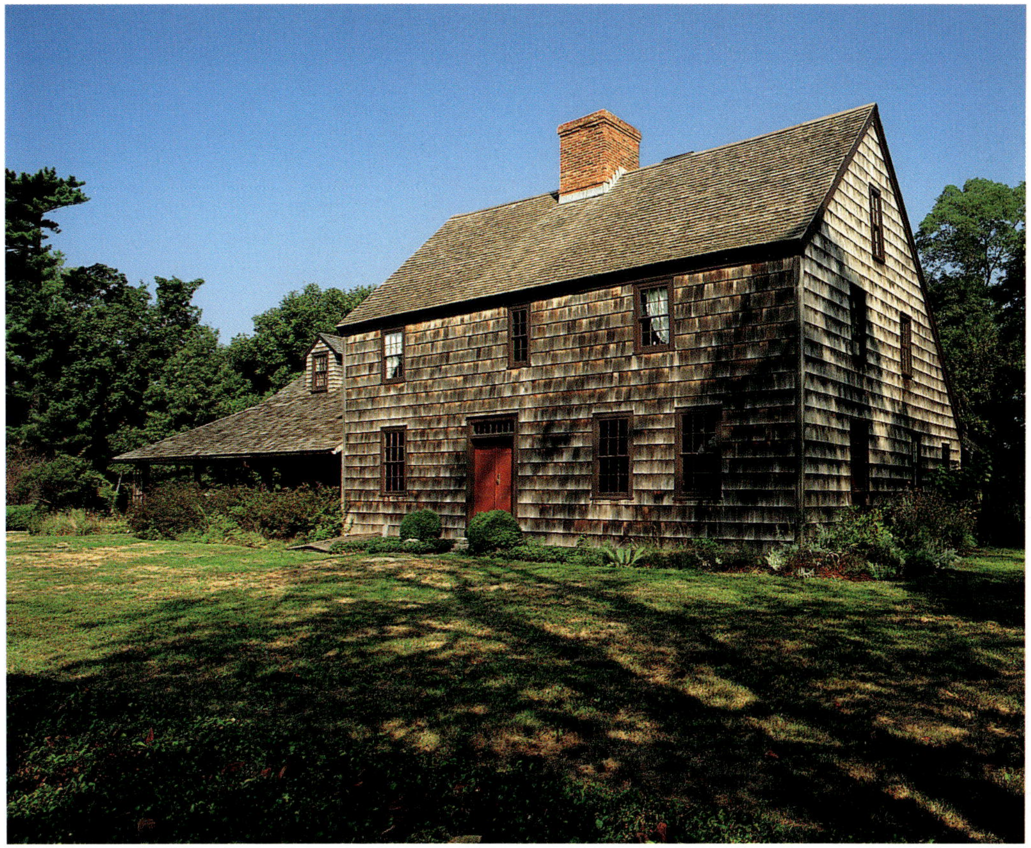
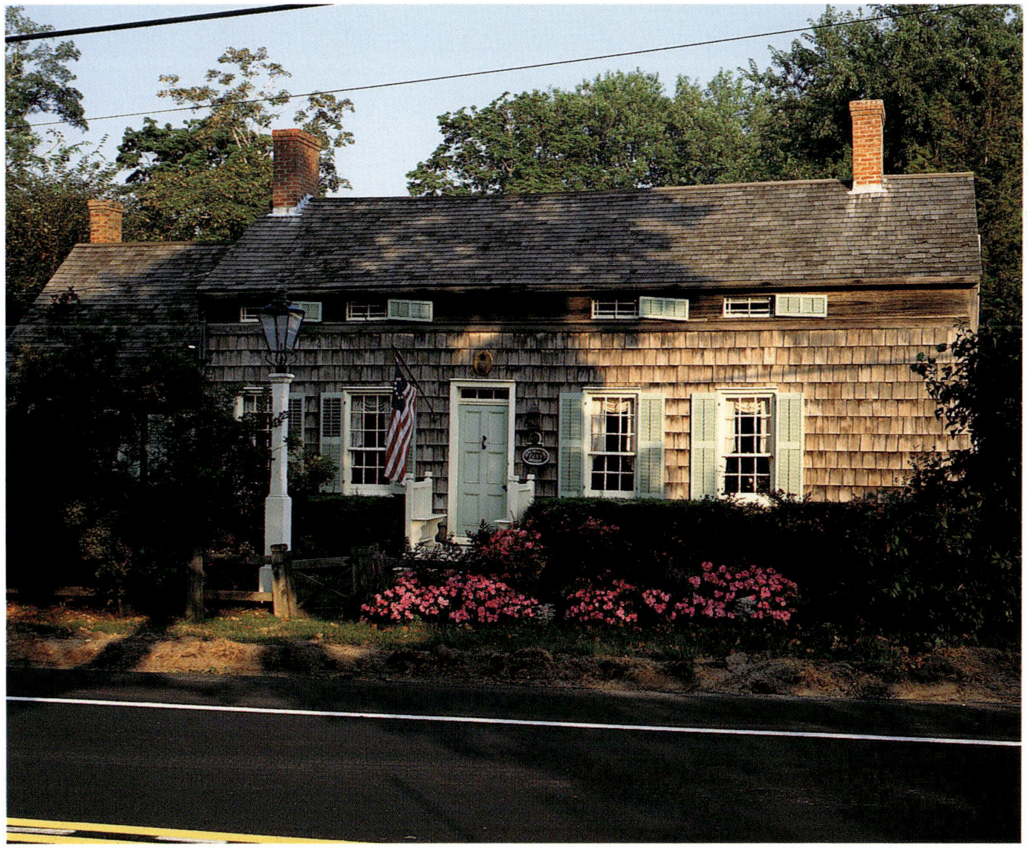

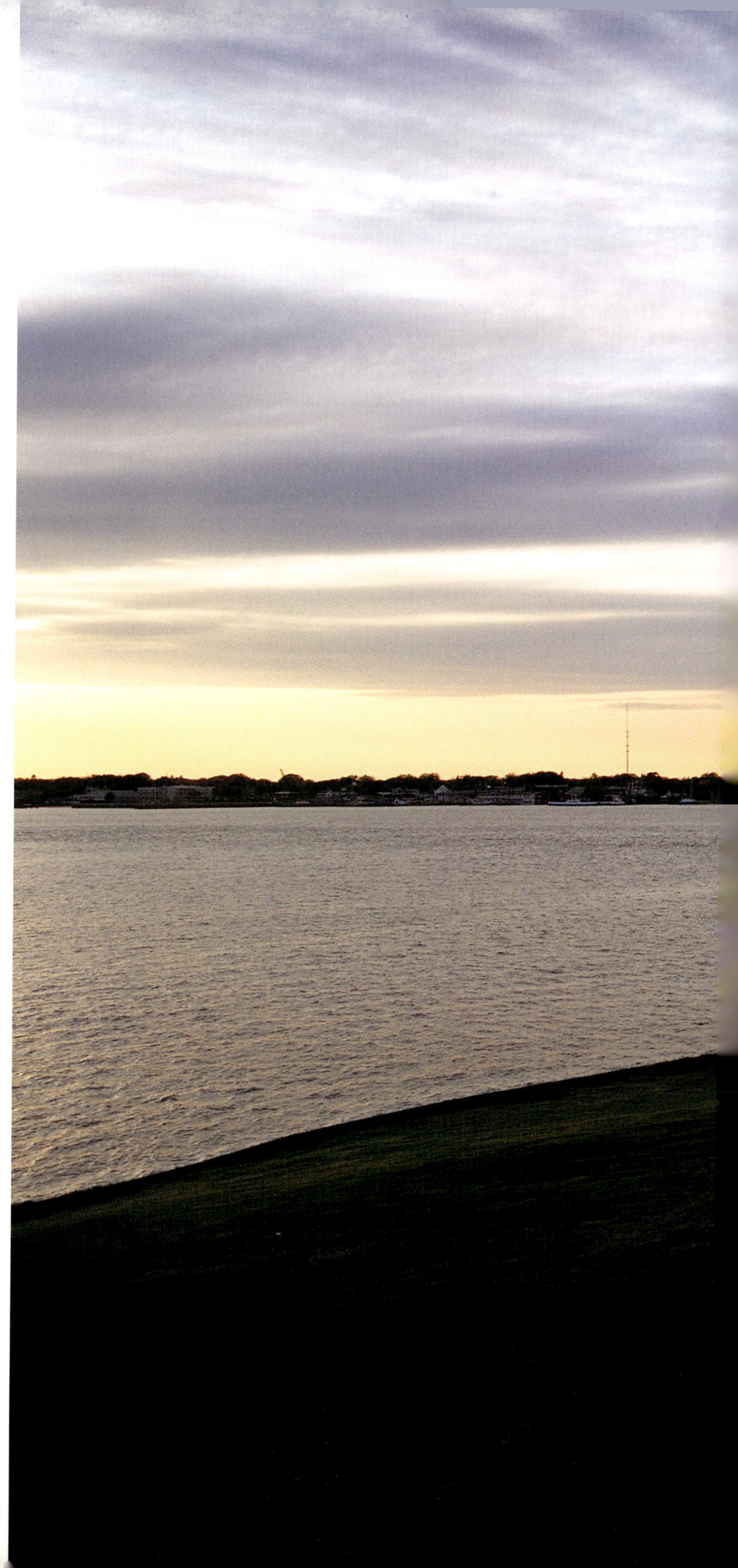

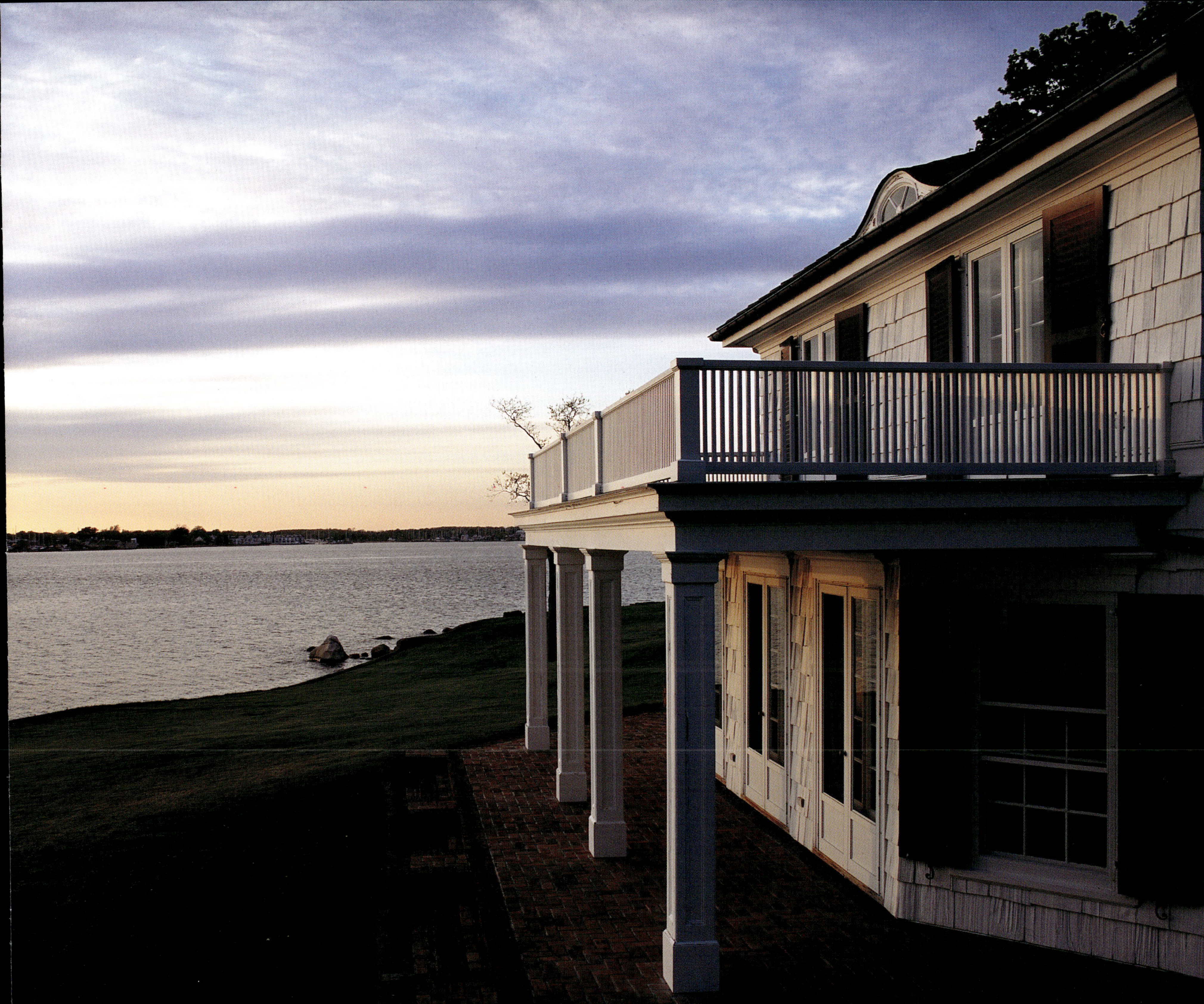

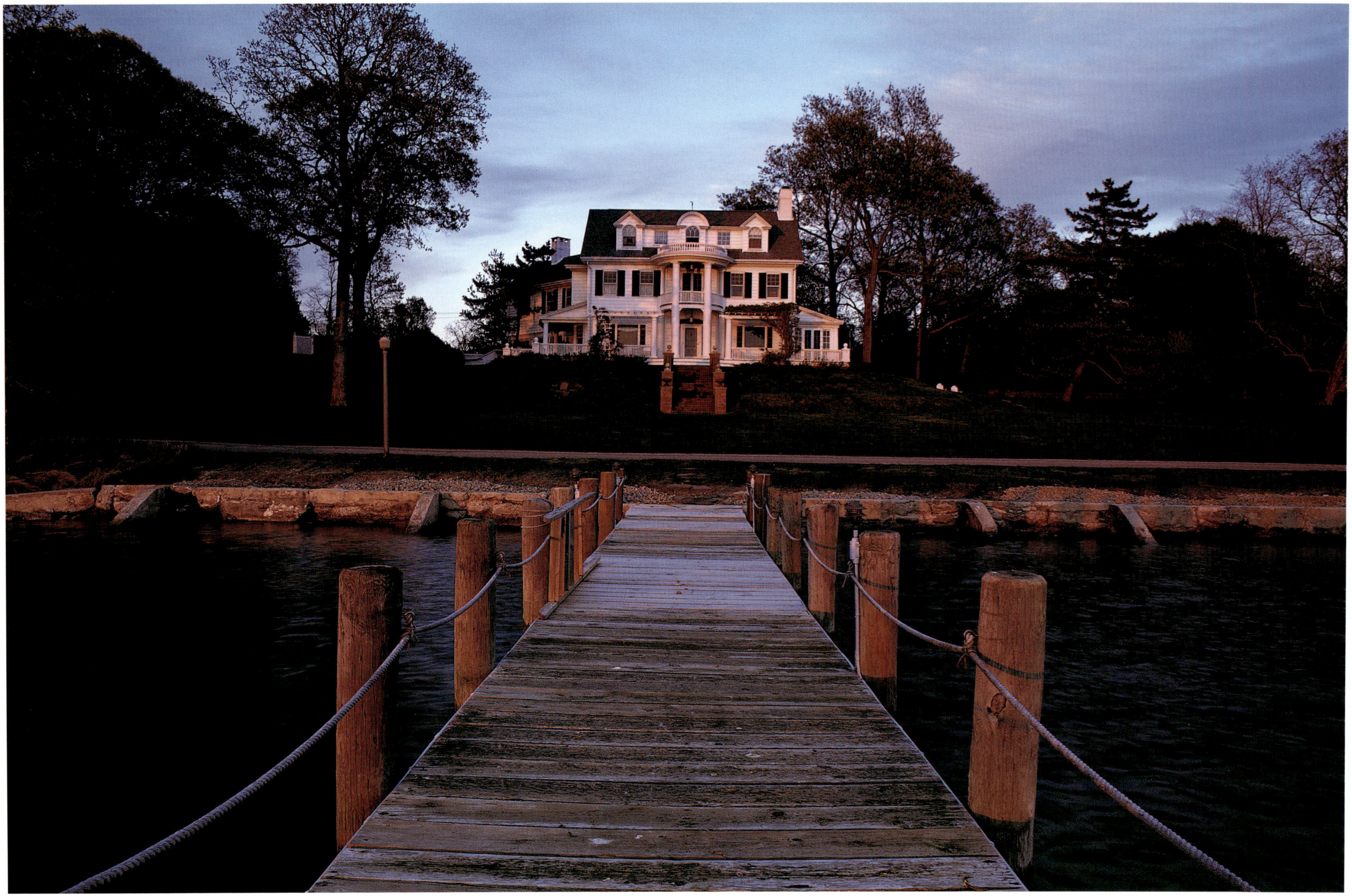

Shelter Island    Ram's Head Inn, Shelter Island

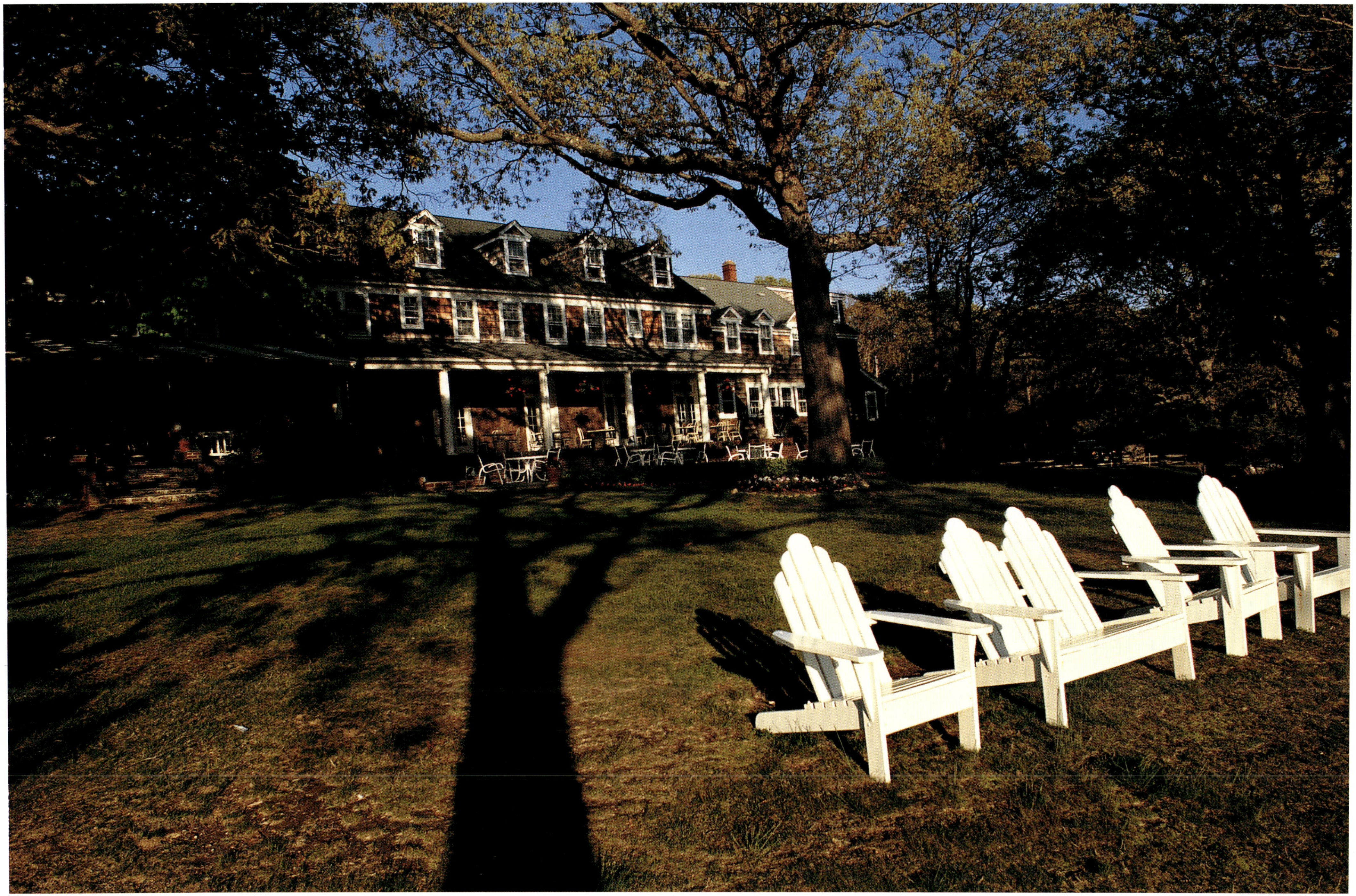

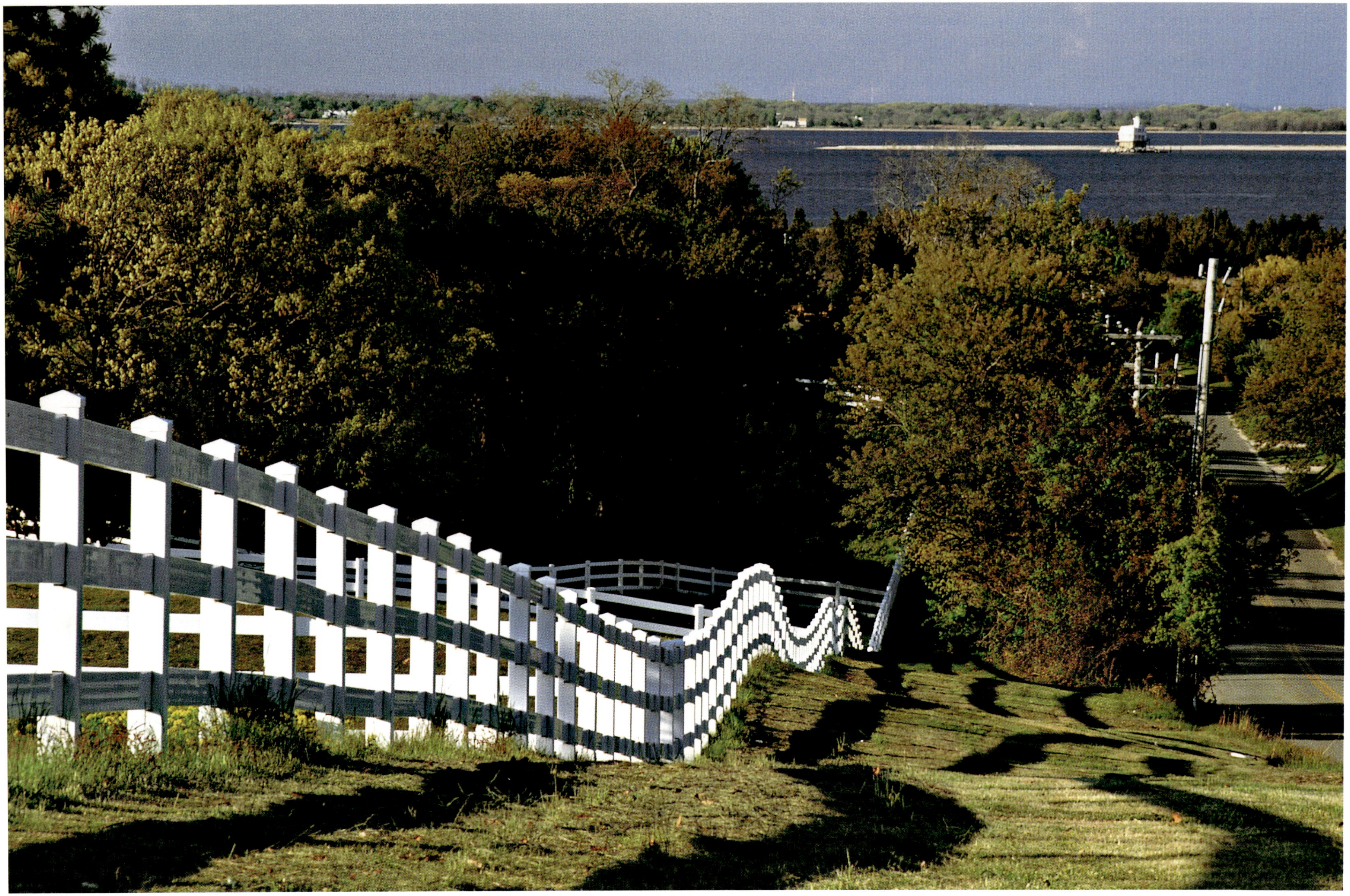

Shelter Island

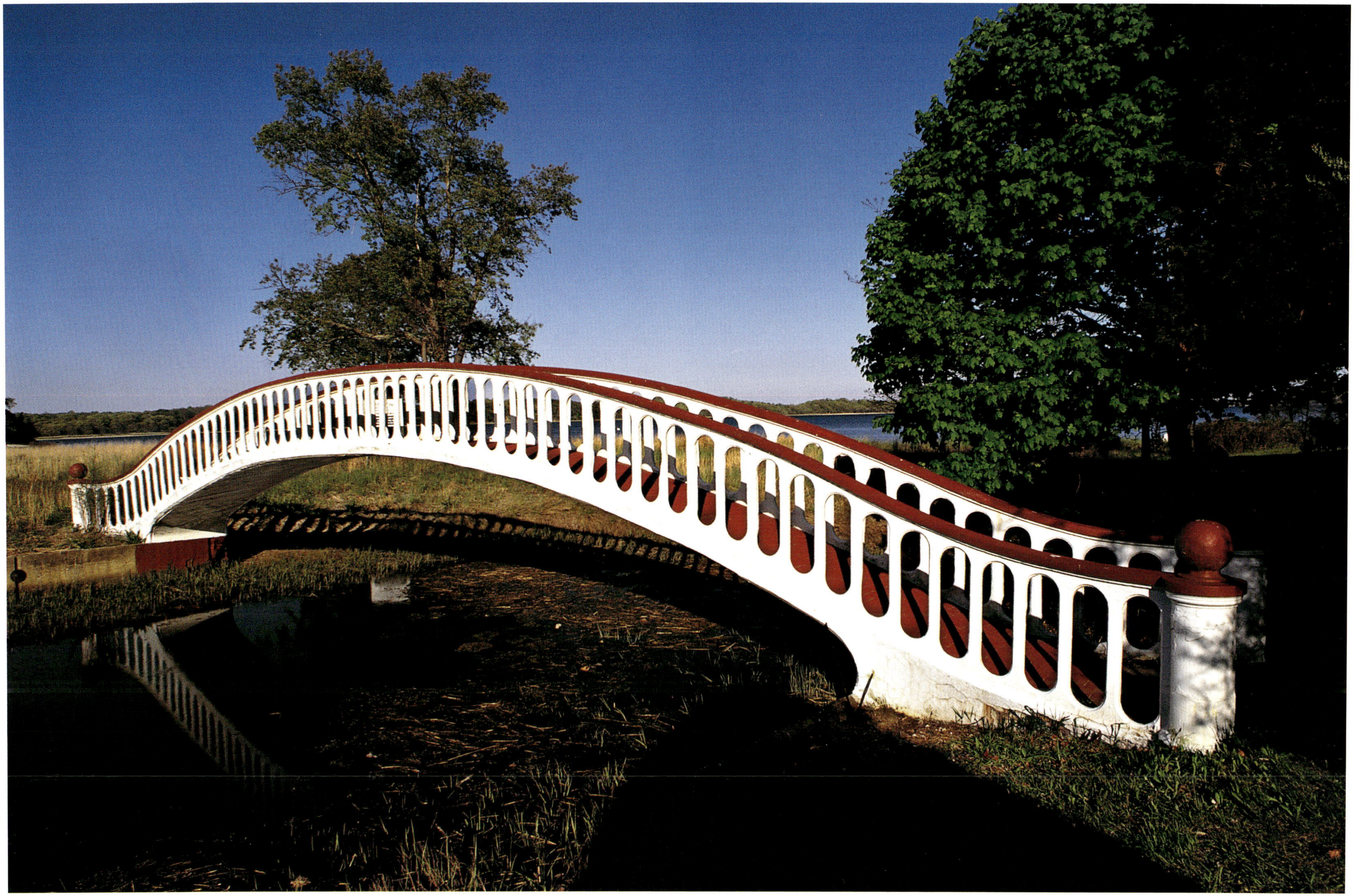

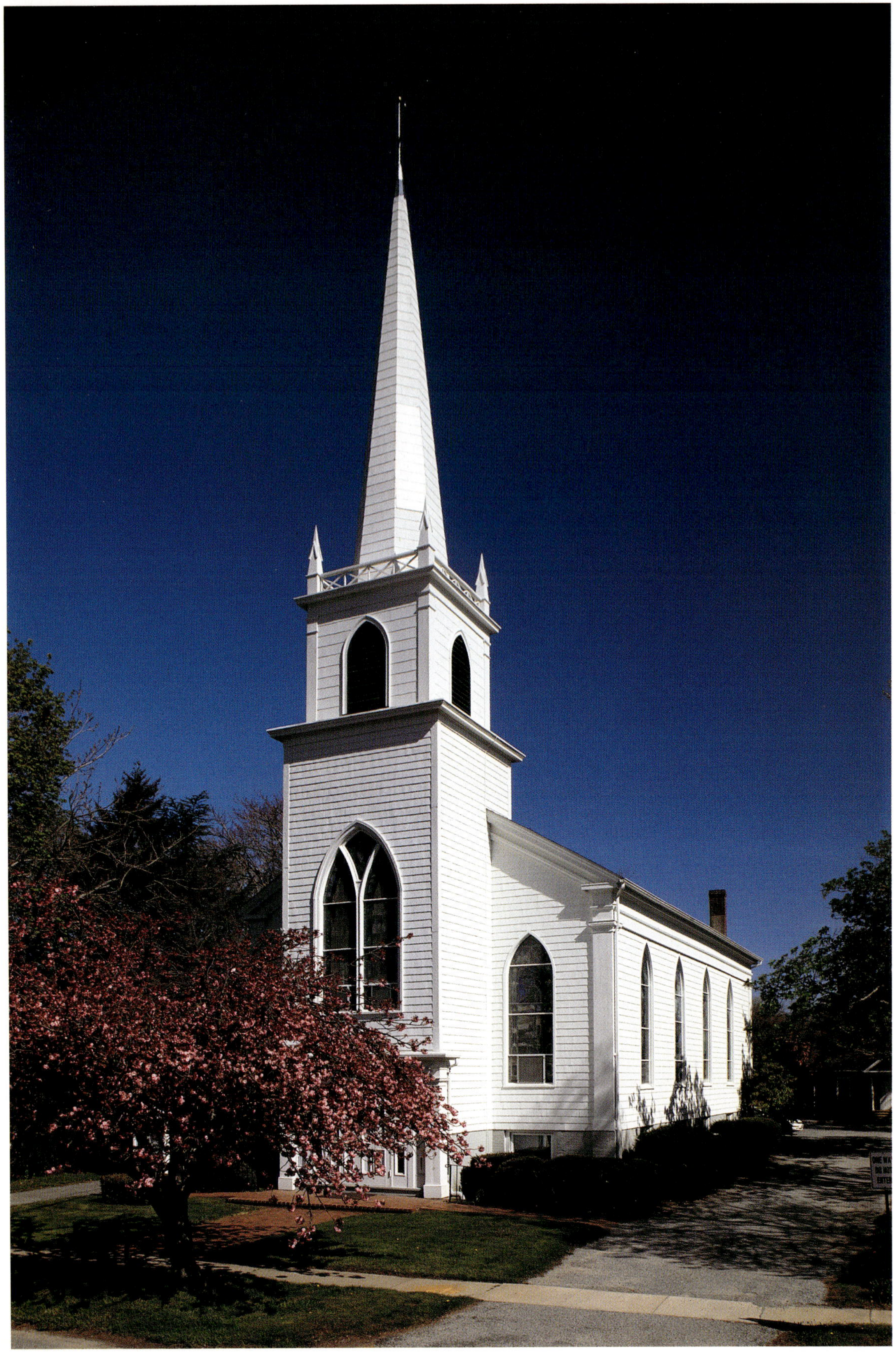

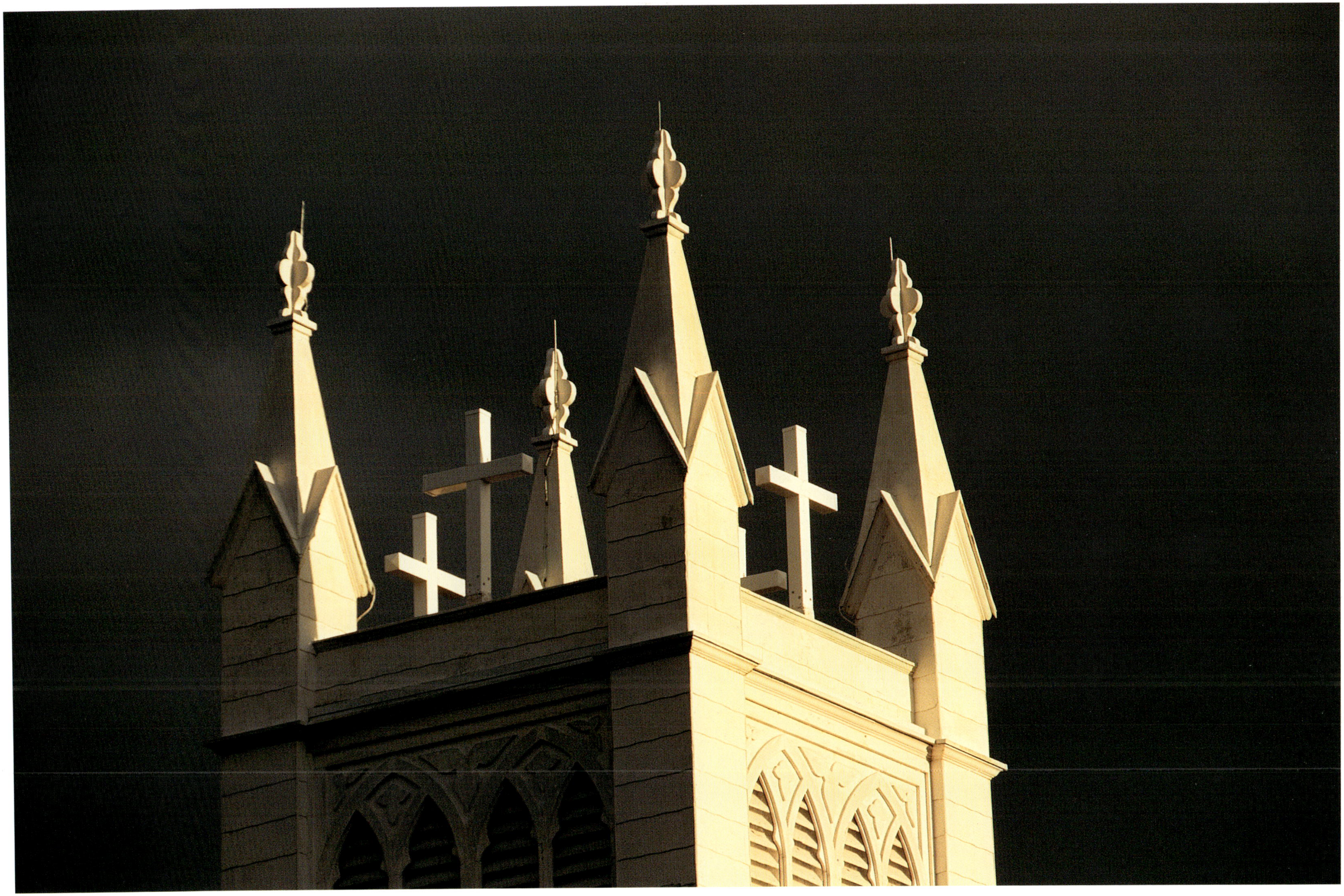

Congregational Church, Orient Saint Agnes Church, Greenport

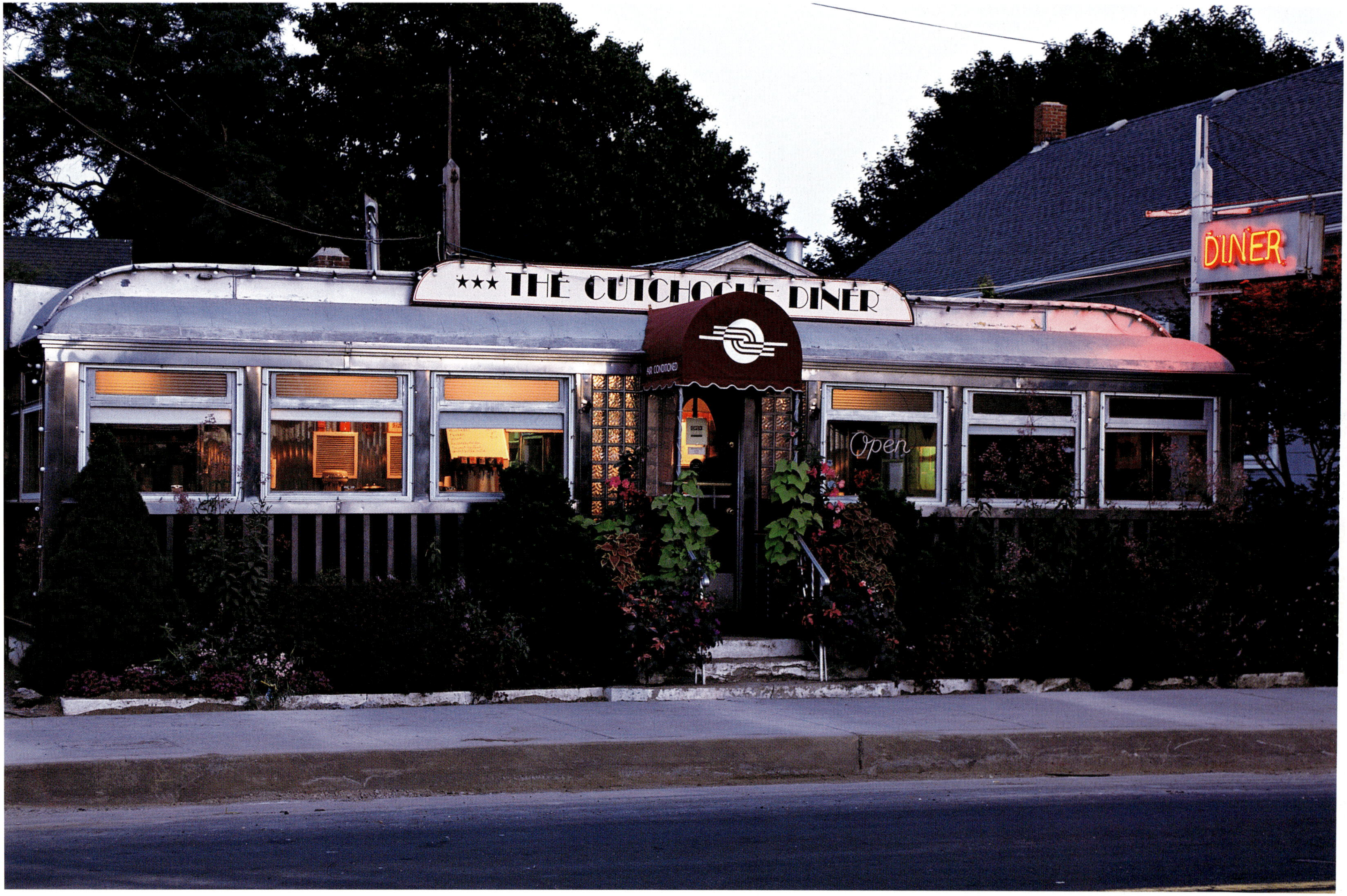
DINER
Open

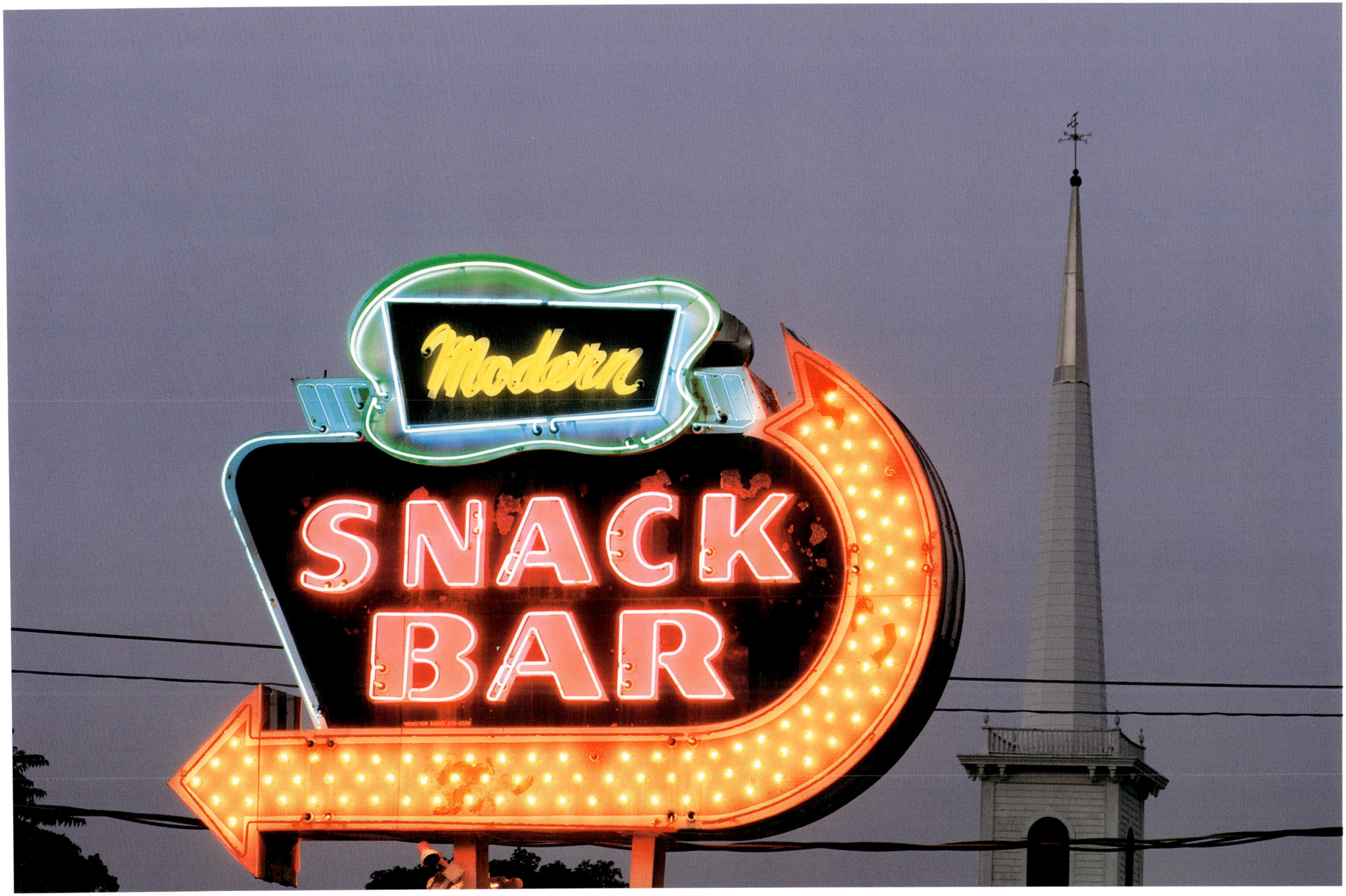
Modern
SNACK
BAR

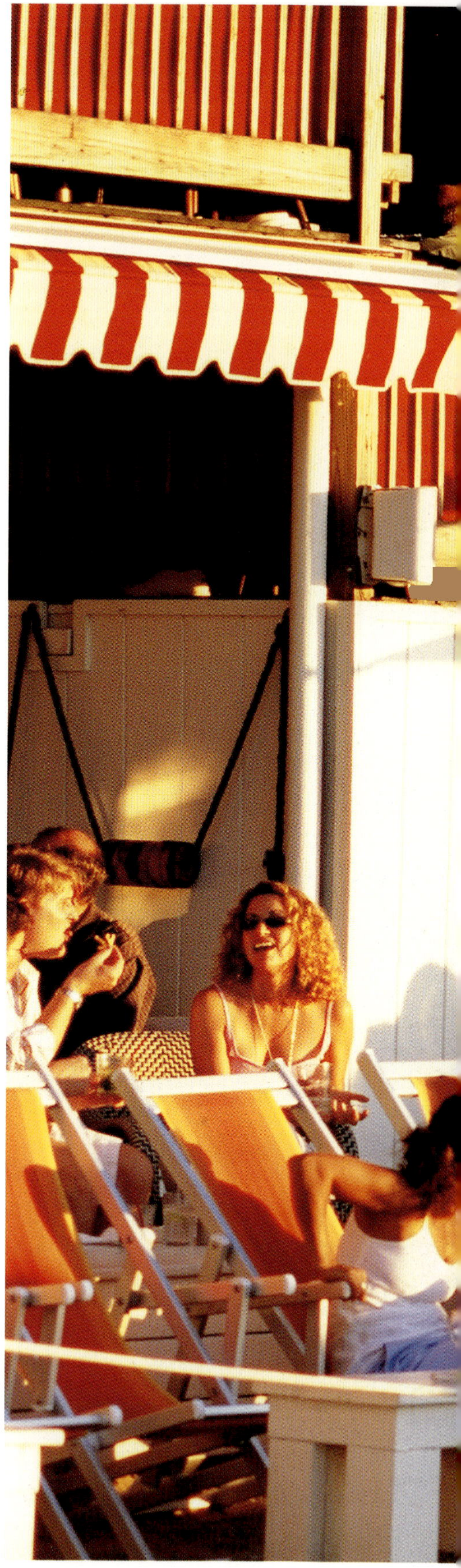

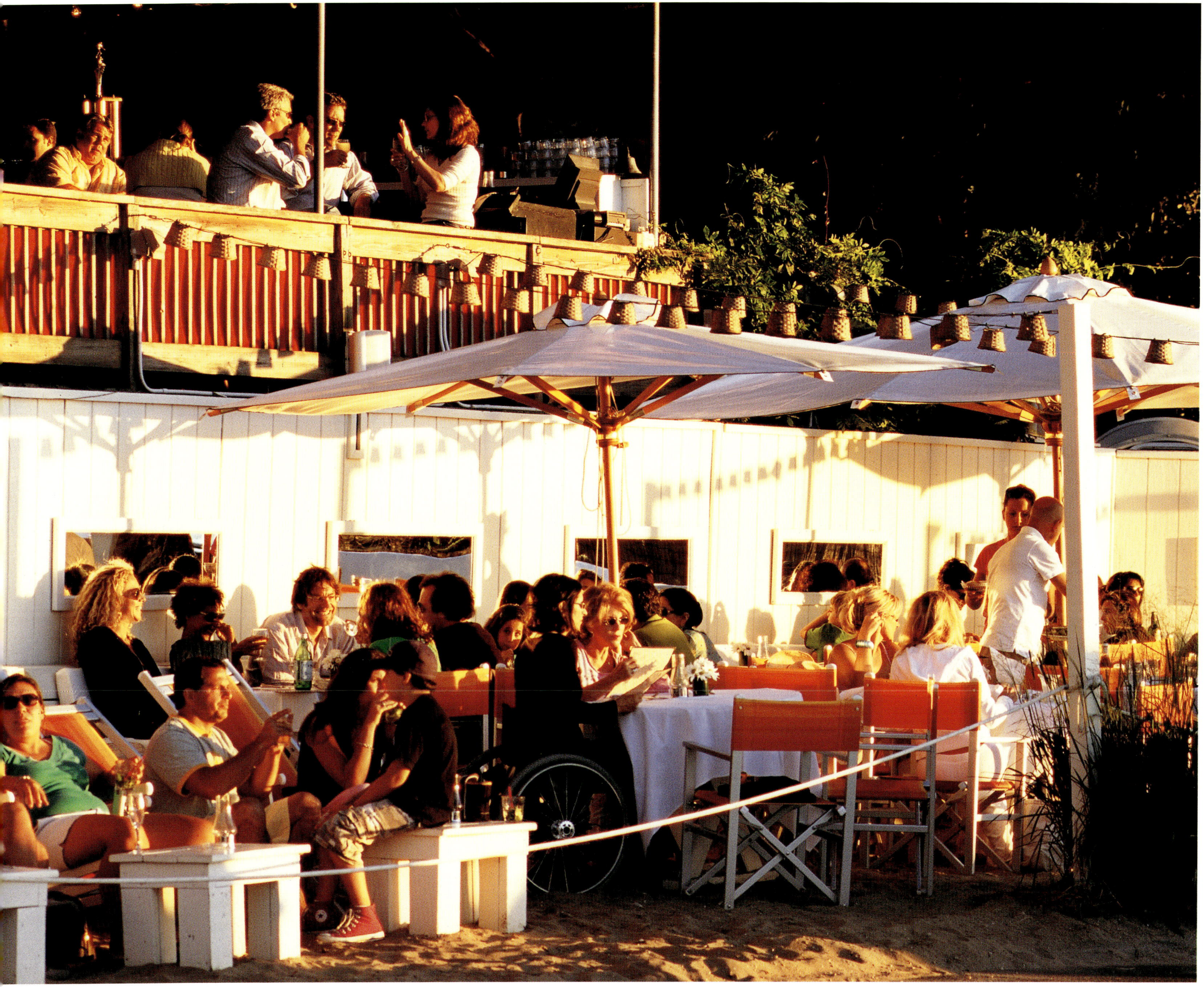

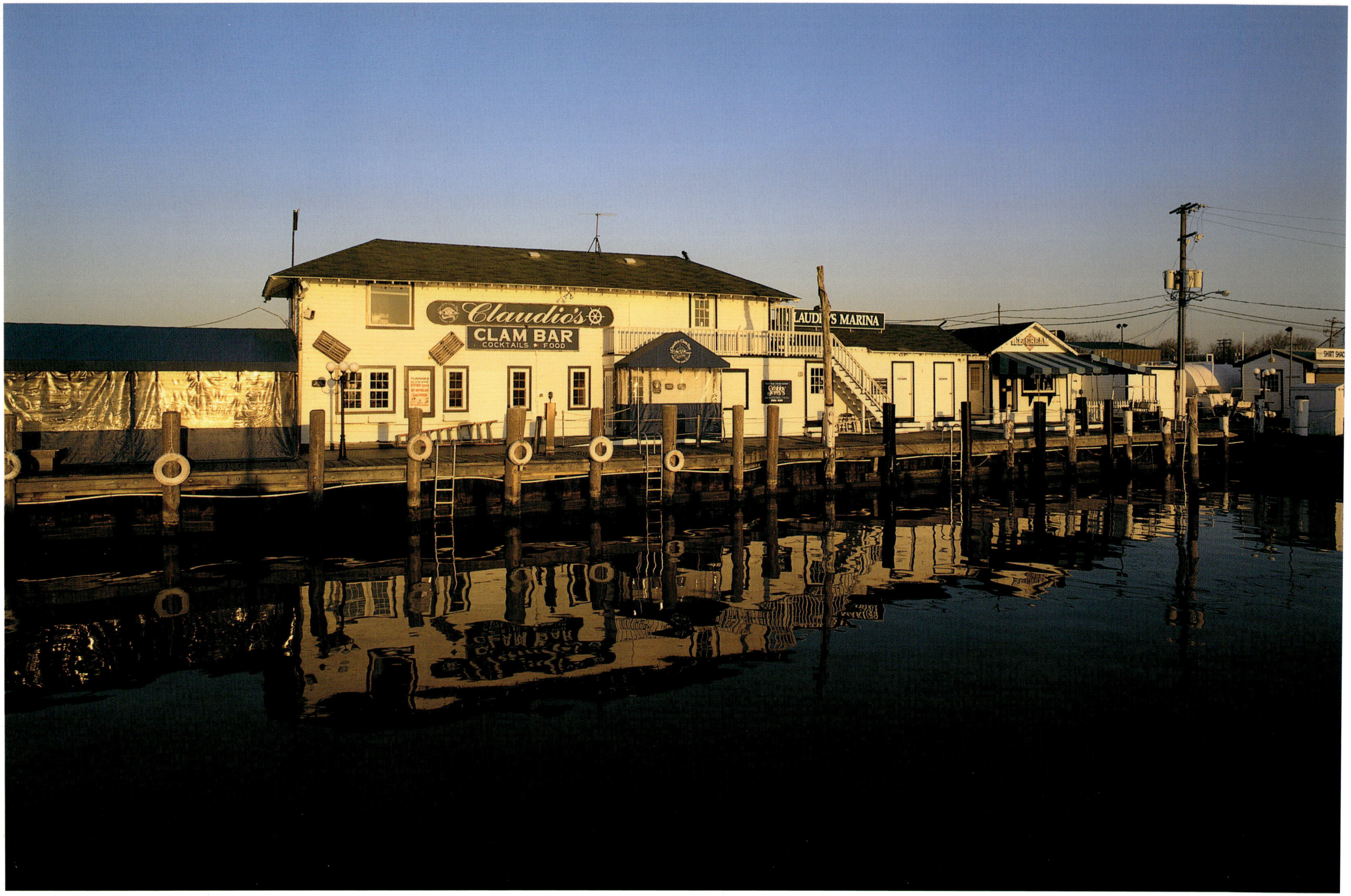


Greenport

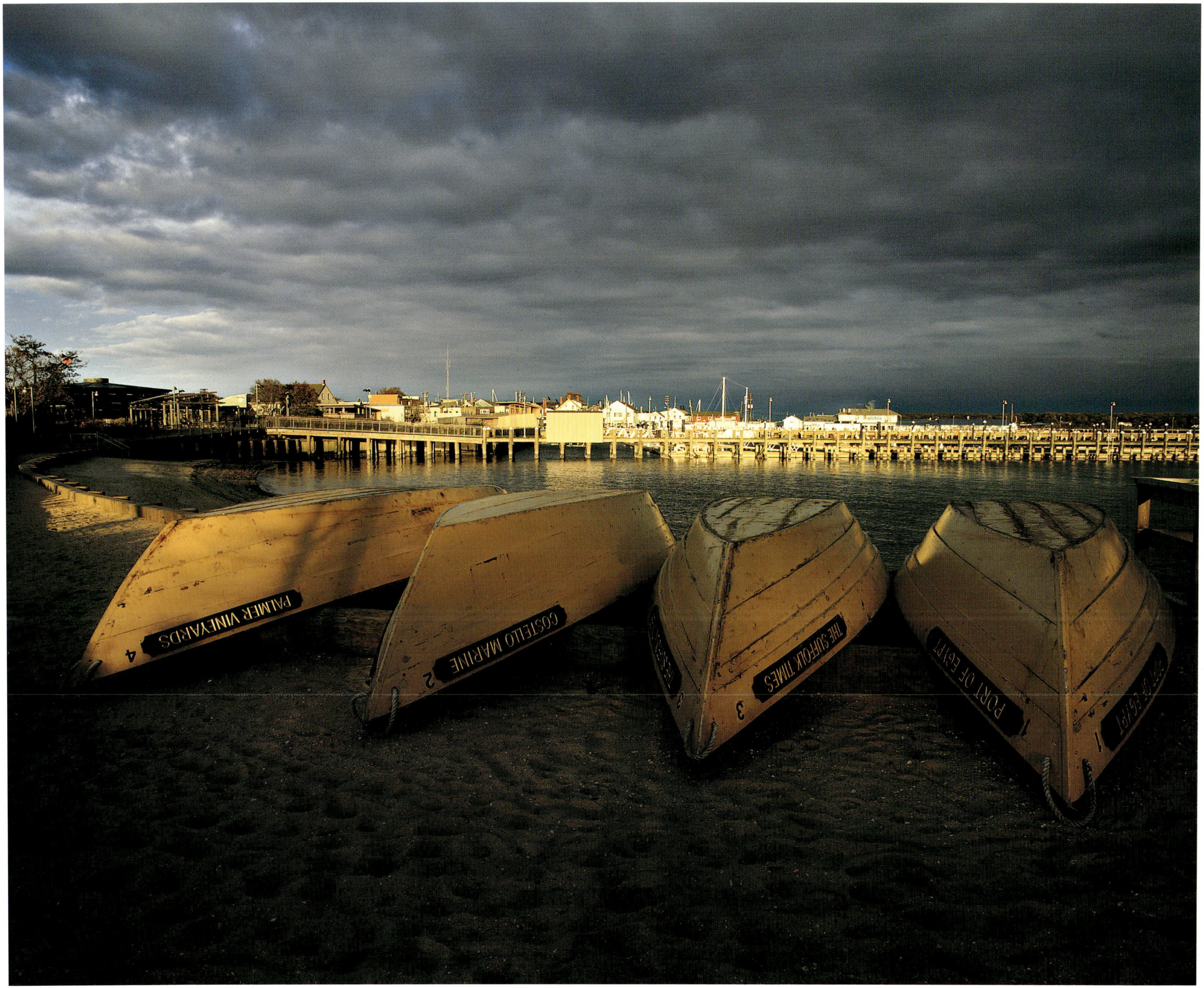

PALMER VINEYARDS
4
COSTELLO MARINE
2
THE SUFFOLK TIMES
3
PORT OF EGYPT
1

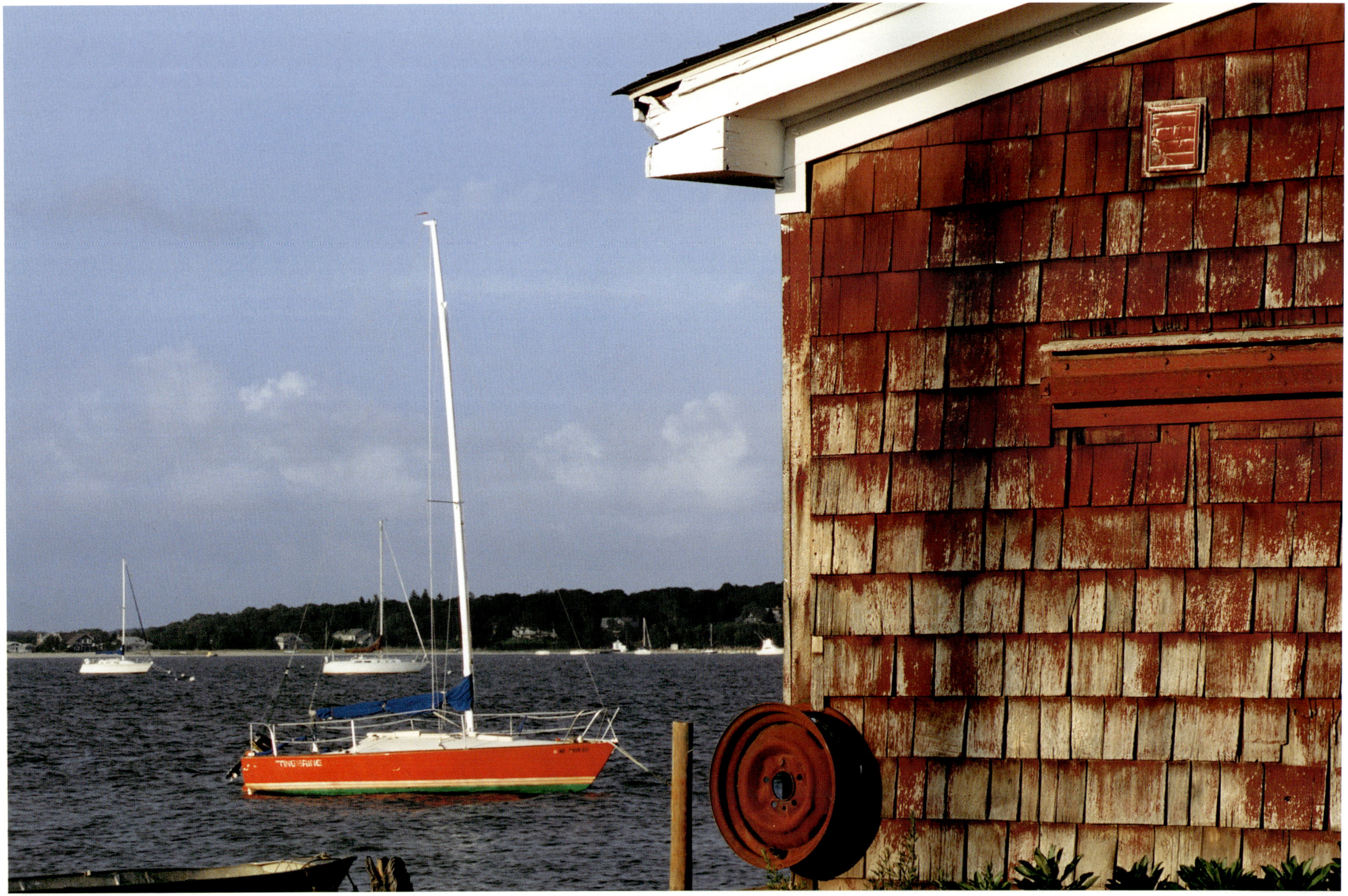

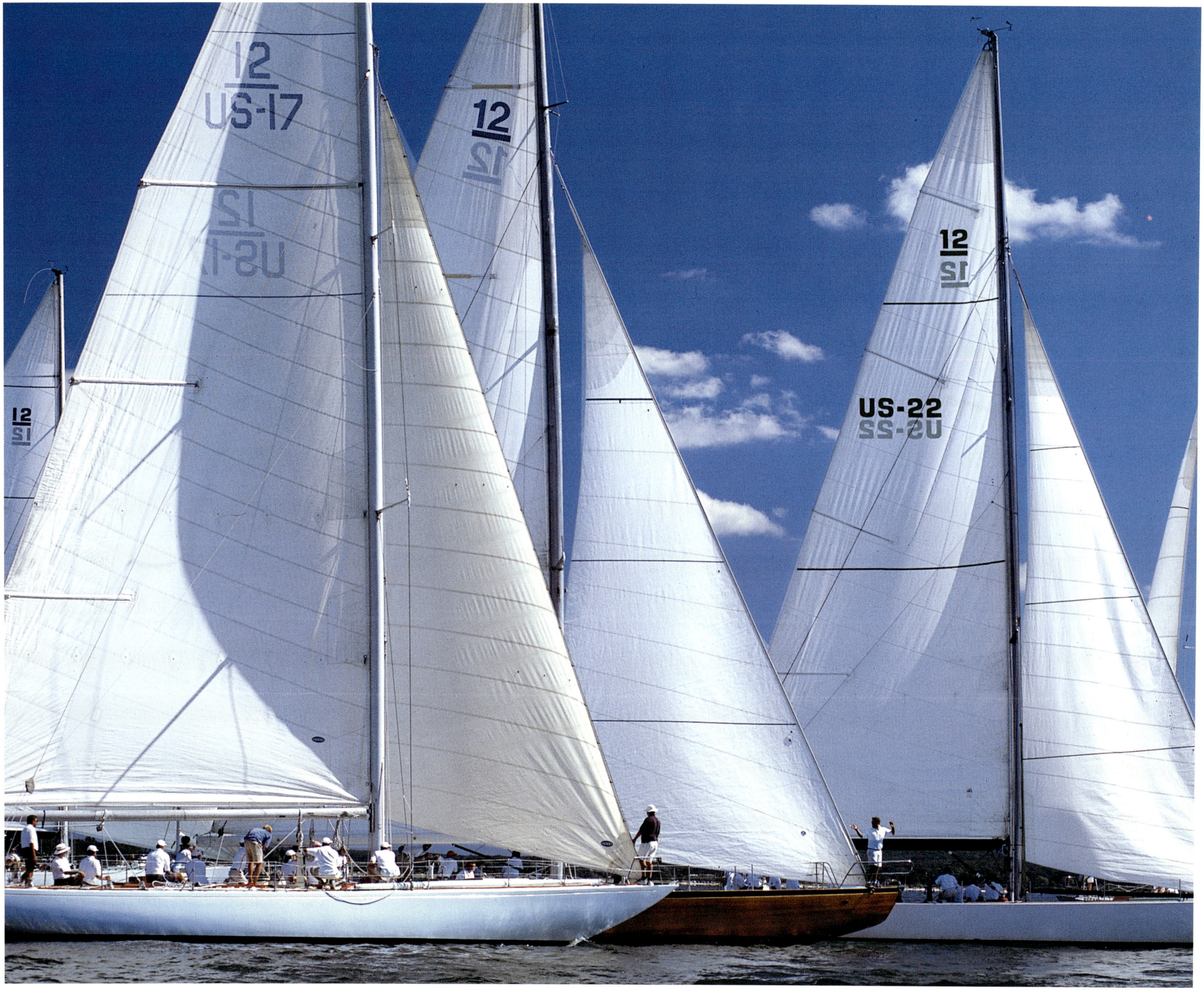
12
US-17
12
12
US-22

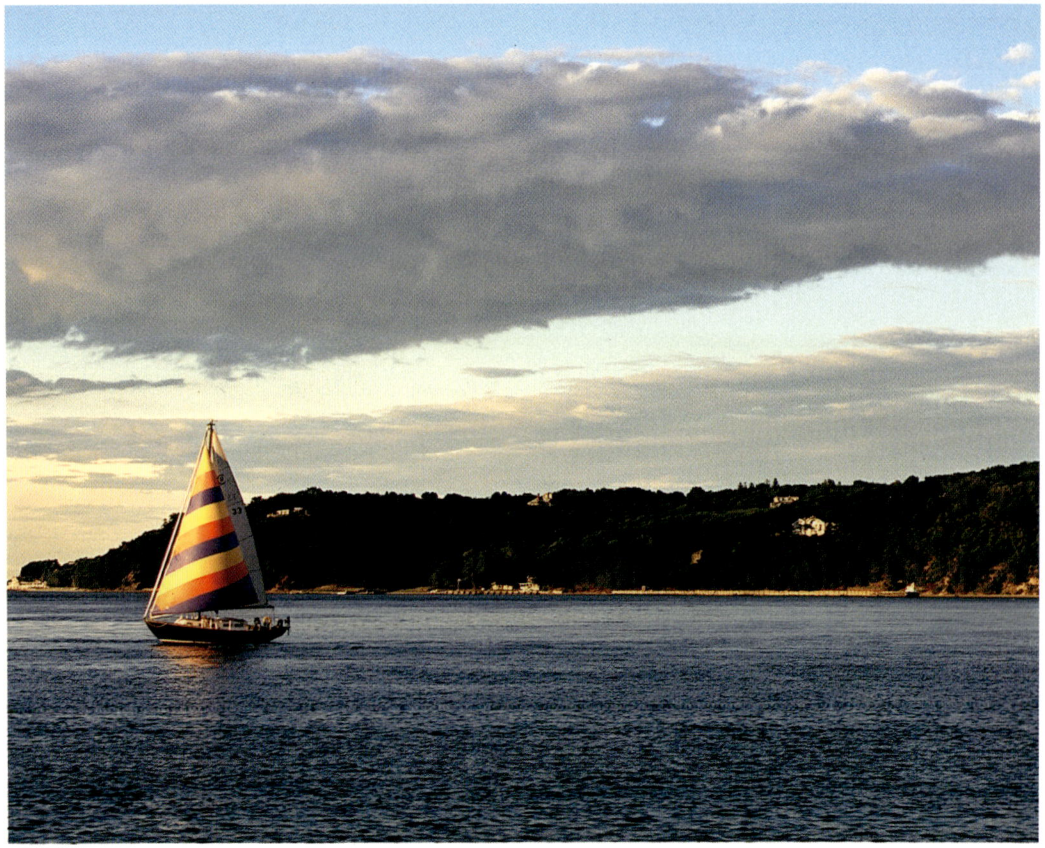

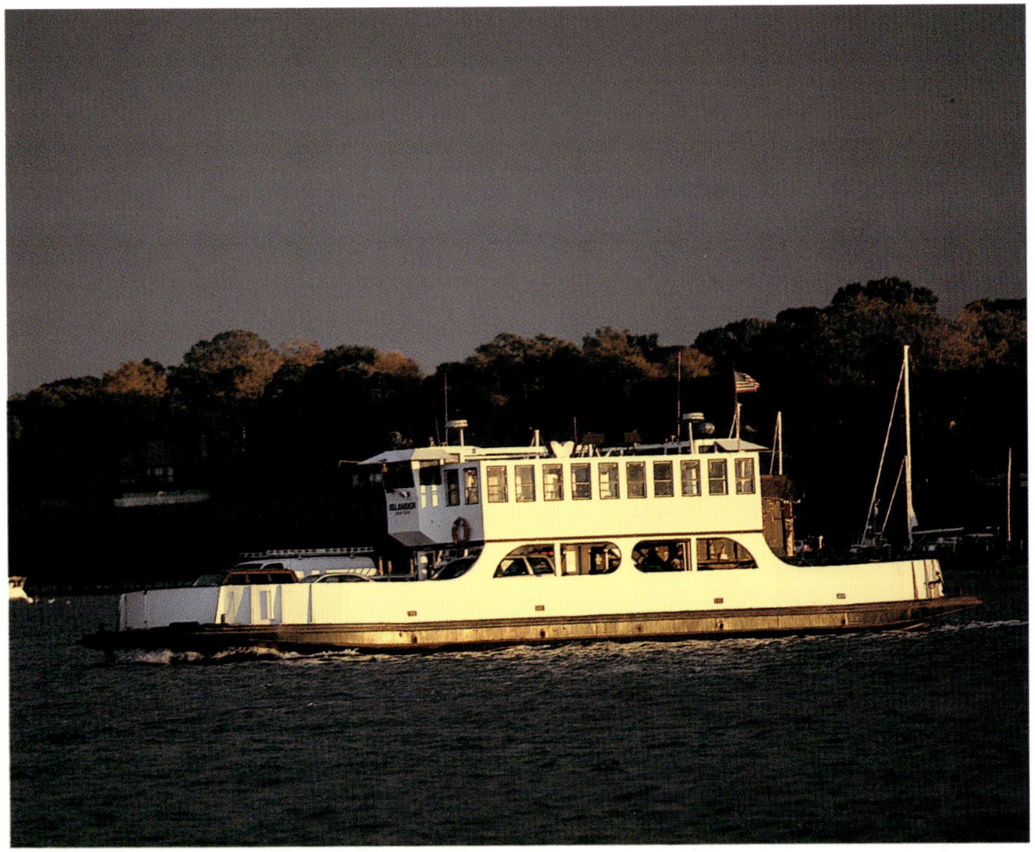

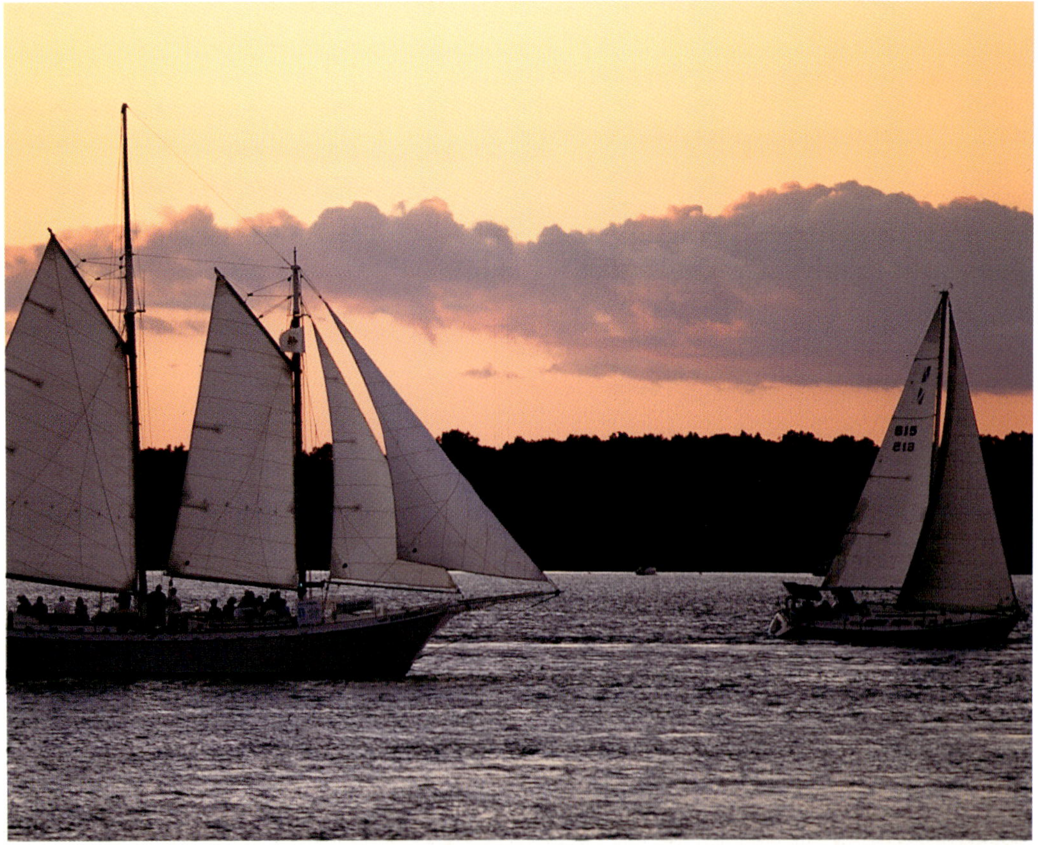

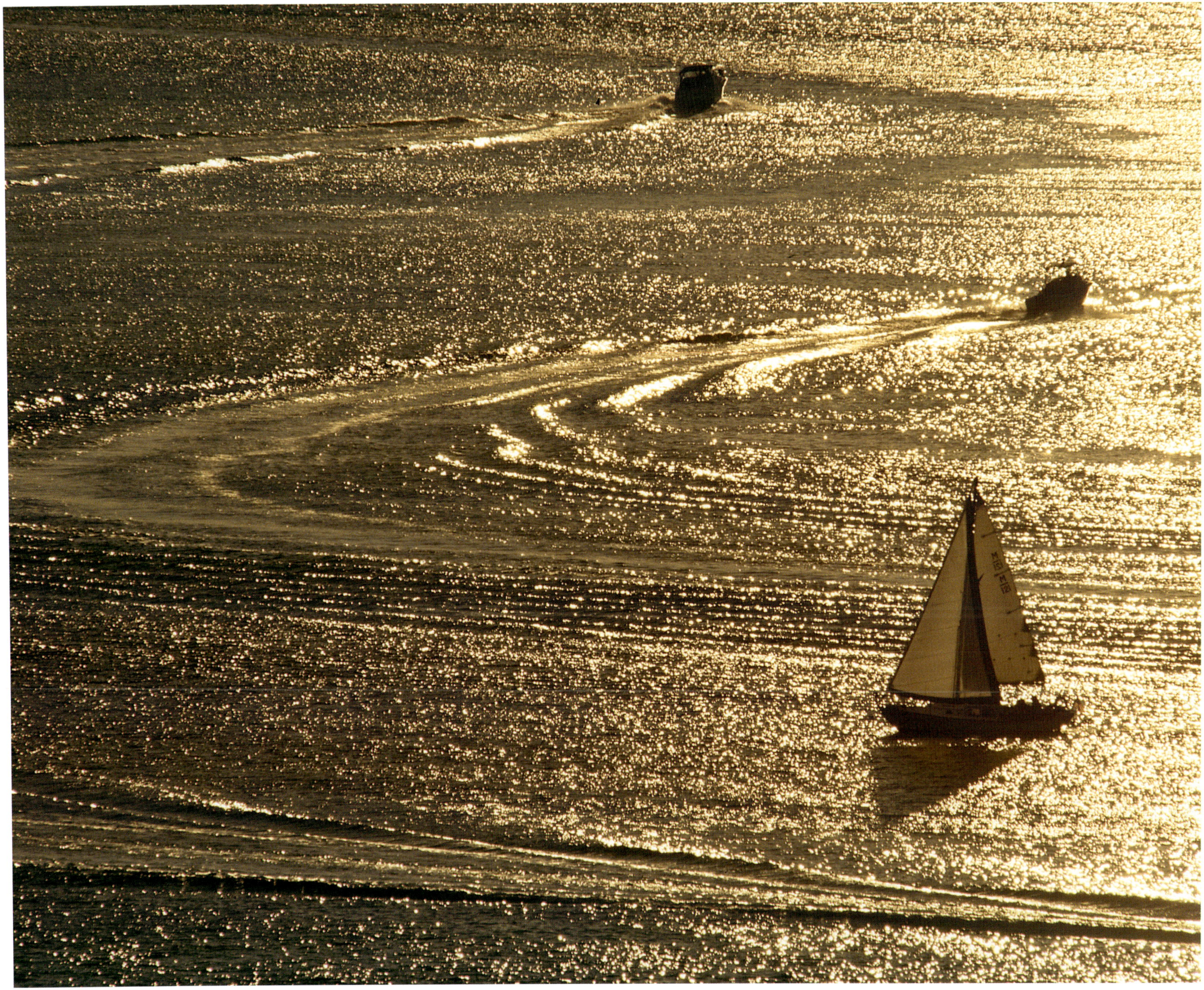

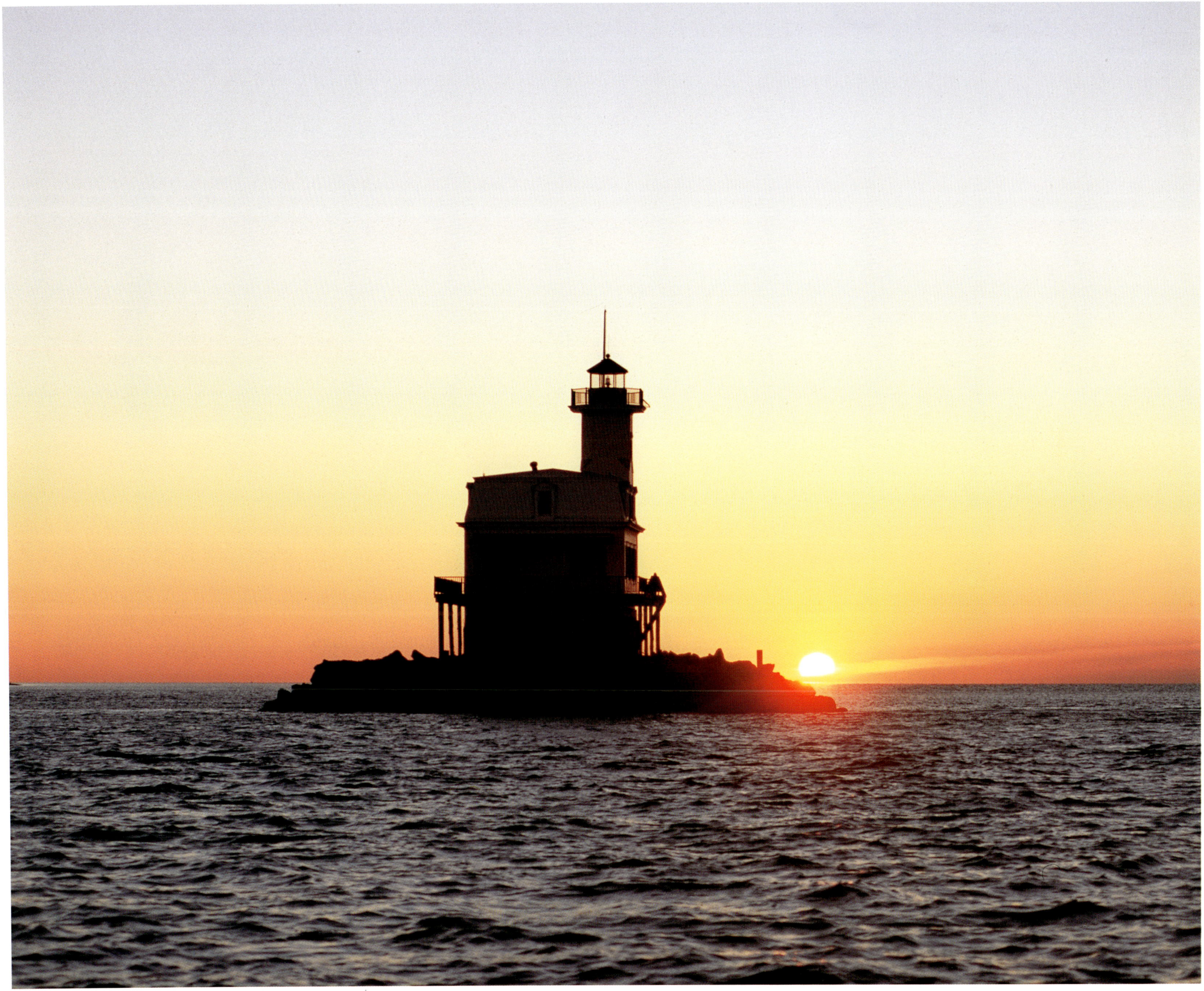

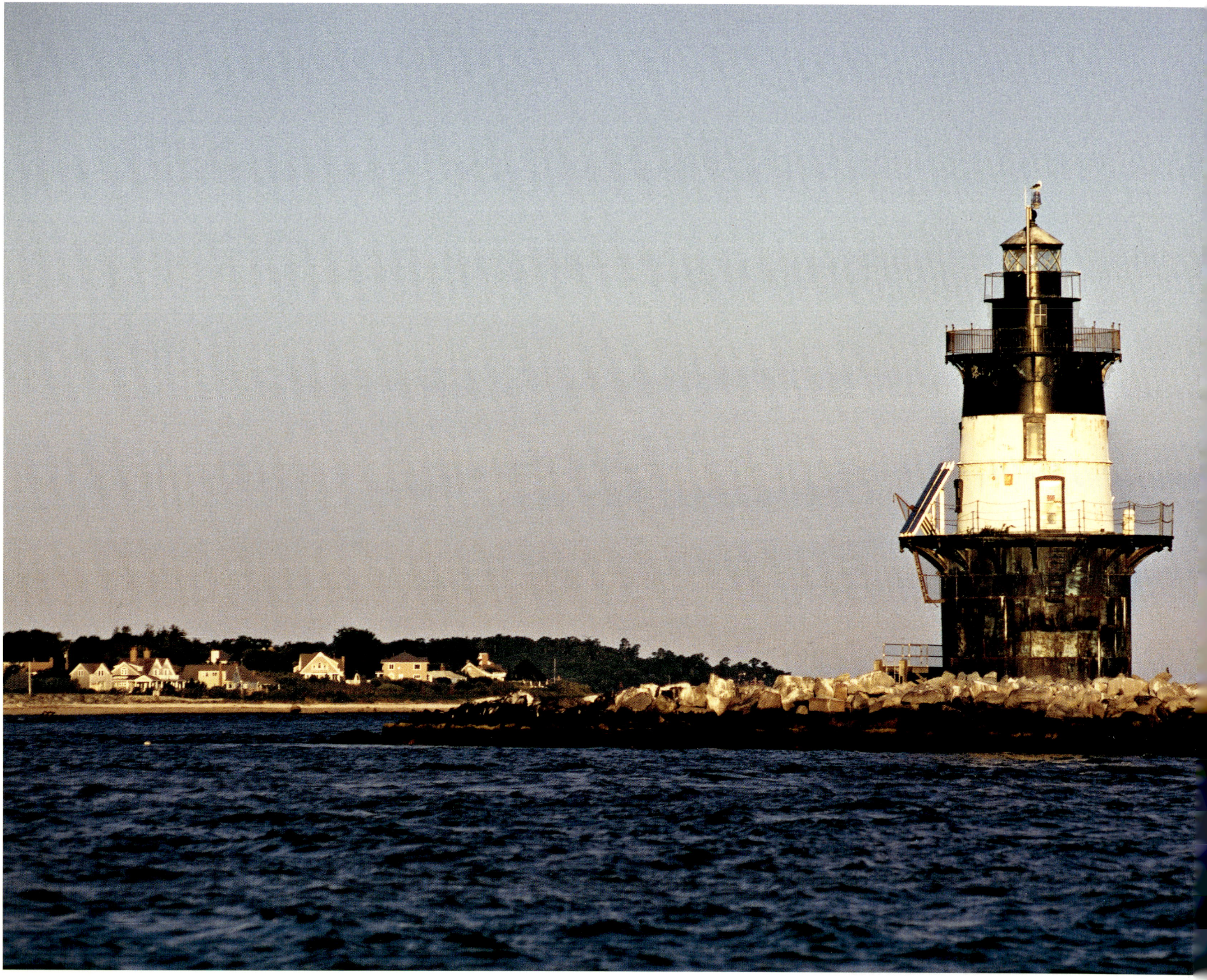

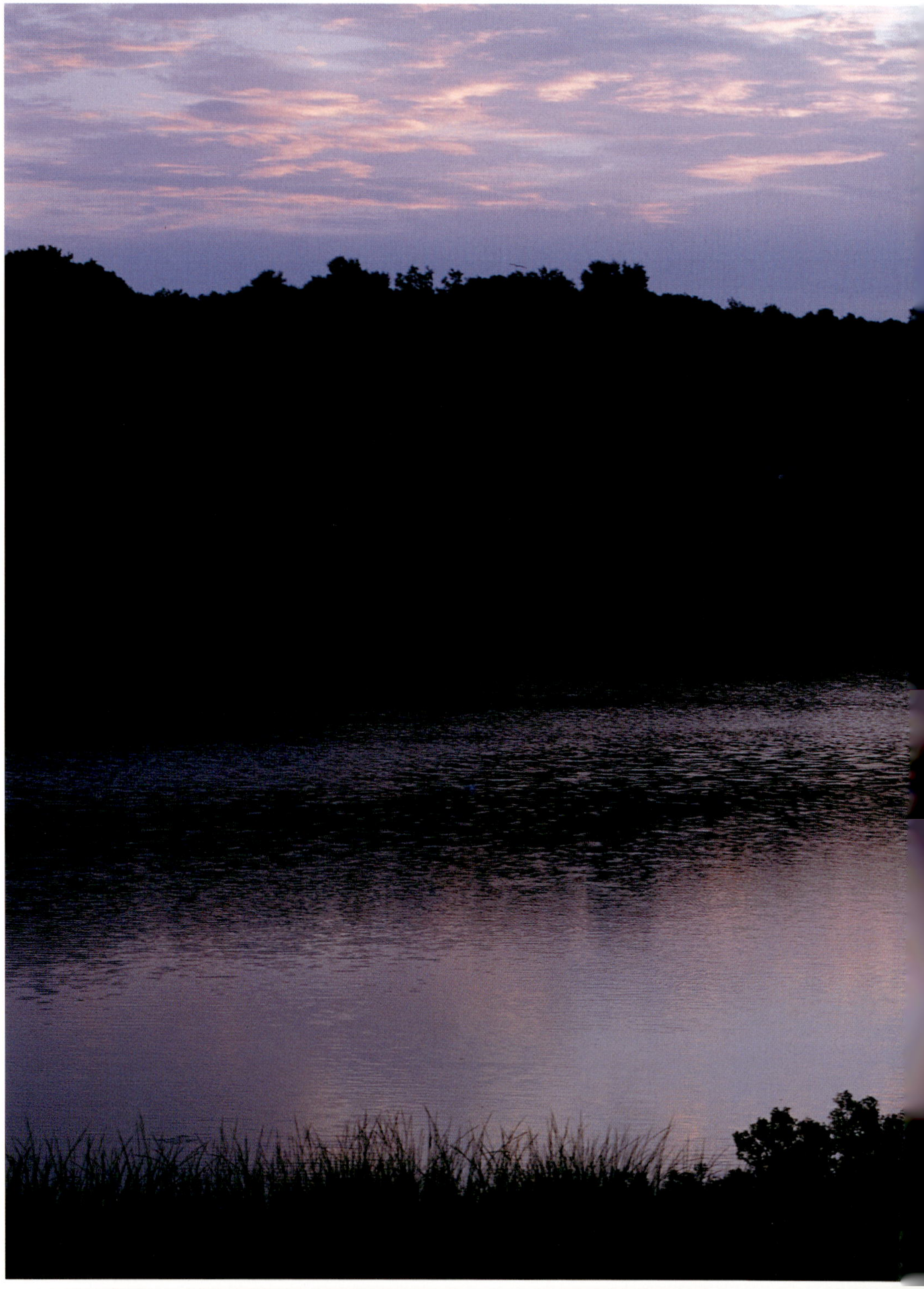

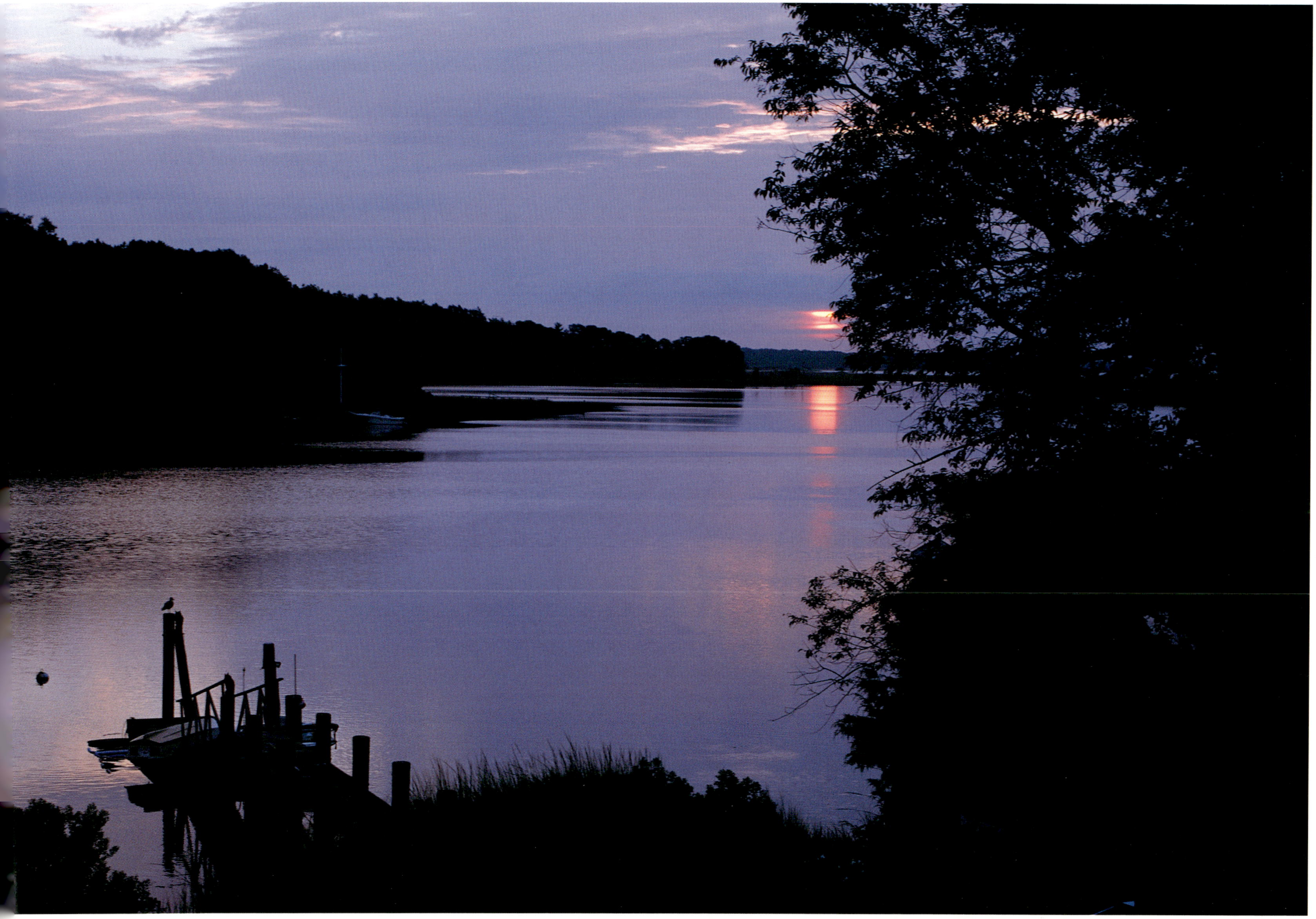

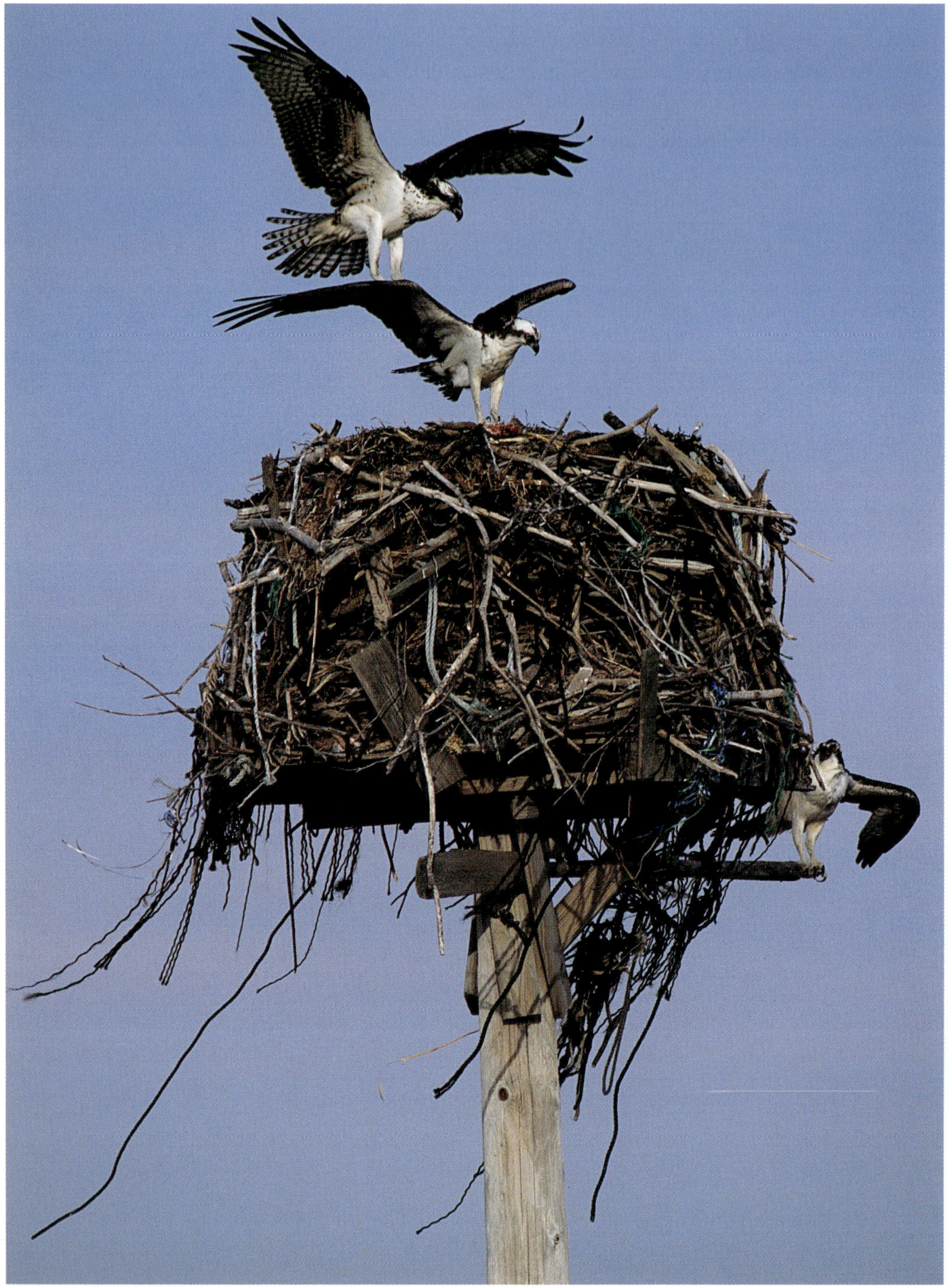

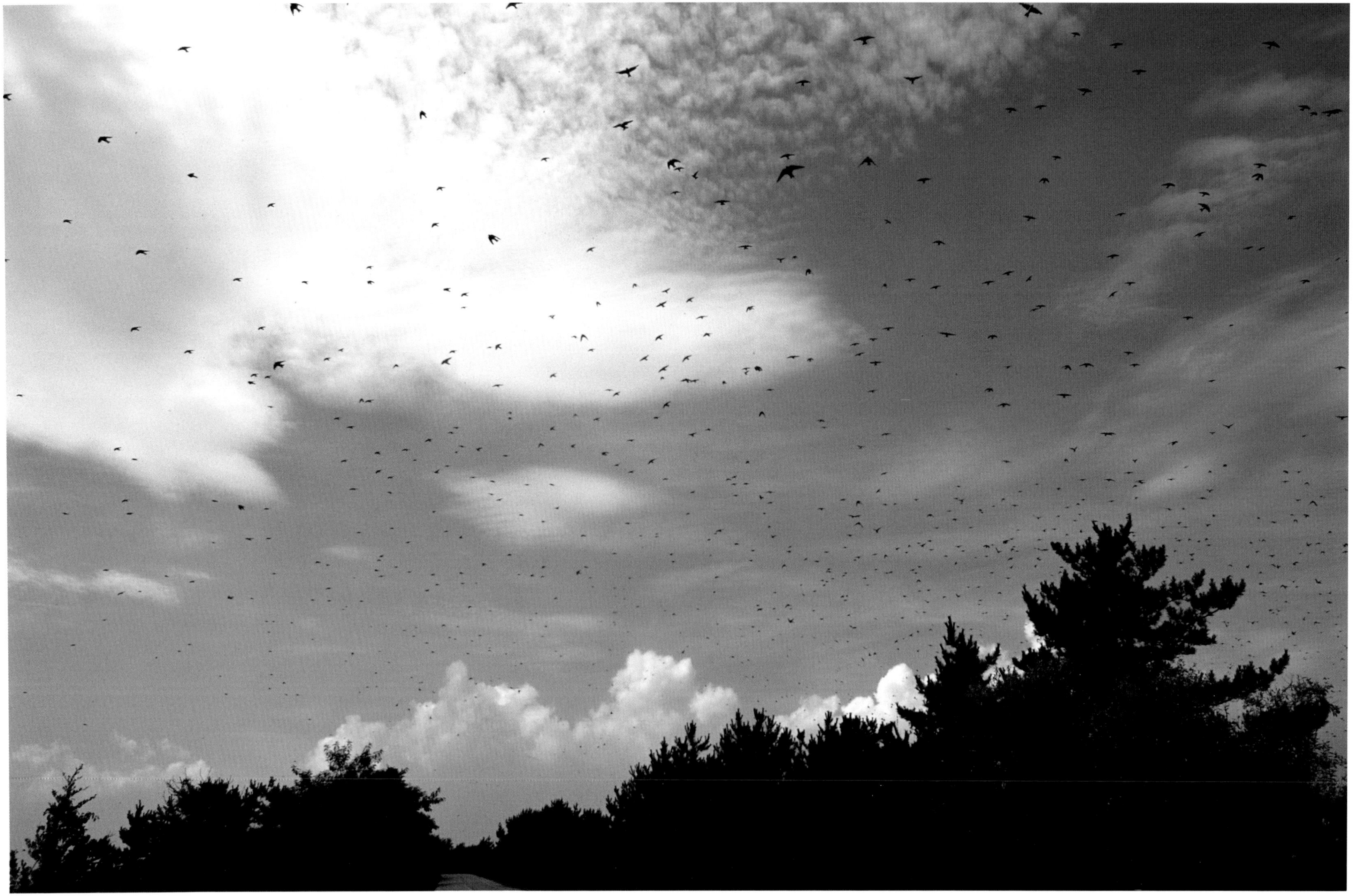

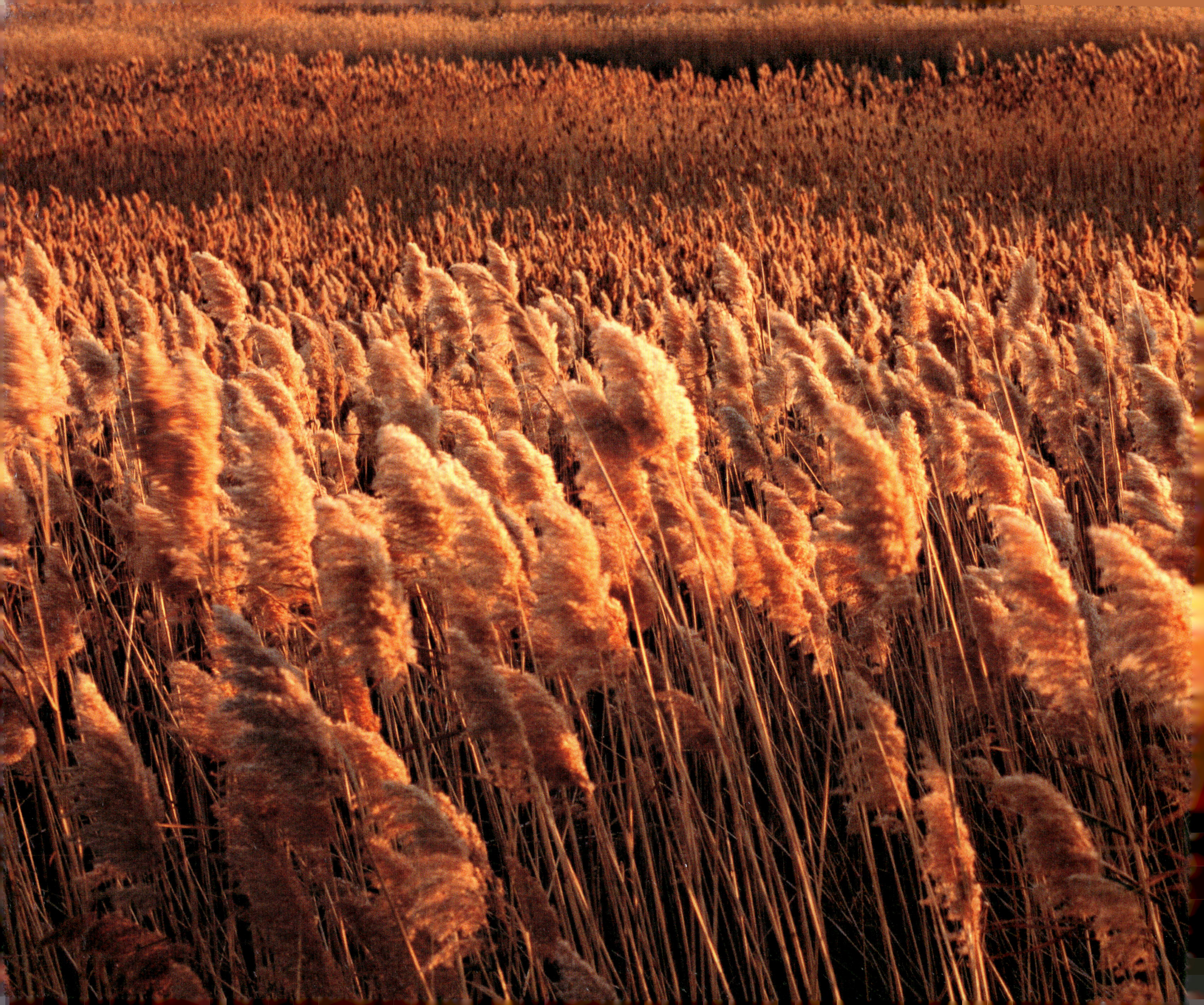

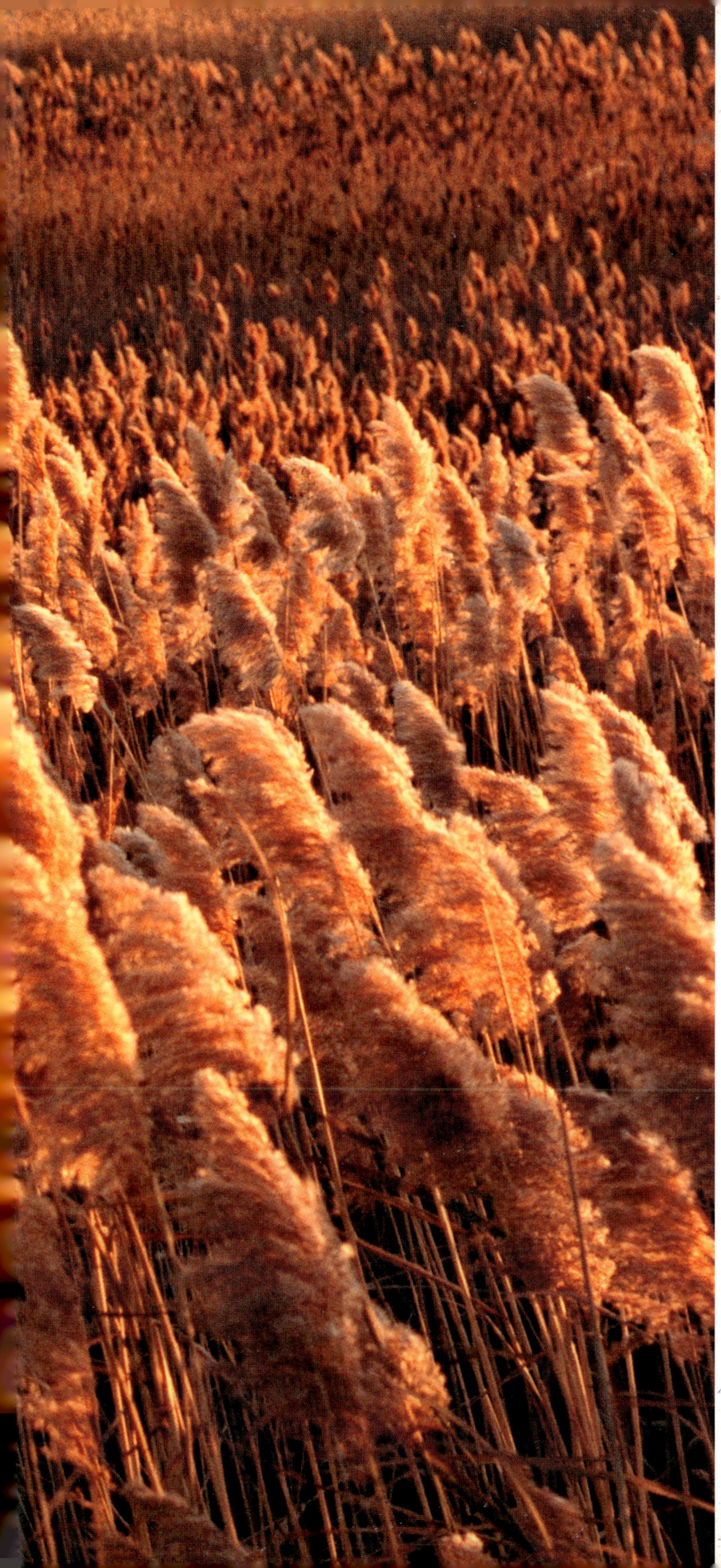

Orient Point

View of Southold Bay from Shelter Island

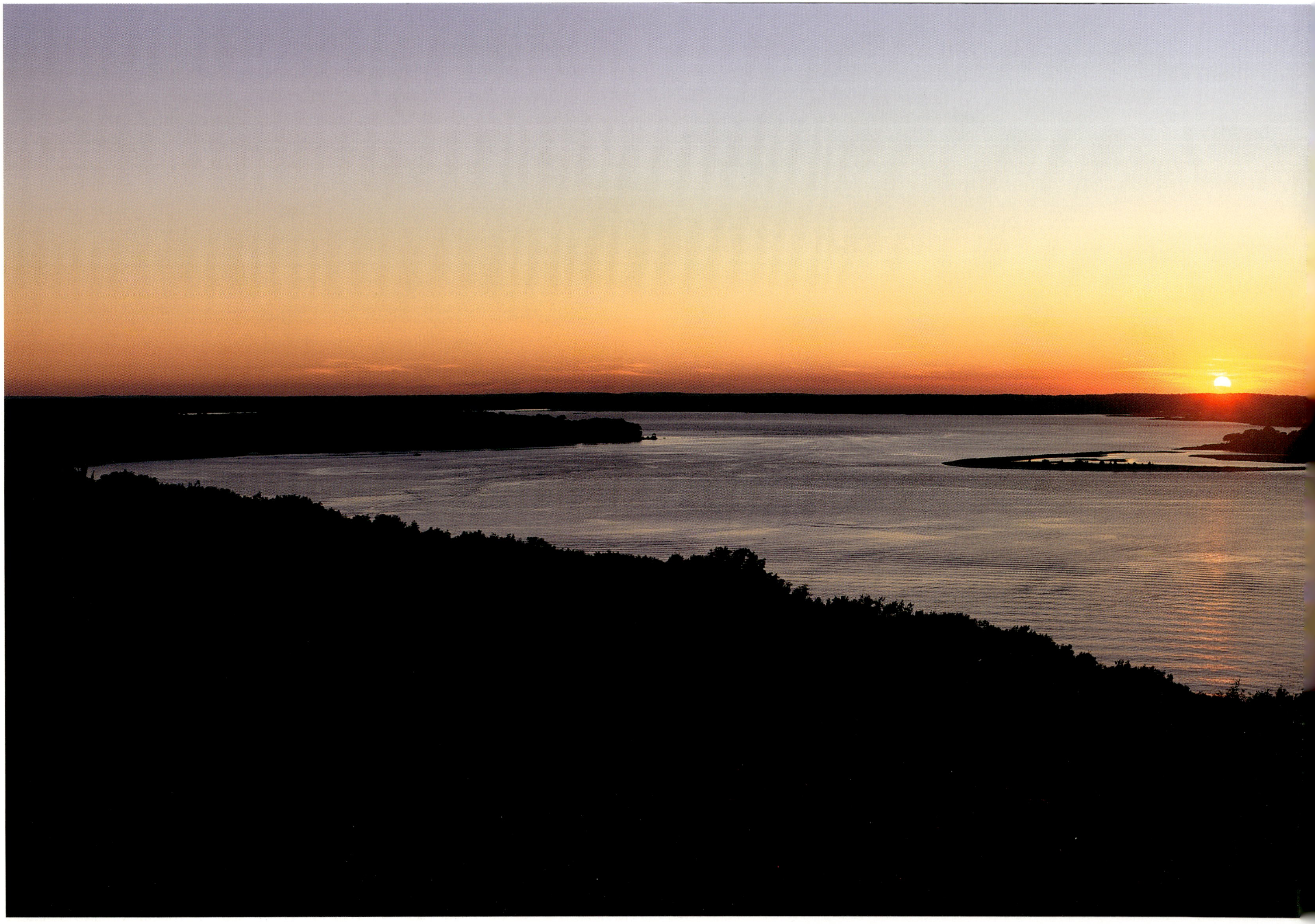

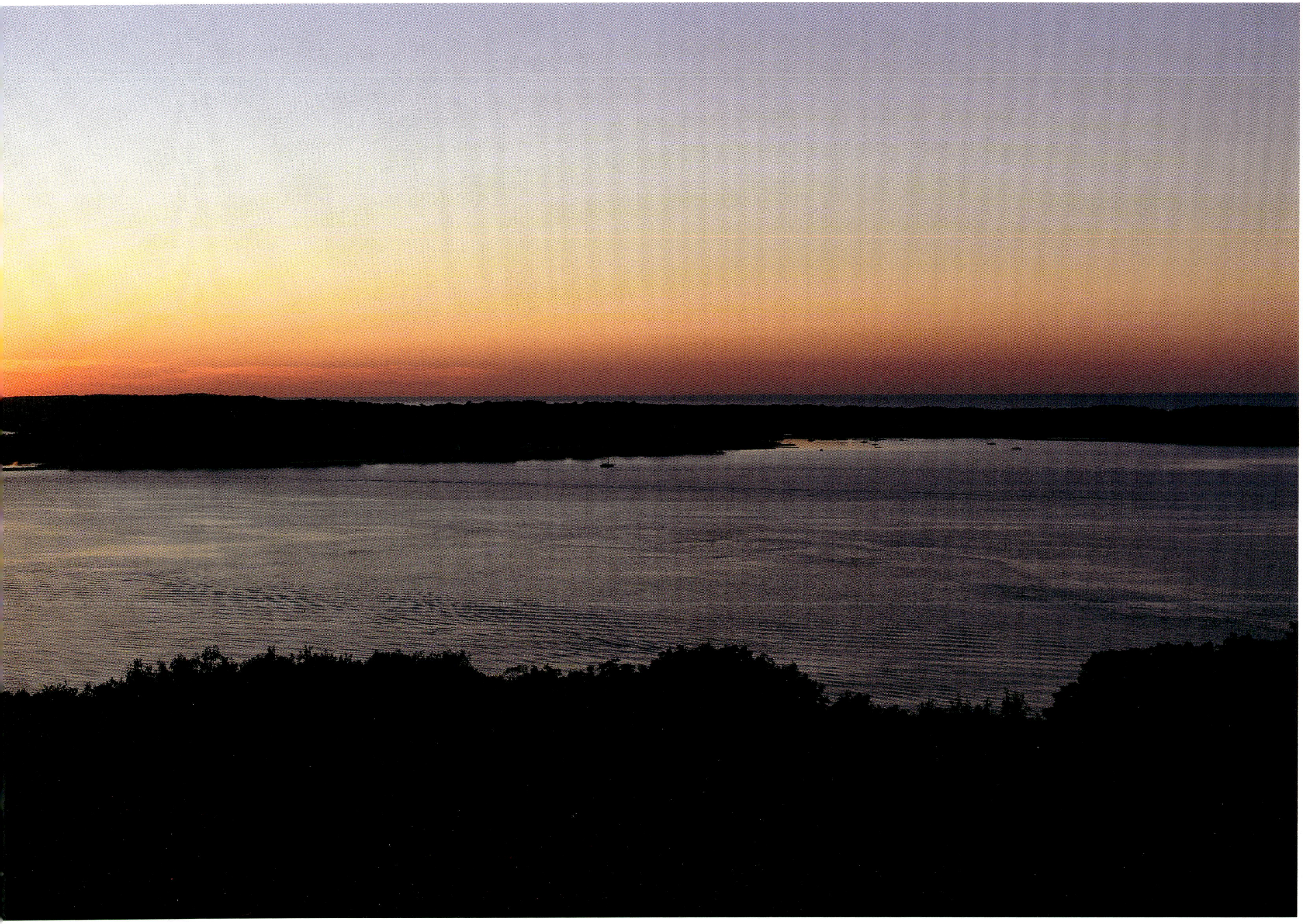

WE USED TO BOAST that our fort had an indoor saltwater pool. It was a half-sunk World War II ammunition barge behind Barstow's Shipyard in Greenport. Not far from there, my sister, Eva, caught a four-foot eel on a bamboo snapper pole. She was about six, and the eel was as longer than she was. Just up the creek, my brother, Dan, taught me how to dive into the water from the towering booms of dock building cranes. After dinner, my parents would take us to swim in the Sound, dive from rocks, collect beach glass, and watch breathtaking sunsets. I can't imagine any other childhood, and I always wanted my children to have the same.

When my son, Justus William Horton, was born, he became the thirteenth generation of my family to call the North Fork home. I couldn't wait to introduce him to my favorite spots in Southold Town and watch him gradually awaken to the North Fork's depth of natural beauty, history, sense of community and the profound freedom that comes with knowing who you are and where you're from.

Our "driving tours" began shortly after he came home from the hospital. Most of the time I was a tour guide to a sleeping boy, navigating through the many places integrated into the landscape of our family—the beach where our ancestors first landed in the early 1600s, buildings my great-grandfather built, the bay where my grandfather sailed, my dad's favorite clamming spots, and the shores of the Sound where I watch the current silently move boulders several feet each year. Justus will join our family in being able to smell the difference between winter and spring, the Sound and the bay, the woods, and the farms.

During this exciting time, I was completing my second term as Southold Town Supervisor. For the first time in many years, our community was unified in understanding that creative solutions were needed to curb development, preserve farmland, and sustain our community's socio-economic diversity. The reasons I ran for office and spent two terms fighting to preserve the North Fork are laid out masterfully in this book. Jake Rajs captures what I know the North Fork to be and visually explains a way of life worth fighting for.

My true appreciation for the dynamic beauty of the North Fork was defined during the decade I spent traveling around the world as a mariner. Once, as the Caribbean sun began to drop on the horizon, my ship's captain asked me, "Where were you when you saw the most magnificent sunset?"

I answered without hesitation, "On the North Fork of Long Island, standing on a bluff overlooking the Sound."

He looked at me in disbelief. "Long Island? I don't recall ever seeing a sunset worth remembering on the Long Island Sound."

Inwardly delighted by his reaction and firm in my sunset resolve, I politely replied, "Perhaps you were sailing east, sir."

I will be sending a copy of this book to that gruff old sailor.

Thank you to Jake Rajs for telling the story of this special place.

JOSHUA Y. HORTON
GREENPORT, NEW YORK

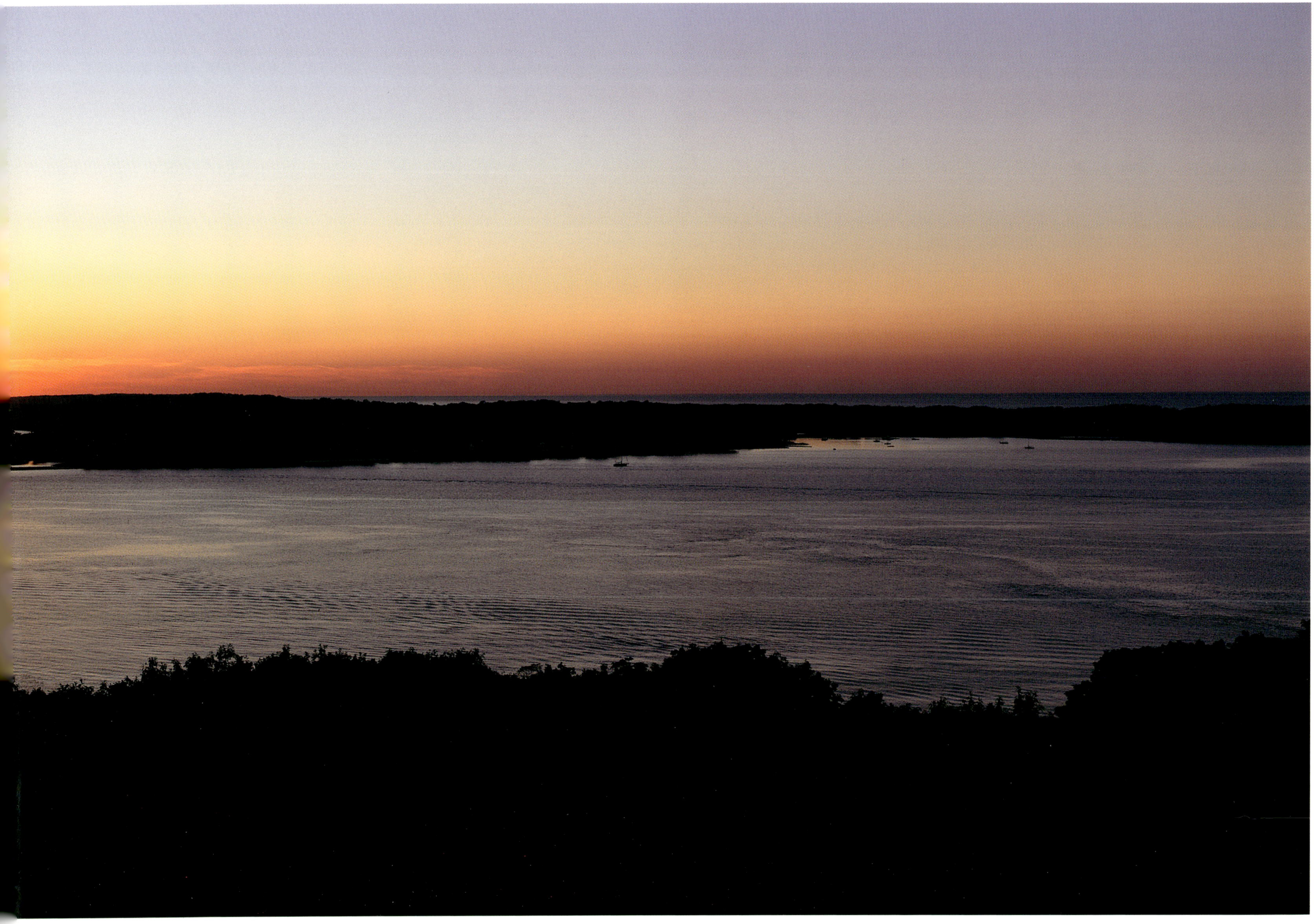

We used to boast that our fort had an indoor saltwater pool. It was a half-sunk World War II ammunition barge behind Barstow's Shipyard in Greenport. Not far from there, my sister, Eva, caught a four-foot eel on a bamboo snapper pole. She was about six, and the eel was as longer than she was. Just up the creek, my brother, Dan, taught me how to dive into the water from the towering booms of dock building cranes. After dinner, my parents would take us to swim in the Sound, dive from rocks, collect beach glass, and watch breathtaking sunsets. I can't imagine any other childhood, and I always wanted my children to have the same.

When my son, Justus William Horton, was born, he became the thirteenth generation of my family to call the North Fork home. I couldn't wait to introduce him to my favorite spots in Southold Town and watch him gradually awaken to the North Fork's depth of natural beauty, history, sense of community and the profound freedom that comes with knowing who you are and where you're from.

Our "driving tours" began shortly after he came home from the hospital. Most of the time I was a tour guide to a sleeping boy, navigating through the many places integrated into the landscape of our family—the beach where our ancestors first landed in the early 1600s, buildings my great-grandfather built, the bay where my grandfather sailed, my dad's favorite clamming spots, and the shores of the Sound where I watch the current silently move boulders several feet each year. Justus will join our family in being able to smell the difference between winter and spring, the Sound and the bay, the woods, and the farms.

During this exciting time, I was completing my second term as Southold Town Supervisor. For the first time in many years, our community was unified in understanding that creative solutions were needed to curb development, preserve farmland, and sustain our community's socio-economic diversity. The reasons I ran for office and spent two terms fighting to preserve the North Fork are laid out masterfully in this book. Jake Rajs captures what I know the North Fork to be and visually explains a way of life worth fighting for.

My true appreciation for the dynamic beauty of the North Fork was defined during the decade I spent traveling around the world as a mariner. Once, as the Caribbean sun began to drop on the horizon, my ship's captain asked me, "Where were you when you saw the most magnificent sunset?"

I answered without hesitation, "On the North Fork of Long Island, standing on a bluff overlooking the Sound."

He looked at me in disbelief. "Long Island? I don't recall ever seeing a sunset worth remembering on the Long Island Sound."

Inwardly delighted by his reaction and firm in my sunset resolve, I politely replied, "Perhaps you were sailing east, sir."

I will be sending a copy of this book to that gruff old sailor.

Thank you to Jake Rajs for telling the story of this special place.

JOSHUA Y. HORTON
GREENPORT, NEW YORK

# A Note from the Photographer

THREE YEARS AGO, at work on a book about the Atlantic Ocean, I found myself on the North Fork. I was excited by the light, the land, the sea. Photographing a sunset and experiencing the afterglow was akin to watching nature create a Mark Rothko painting: bands of light in red, orange, purple, and yellow. Then I discovered that Rothko indeed lived on the North Fork; in fact, he is buried here. Did the North Fork light influence him too?

Each book has its own story. Certainly the backbone of any book on the North Fork is the heritage of farming and fishing. The local farmers and fishermen are grateful for the abundant harvest from the soil and water, and proud of their ability to band together into a community. They shared with me their own sense of this place, from gardens to historic farmsteads to a whale-shaped rock. I was grateful for this opportunity to see a balance between humanity and the environment, a balance we are so often lacking.

Like so many before me, I have come under the spell of the atmosphere and the life of the East End. For a photographer drawn to the great works of nature and of humankind, the North Fork has an abundance of sights: the farmer on his tractor, the clammers in the water, the fishermen leaving the dock. And because this area retains a sense of openness, these things are accessible and without pretense. Here, I can see.

The North Fork retains its rural quality; time is measured by what the farmers are doing and which fish are running. A bud on a grapevine and tender sweet stalks of asparagus announce spring. High summer is filled with corn, peaches, and tomatoes. Netting means fall, and with luck a bountiful harvest of apples, pumpkins, grapes, and root vegetables. Trucks full of fencing herald the imminent arrival of snow. To be here is to find a harmonious rhythm shared by humankind and nature, a dance with the earth and a dance with the sea.

When I photograph a landscape, I try to capture the miracle that there is nothing more beautiful and more perfect then what is created by nature. The natural world has a soothing yet inspiring influence on our spirits, reminding us to appreciate each day. As we watch a sunset or a moonrise, a wave breaking or a leaf spinning, we repossess our souls and we believe in life. We open ourselves to the beauty that nature creates, knowing that the moment, though never to be repeated, is timeless.

JAKE RAJS
CUTCHOGUE, NEW YORK

# Acknowledgments

I would like to thank the following people and institutions for their kindness and assistance in helping to make this book possible:

Alexander Aquino, Chris and Roz Baiz, Scott Bennett and Eastern Long Island Hospital, David Blankenship, Jesse Browner, Carol Coakley, Connie Cross, Matt Gillies, Richard Gluckman, Suzanne Hahn and Brown Harris Stevens of Greenport, Joann and Bob Hamilton, Japp Hilbrand and Mary Ann Zovko, Joshua Y. Horton, Nicholas Iversen, John Karpinski, David Kapell, Bud and Lucy Koehler, Karen and Fred Lee of Sang Lee Farms, Yvonne Lieblein, Joe Macari Jr., Bill McNaught and the Oysterponds Historical Society, Mashomack Preserve, Jim and Barbara Miller, Eugenia and Gianfranco Monacelli, Andrea Monfried, The Nature Conservancy, Peconic Land Trust, Bill Ryall and Barry Bergdoll, Phil Schmitt, Eric Schnakenberg, Dennis Schrader and Bill Smith of Landcraft Environments, Robert Schreiber, Mark Speed, Dave Steele, Joseph Townsend, Van Bourgondien Nursery, Elizabeth White, Tom Wickham, Richard and Nancy Wines, Sherry and Robert Wolfang, Joan Woodle and John DeGennaro, and Cece Lia Zaleski.

A special thank you to all of the wineries for their cooperation: Bedell Cellars, Duck Walk, Lieb, Macari, Martha Clara, Mudd, The Old Field, Osprey's Dominion, Peconic Bay, Pellegrini, Pindar, Raphael, and Shinn Estate.

And most important, my wonderful family: Amy, Chloe, Jack, Olivia, Sean, and Grace.

First published in the United States of America in 2006 by
The Monacelli Press, Inc.
611 Broadway
New York, New York 10012



Pages 4–5: Southold Bay
Pages 6–7: Wickham's Fruit Farm, Cutchogue
Pages 8–9: Narrow River Road, Orient



LOC Control Number: 2006931680
ISBN: 1-58093-179-0

Designed by David Blankenship

Printed in Italy

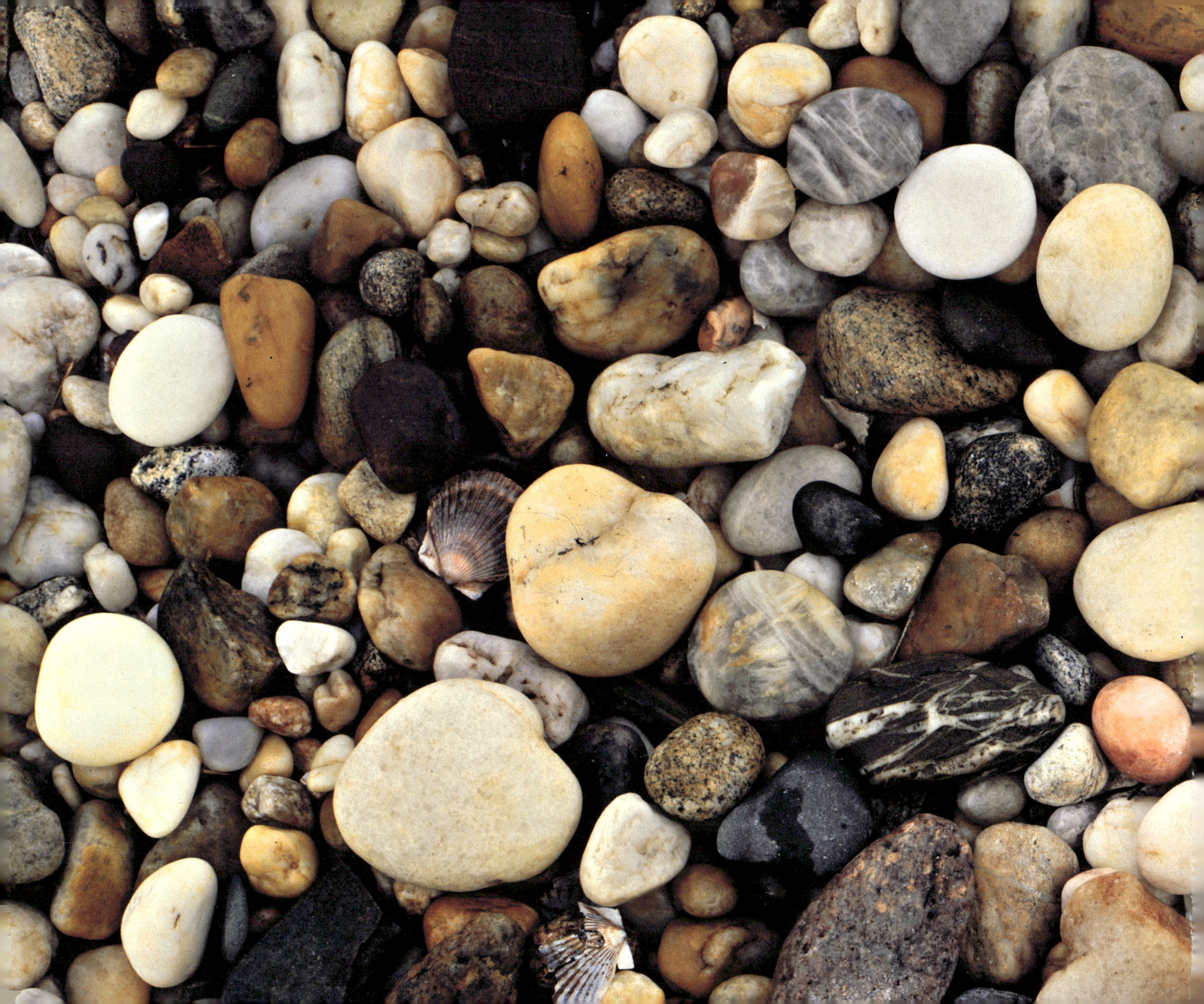